Cornelia Müller and Hermann Kappelhoff
**Cinematic Metaphor**

# Cinepoetics

Edited by
Hermann Kappelhoff and Michael Wedel

## Volume 4

Cornelia Müller and Hermann Kappelhoff

# Cinematic Metaphor

Experience – Affectivity – Temporality

In collaboration with
Sarah Greifenstein, Dorothea Horst,
Thomas Scherer, and Christina Schmitt

DE GRUYTER

ISBN 978-3-11-070907-0
e-ISBN (PDF) 978-3-11-058078-5
e-ISBN (EPUB) 978-3-11-057978-9
ISSN 2569-4294

Disclaimer (figures): All figures were created by the authors. Drawings within figures: Mathias Roloff. All screenshots were captured by the authors.

**Library of Congress Control Number: 2018951330**

**Bibliographic information published by the Deutsche Nationalbibliothek**
The Deutsche Nationalbibliothek lists this publication in the Deutsche Nationalbibliografie; detailed bibliographic data are available on the Internet at http://dnb.dnb.de.


This volume is text- and page-identical with the hardback published in 2018.
Cover image: Collage of a drawing by Mathias Roloff and a detail of a film poster for JEZEBEL (William Wyler, USA 1938)
Typesetting: Integra Software Services Pvt. Ltd.
Printing and binding: CPI books GmbH, Leck

www.degruyter.com

# Acknowledgements

Many people have contributed in developing the theoretical and methodological approach presented in this book. This transdisciplinary collaboration of film studies (Hermann Kappelhoff) with linguistic metaphor research (Cornelia Müller) began in the interdisciplinary research center *Languages of Emotion* at the Freie Universität Berlin, and was further developed at *Cinepoetics*, Center for Advanced Film Studies at the Freie Universität Berlin. We gratefully acknowledge the vision and support of the German Research Foundation (2009 to 2013, and since 2015) in funding these projects.

In its first year, Cinepoetics brought together a wide range of researchers in film and media and in metaphor, working towards a transdisciplinary understanding of, and approach to discuss metaphor in relation to 'Film Images, Cinematic Thinking, and Cognition' (2015/16) under the leadership of Cornelia Müller, Hermann Kappelhoff, and Michael Wedel. We benefited greatly from discussions about our research with invited research fellows, project associates, and other visitors to Cinepoetics, who brought expertise from very different, and sometimes opposing, disciplinary backgrounds. With this group of scholars, we discussed our premises from film theory and theses on audiovisual metaphors over the course of several workshops, reading colloquia, lectures, and a symposium. Against the background of these always fruitful exchanges – including critical, differing, and converging positions – we developed the theoretical framework and methodology of Cinematic Metaphor. We are grateful to all the fellows who visited Cinepoetics in its first year for their engaging and inspiring contributions to our work.

*Cinepoetics Research Fellows*:
Warren Buckland (Film Studies, Oxford Brookes University, GB)
Lynne Cameron (Applied Linguistics, Professor Emerita, Open University, UK)
Alan Cienki (Cognitive Linguistics, VU Universiteit Amsterdam, NL, and Moscow State Linguistic University, RUS)
Kathrin Fahlenbrach (Film and Media Studies, Universität Hamburg, GER)
Raymond W. Gibbs, Jr. (Psychology, UC Santa Cruz, CA, US)
Irene Mittelberg (Cognitive Semiotics, RWTH Aachen, GER)
Eve Sweetser (Cognitive Linguistics, UC Berkeley, CA, US)

*Cinepoetics Associates*:
Gabriele Brandstetter (Dance Studies, Freie Universität, GER)
Jan Distelmeyer (Media Studies, Fachhochschule Potsdam, GER)
Anne Eusterschulte (Philosophy, Freie Universität Berlin, GER)
Gertrud Koch (Film Studies, Freie Universität Berlin, GER)

https://doi.org/10.1515/9783110580785-201

*Cinepoetics Invited Guests*:
Charles Forceville (Linguistics and Media Studies, University of Amsterdam, NL)
Petra Gehring (Philosophy, Technische Universität Darmstadt, GER)
Naum Kleiman (Eisenstein-Centre Director, RUS)
Oliver Lubrich (Comparative Literature, University of Bern, CH)
Martin Vöhler (Classics, Aristotle University of Thessaloniki, GR)
Rüdiger Zill (Philosophy, Einstein Forum Potsdam, GER)

Lynne Cameron was a wonderful companion throughout all the stages of the emergence of this book. Being a leading expert on the discourse dynamics of metaphor as well as being a painter she was a mentor of our transdisciplinary work from its very beginnings; the discussions with her provided crucial support and inspiration. Lynne worked with us for two years as scholar and as artist in residence. During her stay, she offered a series of creative workshops exploring the poiesis of film-viewing as an artistic practice that contributed vitally to broaden our understanding of metaphorical meaning-making as experiencing and 'doing', i.e., as a performing. Sharing her experience, lucidity, and creativity turned the collaborative process of 'doing' the book into an interaffective pleasure.

In 2016, we organized the biennial conference of the *Researching and Applying Metaphor* organisation (RaAM) in Berlin, with a Cinepoetics Roundtable, including contributions from Lynne Cameron and Ray Gibbs, that presented and discussed our approach with the international community of metaphor scholars. We thank the contributors for their insightful comments and reactions and the RaAM executive committee for its support.

The book integrates findings from earlier projects into the new transdisciplinary theoretical perspective. These include:
- "Multimodal Metaphor and Expressive Movement" (Hermann Kappelhoff, Cornelia Müller), interdisciplinary research center *Languages of Emotion*[1] (DFG – German Research Foundation) at Freie Universität Berlin. We thank Susanne Tag, Stefan Rook, and Franziska Boll for their contributions to this project.
- "The Mobilization of Emotions in War Films" (Hermann Kappelhoff), interdisciplinary research center *Languages of Emotion*[2] (DFG – German Research Foundation) at Freie Universität Berlin.

1 For more information please visit www.loe.fu-berlin.de/en/index.html; www.empirische-medienaesthetik.fu-berlin.de/en/affektmobilisierung/index.html.

2 For more information please visit www.loe.fu-berlin.de/en/index.html; www.empirische-medienaesthetik.fu-berlin.de/en/metapher/index.html.

- "Staging Images of War as a Mediated Experience of Community" (Hermann Kappelhoff) (DFG – German Research Foundation) at Freie Universität Berlin.
- "Body Language of Movement and Dance: Emergence of Meaning, 'Languageing' and Therapeutical Application" (Cornelia Müller, Thomas Fuchs, Sabine Koch) (BMBF – German Ministry of Education). Thanks go to the co-directors of the project and specifically Silva H. Ladewig and Lena Hotze.

We are grateful to all the participants in empirical studies for their permission to use the data. Specific thanks go to artist Mathias Roloff whose drawings brought the data to life (mathiasroloff.de).

An extensive project such as this book could not happen without the work of a team of post-doctoral research assistants, doctoral students, and student assistants. We thank them for their contributions: we particularly thank Christian Lippe, Philine Mayr, and Raphael Schotten. We also thank Kaspar Aebi, Jan-Hendrik Bakels, Hanno Berger, Derya Demir, Maximilian Grenz, and Yvonne Pfeilschifter. We acknowledge their manifold contributions in preparing the manuscript for publication.

We thank Daniel Hendrickson for translating the following film analyses: DEATH AND THE MOTHER, REAR WINDOW, DER KRIEGER UND DIE KAISERIN, MAGNIFICENT OBSESSION, JEZEBEL, quotations from Helmuth Plessner, and for translating a draft version of Part I.

We thank Lynne Cameron for meticulous reading, for polishing the English throughout the book, and for turning the preparation of the manuscript for publication into a series of delightful moments. We are also extremely grateful to Ray Gibbs for close reading and commenting on a draft version of the book. Ray's comments were absolutely vital in sharpening and clarifying the arguments throughout the book.

Eileen Rositzka was a wonderful 'human interface' making the communication between the publisher and the authors efficient and clear. We thank Stella Diedrich and Anna Hofsäß from De Gruyter for ample support and advice in preparing the book for publication.

Berlin, May 2018

Cornelia Müller, Hermann Kappelhoff,
Sarah Greifenstein, Dorothea Horst,
Thomas Scherer, Christina Schmitt

# Contents



## Part I: **Setting the Stage for Cinematic Metaphor**

## Part II: **Cinematic Experience and Audiovisual Figurativity**



## Part III: **Cinematic Expressive Movement: Affectivity and Metaphor**

# Conventions

Transliteration
Expressions and utterances in case studies are documented with quotation marks

Translations
Example [*Beispiel*] – Original German in italics and square brackets after the English translation
lit. – literal translations

Films & other audiovisual sources
TITLE – The titles of all audiovisual sources are in small caps
ORIGINAL TITLES of films and broadcasts are used

Figures
Drawings refer to non-published video-recorded face-to-face interactions
Timecode format is hh:mm:ss

https://doi.org/10.1515/9783110580785-202

# Introduction

*Cinematic Metaphor* reflects a truly transdisciplinary approach to metaphors in film, television, and video. It is a result of longstanding transdisciplinary work on metaphors in audiovisual media and face-to-face interaction. Collaboration between film studies (Hermann Kappelhoff) and linguistic metaphor research (Cornelia Müller) began in the center of excellence *Languages of Emotion* at the Freie Universität Berlin and came to fruition through the work of *Cinepoetics*, Center for Advanced Film Studies.

In the first year of Cinepoetics and under the rubric of 'Metaphor – Film Images, Cinematic Thinking, and Cognition', we engaged in a substantial integration of disciplinary approaches with very different theoretical assumptions, different theoretical traditions, and different academic realms of discourse. Metaphor theories and philosophical metaphorology were debated with a group of international scholars representing different approaches to metaphor in audiovisual media. In particular, the idea was to bring linguistic perspectives on metaphor – cognitive, discourse, multimodal – to film and media studies, and to have metaphor scholars from linguistics and the psychology of metaphor discuss with film scholars how metaphors work in cinematic thinking.

## Why we speak of cinematic metaphor

One of the most important outcomes of this transdisciplinary work is reflected in the title of the book: *cinematic metaphor has replaced the term multimodal metaphor for the analysis of audiovisual media.* Our theoretical as well as empirical starting point is the specific mediality, the media character of the cinematic, be it film, television, or video. Starting from theories of cinema that address this media specificity, we extend them to other audiovisual forms such as television news, campaign commercials, or music video. Despite their differences, these forms share a fundamental mode of perceptual experience that Sobchack has characterized as "An expression of experience by experience" (Merleau-Ponty 1968 [1964], 155, quoted in Sobchack 1992, 3). The concept of cinematic metaphor that we have developed therefore fundamentally differs from Whittock's, that takes metaphor in language as reference point (Whittock 1990, 5–36, 49–69). It also stands in contrast to the notions of audiovisual and multimodal metaphor (Fahlenbrach 2010, Forceville 2006, 2009a, 2016).

Why not describe metaphors in film as multimodal? Because audiovisual media in themselves constitute a specific mode: they are *movement-images*.

https://doi.org/10.1515/9783110580785-001

Acting, gesturing, speaking within a film all become elements of a movement composition, a movement-image. An important result of our transdisciplinary work was that it became clear that the notion of multimodality reaches certain limits when considering audiovisual media. While it appears to make sense to conceive of gestures or spoken language as different modes, this does not hold for audiovisual media. Audiovisual media cannot appropriately be described as an accumulation of articulatory modes that 'represent' some moving content and 'communicate' through the different senses (hearing, seeing, etc.) (cf. also Schmitt forthcoming/2019). Rather, sound, camera movement, framing, editing, light, color, acting all merge in a movement-image, constituting a specific media mode. Movement-images structure the process of film-viewing as a media-specific form of perception. We consider cinematic metaphors as emerging from this media-specific mode of perceiving, orchestrated by cinematic movement-images. In short, film images are not composed from different modalities. As movement-images they *are* a mode *sui generis*.

Following Sobchack's neo-phenomenological understanding of cinema (Sobchack 1992), we conceive of the narrative, the film, to be produced by spectators in their embodied experiences of film-viewing. Narratives are thus not the starting-point, but the product of metaphorical thinking; they are 'done' by the spectators.

In the following, a brief analysis of a German news feature serves to illustrate our transdisciplinary perspective on cinematic metaphor. It illuminates how cinematic metaphor orchestrates a feeling for a troubled banking system.

## Cinematic metaphor in a TV News feature: TAGESSCHAU

The news feature was produced in 2008 as German banks began to feel the consequences of the financial crisis, and broadcast as part of the main evening news show on German national television (TAGESSCHAU, ARD, GER 20 October 2008).[1] The topic it addresses concerns a financial rescue package that the German government had offered to the banking sector; it explores the reactions of the banks, and concentrates specifically on the Bavarian State Bank [*Bayerische Landesbank*] because this bank was among the first in Germany to face a severe threat of collapsing. With a running time of less than two minutes, the news

1 The analysis was developed in the context of the research project "Multimodal Metaphor and Expressive Movement", and further worked on within the Cinepoetics' research focus 'Metaphor – Film Images, Cinematic Thinking, and Cognition' by Thomas Scherer. The version for this book was prepared by Cornelia Müller, Lynne Cameron, and Thomas Scherer.

feature incorporates a high frequency of metaphors and metonymies. What appears, at first, as a rather random assembly of single multimodal and monomodal metaphors turns out to unfold as a metaphorical structure, a cinematic metaphor for the bank's loss of power, which emerges from the viewer's experiential engagement with the temporal aesthetics of the feature.

The feature begins by metaphorically introducing the acceleration of the banking rescue package as a horse-drawn carriage moving very slowly across the screen. Shortly after, the metaphorical and metonymical theme is introduced as the voice-over states that "the Bavarian lion roars loudest [...] for help" [*Am lautesten brüllt der bayerische Löwe um Hilfe*], and the screen shows a massive statue of the Bavarian heraldic animal placed in front of a building of the Bavarian State Bank (Figure I.1, first two images).

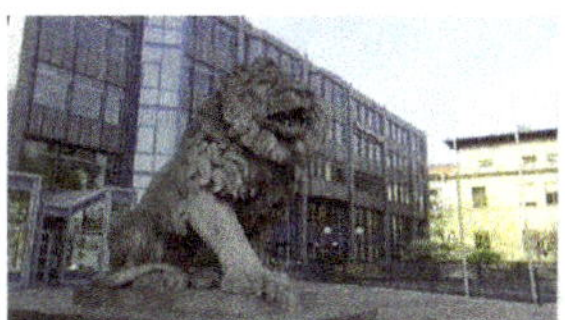
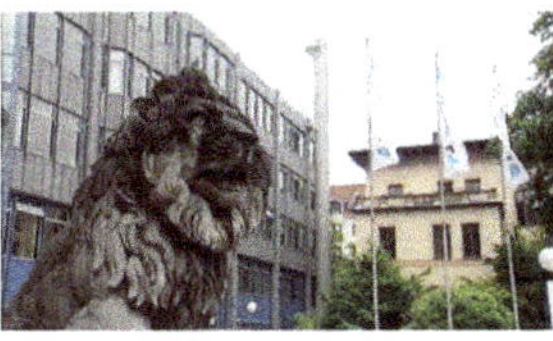
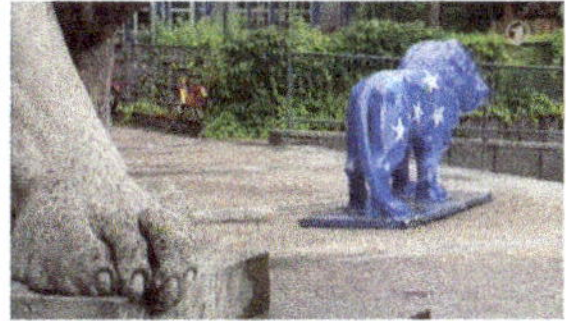

**Figure I.1:** The transformation of the Bavarian State Bank from a strong to a weak lion (TAGESSCHAU, 20 October 2008)

This first shot of the lion metonymically connects the Bavarian State Bank with Bavaria's heraldic animal, and also marks the beginning of the emergent cinematic metaphor. The massiveness of the stone statue of the Bavarian lion is further highlighted by a zooming-in movement which, after first approaching the lion's roaring face, moves past the lion to reveal the logo of the Bavarian State Bank on the building, with a voice-over commenting that "[...] the regional bank is lacking up to five billion Euro" [*(...) der Landesbank fehlen (...) bis zu fünf Milliarden Euro*]. Together, this zooming-in movement and the voice-over transform the perception of the Bavarian Bank from a strong powerful animal into one that is in big trouble and badly needs the financial support offered by the government. At the same time, the zooming-in movement past the lion and towards the logo singles out the Bavarian Bank as example of the critical situation of the German banking system. Together with the preceding zooming-out movement, which was connected with the stable banks not in need of support from the government, a dynamic of moving away versus narrowing down is visually established. The two opposed camera movements distinguish the stable from the troubled banks experientially (Figure I.2). This pair of camera movements are not primarily perceived as a movement in a represented space, but as transformation of the Bavarian State Bank.

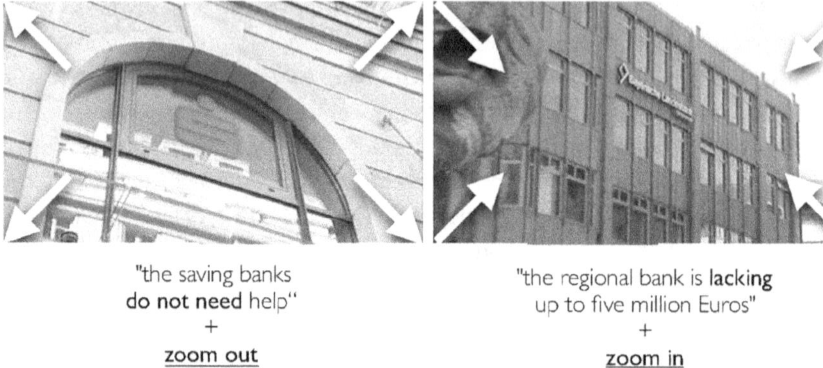


**Figure I.2:** Zooming-out and zooming-in: opposing camera movements experientially distinguish stable from troubled banks (TAGESSCHAU, 20 October 2008)

Then, with a shift to a high-angle shot, several bank buildings along a river come into view and are connected by the voice-over with the private banking sector: "The private banks [that] will also board the state-run rescue boat." [*Auch die privaten Banken werden mit ins staatliche Rettungsboot steigen*] The "rescue package" metaphor is elaborated into a "state-run rescue boat", with metaphoricity emphasized by the visual connection of the river with the governmental rescue boat, and an ironic tone once again brought to the report. The skyscrapers along the river bank metonymically stand for the private banks that will need financial support from the government. With an abrupt cut to a low-angle shot of a skyscraper – apparently the building of the biggest private bank – the voice-over commentary quotes a statement issued by *Deutsche Bank*: "Industry leader Deutsche Bank declares that it is still doing reasonably well." [*Branchenprimus Deutsche Bank erklärt zwar noch es gehe auch so (...)*] The statement, when put together with the shot, however, creates an impression of instability rather than the opposite (Figure I.3).

The two montage sequences of the buildings (zoom-in/zoom-out, high angle/low angle) form a decisive movement pattern and vary the theme just previously set: shifting from a group of banks to one bank as a narrowing down from a broad to a focused perspective. The banks differ with regard to how much in trouble they really are: while the Bavarian State Bank needs financial support right now, the Deutsche Bank does not need help from the German government's rescue package, yet. A further metaphor from the domain of maritime disasters, heard in the voice-over, accentuates and dramatizes the fragile financial situation: "The governing body however predicts various castaways." [*(...) der Dachverband aber rechnet mit vielen Schiffbrüchigen*] Without the rescue package, the troubled banks will be in existential danger.

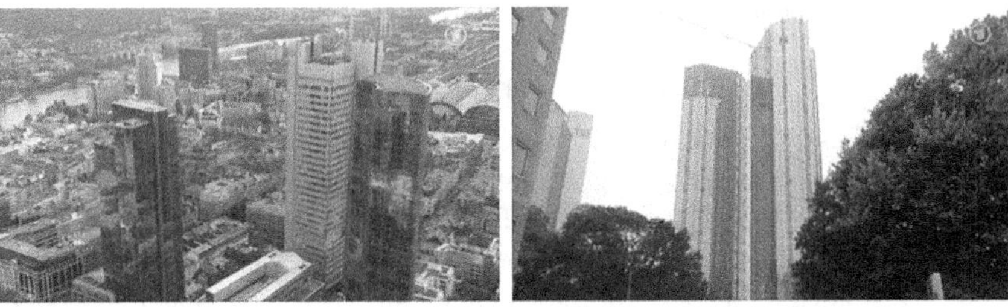


**Figure I.3:** Two opposed camera angles distinguish stable from troubled banks experientially (TAGESSCHAU, 20 October 2008)

The news feature ends with a compound camera movement that begins once again with a close-up shot of the lion statue but then pans down and to the right, zooming in on a statue of a small blue lion (Figure I.1, third image). The camera movement takes up and transforms the two movement patterns to create an ironic twist. The zooming-in that was earlier connected with the weakness of the Bavarian State Bank, and the looking down on the private banks that will at some point also need financial support, are blended in one 'concluding' camera movement that zooms-in and with a pan to the right establishes a downward orientation. When the voice-over comments, "Tomorrow the governing board of the regional banks meets and will finalize how much help the big lion needs" [*Morgen tagt der Verwaltungsrat der Landesbank und wird festlegen, in welcher Höhe der große Löwe Hilfe benötigt*], the zooming-in and the downward pan of the camera creates a metonymical and metaphorical framing of the Bavarian State Bank.

A complex cinematic metaphor has emerged through viewers' experiencing of the movement-images in the news report. It is not simply that the Bavarian regional bank, which was briefly a large roaring lion, has been transformed into a small weak lion that urgently needs help, and that the banking crisis and the government's package of help is like a maritime disaster where rescue boats cannot help everyone and some will be cast adrift. In analyzing cinematic metaphor, we go beyond represented content and verbal metaphors, and take account of the temporal media experience of viewers: camera moves, varying angles of shots, patterns of contrast and variation, connections and contrast between voice-over merging in movement-images and creating a temporal and affective parcours which viewers experience bodily.

## Starting from the media-character of audiovisual images

The starting point of our argument is the question: what is the specific media-character of audiovisual images? In the framework presented in this book, the fact that audiovisuals are 'movement-images' rather than 'moving images' which present contents that move constitutes the theoretical and methodological starting point. We assume that *cinematic movement-images* – and this is what they share with metaphors – create dynamic correlations between various domains of experience, and can accordingly model and alter forms of perception and perspective that constitute a commonly shared reality. Strictly speaking, the function of cinematic images, exactly like that of metaphors, is not so much "communicating [given] information or truths" (Blumenberg 1987 [1981], 433) or representing them, but producing "understanding, agreement, or toleration" (Blumenberg 1987 [1981], 433) between particular experiential perspectives. Both – film and metaphors – offer a dynamic structure of this production of understanding by expressing one experience in terms of another experience (Sobchack 1992).

But what does it mean if we take the thesis seriously, and assume neither given representations nor universal perceptual schemata as claimed by cognitive film and metaphor studies? If we also, and precisely at the level of analyzing the discourse of film images, assume that the conditions of perception continuously change, historically, culturally, and technically? In *The Address of the Eye*, Vivian Sobchack proposes a perspective in which she conceives the historical changing cinematic operations as embodiments and formations of meaning to equal degrees. She outlines the developments of film technology as an arrangement of cinematic forms of expression and perception, which she calls the "history of cinematic embodiment" (Sobchack 1992, 256). What, then, if we understand film images themselves as agents of this change, which in no way reproduce poetic conventions and patterns from the aesthetics of effect, but model a-priori forms of human perceiving, sensing, and thinking? The consequences of such a position for metaphors in audiovisual media form the subject matter of the book.

## Cinematic metaphor: Basic theoretical assumptions

The book is divided into four parts. While Parts II, III, and IV each zoom in on one theoretical facet of cinematic metaphor – experience, affectivity, temporality – Part I presents a detailed exposition of the film and media-theoretical assumptions for cinematic metaphor that begin from the media specificity of audiovision. Here are the fundamental assumptions:

> Audiovisual images are movement-images, not moving pictures. Cinematic metaphors emerge from movement-images.
>
> Movement-images are dynamic, and they come with a particular movement quality: an affective quality. Sense constructions are always based on that affective experience. Cinematic metaphors are grounded affectively.
>
> Cinematic metaphorical meaning is procedural. It emerges from an affective temporal parcours that viewers go through when watching a film.
>
> Viewing films is a specific form of experience. Cinematic experience is embodied, intersubjective, reflexive. Understanding films is historical, multiperspective, and grounded in the aesthetics of cinematic experience.
>
> Cinematic metaphor emerges in this embodied, intersubjective, and reflexive process of understanding.

Understanding metaphors in film, television, and audiovisual media more broadly, presupposes a theory of what audiovisual media are and how they function. Marshall McLuhan provided the radical insight in 1964 that the "medium is the message" and not the 'information encoded' (McLuhan 1964, 23–35). Media and cultural studies take this as a given, and yet, the actual nature of the media seems to be largely neglected in theories and analyses of film, television, and other media. This holds too for cognitive media studies of metaphors (eg. Fahlenbrach 2005, 2008, 2010, 2016, Coëgnarts and Kravanja 2012b, 2014, 2015, Ortiz 2014, 2015) for multimodal metaphor analyses of audiovisual media (e.g., Forceville 2008, 2016, Forceville and Urios-Aparisi 2009), cognitive-linguistic blending analysis (Oakley and Tobin 2012), and multimodal research on audiovisual media more generally (e.g., Wildfeuer and Bateman 2017, Bateman, Wildfeuer, and Hiippala 2017, Wildfeuer 2017, Schmitt forthcoming/2019 for a critical discussion). Such a misalignment ignores the media character of film. Here is where this book proposes an alternative approach. *Cinematic Metaphor* develops a framework for metaphor in audiovisual media which starts in particular from the specific character of film images as movement-images.

## Overview of the book

Part I develops a framework for cinematic metaphor as performative action, as sense-making, which is grounded in the dynamics of viewers' embodied intersubjective experiences with the film and entangled affectively with cinematic movement-images, temporally orchestrated on every level.

Chapter 1 sets off with some critical questions concerning the media specificity of audiovisual images and proposes a framework rooted in the history of film theory. By putting the concept of movement-image center stage, Chapter 1 suggests a model of cinematic metaphor as poiesis of film-viewing that goes beyond conceptual metaphor and cognitive film studies. By taking the mediality of audiovisual images as vantage point for theorizing metaphor, film-viewing as a specific mode of experience becomes a starting point of a theory. We develop a rhetoric-based position to metaphors in audiovision informed by philosophical theories of metaphor (Max Black, Hans Blumenberg, Friedrich Nietzsche) Metaphoricity emerges with the movement experience of film-viewing. Considering cinematic metaphor as poiesis of film-viewing replaces the idea of a spectator as information-processing computer as in cognitive approaches to film and heals the break with rhetoric established by conceptual metaphor theory.

In Chapter 2 cinematic metaphor is discussed in relation to a media-specific mode of experience. The model of cinematic metaphor adopts Black's idea of metaphors as cognitive instruments, and Lakoff and Johnson's early formulation of metaphors as multidimensional experiential gestalts. The idea of cinematic metaphor differs, however, profoundly from the later applications of conceptual metaphor theory to audiovisual media. Rather than conceiving of metaphors as instantiations of image schemas or primary metaphors, we consider metaphoricity to be emerging locally from the spectator's experiencing of movement-images in the moment of film-viewing.

Chapter 3 is about the 'doing' of cinematic metaphor: perception, feeling, and affective entanglement. We suggest that cinematic metaphors are 'done' by the spectators and, like metaphors in discourse and face-to-face communication, are dynamic, emergent, always changing. Obviously, this 'doing' of metaphor is not a deliberate process, it happens as viewers are perceiving and sensing the film; it happens as they are entangled affectively with the unfolding of cinematic movement-images. Cinematic metaphors thus evolve from perceptual sensations, from the viewer's engagement with what we describe as 'cinematic expressive movements'.

Chapter 4 addresses cinematic metaphor and embodiment: intersubjectivity, dynamics, the 'We' and the other 'I'. Here we lay out an understanding of embodiment that is informed by phenomenology and that has been extremely influential in contemporary film theory. Embodied experience is taken to be intersubjective, reflexive, and dynamic, and integral to cinematic meaning-making. We show how this differs from the universalist and individual model of embodiment advocated by cognitive film and metaphor theories. 'Doing' cinematic metaphor is a co-production of two agents: the viewer and the film. Alongside intersubjectivity, we consider the role of reflexivity and consciousness in the 'doing' of metaphor. Meaning-making in cinematic metaphor becomes the joint sharing of an always changing reality.

Chapter 5 addresses the phenomenological concept of embodiment especially with respect to the fundamental and meaning-making role of experience. Shortcomings of the embodiment concept prevalent in cognitive analyses of metaphor are discussed. Our critique comes with an argument for a phenomenological concept of embodiment, which involves three essential aspects: dynamics, intersubjectivity, and reflexivity. With reference to Blumenberg's metaphorology, Nietzsche's philosophy of rhetoric, and Black's reality-constructing power of metaphor and of film, it argues for a return to rhetoric and poetics in metaphor theory – a plea that affects not only audiovisual media.

The subsequent parts of the book explore more deeply three key dimensions of *Cinematic Metaphor* resulting from this framework: *Experience – Affectivity – Temporality*. This is done with extensive use of illustrative analyses from film, television, video, and face-to-face interaction, and further discussion of theoretical points.

In Part II, we consider closely 'experience' as a key characteristic of cinematic metaphors. Cinematic metaphors are produced within the process of film-viewing, i.e., the interaction between spectator and audiovisual image as a process in which the temporal structure of the audiovisual composition is embodied in viewers as a temporal gestalt of perceiving, thinking, and feeling. In film-viewing, spectators are 'doing' metaphors, they create fictive realities, and connect them with everyday reality. This process is described as an artistic production, a poiesis of film-viewing that defines the specific character of the media mode of experience of audiovisual images, i.e., *cinematic experience*. We illustrate the consequences of this understanding of cinematic experience, not only for metaphor but also for metonymy, with a series of analyses.

In Chapter 6, a comparative analysis of multimodal interaction in a dance lesson and film-viewing is offered. Suggesting that embodiment – reflexivity, intersubjectivity, and temporality – structures metaphorical meaning-making, we argue that this is one of the dimensions that multimodal face-to-face interaction shares with the poiesis of film-viewing.

In Chapter 7, a series of further case studies documents how, from cinematic experience as a media-specific mode of perception, cinematic metaphor as well as metonymy emerges. Examples include different media formats, ranging from a TV news feature to classical Hollywood cinema, music video, and election campaign commercial.

In Part III, we illustrate how cinematic metaphors emerge from the affective involvement of the spectator with movement-images. The key concept here is the notion of *expressive movement*. It is important because it allows us to describe the process of film-viewing in its affective dynamics.

To introduce the notion of cinematic expressive movement as a form of cinematic composition that modulates affective experiences of film viewers, Chapter 8 presents three short example analyses from different media formats, including German feature film, Hollywood cinema, and TV news.

In Chapter 9, we outline the film-theoretical frame against which the notion of cinematic expressive movement has been developed. The chapter includes theoretical reflections and an illustrative case study of expressive movements in face-to-face interaction. It includes a sketch of the idea of body movements as expressive, as discussed in philosophical anthropology, psychology, and linguistics, illustrates how metaphoricity emerges in a small group discussion within an interaffective dynamics of gesture, speech, and body movements, and describes the parallelism between body movement and cinematic movement expressed by the notion of movement-image. It shows the historical roots of this idea in the aesthetic strategies of affect modulation, developed within the concept of melodrama in theatre and film.

In Chapter 10 we illustrate how the notion of cinematic expressive movement applies not only theoretically, but also as a methodological tool to the analysis of metaphors in a Hollywood film and a report from a TV news show.

In Part IV, temporality as a third key characteristic of cinematic metaphor is introduced. It concerns a fundamental characteristic of face-to-face as well as of cinematic meaning-making, and, as such, is a theme that runs through the entire book. The poiesis of film-viewing cannot be conceived without recourse to the temporal structure of cinematic images, of audiovisual media and embodied experience in general. We illustrate how the temporality of cinematic metaphor affects all levels of cinematic staging, from cinematic expressive movement units to the unfolding of an entire film.

In Chapter 11, we document the commonality between the dynamics of discourse and the temporality of audiovisual images with two case studies, showing how emergent metaphorical scenarios as temporal forms of meaning-making apply to processes of multimodal face-to-face interaction as well as to the cinematic mode of perceiving.

In Chapter 12, the macro level of cinematic metaphor is illustrated with an analysis of a TV-news report. We describe how metaphorical themes intertwine and orchestrate the entire television news feature, and illustrate how, methodologically, analyses of the micro level of cinematic expressive movements connect with larger levels of metaphorical themes.

In Chapter 13, this approach is applied to the analysis of two metaphorical themes running through an entire Hollywood film. We show how, from the temporal parcours of experiencing a recurrent pattern of cinematic expressive movements, metaphorical themes evolve and intertwine – forming cinematic systematic metaphors.

We believe that the study of cinematic metaphor has important implications for how metaphor should be theoretically characterized and how it should be studied more generally. Throughout the book, we suggest that the core theoretical and methodological positions we develop for cinematic metaphor also apply to the study of processes of meaning-making in multimodal face-to-face interaction, including hand-gestures, body-movements, and speech in interaction. The conclusion further explores implications of the theoretical and methodological positions developed that go beyond metaphor in audiovisual media.

The book closes with an appendix that offers an introduction to the methods for analyzing cinematic metaphor as an affective temporal form of 'doing' metaphor and a dynamic form of meaning-making. The appendix illustrates how these methods apply to the analysis of audiovisual material and to multimodal face-to-face communication. Along with a hands-on outline of the methods, diagrams visualizing different aspects of our analyses are presented.

# Part I: **Setting the Stage for Cinematic Metaphor**

# Introduction

Nothing is so obvious as the fact that large parts of our everyday communication are structured through the use of audiovisual images. At the same time, nothing is as taken for granted as the fact that we all understand them. The power of audiovisual images is frequently so emphasized – and indeed countless examples could be named which prove their power. And yet we still have a highly underdeveloped idea of what this power actually consists in. What is it, for instance, that distinguishes communicating with audiovisual images from other, primarily language-based, forms? Can audiovisual images be described in terms of communication at all? And what might be lost when we consider social interaction structured by audiovisual images as 'communication'? What is the specific media-character of audiovisual images?

Despite a long history in film theory, these questions are hardly recognized by current scholars of multimodal metaphor and cognitive approaches to film and audiovision more generally. We thus face a kind of absence in current theory and research on metaphor in audiovisual media. Part I of the book considers some of the consequences of this neglect, while at the same time developing a theoretical framework that not only accounts for the specific media-character of audiovisual images but takes it as starting point for a theory of metaphors in audiovisual media.

As a rule, audiovisual images, in their obvious comprehensibility, get assigned to a representational regime that assumes, on the one hand, a model of representational pictoriality and, on the other, a primarily verbal model of human communication. The turn to "visual culture [*Bildwissenschaft*]" has largely been carried out without taking moving images of audiovisual media – and the theoretical tradition related to them – into account (Mitchell 2008, 2009). Moving images are all too frequently understood in terms of 'an image', that is, as a discrete, iconic representation; and if they then become the object of theoretical reflection after all, this is done with reference to linguistic forms of expression and their corresponding theoretical concepts, such as code, text theory, or narrative. Furthermore, a methodology which would allow a description of how audiovisual images structure viewers' thinking when watching a film, and that relates such a description to affect, movement and action, is largely still lacking, notwithstanding the fact that a casual reading of the history of film theory (from Sergej Eisenstein to Gilles Deleuze) suggests the development of a poetology of film that conceives of audiovisual movement-images as specific mode of experience.

https://doi.org/10.1515/9783110580785-partI

If more and more research from the field of conceptual metaphor theory has turned to audiovisual images in recent years, this has occurred not only in response to the enormous significance that audiovisual media have for political, social, economic, scientific, religious, and pedagogical spheres of communication. The orientation of conceptual metaphor theory to the multimodality of forms of human expression emphasizes its constitutive hypothesis, namely that metaphorical concepts are fundamental cognitive schemas from which linguistic metaphors are derived and which, as a consequence, are considered as being prior to language. Indeed, both in view of gestural and audiovisual modes of expression, processes of metaphorical meaning emergence can be shown that are not formulated linguistically (Cienki and Müller 2008a, Forceville and Urios-Aparisi 2009). Research on gestures has demonstrated that conceptual metaphor theory addresses embodied processes of meaning-making which are primarily structured by physical interaction, inter-affective involvement, and synchronization of gestural movements as behavioral expression (see Chapters 4 and 5 for a critical discussion of CMT's notion of embodiment; see alsoHorst et al. 2014, Kappelhoff and Müller 2011, Müller and Schmitt 2015).

Clearly, conceptual metaphor theory, including a variety of its internal strands, only captures one specific area within contemporary metaphor research. In fact, the field, including theory and application is broad and diverse, and includes highly controversial positions (Gibbs 2008, Hampe 2017, Haverkamp 1983, 2007b, Müller et al. 2013, 2014, Ortony 1993).

However, very broadly speaking, we can distinguish two profoundly distinct positions: on the one hand, (neuro-)cognitive research on cognitive concepts and schemas, which assumes a biological grounding of human thinking; on the other, philosophical anthropology, which conceives of history as cultural history and as history of thought. Philosophical anthropology pursues the study of historical development of forms of thought, including abstract concepts of human thinking and media. In very simplified terms, we can say that there are two key approaches to metaphor that are, however, diametrically opposed with regard to their epistemological and their academic goals. While both claim to study the forms of human thinking, their respective understanding of 'what thinking is' is sharply opposed: philosophical anthropology conceives of thinking as historically reconstructable (cultural), cognitive neuroscience considers thinking as processing of universal neurocognitive schemata.

The two approaches mark opposed endpoints on a range of contemporary positions to metaphor. One side is occupied by Lakoff and Johnson's conceptual metaphor theory, which continues to dominate the discourse of/on metaphor in linguistics and cognitive sciences more generally. Notably, this theoretical position defines itself explicitly by a radical break with the rhetorical and poetological tradition of human forms of expression (Lakoff and Johnson 1980a, b). On the other side, we have Hans Blumenberg's *metaphorology* (Blumenberg 1981, 1987 [1981]), which has significantly influenced the discourse on metaphor within philosophy, and continues to do so (Buch and Weidner 2014, Gehring 2009a, Haverkamp 1983, 1998, 2007a, b, Kopperschmidt 2000, Kroß and Zill 2011). Blumenberg's philosophical perspective on metaphor links back to the tradition of rhetoric and poetology and his work on metaphor aims to grasp the rhetorical dimension of linguistic utterances in their epistemic relevance: we understand the world relative to its media- and symbolic instruments of representation. In relation to our account of cinematic metaphor, these two perspectives appear as indispensable as they are incompatible. For one thing, conceptual metaphor theory brings a model of bodily experience into play that makes it possible to describe processes of understanding in their relation to concrete sensory experiences of perception and action. This 'embodied' perspective addresses directly what constitutes the process of understanding audiovisual images and what characterizes audiovisual images as a specific media-mode of experience: the concrete experience of a perceptual sensation of film-viewing and -hearing which grounds all processes of film understanding (cf. Section 1.3) Blumenberg's metaphorology, on the other hand, promises access to the cultural history of human thought, which is precisely the history of development and change of symbolic forms in which human thinking sediments: its media, its artefacts and its languages. Blumenberg's philosophical rhetoric provides access to an understanding of reality, which is always a shared reality of a cultural community. Each theory of audiovisual images that claims to grasp film images themselves as a genuine form of human thinking and that aims at reconstructing the function of film-images for the modeling of cultural horizons of meanings is to be situated within such a historical perspective.

Starting from a cultural-historical film studies perspective thus implies – this is our basic thesis – that every question on metaphors and metaphorical concepts in audiovisual images is inseparably linked to the question of the historicity of media modes of experience, that is, their cultural-historical positioning. Against this backdrop, there can be no understanding of the processes of meaning-making of audiovisual images which ignores the fundamental historicity of cultural processes of meaning-making. Already a systematic analysis that simply aims at describing the interaction between viewers and audiovisual images as a process of meaning-making from a linguistic perspective, e.g., to pursue the dynamics of verbalizing audiovisual images, will have to take into consideration the historical dimension of its media form of experience. Why this is so will be considered more carefully over the course of our argument.

At this point, it appears necessary to also determine the specific interest that drives media theory, and specifically film theory towards engaging with current discussions in metaphor theory. What can media studies learn from metaphor research? And vice versa, how can the extensive research on metaphors in images of audiovisual media profit from the theory of cinematic images? Is it possible at all to relate these very different concepts of metaphor outlined above with one another? Or, do they perhaps have nothing more in common than naming a phenomenon that is subsequently defined as theoretical object in completely different and even incompatible ways? In order to provide an answer to these questions, initially we would like to discuss conceptual metaphor theory analysis of audiovisual images as well as cognitive theories of film understanding. We do this because what they have in common is the neglect of the historicity of audiovisual images as a mode of experience, whereas for us the historicity of the mode of human experience is a constitutive axiom of any kind of meaning-making.

# 1 Cinematic Metaphor as Poiesis: The Movement-Image as Starting Point

This chapter offers a critique of how audiovisual metaphors are analyzed within conceptual metaphor theory and cognitive media studies. Some of the fundamental criticisms are illustrated with an analysis of the short film DEATH AND THE MOTHER (Ruth Lingford, UK 1997) suggesting an alternative proposal to the idea of a cognitive instantiation of conceptual metaphors in audiovisual images: the grounding of metaphor in the viewer's engaging with films as movement-images. Since this involves a model of film-viewing that is profoundly different from common cognitive models of film reception, we then offer a critical review of cognitive theories of film understanding before introducing our alternative model: cinematic metaphor as emergent from the poiesis of film-viewing.

## 1.1 A Critique of Cognitive Analyses of Metaphors in Film

In conceptual metaphor theory and in cognitive film studies, the historical-cultural dimension of human thinking only contributes incidentally to analyses of visual representations. By explaining the meaning of visual representations through recourse to a physiological level of universal hard-wired cognitive structures (Johnson 2007, Lakoff and Johnson 1980b, 1999, Lakoff 2008), the concrete situatedness of meaning is turned into something secondary. From such a perspective, all historical and cultural formations of metaphorical thinking are ascribed to basic schemas of human cognition – and rather paradoxically are explained by them at the same time (for discussions of the circularity of CMT, see, e.g., Cienki and Müller 2008b, Gibbs 1998, Müller 2008a, b). In contrast, for us, the situatedness of meaning-making is essential, as is the character of the medium in which this happens. For our framework of cinematic metaphor, the historicity of audiovisual images as a human mode of experience is constitutive and affects every aspect of meaning-making. This cultural-historical dimension of metaphoricity in audiovisual media is irreducible – and correspondingly can in no way be circumvented by appealing to general principles of human thinking. We can maintain, however, that models of cognitive processes are instructive about the physiological or psychological bases of mental activities – but not about the concrete, historically situated sense-making interactions in each specific case.

https://doi.org/10.1515/9783110580785-002

### The historicity of metaphorical meaning-making

The historicity of metaphorical meaning-making relates to two traditions, poetics and rhetoric, that contemporary metaphor theory has cast aside. Charles Forceville, one of the leading figures in applying conceptual metaphor theory to audiovisual media analysis, highlights the break with these traditions:

> From [Lakoff and Johnson's conceptual metaphor theory] on, metaphor was no longer one of a series of tropes that could enhance or embellish the aesthetic meaning of a poem or the persuasive power of speeches (as had been its primary claim to fame since Aristotelian times), but one of the conceptual tools for human beings to make sense of the world. (Forceville 2016, 17)

Forceville positions conceptual metaphor theory as the origin of theorizing metaphor as a "conceptual tool" (Forceville 2016, 17–18). Since Lakoff and Johnson's concept is explicitly situated as a break with the traditions of poetics and rhetoric, these dimensions are removed from a media analysis based on conceptual metaphor theory. What's more, by shelving aesthetics, and marginalizing the persuasive dimension of aesthetic figurations, which is crucial for rhetoric, we lose the idea of audiovisual images as a mode of perceptual experience, so central to cultural and film studies, and, as a consequence, it disappears from the focus of media analysis.

### Audiovisual images as moving images

In fact, from the viewpoint of media theory, a fundamental objection to the conceptual metaphor analysis of audiovisual images can be made. They refer to audiovisual images as sequences of static images, rather than as *moving* images, which means that such analyses ignore a fundamental facet of the media-specific nature of audiovisual images. Moreover, they typically refer to 'content' as if it was 'contained' within the image and readily interpretable. Instead of considering the image in its media and aesthetic composition, it is immediately identified as an audiovisual *representation* of some real-world circumstances. In this way, audiovisual images are not categorically distinguished from texts or paintings, and as a consequence they are not considered in terms of their particular media format.

For conceptual metaphor analyses of audiovisual images this entails a (seemingly) 'useful' simplification. If, by rejecting the traditions of poetics and rhetoric, one dismisses all the differentiations that art theory, cultural theory, and media theory have developed about the audiovisual image, it becomes quite simple to describe any media phenomenon in terms of cognitive schemas. This also avoids dealing with the phenomenon of film images as moving images.

The contrast that conceptual metaphor theory establishes with poetics and rhetoric only makes sense if one seriously claims that, for an analysis of language and media, the identification of a universal cognitive schema would fully answer questions of meaning and function – which is indeed how works from a conceptual metaphor theory point of view tend to present their analysis (Coëgnarts and Kravanja 2012c, Forceville 2017). To speak allegorically, such a process corresponds to the viewpoint of visitors to a museum in front of a Picasso painting who recognize a face in the composition that is made up of two, three or perhaps four faces. Instead of seeing the painting in relation to the history of western portraiture and as a new form of seeing a face brought into the world through painting, they identify it as the representation of a deformed human face and interpret the multifaceted face as a metaphor – let's say, metaphorically portraying a multiple personality or a crisis of identity. What gets interpreted in this way, however, is merely the 'naked' representation (the face of a human person, or are there two or three persons in one face?) and not the poetic dimension of the painting, that is, a pictorial composition that does not stand by itself, but in its relation to the history of the rhetoric of the portrait and that brings a new reality into being (instead of re-presenting an already given reality). When such analyses are made, what gets lost is a reflection of the media-specific and historical character of paintings or of film, i.e., exactly what is the object of concern of media-studies.

### Discourse dynamics of metaphor

Our recognition of the crucial theoretical importance of the media-specificity of cinematic metaphor resonates with dynamic approaches to metaphor in discourse developed for verbal metaphor and gesture that also attempt to deal with the shortcomings of conceptual metaphor theory (Cameron 2011, Müller 2008a, b). For example, not only do gestures share several fundamental features with audiovisual images, they also display the situatedness, the ephemeral, constantly changing forms of metaphorical meaning as intersubjective bodily experience. Formulating a counter position to the conceptual metaphor idea of linguistic metaphors as instantiations of pre-existing conceptual metaphors, the Discourse Dynamics approach holds that verbal metaphors emerge in interaction in a quest for mutual understanding, a continuously unfolding process in which metaphoricity is adaptive, changing and emergent (Cameron 2008a). In Cameron's Discourse Dynamics approach, there is only discourse.

Connecting cultural-historical film theory with linguistic gesture research and with discourse dynamic metaphor theory allows us to grasp and to describe the emergence of cinematic metaphors as a media-specific situated process of embodied intersubjective meaning-making: it will help us to develop the idea of cinematic metaphor as poiesis.

## 1.2 Metaphor and the Movement-Image: DEATH AND THE MOTHER

Without a media-theoretic understanding of the audiovisual image as a cultural artefact, every media and modality difference simply disappears. What's more, the basic grounding of the audiovisual image as a movement-image disappears. Across the various media formats, from web videos to films for the cinema, audiovisual images are characterized by the fact that they are *not* a succession of isolated, immobile pictorial representations, but rather generate temporal gestalts. These gestalts are created in a similar way to hand gestures, as a changing flow of shapes, positions and movement qualities. The movement of audiovisual moving images is, along with its temporality, constitutive of the media mode that brings audiovisual representations into existence, in the first place. As a consequence, any theorization of audiovisual images that takes their media specifics seriously must begin from movement and temporality. Therefore, we speak of movement-images (Deleuze 2008 [1983]).

An application of conceptual metaphor theory to media analysis also requires a media-specific understanding of audiovisual images before being in a position to attribute metaphorical concepts to moving images. In addition, we must have an understanding of the moving image that does not consider the various modalities (e.g., "visuals, written language, spoken language, non-verbal sound and music", Forceville 2009b, 383) as signaling systems or modes in isolation; rather, we must address the overall dynamics that allows these modalities to merge into a combined audiovisual perceptual whole. In short, we need an analytical approach that does not take audiovisual images to be a loose combination of different modalities, but which can grasp their specific perceptual quality as the basic feature of the cinematic mode of experience itself – and thus in contrast with texts, paintings, photographs, etc.

Here the term multimodality appears to be relevant. Indeed, it seems to precisely address this dynamic complexity of audiovisual images. However, this term also needs to be clarified theoretically. In the context of metaphor theory, 'multimodality' refers to distinct (human) expressive modes, such as spoken and written language, gesture, or pictures. Now, film theory has made a categorical distinction between the idea of 'movement-image' and the term moving image, which refers simply to pictures that move. The audiovisual movement-image is seen as a quite distinct media mode of representation in itself, characterized precisely by the fact that it can consolidate all possible aspects of acoustic and visual perceptual dimensions in a temporal gestalt. The movement-image is defined, through its multimodality, as a specific expressive mode, and, at the same time, it implies a particular way of perceiving in multimodal movement gestalts. This contrasts with the additive understanding of multiple modes which typically characterizes research on 'multimodal metaphor'.

This is why we make a terminological distinction between audiovisual moving image and cinematic movement-image (Deleuze 2008 [1983]). Moving image as a term designates media artifacts, that is, all audiovisual images, quite regardless of their media-technological type and completely in the sense that these images can be understood as isolated illustrative representations of contents that move. The term movement-image, on the other hand, designates the overarching context of the temporal shape of a film, video, or television report; it refers to the staging, poetic, or rhetorical regime under which the isolated moving images, that is, short audiovisual representations, can be conceived as elements of the entirety of a cinematic movement-image unfolding in the time of its viewing. The movement-image constructs, and is constructed within, its own space and time. It functions as an aesthetic and logical framing which turns individual audiovisual representations into a meaningful whole.

We will illustrate the difference between a focus on audiovisual moving images and a metaphor analysis which starts from the aesthetics of cinematic movement-images with a discussion of the short film DEATH AND THE MOTHER (Ruth Lingford, UK 1997).[1] Charles Forceville has published a conceptual metaphor analysis (Forceville 2017) of this film and we choose this as an example of an analysis that targets the succession of isolated audiovisual representations in terms of a narrative logic of action and as instantiation of universal cognitive structures (image schemas). We contrast this approach with an analytic perspective that starts from the gestalt-like whole of the movement-image, and which conceives of its aesthetics as the experiential grounds (the felt sensations) from which metaphorical meaning emerges in the situated process of film-viewing.

The film DEATH AND THE MOTHER is based on a fairy tale of Hans Christian Andersen. It describes the fate of a mother living in a lonely house in the forest. She is visited by Death, who, in an unobserved moment, takes away her child.

1 Analysis by Hermann Kappelhoff, carried out within the Cinepoetics' research focus 'Metaphor – Film Images, Cinematic Thinking, and Cognition'. The English version for this book was adapted by Cornelia Müller and Dorothea Horst.

She pursues him and, in order to find the right path, has to give away her skin, eyes, and hair. When she arrives and demands her child back, Death shows her that the child will live in poverty and misery, whereupon she finally decides to leave the child with him.

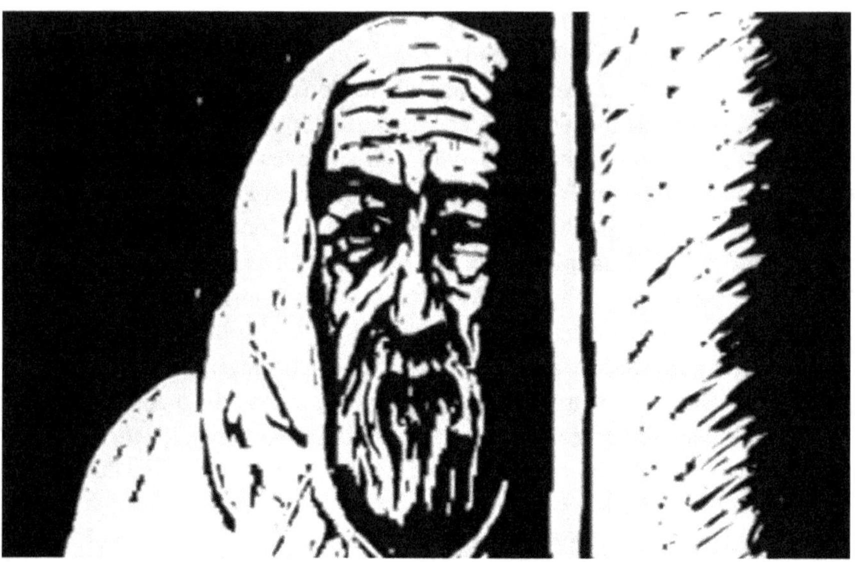

**Figure 1.1:** Animation in the style of woodcut prints in DEATH AND THE MOTHER

The video uses animations in the style of woodcut prints (Figure 1.1). This is extremely important for the poetics and aesthetics of the short film because the audiovisual images here are based on a highly abstract, dynamic interplay between light and dark surfaces, dense and less dense cross-hatchings. And indeed, it is above all the constantly alternating status of individual omissions, surfaces, and hatchings, that is, instantaneous perceptual shapes, which mark the meaning of individual audiovisual images – within a poetic logic of the cinematic movement-image. For instance, a black space between white tree-like shapes changes from the negative of omission in one moment to the positive of a gestalt-like surface of Death in human shape in the next and vice versa. It is, thus, only through the animated movement that object-like figurations appear from the hatchings and shadowings: the forest, the mother's lonely house, Death, the mother and her child. These figurations do not feature continual or self-contained contours. Due to the woodcut style, they are always rough, angular, and jagged. This unpolished and rough quality throws their haptic qualities into sharp relief: the angularity of the trees, the sharp angles of the paths, the sharpness of ice sheets on a lake, the agony in the mother's face, all become an immediate experience in the act of watching. Moreover, these figurations never have an ultimate, fixed form for the spectator. They are continuously quivering and oscillating, caught in an overall movement, a permanent metamorphosis from one instantaneous perceptual shape to the next. This continuous flow of becoming and decaying, that is, the non-existent permanence, is what becomes the object of perception in a very explicit manner here, and thus brings death – one central aspect of the story – as a concrete experience into being. Indeed, every move of the appearance of the figuration is linked to the dynamic perceptual sensation of a spectator, who attempts to grasp what is only hatchings and surfaces in the next moment, and vice versa (Figure 1.2).

The potential of these audiovisual images to affect us does not lie in the individual representations, but in that dynamic of constant transformation, of ambiguous figures and metamorphoses. That is, there is an uninterrupted connection between the metamorphoses of the animated woodcut pattern and the dynamics of the transforming perceptual sensations of the viewer. The movement-image emerges from an interaction between audiovisual moving images (that is, the animations) and the perceptual process (that is, the flowing metamorphoses of the individual phases of animation within the spectator's perception); the technologically animated movement as affecting force is inseparably intertwined with the embodied experience of the viewer.

From the woodcut hatchings and shadowings, we, the spectators, effortlessly recognize the figurations of a fairy-tale-like plot: the wrestling between mother and Death over the life of the child. In addition to being bodily affected in the very reception process, this recognition can be traced back to a diffuse knowledge about allegorical figures and iconographies from fairy tales that spectators bring, such as Death as an old man taking doomed people with him, or the unconditional love of a mother towards her dying child that recalls the iconography of countless *pietà* representations, in which Mary, as suffering mother, holds the body of Jesus. Only in this constellation, that is, in the union of cultural-historical context and present experience can the animated movement of the audiovisual image, the dynamically transforming relationship between pattern, hatchings, and emptiness, become the shape of a mother holding her dying child in her arms, struggling not to relinquish it to death. For the viewer then a cognitive/perceptual relation between figure and ground arises from a strong and visually dynamic black-and-white surface structure in the style of a woodcut.[2]

---

2 It is such an emergence 'becoming' of the representation or 'content' (i.e., the figure) from its respective media-specific environment (i.e., the ground) that McLuhan is referring to with his famous statement "The medium is the message" (cf. McLuhan 1966).

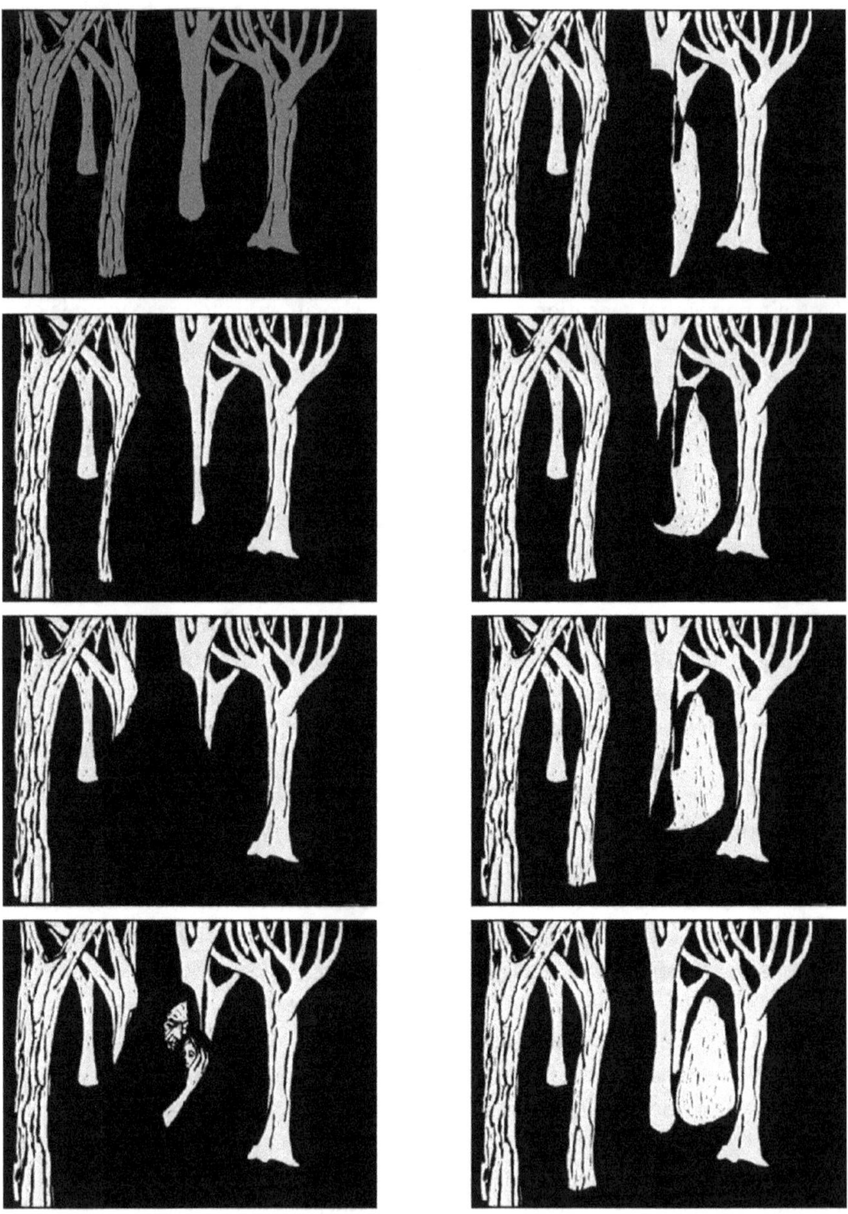

**Figure 1.2:** Instantaneous perceptual shapes in DEATH AND THE MOTHER

Forceville's (2017) analysis of metaphorical FORCES in the animated short film applies, however, directly at the level of the action of the fairy tale (a mother who is meant to relinquish her child to death). That is to say, by analyzing the film directly on the level of its representation, characters and narratives are treated as givens. The perceptual process that allows for a movement-image to emerge from the black-and-white schema of light and dark hatchings, in the first place, is thus ignored. Such an analysis also ignores that the narrative emerges from the viewer's engagement with movement-images rather than being encoded in an audiovisual form (as a sender-receiver model of communication would assume). From the point of view of film-viewing, the narrative emerges from the viewer's experiential engagement with movement-images in a process of 'fictionalization':

> Visual representations are not already given with the image, but are themselves the result of complex processes of fictionalization. For any understanding of what is represented in the image, the audiovisual data of the moving film image must above all already be realized as the embodied experiences of the senses. (Kappelhoff and Greifenstein 2016, 184)

In Forceville's analysis, in contrast, all figures (e.g., Death, the mother, the child) and actions (e.g., the stealing of the child, the search of the mother) are taken for granted, as if they were 'contained' in the audiovisual images. These audiovisual representations are considered to convey "*manifestations* of the FORCE schemas" (emphasis CM & HK), which act as source domains for the metaphorical conceptualization of the narrative. For example, Death's walk towards the mother's house is conceived of as an instance of the ENABLEMENT schema. Forceville defines the ENABLEMENT schema as follows: "Some sort of internal or external force provides the means for the agent or entity to move into the desired direction" (p. 243). Drawing upon presumably shared cultural-historical background knowledge and another cognitive schema, Forceville explains the represented movement of Death '*on*' the screen: "but we know from myths and fairy tales that Death has a desire to take people with him, so we could say that Death is here drawn to the sickly child, a candidate to be seized away from life by him (ATTRACTION)" (p. 246). On these grounds, he argues that viewers would interpret these kinds of FORCES not just literally but also metaphorically as a source domain for Death's desire or compulsion to take away the child (DESIRE IS PHYSICAL ATTRACTION or COMPULSION IS A COMPELLING FORCE).

Rather than conceiving of metaphoricity as a gestalt that arises from the process of perception, it is described in terms of static relations between audiovisual representations. Moreover, the elements of metaphor, i.e., target and source, are treated as if they were incorporated in the audiovisual images themselves. Forceville's definition of multimodal metaphors indeed labels them as "metaphors whose target and source are each represented exclusively or predominantly in different modes" (Forceville 2009a, 24) as if audiovisual images additively combine different modes to represent metaphorical instantiations, a given fairy tale, a given story. The audiovisual composition is thus treated as a direct representation, a depiction of metaphors[3] (e.g., Death's walk towards the house as the child's lethal fate) whose recognition and understanding on the part of the viewers is justified by the argument that they rely on "directly meaningful, preconceptual structures rooted in the body's movement through space, perceptual interaction with the environment, and the handling of objects" (Forceville 2017, 242). What is being analyzed are the elements of the narrative depicted audiovisually, i.e., of images as representations rather than as movement-images. What is being analyzed is the narrative that the researcher has produced by watching the film, not the process of film-viewing. In this way, audiovisual representations are considered self-evident. The crucial question of how we get to those media representations at all when viewing audiovisual images remains completely disregarded in such a restricted focus on those representations. It is as if what actually is to be analyzed in terms of the movement-image were completely self-evident. However, it is only because of a perceptual process, i.e., a reception process, that the figuration of a mother who is fighting for her child can be distinguished in the first place.

To summarize, an analysis that directly refers to the fairy tale as a represented action has several problems:

- it neglects the viewer's process that allows for the figuration of a mother-child relation to emerge from experiencing the composition of dynamically changing woodcut patterns as a movement-image and an affective expression in the first place;
- it reduces the aesthetic intention of employing the black-and-white technique of the woodcut for an animated film, which, in fact, opens up a reflexive space that resonates with all other techniques operating with such pure (positive-negative) contrasts, to a simple stylistic packaging of what would otherwise be "only bare, propositional information" (Forceville 2017, 254), i.e., a given narrative presented in a historic print style;
- it takes the audiovisual representation of the mother and the child for granted, cultural-historical contexts are being called up post-hoc as "background frames that are mostly accessed automatically and subconsciously" (Forceville 2017, 253) and get assigned to the representation via cognitive

3 Cf. also Eggertsson and Forceville (2009, 429): "After all, a central tenet of CMT is that human beings conceive certain phenomena systematically in terms of certain other phenomena, allowing for numerous different surface manifestations of a single conceptual metaphor."

analogy. It considers cultural-historical contexts as automatically accessible, fixed, cognitive inventories of cultural-historical knowledge, rather than as an essential element of creating the representation in the process of film-viewing itself – which is what we consider as poiesis of film-viewing.

In brief, in a conceptual-metaphor analysis of Ruth Lingford's short silent movie, the viewer's activity of creating a cinematic image of the suffering mother and her child disappears in the black box of an uncritically assumed pictorial representation. A perspective from media and cultural studies reverses the theoretical model in respect of emotions, affect, and feeling. What, from the perspective of conceptual metaphor theory, is being *subsequently* ascribed to the allegorical figurations as constellations of action is to be traced back, in terms of media aesthetics, to the movement-image itself, to the interaction between animated movement and perceptual sensation, to the co-production of audiovisual image and the body of the spectator. Their interaction forms the foundation on which the figuration can appear as a fairy-tale-like allegory at all. If, in contrast, the mere representation of the mother and her suffering child is placed in the foreground, the interaction between movement-image and an affected spectator's body disappears.

The problem outlined in this section, including the discussion of the metaphor analysis of Ruth Lingford's animated short film, may at first glance appear to be only a matter of perspective – according to whether audiovisual images are considered in terms of representations or whether they are considered as movement-images emergent in the interplay of viewer and audiovisual image. In fact, the problems just discussed lead directly into the heart of current film theoretic debates concerning cognitive models applied to analyzing audiovisual images, and reach far beyond questions of metaphor in film and television. What is at stake is no less than the fundamental question of how viewers understand the films they see.

## 1.3 Critical Review of Cognitive Theories of Film Understanding

Film studies as an academic discipline started from the goal of asking *how* spectators understand a film rather than the popular question in film and cultural criticism of *what* individual films suggest. In this section we sketch out the models which have significantly influenced discourse in film studies about film understanding. It will then be possible to locate and outline our approach more precisely.

From Umberto Eco's semiotics of cinematic codes (Eco 1976), Christian Metz's syntactics of the film text (Metz 1991 [1968]), the imaginary structure of film narration (Heath 1981, Mulvey 1975), through the narrative models of cognitive film theory (Bordwell 2008, Branigan 1992), and on to cognitive psychological models of dealing with film images in the last decade (Coëgnarts and Kravanja 2012a, b, Persson 2003, Tan 1996), the question of film understanding constantly reappears. Admittedly, from Eco on, what is meant is something quite different than would be suggested by the reading of the term "understanding" in hermeneutics. Hermeneutics focuses on the historically and culturally determined distance between the understanding subject and the text, in the light of which meaning-making appears as a highly precarious act, while at the same time pointing out that it is just this distance that allows the construction of meaning (Gadamer 1960).

Without this hermeneutic perspective on understanding, what cinematic images represent is obvious. Indeed, the above approaches agree in conceptualizing film understanding in strict opposition to hermeneutic 'sense'. David Bordwell, who has developed the certainly most influential film-analytical model, can therefore formulate the following as a premise of his approach: "By and large, audiences understand the films they see." (Bordwell 2008, 135) If, nonetheless, large numbers of publications mention the question of film understanding in the title, this indicates a fundamental problem. Metz points to the problem when introducing his extremely influential film theory *The Semiotics of Cinema* with the following remark: "A film is difficult to explain because it is easy to understand." (Metz 1991 [1968], 69) Put differently: understanding itself might indeed be simple – the theoretical appreciation of this obviousness is complicated. The claim that basic meanings are understood, as a rule lacks a convincing model of how this understanding is accomplished. Instead, what is to be understood from film images is taken for granted, as already given: actors, actions, spaces, objects, treated as a concatenation of isolated pictorial representations.

Because of such a mimetic understanding of representation and the idea of a succession of isolated signs, the traditional code model, as well as film semiotics (Eco 1976, Joost 2008, Kanzog 2007), quickly reach their limits. Indeed, semiotic analysis ends up in a tautology, if visual representations are understood as signs of what the camera reproduces[4] – a theoretical dead end, which Metz already tried to deal with: first by trying to localize the understanding process, not at the level of the image, but at the level of the syntactic structure of a film text;[5] then, in a poststructuralist turn, by choosing the term 'film

4 Attempts such as Eco's (1976) or Pasolini's (1971)dows semiotics of film which do not focus on film representations, but on the cinematic image, only gained influence with Deleuze's taxonomy of film images, or their relation to Peircean semiotics.

5 Current attempts to outline the term 'text' also aim at accounting its pragmatic dimension by asking how the text functions in communication processes (Grauwe 2000, Wildfeuer 2013).

text' as the basis for a theory of the film imaginary (Metz 2000 [1975]). What is significant here is how explicitly this turn is tied in its argumentation to a tautological grasp of visual representations. In the tradition since Metz, psychoanalytic film theory becomes convinced that, if the film image is identical with what it represents, if it is understood as a depiction of our everyday reality, then this is the effect of a deception, a deception that as process of imagination structures film understanding (Heath 1981).

Exactly at this point in the history of theory, cognitive film theory finds its starting point. It counters this understanding of film as text, including its critique of ideology and its assumption that a viewer's consciousness is ideologically preformed, by introducing the notion of an active viewer who takes part in the construction of meaning (Bordwell 1989, Carroll 1996).

Correspondingly, approaches from cognitive film theory do not relate cognitive operations to the structure of the 'film text', but to the temporal form of the narrative process. The operations themselves are based on schemas from everyday perception of space, time, and causality, as well as on repetitive patterns in which the result of film representation as information is assessed (Grodal 2009, Persson 2003, Plantinga 2009, 2013, Wuss 2009).[6] *From this perspective, the world depicted is not directly represented in the film images, but emerges from the causal-logical combination of discrete pictorial representations* (Branigan 1992, Carroll 1996). *Meaning therefore appears as a construct, in the form of the narrative that the spectators produce out of this combination.*

This conceptual link between cognitive theory and narratology has been developed by David Bordwell (1989) as a prototype for Hollywood cinema and, with recourse to Formalism, has been linked back to a historical poetics of the cinema. The latter puts the focus on the history of stylistic and technical innovations, of narrative conventions and poetic rules as cultural or film-historic knowledge, genre knowledge, or genre awareness (Bordwell 1985, Carroll 1996, Grodal 1997). This results in a theoretical model that is secured through two hypothetical premises which mutually support each other. On the one hand, universal schemas of ordinary perception are presumed and transferred to film. The second premise refers to knowledge of poetic conventions, genres and folk psychology. Whatever cannot be explained with one premise, is allocated to the other and vice versa. What remains hidden is the question of the relation between cognitive processes of film understanding and shifting historical, cultural, and media conditions of perception.

---

6 On narration as a category, which examines film in parallel to other 'text', Hogan (2011, 2013). On the term information, cf. the introduction to Nannicelli and Taberham (2014, 1–24).

Research operating from this perspective has resulted in two equally unsatisfactory responses. Either it concentrates on the discourse-analytical reconstruction of knowledge and the historical circumstances that determine production, distribution, and reception of film images, largely dropping the question of how film is understood (Caldwell 2008, Hall and Neale 2010, McDonald et al. 2015, Neale 2000). Or it continues to develop the narrative model outlined above, taking account of recent neurocognitive studies – thus abandoning any attempt to bring a historical perspective to the construction of meaning in film. This second direction is not only pursued by film research informed by cognitive psychology (Grodal 2009, Plantinga 2009, Shimamura 2013), but also by a series of works under the growing rubric of 'film as/and philosophy' (Carroll 2008, Frampton 2006, Sinnerbrink 2011, Smith and Wartenberg 2006, Wilson 2011). Over the course of these debates, research interest has shifted to the function of affect in cognitive processes (Grodal 1997, 2009, Plantinga 2009, Smith 2003, Tan 1996).[7] The speculative model of spectator understanding is countered by the 'hard-wired' aspects of film perception, that is, unconscious neuronal operating processes (Bordwell 2011, 96ff, Grodal 2009). This has enormously extended the spectrum of assumptions about schemata as framings for processes of reception in film. One no longer speaks, as in Bordwell's early work, only of perception schemata on the one hand and narrative schemata on the other, but of appraisal processes, affect scripts, image, action, or motor schemata.

Moreover, every importation of neuroscientific terms constitutes a clear tendency toward schematism in terms of effect aesthetics (Bordwell 2013, 29). This is seen above all in an extremely truncated understanding of the phenomenological term 'embodiment'. Corresponding analyses use a concept of embodiment that imagines it as summarily doing away with the reflexivity of human cognition. Every historical, cultural, or technological differentiation of the conditions of film cognition disappears in a cognitive model of the physiological processing of audiovisual images; a model, the empirical validity of which is highly dubious.

Importing models of cognitive psychology into film and media studies has intensified the problems outlined above. Indeed, these approaches (Fahlenbrach

7 On the scope of the spectrum, cf. the contribution in Anderson and Fisher Anderson (2007). Many works from this field focus on an relation of empathy or simulation to the characters represented in the film (cf. Brewer 1996, Bruun Vaage 2009, Eder 2008, Schick and Ebbrecht 2008, Smith 1995, Tan 2013, Vorderer, Wulff, and Friedrichsen 1996, Wulff 2003, Zillmann 1996), which sometimes are tied to formal aspects of genre poetics and dramaturgy (Cutting, Iricinschi, and Brunick 2013, Frome 2014, Gendler 2012, Grodal 1997, Smith 2003, Visch 2007, Visch and Tan 2009). In the German-speaking realm there are comparable articles, primarily in communication studies and in research on media effects (cf. Dohle 2011, Suckfüll 2004); the focus here is often on the concept of meta-emotions, which evaluate the feelings of spectators in the reception process (cf. Bartsch 2007, Oliver 1993).

2010, Forceville 2008, Grodal 2009, Persson 2003, Tan 1996) resort to the fact that audiovisual images are first and foremost perceptual events which cannot be directly read as texts or text-like narratives. They do, however, regularly resort to perceptual models that function like structural systems for generating meaning. The recourse to cognitive-psychological or neuropsychological empiricism is used to justify interpretations of audiovisual images as reconstructions of cognitive processes.

In place of a grounded argument, comes the more or less explicit claim that a recourse to the most general principles of human cognition could explain the meaning-making of spectators in their interaction with audiovisual images of a film, a video, or a television broadcast. Reference to the empirical knowledge of cognitive science replaces the image-analytical justification of interpretive operations.

These models do not relate cognitive processes of reception to the level of visual perception, but to the temporal arrangements of events 'represented' in audiovisual images. This becomes clear, particularly in recent theories which extend cognitive narratology and cognitive film theory as a transmedia concept in the sense of a cognitive media theory (cf. Kuhn, Scheidgen, and Weber 2013, Nannicelli and Taberham 2014). *Detached from its media specificity, the film narrative becomes the representation of an event that took place in front of the camera* (Kuhn, Scheidgen, and Weber 2013, Prince 2003). As a result, it makes no difference whether the identity of the film image and isolated audiovisual representations are traced back to perceptual schemas derived from evolution (such as image schemas). Either way, the perceptual, affective, and cognitive processes disappear into the black box of a pictorial-mimetic understanding of representation. In this way, we lose the 'work' that the spectators themselves are doing over the course of viewing.

Such a reduced conception of the process of film reception – of meaning-making and, with it, the poiesis of film-viewing – can only be accepted as long as audiovisual representations are considered to represent a given reality, before any media and aesthetic involvement. Only a robust realism that radically abandons the media and cultural mediation of a jointly shared reality would allow this, and this seems highly questionable/problematic. What then might a theoretical approach look like that seeks to liberate that activity of the spectator from the black box of a simple model of pictorial-mimetic representation?

## 1.4 The Alternative Proposal: Cinematic Metaphor as Poiesis of Film-Viewing

Our alternative proposal is a cultural-historical poetology of film and audiovisual media which starts theoretically as well as methodologically from the process of media perception as poiesis of film-viewing. Rather than being instantiated, cinematic metaphors emerge from the poiesis of film-viewing. We thus suggest a media-aesthetic framework for cinematic metaphor which is marked by an essential difference to the models outlined above, which apply cognitive theories to the analysis of audiovisual images. In the following, we discuss these differences by developing a media-aesthetic perspective on audiovisual images as cinematic movement-images and cinematic metaphors as emergent forms of meaning-making.

### A specific mode of perception

We have already repeatedly underlined the specific media-character of audiovisual images as movement-image; we have also argued that audiovisual images are not appropriately accounted for as sequences of images that move, nor as representations of contents that move. We would now like to highlight that their mediality involves, in fact, a specific perceptual mode. Our perhaps most substantial premise is: audiovisual images *in no way* reproduce the spatio-temporal structures of everyday perception patterns as a priori structures of experience shared by all human beings (as the idea of image schema for instance would suggest). Interpreting audiovisual images in terms of everyday perception misses the point that perceptual patterns (everyday and cinematic) are always realized in concrete contexts in which they occur and from which meaning is made. It also misses the point that different contexts imply different forms of perception and, with it, the difference between a media context and an everyday context. Perceptual patterns are always realized as concrete figurations of space and time and, precisely with regard to these space-time structures, audiovisual images are significantly different from our everyday perception, just as they differ from other media and arts. *Audiovisual images set up their own space-time logic and cinematic perceiving engages with this cinematic space-time composition to create a narrative, be it on the level of a feature film or of a television broadcast.*

The cinematic movement-image can thus neither be understood as a mental representation of given objects, actions, or agents that exist independently from the mediality of the image, nor as the reconstruction of a narration or plot based on cognitive processes that bring isolated audiovisual representations into a particular temporal-logical cause and effect arrangement. On the contrary, analyses of the viewers' process of meaning-making with audiovisual images can only be done through reconstruction of the framing conditions of the viewers' aesthetic experience. This does not mean that the analytical focus shifts away from concrete images toward an abstract idea of aesthetic experience. Rather, the cinematic image in its concrete aesthetic composition is reconstructed as the media and aesthetic framing of a perceptual process that puts all audiovisual representation under the regime of a specific spatio-temporal sensibility. For the analysis of such images, this means that they cannot be grasped as the sum of isolated single representations. Instead the cinematic movement-image must first be reconstructed in the analysis itself – and here indeed is its constitutive difference to how everyday perception works.

If we skip this step, which is often the case in film analysis informed by cognitive theory, and pay no attention to the concrete media and aesthetic conditions of the cinematic movement-image, that is, the dynamic of a continuous perceptual process structured by media, then instead of analyzing film images, we merely analyze isolated audiovisual representations (such as characters, plots, objects, or places). Disregarding the aesthetic-media framing of the cinematic movement-image leads to an interpretation of single audiovisual representations in terms of the most general cognitive principles, just as if the issues represented were carried out within an all-encompassing everyday world. *What is missing in such an analysis is precisely the object that is to be analyzed: the cinematic movement-image itself.*

### Cinematic movement-image as media-aesthetic framing

When we speak of media-aesthetic framing with regard to a cinematic movement-image, we are thinking of a completely open logic of bringing together objects, actions and figures, as well as every single representation, under a specific aesthetic order. This media-aesthetic framing may be understood as a particular perspective in which everyday reality becomes the reality of a different consciousness, that can seem unfamiliar and even quite impossible to film viewers (Sobchack 1992); this framing follows the law of a fictional world (Koch and Voss 2006). It can be understood as a space of absolute significance, in which every single object, every character, every action designates something other than itself – that is the power, the poetic logic, or the thinking, an expression of the inner law of the diegetic world that the film unfolds; it may even express nothing more than a subjectivity which we encounter as foreign and inaccessible.

Of course, we have good reason to presume that activating basic perceptual and action schemas of our everyday perception processes does play an important role in the reception of audiovisual images, photographs, and even of paintings and sculptures. Nonetheless, analytically we must maintain that even the specific representation of something happening within the scope of a widely shared reality (for instance, film images of historical events or news broadcast) only comes out of interaction between recipients and audiovisual images. The relation to reality is a product that is actually created in this process. There is no reality out there that is being mirrored audiovisually. Rather, audiovisual images create a fictional reality that is only produced in the reception of the film, during the time of film-viewing (Kappelhoff and Greifenstein 2016, 184).

This is why, with regard to the emergence of meaning in audiovisual images, we prefer not to speak of 'communication', but of film images as a product of the interaction between viewers and audiovisual images; we take this interaction to be a genuine process of creation which is thoroughly comparable with that of artistic production. Poiesis of film-viewing addresses an act of creative production that is to be located in the media consumption itself (Certeau 1984 [1980]).

Since we address the media format of fiction film and documentary film as the basic form of all audiovisual images, we speak of a poiesis of film-viewing to refer to this creation process. The term cinematic movement-image refers to all possible audiovisual images, beyond the actual domains of cinema and film, as long as they indicate a minimum of rhetorical or poetic design beyond immediate audiovisual reproduction. Against this backdrop, we suggest that it is the poiesis of film-viewing that transforms audiovisual material into an image, that is into a cinematic movement-image. The poiesis of film-viewing is not describable in terms of a communication model that assumes fixed positions of agency. Rather, the poiesis of film-viewing involves the interaction of an indeterminate plurality of spectators with audiovisual images of an indeterminate diversity of cultural production.

Such a theoretical position has important methodological implications: namely that an analysis of audiovisual media has to start from a reconstruction of the cinematic movement-image and not with a description of the narrative, for example. Only based on such an aesthetic analysis can the diegetic world that a film unfolds, can metaphorical meaning, and can the film's specific relation to reality be accounted for appropriately.

### Film images create and express a shared reality

In that sense, film images create and express a shared reality. They bring about a complex network of relations which cannot be appropriately accounted for in terms of image schemas, or universal cognitive schemas more generally. The poiesis of film-viewing, no matter how reflective, conscious, or unconscious it may be, is embedded in the history of rhetoric and poetic formations of a shared reality. It is the cultural production that is always silently at work before we are involved in making even everyday issues tangible. What we assume as a jointly shared reality in our actions and thinking is essentially produced through this history. Cinematic metaphors are part of this cultural-historical production of shared reality. One will therefore always have to consider such images within the historical ramifications of differing media formats, art forms, genres, narratives and iconographies, if one wishes to analyze the concrete interaction between the sensing body of the viewer and audiovisual image. In contrast, as long as one assumes a communication model with fixed relations between authors and recipients, the audiovisual representation is regarded as self-evident. In brief, the critical question is how, in the process of reception of audiovisual images, one comes to the representations at all. This question remains unnoticed as long as one attributes a model of communication that defines audiovisual images as mediating instances of a message 'to be understood' in the communication between distinctly localizable agents. The poiesis of film-viewing thus formulates a counter position to the sender-receiver model of communication which cognitive approaches to film and metaphor follow; only that codes have been replaced by cognitive schemas. It formulates an alternative to their assumption of fixed positions of agency implied in that model. We assume an indeterminate plurality of producers and recipients, whose agency branches out in a web of interactions between media (of cooperation), cognitive schemas, historical-cultural horizons of sense. Rather than assuming that communication takes place between filmmaker and film viewer, that the film is a transmitter of information and that the film viewer is a cognitive decoder of audiovisually encoded information, we start from the engagement of film viewer and film, and not from a producer that transmits an intention to a spectator as receiver of a message: in short, the poiesis of film-viewing differs fundamentally from a code model idea of communication.

This not only holds for artistic forms of audiovisual images, but also for the audiovisual rhetoric of everyday media realities. It is the case with quickly produced news shows and news reports as much as it is for humorous or horrifying YouTube videos, for films in the cinema, and for socio-politically engaged reportage or private video messages.

### The as-if

But what does it mean to assume neither a self-evident, given everyday reality nor universal perceptual schemata when analyzing audiovisual images? How can the poiesis of film-viewing be conceived at all if it cannot be defined solely by using isolated audiovisual representations? Can anything methodologically distinct at all be said about a reception process if this is modeled as an interaction of image and recipient, open on all sides in its operative networks between affects, cognitive schemata, and cultural semantics? And can it contribute to an understanding of metaphor in audiovisual media?

In order to be able to answer these questions, another fundamental premise of cognitive approaches to understanding film needs to be discussed in more detail. If spectators construct a diegetic world in the process of viewing a film, which they relate to *as if* they were interacting with a real world surrounding them (e.g., by simply applying everyday perception processes)[8], it is just this as-if that designates the crucial point. It is this as-if which makes perception of film fundamentally different from everyday perception and, as mentioned earlier in this section, which involves, in fact, a complex process of fictionalizing, of creating a pretense world (Kappelhoff and Greifenstein 2016, Koch and Voss 2009). Fictionalizing may include metaphorizing, but it is not identical with it.

The cinematic movement-image and the film itself is accessed by the viewer in the mode of 'as-if'. It is the sensorily experienced world of another 'I', which viewers experience physically and with their senses, and which they experience precisely not as everyday reality, but as-if it were their own reality (see also Geary 2011). In this way film images as aesthetic experience do not conform at all to any ordinary reality of life; *for the moment of their reception, they replace this by an apparent reality* (Kappelhoff 2018a, b).

In a sender-receiver-code model of communication, in narrative film theory and in an understanding of film as representation of 'contents that move' this as-if is not entailed. However, this process of fictionalizing, that is of 'as-if-I-were-interacting-with-a-reality-surrounding-me' should be constructed as an interaction between affects, cognitive schemata, and cultural semantics that is carried out in the interaction between cinematic movement-images and the sensing bodies of the (seeing and listening) viewers.

The interaction in the mode of as-if brings a mode of experience into view addressed in Lakoff and Johnson's original formulation of metaphor as linking two domains of experience through an as-if relation: metaphor as "understanding and experiencing one kind of thing in terms of another" (Lakoff and Johnson 1980b, 3). Following this definition, metaphorical meaning itself is reconstructed as an as-if relation – which does, however, not imply that all as-if relations are metaphorical (Gibbs 2018a).

---

**8** This aspect of film reception is the focal point of the discussion about immersion (cf. Curtis 2008, Grau 2003, Griffiths 2008, Ryan 2001, Visch, Tan, and Molenaar 2010, Voss 2009).

### Experiencing one thing in terms of another as a process of fictionalizing

For cinematic metaphors this means that it is the viewers who perform a process of fictionalizing (Kappelhoff and Greifenstein 2016); it is their process of viewing that creates cinematic movement-images, sometimes with a metaphorical meaning. It is the viewers who perform the "seeing as", "seeing through", or "seeing one thing in terms of another" in the process of film-viewing (Müller 2008a). This process then gives rise to a constructed, a fictional reality in every single facet of cinematic movement-images. It also gives rise to metaphorical meaning. With it a scene is proposed, a framework of spatio-temporal relations is set, and positions of characters are established; only within this emergent creation can a viewer's understanding unfold as a reconstruction of an action, of a narrative. This is the sense in which we see the viewing of film images as a poiesis, an act of creative production.

The fundamental media mode of cinematic metaphor can then be described as the creation of metaphorical meaning on the basis of bodily processes of perception – in the mode of as-if experiencing another experience. This alludes to an understanding of metaphor that Max Black already established in conceiving of metaphor as interaction, and to which we return below (in Sections 4.3, 5.2).

# 2 Cinematic Metaphor and Experience: Creating Fragile Realities

The sketch of cinematic metaphor as poiesis of film-viewing, that we have outlined in the previous chapter assumes an active participation of the viewer in audiovisual metaphors as well as the idea of movement-images as orchestrating processes of meaning-making on the side of the viewer. We now move on to discussing Black's idea of metaphors as cognitive instruments that create new realities and relate this to Lakoff and Johnson's early formulation of metaphors as multidimensional experiential gestalts. With an analysis of Hitchcock's REAR WINDOW (USA, 1945), we illustrate how cinematic metaphor emerges from the experience of movement-images as multidimensional gestalts and – instead of instantiating pre-hoc existing conceptual patterns – creates new realities.[1]

## 2.1 From Metaphors as Cognitive Instruments to Metaphors as Experience

It was Max Black who noted, in a revision of interaction theory in 1977, that it would be a significant step for metaphor research if metaphorical statements were conceived as instruments of thinking and bringing new relations into the world that had previously not existed:

> If some metaphors are what might be called 'cognitive instruments,' indispensable for perceiving connections that, once perceived, are *then* truly present, the case for the thesis would be made out. Do metaphors function as such 'cognitive instruments'? I believe so. (Black 1993 [1977], 37)

One thing that is interesting about this line of thought is its entailment: a shared reality is available to us, to the degree that there are metaphors that can describe this reality. When we attempt to evaluate Black's argument in retrospect, it becomes clear that his arguments, in their inner logic, go in the direction of breaking with the then dominant linguistic paradigm. His reflections on the dynamics of metaphor as interaction (cf. Winkler 1989) go indeed beyond the scope of a structurally defined language system that necessarily precedes thought.

---

1 For a philosophical perspective on this film see Anne Eusterschulte's (2018) chapter "*Actio per distans*: Blumenberg's Metaphorology and Hitchcock's REAR WINDOW" in *Cinematic Metaphor in Perspective. Reflections on a Transdisciplinary Framework.*

https://doi.org/10.1515/9783110580785-003

Black's reflections imply three basic aspects that are central for the relation between film images and metaphors:

1. Metaphors are tools of thought.
2. They relate both to sensorily perceived reality and to the symbolic structures of that reality.
3. This reality is not objectively given, but is always related to certain perspectives and aspects of its description.

All three aspects actually mark a fracture in linguistic theory, but it was only the conclusion that Lakoff and Johnson drew from these insights that achieved a fundamental paradigm change.

> The general principles [of how people understand their experience; CM & HK] involve whole systems of concepts rather than individual words or individual concepts. We have found that such principles are often metaphoric in nature and involve understanding one kind of experience in terms of another kind of experience. (Lakoff and Johnson 1980b, 116)

Now it is no longer the structures of meaning systems or generative rules that are held to determine human thinking, but systems of cognitive schemas that, as such, motivate language.

In the ubiquity of metaphors in ordinary language use, a principle of such cognitive operations becomes graspable, to which Lakoff and Johnson assign an encompassing paradigmatic value, characterized as the relation between distinct realms of experience: "We have talked throughout of metaphorical concepts as ways of partially structuring one experience in terms of another." (Lakoff and Johnson 1980b, 77)

A range of different research perspectives result from this change in perspective. Here we focus on the three currently predominating ones:

1. One can examine the occurrence of metaphorical concepts in various cultures, media formats, and various forms of communication to get to theoretical models about fundamental (physiologically grounded) processes of human thinking – and, in turn, make this the basis of empirical studies of the mind.
2. One can use theoretical models of cognitive processes to explain or interpret metaphorical concepts in all kinds of utterances, texts, or other media forms. And then these metaphorical concepts can be traced back to general cognitive principles, such as, for instance, image schemas. With recourse to such models, phenomena can be causally explained or interpreted, and, in this way, a basis of universally valid facts can be established under a nearly endless play of permanent modulation of what we understand as a commonly shared reality.

Or

3. One can take the theoretical insights into the way metaphorical concepts work as a starting point to investigate the dynamics of media interaction and the cultural-historical processes with their situatedness in concrete social interactions, assuming that they may indeed alter and shape our reality by yielding new descriptions or new perspectivations of reality.

Quite a substantial number of problems that arise in the application of conceptual metaphor theory to audiovisual images originate from the lack of differentiating their respective claims of validity. Against the backdrop of the argument developed thus far, the analysis of cultural potentials of meaning of audiovisual images that we are advocating concerns the third option.

How then, can a cognitive understanding of metaphorical concepts as "structuring one experience in terms of another" (Lakoff and Johnson 1980b, 77) be made fruitful for an analysis of audiovisual images that targets the dynamics of media interactions in their reality-constituting aspects? A brief analysis of cinematic metaphor in Alfred Hitchcock's film REAR WINDOW will serve to illustrate this.

## 2.2 Cinematic Metaphors as New Descriptions of Reality: REAR WINDOW (1)

In the following example, one of the most powerful supporting actresses in classical Hollywood cinema – Thelma Ritter as Stella (James Stewart's nurse) in REAR WINDOW (Alfred Hitchcock, USA 1954) – is trying to explain her idea of marriage to her patient Jeff, who seems unable to make up his mind about marrying Lisa (played by Grace Kelly, before, in the real world, a European prince shows up to steal his thunder).[2] Stella resorts to a metaphor:

> STELLA: Look, Mr. Jefferies. I'm not an educated woman, but I can tell you one thing – when a man and a woman see each other, and like each other – they oughta come together – wham, like a couple of taxis on Broadway. Not sit around analyzing each other like two specimens in a bottle.
>
> JEFF: There's an intelligent way to approach marriage.
>
> STELLA (scoffing): Intelligence! Nothing has caused the human race so much trouble as intelligence. Modern marriage![3]

2 Analysis by Hermann Kappelhoff, carried out within the Cinepoetics' research focus 'Metaphor – Film Images, Cinematic Thinking, and Cognition'.

3 Thelma Ritter as Stella in REAR WINDOW, 00:10:40–00:11:10.

When looking only at this dialog, we might conclude that the metaphor she is using might be “men and women are like two taxis on Broadway.” However, this changes if we leave aside the verbal side and even the gestural side of the dialog and focus on the dynamics of perceiving the cinematic image in its unfolding gestalt. In this scene it is neither the meaning of the words nor the iconicity of the gestures – Stella’s words are accompanied by a clapping gesture, she hits her open palm with her closed fist – that establishes the metaphor. It is, rather, a kind of gesture performed by the cinematic image itself, arranged in the rhythm of staging, acting, and speaking that literally makes sense over the course of the entire scene. The metaphor that emerges along this scene can be paraphrased as: falling in love is a car crash. Watching the film sequence, the idea is grasped instantly. But if we just consider the dialog: “when a man and a woman see each other”, neither ‘love’ nor ‘car crash’ are mentioned. So why do we get that idea? The answer seems quite simple. We, that is, the viewers, get this metaphor because we are able to connect two experiential domains: traffic in a big city and personal relationships. However, in order to do so, we have to bring together several dimensions of the audiovisual image: the style of acting, the literal meaning of the dialog, and a physical, embodied feeling that is intimately tied to the audiovisual composition of the moving image.

To begin with, the metaphor of ‘falling in love being a car crash’ is rooted in the intertwining of dialog and gesture. The verbal utterance “a couple of taxis on Broadway” is complemented by a strong gesture: the clapping hand accompanied by a seemingly meaningless verbal expression: “wham”. By itself, this gesture does not represent the idea of a car crash either. But the clapping gesture works as a metonymy in two ways – and both of these ways are rooted in sensory experience rather than in iconic representation. First, the sheer sound of clapping serves as a non-verbal, sonic reference to the experience of crashing. Second, the movement of the clapping hands activates the felt impression of two antagonistic forces clashing. From the viewer’s perspective, this gesture is a bodily enactment of two forces crashing loudly: “wham”. Only in bringing together this embodied simulation (Gibbs 2006, 2018b) with the notion of the couple of taxis on Broadway is the source domain established: a head-on collision between two cars. But what about the target domain? The dialog contains notions of “a man and a woman” and “marriage”, but a concept like ‘falling in love’ is, again, not mentioned at all. So why is it, once again, looking at the scene, so obvious that the metaphor displayed here is ‘falling in love is a car crash’?

The answer is similar to that regarding the source domain; it is, so to say, an audiovisual gesture – a cinematic composition or staging that provides an embodied simulation here. First of all, we have to highlight the great acting by Thelma

Ritter. The way she moves across the room, the fast, precise rhythm in which she is speaking, all of this serves the dynamic experience of a forceful vitality, which becomes the experiential ground for the emerging metaphor. An experience that is amplified by the audiovisual image itself. The fast call-and-response rhythm of the dialog is accentuated by the rhythm of the cuts; the actress's forceful movements across the room are synchronized with a rhythm of fast camera movements to the left and right. This way, the subjective view of the spectator, the embodied experience of an audiovisual gaze, creates the experience of participating in a forceful vitality from a first-hand perspective. The clapping gesture lets the forces clash, but, through the rhythm of staging, the experience of force permeates the whole sequence. The meaning of utterances like "a man and a woman" and "marriage" is modulated towards the metaphor of 'falling in love' only by the experience of being moved forcefully in a vital rhythm. The feeling that comes with watching the cinematic image as it unfolds in time, provides the basis for creating a metaphorical conceptualization that we describe for now as: 'falling in love is a car crash'.

Love is quite an abstract concept. It is almost arbitrary how we conceive the 'thing called love'. It is almost always comprehended in terms of some other concept easier to grasp. Hitchcock makes use of all the means of audiovisual staging to come up with an audiovisual metaphor that is neither uttered within the dialog nor signified within a single gesture. Instead, the scene draws on the temporal structuring of the audiovisual image on every level of cinematic composition in order to modulate the meaning of utterances like "two taxis on Broadway" towards an emergent, implicit, yet crystal-clear metaphor that can be described as 'falling in love is a car crash'.

Summing up, it is on the level of the scene that the cinematic metaphor emerges. First, the idea of a car crash is established as a source domain by a metonymical gesture tightly embedded in the dialog.[4] A car crash is two opposing forces clashing loudly. Second, this highly specific, embodied simulation of a car crash is embedded in the multidimensional temporal gestalt of the audiovisual image which on the one hand orchestrates the rhythm out of which the experiential qualities of a car crash emerge while on the other hand establishing the concept of falling in love. Only by connecting these two experiential domains do we come to conceive a metaphor that is never uttered or explicitly signified.

---

4 Ladewig (forthcoming) investigates syntactic and semantic integration of gestures into verbal utterances, showing that gestures can be inserted into the verbal utterance and may often complete them (which is the case in Stella's dialog too).

## 2.3 Cinematic Metaphors as Multidimensional Experiential Gestalts: REAR WINDOW (2)

'Love' is indeed quite an abstract concept.[5] Yet, at the same time, the meaning of a phrase like 'falling in love' is very subjective, or, let us say: it is very specific with regard to particular communities and cultures. But by metaphorically connecting it with the experiential qualities of a car crash, an intersubjective, common ground for all spectators is offered. This is achieved by an orchestrated multidimensional experiential gestalt, that is, the audiovisual image, which structures a process of embodied simulation for the perceiving viewers of this scene, and this is what Lakoff and Johnson might have had in mind when they formulated their early definition of conceptual metaphors:

> The metaphors come out of our clearly delineated and concrete experiences and allow us to construct highly abstract and elaborate concepts [...]. (Lakoff and Johnson 1980b, 105)

Adopting such a position implies three assumptions for the analysis of audiovisual images and hence for cinematic metaphor:

1. Metaphorical concepts are not fixed structures of meaning, but structure thought processes by juxtaposing different domains of experience and bringing them into a dynamic relation.
2. Metaphorical concepts always relate to both aesthetic aspects, along with the sensorial-perceptual dimension of such domains of experience, and to semiotic or textual structures.
3. From this perspective, a metaphorical concept has the function of unlocking realms of experience (by way of building analogies), which are, otherwise, logically and sensorially inaccessible.

The full weight of the argument therefore rests on the term 'experience', a point that easily gets lost from view. If we follow the research on metaphor in cognitive paradigms, it is often with reference to Lakoff and Johnson's: "The essence of metaphor is understanding and experiencing one kind of thing in terms of another." (Lakoff and Johnson 1980b, 5). The metaphorical 'as' relation is, however, all too often understood as a purely logical one. In many studies, metaphors continue to be considered as purely cognitive, disembodied, abstract conceptualizations (see Gibbs's critique: Gibbs 2005, 121–122). However, just as with the term 'embodiment', when physiological aspects become a focal point

5 Analysis by Hermann Kappelhoff, carried out within the Cinepoetics' research focus 'Metaphor – Film Images, Cinematic Thinking, and Cognition'.

of conceptual metaphor theory (Gibbs 2005, Johnson 2007, Müller 2008a), a dimension of experience is foregrounded which concerns aesthetic correlations – put differently, analogy and comparison also operate on the level of perception and affect. The experiential dimension of metaphor is not graspable on the level of logical operations and meaning constructions. From such a perspective, metaphors thus combine two domains that are mutually related in their affective, perceptual, and sensory dimensions as concrete, embodied experiences.

Lakoff and Johnson initially used the term "multidimensional gestalt" (Lakoff and Johnson 1980b, 81) to describe experience as a coherent unit before they switched to describing the mapping processes between cognitive domains in neurological terms (Lakoff 2008).

> [...] multidimensional structures characterize *experiential gestalts*, which are ways of organizing experiences into *structured wholes*. [...] Structuring our experience in terms of such multidimensional gestalts is what makes our experience *coherent*. [...] As we saw above, *experiential gestalts are multidimensional structured wholes*. (Lakoff and Johnson 1980b, 81, emphases in original)

We prefer their early terminology, because the description of experience in terms of experiential gestalts that are multidimensionally structured targets the level of everyday perception and everyday consciousness, while later terms, such as "image schema" or "primary metaphor" address the physiological level of human cognition, which implies a shift from an experientialist, cultural-historical understanding of experience to a physiological one. We will return to this point later in the context of our discussion of embodiment in relation to cinematic metaphor (cf. Chapters 4 and 5).

On the other hand, we need a concept such as embodied simulation (Gibbs 2005, with reference to Lawrence W. Barsalou's work on a system of perceptual symbols, Barsalou 1999) to grasp how the temporal composition of audiovisual images can interact with the viewers' bodily sensations over the course of a film. In this way, the other side of the interaction, the involvement of actual viewers in the temporality of the cinematic movement-image, can be modeled. It offers a way to understand how a distinct feeling of one's own body, structured by the audiovisual composition, can work for the viewer as a source of metaphorical meaning. The viewers' bodies, in all their physiological and intelligible possibilities, thus ultimately form the material of the film image.

One might object that the brief analysis of the scene from REAR WINDOW as a whole is nothing more than simple interpretation; because indeed, it only builds on what we can describe as aesthetic experience and what is describable at all. Moreover, it might be objected that the metaphor dissected from it does not meet the definition of metaphorical concepts of the type of 'A is B' and therefore lacks evidence of being derived from conceptual links.

We would not wish to contradict these objections, because they concern metaphor analysis of audiovisual images more generally. They point, however, to three basic aspects that are central for audiovisual media analysis:

1. Any analysis of audiovisual forms of art and entertainment must address the problem of the communicability of aesthetic experiences. It always strives to explain the viewers' participation in a specific aesthetic and media-specific perceptual experience, which cannot be formulated in terms of factual knowledge. This is so central because the media-aesthetic framing determines individual experience precisely through its difference from a commonly shared, everyday reality. This is exactly why the audiovisual image cannot be related ahead of time to a self-evidently given reality of the everyday *world* in order to derive its meaning – whether this be in recourse to semiotic, narratological, or genre-poetic systems, whether it be with regard to the everyday perception of structuring cognitive patterns of perception and action – directly from identified representations of images.
2. As a matter of fact, our film analytical studies suggest that metaphorical conceptualizations in audiovisual images cannot be grasped as static entities that can be described according to the formula 'A is B'. Rather, they should be understood as networks of interlocking figurative interactions that can extend over the entirety of a film, video, etc. as a dynamic process. They are thus a matter of a compositional whole, the cinematic discourse. Only if we detach individual audiovisual representations from their compositional structure can they be identified as isolated metaphors of the type 'A is B' (Cameron 2018). But then they have no relation to the metaphorical network of the entirety of the cinematic movement-image.
3. As a consequence, analyzing the meaning of audiovisual images can only be achieved by reconstructing the process of an unfolding cinematic movement-image as a viewer's sensed experience. Only on the basis of reconstructing this as an embodied experience, can the analysis refer to previously existing semiotic systems, cultural semantics, or cognitive models of understanding. The framework within which the process of meaning-making unfolds must be first reconstructed, for each particular case, as a specific media-aesthetic framing. This must be done before it is even possible to analyze the process of meaning-making, because the aesthetic framework of a given film shapes the viewer's understanding in the first place.

If we ignore the dimension of perception of an aesthetically-involved and reflecting viewer, who, through interacting with the movement-image, produces a specific subjective experience, then all we see in our short scene from REAR WINDOW is a man with a broken leg (Jeff), sitting in a room in front of his rear window, stuck in his wheelchair, and wishing for just one thing: he wants something to happen in the courtyard that will make the boredom bearable. We learn from the dialog with the nurse (Stella) that he actually has an exciting job as a successful photo journalist and a beautiful girlfriend whom he does not necessarily want to marry. We will follow him in his mildly perverse pleasure and spy on the neighbors in the courtyard. We will look on in amusement as the two women (Stella and Lisa) are drawn into the fascination of the voyeur – and then we, like they, will speculate on the mysterious behavior of the neighbor who quite obviously is committing a murder to get rid of his wife. For affectively involved spectators who follow the film into its finale, a sure sense for the entirety of the film world will only be reached from this ending. And only from the sense for the whole of the situation that is unfolding in the physical presence of their perceptual sensations, exactly to the degree that they are affected and become entangled in the unfolding movement-image – only from this feeling for the entirety of the situation, and one's own being-entangled, is the metaphor disclosed as a complex interactive process.

A viewer involved in this way in the dynamically developing situation will in fact only grasp the metaphor outlined above in its multiple metaphorical and metonymical ramifications and overlappings, which finally end in another accident for the protagonist as he falls out of the rear window. His physical situation can be understood by an affectively-involved viewer as a metaphor for his or her own perceptual experience. Viewers in the cinema are heavily restricted in their freedom of movement, very much like the protagonist in his wheelchair; and much like him their eyes are glued to the screen, more or less greedily on the lookout for sex and crime, for instance, or perhaps hoping more for a romantic love story or a melodramatic tearjerker.

Engaged viewers will get all of this: erotica, thrill, suspense, horror, melodrama, and romantic love. Over the course of the film, the modes of genre cinema are related in oppositional and conflict-laden ways, much like the man with his legs in a cast desires freedom of movement. The viewers are led through a jumble of emotions into the dramatic collision of affective modes of classical Hollywood genre cinema, which provides access to ambivalences, resistances, and defensive positions as a feeling for the world of the film, and all of these will be shown from the very beginning as an inner conflict of the dramatis personae: between the wish for individual self-determination and the longing for community – whether this be called marriage or love.

A viewer involved in this way over the course of the film may only be able to put the metaphor of the car crash together with the idea of 'falling in love' from the end, only after having seen the hero fall from the window. When the protagonist, robbed of any capacity to flee or of even any autonomous movement, seems to have finally consented to marriage – and exhausted and worn out, consigns himself to the beauty of Hollywood. Such a viewer may develop one last attempt to construct a metaphor from the final apotheosis, in which the resolute nurse, in the rhetoric of American screwball comedies, sets out on the path of a long process of elaborating metaphorical concepts through ever new ramifications, intersections, impressions with other metaphorical relations, while she massages the naked back of the patient, who is as impatient as he is helpless.

In the convergence of the events of the plot and of the audiovisually-figured subjectivity, the protagonist's fall from the window offers itself to the viewer as a final element in a series, which together allow their increasing affective engagement to crystallize into a feeling of the protagonist's sense of self. Only in this way does the feeling for the whole of the fictional world of the film reach a certain stability. Related to the fictional reality of the film, even the tension between marriage and freedom in the hero's sense of self is a metaphor for a fundamental topos of American genre cinema: the question of the possibility and boundaries of a self-determined life.

Summing up, we argue that Black's idea of metaphors as cognitive instruments and creating new realities applies equally to metaphors in audiovisual formats. As formulated in Lakoff and Johnson's early work – before concepts such as image-schemas and primary metaphors lead to a neurocognitive turn in their theory – we conceive of metaphors as multidimensional experiential gestalts. The idea of cinematic metaphor, differs, however, profoundly from later applications of conceptual metaphor theory to audiovisual media. Instead of grasping metaphors as instantiations of image-schemas or primary metaphors, we regard metaphoricity to be emerging locally from the spectator's experiencing of movement-images in the moment of film-viewing. The following chapter will take a closer look at the viewer's active participation, it will lay out what the 'doing of cinematic metaphors' (cf. Gibbs 2018b) involves, which includes an exploration of the role of perception, feeling and affective entanglement in this process.

# 3 'Doing' Cinematic Metaphors: Perception, Feeling, and Affective Entanglement

'Doing' cinematic metaphors involves a specific kind of perceptual, affective, felt experience. (cf. Dewey 1980, 36–59) Audiovisual images emerge from aesthetic experiences and the figurations of subjectivity that mark these experiences. Only by reconstructing the affective entanglement[1] of the viewer with the film, by reconstructing the position from which a 'sense for the entirety of the situation' (cf. Kappelhoff 2006) is disclosed, can the position of the understanding subject be specified – indeed, in its physical sensations it is inseparably involved in the unfolding film image. Mark Johnson alludes to these connections when he writes:

> In the visual arts, it is images, patterns, qualities, colors, and perceptual rhythms that are the principal bearers of meaning. The obvious fact that we usually cannot put into words, what we have experienced in our encounter with an artwork does not make the embodied, perceptual meaning any less a type of meaning. (Johnson 2007, 234)

The visual arts, according to Johnson, are paradigmatic for illuminating aesthetic ways of experiencing, which he acknowledges as offering important resources for human understanding. In Johnson's sense, the perceptual, aesthetic, and pictorial qualities of artworks cannot be reduced to a linguistic-conscious level ("we usually cannot put into words"). Rather, they get their value from the concrete act of an aesthetic experience, an experience that does not require previous concepts, but in a certain sense completes and sets in motion the process of conceptualizing in the first place (Kappelhoff and Greifenstein 2016).

This very process of conceptualization, however, is only graspable for film analysis, through aesthetic experiences. Film analysis, therefore, must always proceed via reconstructing aesthetic experience: its appearance, performance, composition. Appearance refers to the audiovisual moving image in the context of a specific film or media setting. Performance here refers to the temporal structure of how the moving image unfolds. Composition of a scene describes, how the succession of movement-images comes to form a meaningful whole in the process of film-viewing. The movement-image, assembled in the composition and realized in the process of viewing, is therefore an embodied image, which cannot be derived from isolated audiovisual representations (moving pictures),

1 Entanglement is used terminologically in the book. It translates the German "*Verwickelt-Sein*" and, along with the weaker terms 'involvement', 'being engaged with', seeks to capture the idea of being enmeshed in a film affectively and cognitively. Escape is possible, but would mean missing the film.

https://doi.org/10.1515/9783110580785-004

but can only be conceived as a temporal gestalt embodied in the interaction of movement-image and viewer.

## 3.1 The Spectator-I

This is why analyzing such images can also not be directly based on textual, narratological, or iconographic structure-models, as if viewers were encryption machines that offset their visual perceptions against semiotic systems, iconographic patterns, and poetic knowledge in a computer-like mode of information processing. (The significance of the computer as a source domain for metaphorical conceptualizations (Gigerenzer and Goldstein 1996, Goschler 2008) informing cognitive theories of audiovisual images would certainly be worth examining more thoroughly). Analysis of audiovisual images has to take the detour through reconstructing the process of the spectator's aesthetic experience. In this case, we would have to speak of the spectator-I in the same sense as literary studies speak of the lyrical or the poetic 'I'.[2] This subjectivity, the 'I-position' that comes into play here is itself a product of the cinematic image, a specific positioning of the viewer, who finds him/herself engaged in a kind of bodily entanglement with the movement-image. The spectator-'I' is to be strictly differentiated from the empirical spectator who may assume this position but does not have to. The spectator-I refers to a subjectivity that only emerges in the interaction of the audiovisual image and the perceiving body of the viewer. This subjectivity presumes the affective involvement of the empirical spectator in the audiovisual moving image, its empathetic engagement – without requiring this of each empirical viewer.

Moreover, the spectator-I is also not some kind of implicit or ideal spectator to whom one could ascribe a complete saturation in the semiotic material or even authorial intention. On the contrary, the spectator-I is constitutively dependent on the connection between the temporality of the audiovisual image and the temporal structure of the corporeal process of sensing and thinking; the cinematic movement-image is bound to the actual interaction between image and viewer. It can neither be separated from the materiality of the image nor from the viewers' bodies perceiving the movement-image. It is only conceivable in the joining of the two temporalities, that of the compositional pattern and that of the sensation.

2 Spectator, rather than viewer is used here as a technical term relating to film theory (Baudry and Williams 1975, Metz 2000 [1975], Mulvey 1975).

In a nutshell: the spectator-I is a product of the interaction between the involved body of the viewer and the temporal structure of the audiovisual moving image; it is a product of a subjective perspective that structures what the movement-image offers as something intentionally directed, as a specific way of hearing and seeing (Sobchack 1992). In this sense, this relates to the film-theoretical term as comparable to the lyrical I: the *camera-I*. (Deleuze 2008 [1985], Vertov 1998 [1923])

## 3.2 Feeling as Unity of Experience

The viewer's feeling is thus marked by a specific experience of subjectivity. Viewers always continue experiencing themselves in their self-perception as involved in the dynamically developing situation for the entirety of the fictional film world. Mark Johnson thinks of such a feeling for the whole of the situation, in which we are affectively involved, when he – referring to John Dewey – writes: "[…] every situation we dwell in is characterized by a pervasive felt quality that is the starting point for all our perceptual discrimination and conceptual definition." (Johnson 2007, 18) To put it another way: there is a basic feeling for the situation, an affective arrangement and positioning of oneself.

With regard to film, this brings in a notion of experience which does not refer to the processing of abstract information or the cognitive recruitment of schemas but presumes an interaction between the audiovisual moving image and the viewer's body in the process of film-viewing in which the sensations, reflections, and affective reactions to the audiovisual scenario are combined in a 'feeling for the unity of experience' (Dewey 1980, 36–59) A feeling for being involved that encompasses the situation becomes, for the spectator, a feeling for the entirety of the cinematic movement-image.

Notably, such a 'feeling for the unity of experience' cannot be traced back to a set of physiologically determined image-schemas (Johnson 2007); since it actually consolidates highly disparate cultural, historical, as well as subjective, factors and physiological schemas of movement and action. It is just this interplay that Gibbs has in mind when he uses the term *embodied simulation* on all levels, including those of cultural and historical knowledge. Moreover, this feeling for the unity of experience does not refer to reaction patterns studied within the aesthetics of effect – a tendency to be found, for example, in neurocognitive film research as in Hasson et al. (2008) or in cognitive film studies (Bordwell 2013) – and which cognitive film narratology calls up under the category emotion and affect (Grodal 2009, Tan 1996). We, on the contrary, define experience as duration of sensorial perception and its temporal structure, which can only be grasped reflexively in terms of the viewer's sensations.

Here we are following the idea of Dewey (1980) who makes something palpable in his understanding of experience that to us is central for film. What experience means here is a becoming aware of an object through a deliberate process of perception; it is the unfolding of an object field into a perceived object through a temporally unfolding feeling for the perception of a concrete thing. The term experience therefore denotes the reflexive becoming aware of this operation, which unfolds automatically in our perception process and is completed without an awareness of the developing feeling.

For us, Dewey's reflections offer a way to differentiate film cognition from an understanding of visual representation, and to relate to the temporality of the movement-image as a process of pretending. Constructions of meaning are then based on reflexive self-perception in the process of perceiving film images, which, following Dewey, we take to be a temporal form of feeling. From this perspective, 'feeling' is not to be understood as a synonym for emotion, affective appraisal, or sensation, but as intuitive monitoring ('feeling' in Damasio's [1999] terms), which reflexively combines the various sense impressions, emotions, and affective processes with the cognitive operations into a construction of meaning. In short: the process of fictionalization always includes an act of subjectification – an experience of the unity of feeling of oneself, as a feeling for the given world.

Importantly, films articulate a subjective experience of the world that the viewer realizes as his or her own bodily experience of sensation, and, at the same time, as a specific way of perceiving the world. This mode of perception explicitly does not relate to perceiving the world in terms of everyday schemas but refers to a mode of perception that is different from the everyday one and that articulates a different mode of experience. Dewey distinguishes everyday automatized perception from monitored perceptual processes.

In the following example, we illustrate how cinematic metaphor arises from an aesthetic experience of a subject position that is inherently involved in the unfolding of the movement-image. The analysis of a scene from Tom Tykwer's DER KRIEGER UND DIE KAISERIN describes how a feeling for the unity of experience emerges in this temporal engagement of creating a movement-image, as an "experiential gestalt" that is a "multidimensional structured whole" (Lakoff and Johnson 1980b, 81).

## 3.3 Multi-Perspectival Perceiving: DER KRIEGER UND DIE KAISERIN

The analysis of a car crash sequence from Tom Tykwer's DER KRIEGER UND DIE KAISERIN (THE PRINCESS AND THE WARRIOR, GER 2000) zooms in on the active participation of viewers in creating a cinematic movement-image in the first place.[3] Without their creative 'doing', there would only be single frames, effects of lighting, or digital information – but no film. In this sequence from DER KRIEGER UND DIE KAISERIN, this involves creating a multidimensional experiential gestalt characterized by a multi-perspectival perceiving of a car crash.

In the sequence concerned here (0:14:40–0:26:36), ex-soldier Bodo (Benno Führmann) and the nurse Sissi (Franka Potente) literally crash into one another. While Bodo – on the run from a group of people chasing him – runs through the streets of Wuppertal, Sissi is involved in an accident, leaving her first in front of, and then under a truck. She is at risk of choking from her injuries – but then Bodo turns up at the scene of the accident. With great presence of mind, he saves Sissi's life with an improvised tracheotomy. In the combination of various rhythms and tempi the sequence interweaves different modes of genre cinema. Bodo's escape and Sissi's accident are initially staged as an action sequence in a parallel montage with fast editing and quick camera movements. When Bodo appears at the scene of the accident, the action mode is abandoned, and the sequence skillfully allows suspense – articulated by dull droning in the sound design and slowing moments in the audiovisual movement – and moments of melodramatic introspection – realized in the interplay of close-ups of Sissi's face and a slow, deliberate monolog that she gives as off-commentary, summarizing the scene – into one common sensation. As the film proceeds this scene is revealed as the starting point of a dynamic at the end of which Bodo and Sissi end up as a romantic couple.

In the action sequence, we instantly recognize a multiplying of the perspectives, which are all projected onto the screen like a concert of subjective shots. Each of these perspectives – and this is the hypothesis with reference to Gibbs' concept of embodied simulation (cf. Gibbs 2018b) – is simulated by the spectators, quasi in the I-form: *I am the title heroine at the traffic light; I step onto the street and see a truck racing toward me; I turn around – an unconscious reflex – and push the boy holding onto me away to keep him from ending up under the truck; I am the young man, closely bonded with the woman in front of me, whose shoulder I sense; I hear squealing tires, a strong shove to my chest sends me reeling backwards; I fall, a crack, a scream around me; I am the truck driver – what's that behind my truck?; I yell at the guy that's hanging to the back of the truck; I approach the red light; I sense the thrust of the massive truck – there's no more stopping, no more control; where's the girl? – The impact couldn't be felt; I'm the guy hanging to the back of*

3 Analysis by Hermann Kappelhoff, carried out within the Cinepoetics' research focus 'Metaphor – Film Images, Cinematic Thinking, and Cognition'. In her dissertation, Christina Schmitt offers an extended analysis of this film (Schmitt forthcoming/2019).

*the truck; I jump, a car races toward me, tires squeal, just get away; I am the squealing tires grinding over the asphalt, burning, hot; I am the massive force running over everything, nothing can stop me; I am Sissi, where am I?; I can't breathe, everything's blurry; etc.* (Figure 3.1).

Certainly the perceiving subject, to which each of these perspectives is revealed as part of a whole, is none of the named (or unnamed) persons or objects. Within film theory this subject has been called the camera-I (see above). In *The Poor Man's Couch*, Félix Guattari describes the equally fluid and heterogeneous subjectivity that is experienced in such alternating shapes and positioning as a camera-I (Guattari 2009 [1975]). In fact, the camera does not simulate a gaze, but locates a seeing and hearing that encompasses the entire scene as a dynamic correlation between a wide variety of experiential domains and combines them into a whole.

And yet it is not only the alternating standpoints and perspectives that mark the sequence as a specific aesthetic experience. It is much more the entirety of the audiovisual composition; it is the spatio-temporal dynamics of the cinematic movement-image – of action, of suspense, of melodrama, the expressive modalities of the action genre, the suspense, the melodrama – in which each of these perspectives and aspects adds up to an expressive ensemble, i.e., a continuous, subjective perspective, in which this entirety is formed into the gestalt of an experiential complex. And we as viewers realize this gestalt in a process of perceiving embodiment, as just described, highly fragmentary and in its most basic form. We, the viewers, run through the heterogeneity of the various perspectives of things and persons in our physical sensations – as embodied simulation – and realize them as a temporal entity of the camera's gaze. The composition of the film image becomes the temporal gestalt of a multidimensional experience actually in the sense Lakoff and Johnson employed it in their 1980 book, which feels as if it were my own bodily experience.

But how do we get to understanding a film image of overwhelming violence and brutal physical injury as a metaphorical concept that links the car accident with the experience of 'falling in love'? It is precisely this multidimensional experience that becomes the source domain for metaphorizing the event/process of falling in love. Being run over by a truck and getting your throat cut open – these are not source domains that commonly offer themselves for love metaphors. A complex interactive structure between the experiential areas of love and mortal violence is necessary, which expands over the whole film and includes historical knowledge from the most trivial association with romantic movies to Romantic poetics.

On the one hand, this seems grounded in the staging. If we wish, we can easily see, in the way the man lies over the woman, opening her trachea and pushing a straw into her throat, a highly tasteless metaphorical projection between lifesaving first aid at the scene of an accident and a wide field of associations – from

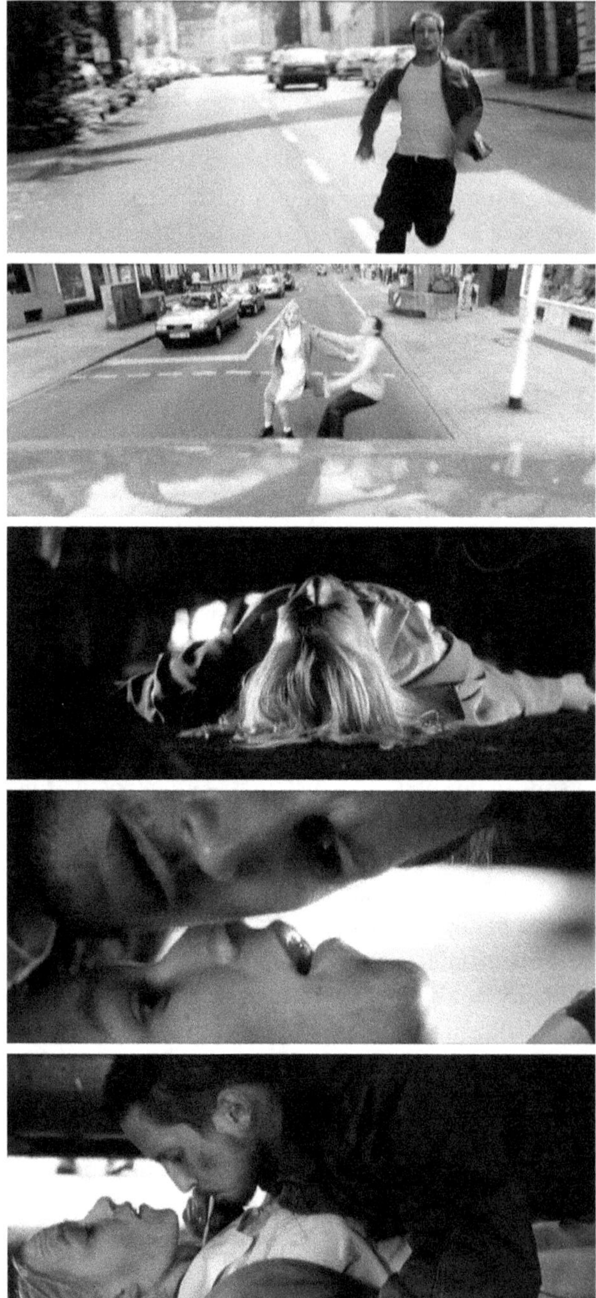

**Figure 3.1**: Multiplied 'I' perspectives of a car crash creating a multidimensional experiential gestalt (DER KRIEGER UND DIE KAISERIN)

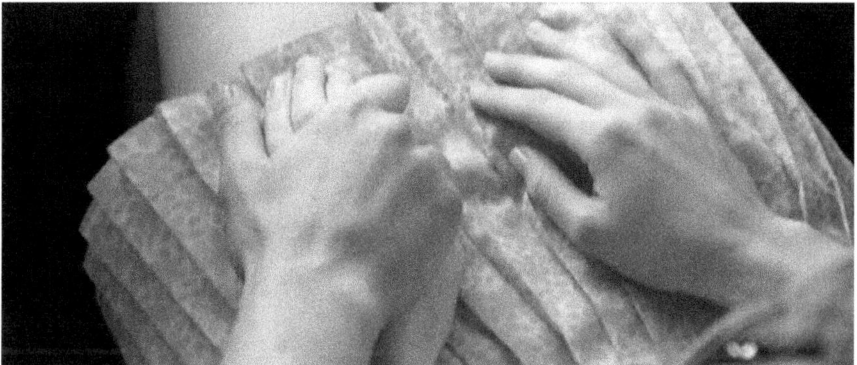

**Figure 3.2:** The end of DER KRIEGER UND DIE KAISERIN

the kiss that wakes Sleeping Beauty to violent deflowering. In fact, over the course of the film it becomes ever clearer that the various scenes play through the inner circumstances and ambivalences of a heterosexual love affair. What is significant in the context of the questions being discussed here, however, is the intersection at which the various perspectives are related to the viewer's physical perception, to the resonating body of a spectator-I.

From this perspective, the scene can be characterized in terms of a metaphorizing consciousness which is desperately in love: *You confronted me with an impact that bowled me over, that took my breath away; the desire for you ran over me like a ten-ton truck; it took my breath away. I was possessed by fear and horror. But your hands gave me the room to breathe and rescued me from my paralysis. Where are you off to? I want to keep you; the only thing left to me is the scent of your sweat.*

Just as, self-evidently, the film scene can be translated into the realm of associations of an 'I' who is in love, so, as a metaphorical concept, it can only be defined through the development (regarding vehicle and topic development, see Cameron 2008b) that goes over the whole course of the film. The metaphor is formed in the repetitions and variations of a single basic motif which carries a wide variety of interpersonal closeness: that of physical touch. Over the course of these variations, all forms of touch become metonymical or metaphorical projections of 'being-one', or of the longing for being-one. Only in this context, does the scene of the accident become the pivotal point in the succession of ever new variations of getting in touch, being in touch, touching gently, being touched as cold as ice or as hot as fire, getting hit, getting punched, getting knocked down, etc. All these moments end in a touch, the representation of which is as stereotypical as it is consistent in its arrangement – the cautious very first touch between two lovers getting closer – and here is where the film ends (Figure 3.2) (cf. also Schmitt forthcoming/2019).

## 3.4 Dynamics of the Metaphorical Process

The variations of audiovisual scenes of bodily interaction in the example above let all possible forms of touching and getting in touch become metonymical and metaphorical projections of the longing for love – from the most childlike need for tenderness to the rawest fantasy of sexual violence; they are formed into a multidimensional gestalt of a realm of experience, just as Lakoff and Johnson describe:

> The multidimensional structure [of the concept war; CM & HK] characterizes experiential gestalts, which are ways of organizing experiences into structured wholes. (Lakoff and Johnson 1980b, 81)

For the spectator, the unfolding of the entity, which Lakoff and Johnson are speaking about here, over the course of the entire film becomes, in the interrelation of *embodied simulations of something like being touched*, a temporal gestalt that can in turn be grasped as a continuing variation of the source domain of a metaphorical concept of love. Love is the difficulty of being touched without being injured. It is therefore the figure or the cinematic image of a specific temporality.

This temporality alludes to the dynamic nature of metaphors used in verbal discourse. Lynne Cameron's Discourse Dynamics model of metaphor formulates such a position, showing how metaphors develop and pattern across temporally extended time periods in spoken discourse (Cameron 2018). Müller's (2003, 2008a, b, 2017) dynamic view of metaphors highlights the cognitive activity, the 'doing', that is involved in the interactive process of establishing metaphoricity over the course of multimodal face-to-face interaction (for an overview, see Horst forthcoming/2018, Schmitt forthcoming/2019). Gibbs also characterizes metaphor in this sense not as a static relation, but as a process, the process of *'doing' metaphors* (Gibbs 2016b, see also Jensen 2017a). With regard to film, this 'doing' appears as a temporal structure in which viewers go through the metaphor as a process performing a metaphor. When Gibbs claims that "we are moving ourselves as part of a metaphorical performance" (Gibbs 2016c) he is addressing the close link between logical and aesthetic structure, cognitive operation and affective involvement through the sensations of the senses, which define the metaphorical process as a whole. The metaphor calls up a scene, a situation – and structures the dynamic involvement of the spectator-I in the fictional reality of the cinematic movement-image. But when the material in which such an involvement is realized is in fact the spectators' perceiving bodies, that is, includes them through sensations and processes of feeling, as a physical being-affected by the film image, the question remains as to how the metaphorical structuring relates to this process of feeling; how does the aesthetic experience of being-involved in the cinematic movement-image – as we have conceived it above, following

Johnson and Dewey, as a feeling for the entirety of the film reality – connect with the metaphorical concept?

## 3.5 Film and Affect: Cinematic Expressive Movement

Taken together, the reflections developed above point to a close connection between film and affect, which is located in a specific dimension of cinematographic or cinematic movement. In our research on the poetology of audiovisual images we have developed an analytical model that is comprehensive and cultural-historically oriented: *expressive movement* (cf. Kappelhoff 2004a).[4] It captures the affective movement of the viewer as a bodily sensation of the unfolding flow of cinematic movement-images. We have briefly alluded to this feeling in the analytical fragment of Tykwer's car crash scene.

The concept of expressive movement captures a media practice that produces and shapes feelings and senses of self of a broad audience (see Part III). Viewed in this light the poetics of expressive movement concerns a basic mode of representation [*Darstellungsmodus*] of Western Art, which is closely connected with the cultural history of sentimental art of entertainment in its diverse melodramatic varieties: theatre, dance, film (Kappelhoff 2004a, 182, 2014). Moreover, and as Part III will elaborate more closely, classical film theory conceived of expressive movement as form within aesthetic practice and the poetics of affect, that targets the affective responsivity of a broad anonymous audience as a collective subjectivity. In such a perspective, the concept of expressive movement does *not* align with the individual psychological idea of a subjective interiority, displayed bodily in an external appearance; on the contrary, and in reverse, expressive movement is conceived as an aesthetic media practice that evokes a feeling for one's own interiority as an effect of subjectivization.

4 For a systematic and historical analysis of the notion of 'expressive movement', see Kappelhoff (2004a, see also Kappelhoff and Bakels 2011, Scherer, Greifenstein, and Kappelhoff 2014). How expressive movement connects with affective grounding of meaning-making in film and in face-to-face interaction was a topic of Kappelhoff and Müller (2011, see also Greifenstein and Kappelhoff 2014, Horst et al. 2014, Kappelhoff and Greifenstein 2016, Schmitt, Greifenstein, and Kappelhoff 2014, Schmitt and Greifenstein 2014).

# 4 Cinematic Metaphor and Embodiment

Following the line of argument developed so far, cinematic metaphor emerges from the viewer's affective entanglement with the cinematic expressive movement. The process of this involvement can be described as an interaction between movement-image and viewer's body. The aesthetic orchestrations of films are realized as subjective bodily sensations which are in an ongoing reciprocal relation with the unfolding of cinematic movement-image and in which the film is bodily realized as the expression of another subjectivity. This process can be described as an interplay between the dynamics of cinematic expressive movements and the 'doing' of cinematic metaphor. The metaphorical 'mapping' is thus captured as a 'doing' that happens in the process of film-viewing (and hearing); a process in which the perceptual, affective and conceptual schemas of concrete staging patterns and expressive qualities of audiovisual images are experienced and related to one another in their heterogeneity as diverse multidimensional experiential gestalts.

Having described the specific bodily subjectivity which characterizes cinematic movement-images as aesthetic experience, along with some of the implications that this has for an analysis of metaphoricity of these images, we now turn to a more detailed examination of a model of film-viewing that differs from effect-aesthetic models of film recipient as well as from hermeneutic speculations about a presumed spectator position. The path towards an alternative conception of the viewer suggests the phenomenological concept of intersubjectivity.

## 4.1 The Intersubjective Dimension of Cinema

From a phenomenological point of view embodied experience is intersubjective experience. Phenomenology has received a great deal of attention in film philosophy in particular through the reception of Vivian Sobchack's influential neo-phenomenological film theory. She has particularly addressed the question of how cinematic expressivity relates to the film viewer's affective experience (Sobchack 1992). Following Sobchack, any movement occurring in the composition unfolds outside the physical film material, outside the screen. It is materialized as bodily sensation of/in the viewer, it is embodied by that viewer (Sobchack 1992, 9) – spectator perception and cinematic expressivity are directly intertwined (Schmitt and Greifenstein 2014, Sobchack 1992, 13). The expressive movement articulated in the medium of cinematic movement-images gains its affective reality as viewer's physical sensations. And it is exactly in this cinematic dimension of movement,

https://doi.org/10.1515/9783110580785-005

through which all constitution of meaning goes, where Sobchack finds the basis for the intersubjective dimension of cinema:

> In a search for rules and principles governing cinematic expression, most of the descriptions and reflections of classical and contemporary film theory have not fully addressed the cinema as life expressing life, as experience expressing experience. Nor have they explored the mutual possession of this experience of perception and its expression by filmmaker, film, and spectator – all viewers viewing, engaged as participants in dynamically and directionally reversible acts that reflexively and reflectively constitute the perception of expression and the expression of perception. Indeed, it is this mutual capacity for and possession of experience through common structures of embodied existence, through similar modes of being-in-the-world, that provide the intersubjective basis of objective cinematic communication. (Sobchack 1992, 5)

In film and media studies, *embodiment* thus does not only refer to the derivation of linguistic meaning from patterns of physical interaction with a given environment, as suggested in Lakoff and Johnson (1999) for example. Rather, it is assumed that the viewing of cinematic images involves a (re-)activation of patterns of experiencing a given perceptual situation that is tied to the body and marked by sensation and emotion. In this model, the spectator understands the film as an individually sensed experience of another body and as somebody else's perception, because it becomes a concrete physical-sensed experience in one's own body. The body of the spectator becomes the physical basis of a feeling for the entirety of the film world, the world of an unfamiliar, other 'I'.

The neo-phenomenological concept of embodiment makes it possible to understand how the cinematic movement-image can be grasped as a medium, one pole of which is represented by an unfolding figuration of movement (cinematic expressive movement), while the other is the process of an emerging-transforming-ending affective experience: the involvement of a spectator in the cinematic movement-image, a spectator feeling (Kappelhoff 2008) which constitutes a transitory subjectivity called the spectator-I. The 'spectator feeling' neither corresponds to any individual affect entity nor to the summary succession of various discrete emotions; it is tied much more to the consistent modeling of a feeling that unfolds over the duration of a film (of a mood, of an atmosphere), which is grounded in aesthetic pleasure (Kappelhoff 2004a). This unfolding feeling is intertwined in a variety of ways with the characters, their actions, and the narration. But at no point is it identical with the emotions being represented at the level of narration (Greifenstein forthcoming/2019). The temporal organization of the aesthetic experience of film itself forms the basis, the matrix of spectator feeling (Kappelhoff 2004a). This feeling incorporates both the dramaturgical logic as well as the compositional arrangement or the elements of the diegetic world.

## 4.2 Dynamic Versus Static

All of this alters the scope of work for film analysis and hence for cinematic metaphor. Put differently, it affects the very task of film analysis. Against this theoretical background the aesthetic organization of audiovisual moving images can be grasped in terms of viewers' affective experience of the temporal dynamics of expressive movement patterns. Gibbs, from the point of view of cognitive psychology, describes this as a continuous chain of viewers' embodied simulations, which, in the process of 'doing' metaphors, are integrated in the temporal structure of cinematic movement-images (Gibbs 2018b). Metaphors in audiovisual images can then no longer be formulated as a fixed constellation of the type 'A is B', as conceptual metaphor theory suggests; on the contrary, they should be reconstructed as dynamic succession of continuing, responding, and connecting metaphorical projections, much in the sense of Cameron's theory of systematic metaphors or metaphor trajectories (Cameron et al. 2009, Cameron 2010, 2018, see also Jensen 2017b, Müller 2008a, 2017). Following the dynamic nature of cinematic movement-images, metaphors in audiovisual media are procedural, continuously connecting and branching out, building up from a multitude of metaphorical projections; they are interwoven with the process of film-viewing and the unfolding of film images as movement-images. Cinematic metaphors are dynamic and emerge from the embodied experiences of the film viewer. We conceive of cinematic metaphor as a process of embodied performance.

What remains the guiding principle for conceptual metaphor theory analyses of audiovisual images, on the other hand, is the idea of a mapping as a static (and unidirectional) relation between two experiential domains; whose relation of similarity can be traced back to fixed conceptual patterns based on universal physical experiences, be they image schemas or primary metaphors (Coëgnarts and Kravanja 2015). A prerequisite of such a conceptual metaphor theory analysis is the reduction of audiovisual images to sequences of static individual audiovisual representations from which the compositional structure is built.

As soon, however, as one refers to the temporal structure of the movement-image as a composition, audiovisual metaphors behave as dynamically as metaphors in written texts and spoken discourse: the individual metaphorical expression is an essential part of a ramified contextual structure (cf. Cameron 2010, Gehring 2009b). The consequence for metaphors in audiovisual images is that viewers are affectively involved with an ongoing succession of perceptual configurations, i.e., their involvement as well as emergent metaphorical meaning are temporally orchestrated. In short, conceiving of metaphor as embodied meaning-making implies the temporal dynamics of metaphor.

## 4.3 Metaphor as Interaction and the Intersubjectivity of Meaning-Making

Despite conceptual metaphor theory's static mapping model, it is possible to relate Lakoff and Johnson's formula of metaphor as "understanding and experiencing one kind of thing in terms of another" (Lakoff and Johnson 1980b, 5) to the modes of cinematic experience in Sobchack's phenomenological sense just outlined as "expression of experience by experience", (Merleau-Ponty 1968 [1964], 155, quoted in Sobchack 1992, 3) and to the affective involvement of a given viewer (cf. Johnson 2007, 234). Black's concept of metaphors as interaction offers a dynamic counter-model to the static unidirectional mapping idea advocated by conceptual metaphor theory.

For Black, a "metaphorical statement" is always tied to an open interaction between a primary and a secondary field of reference; notably, this interaction is not exclusively based on similarities that are realized and reproduced, but can itself newly discover and create such similarities: "It would be more illuminating [...] to say that the metaphor creates the similarity than to say that it formulates some similarity antecedently existing." (Black 1962, 37) Black's notion of metaphor assumes that certain qualities of the subsidiary subject come forth from experiencing the principal subject, in which quite particular qualities of the first are "projected upon" the second (Black 1962, 41), or that the first "filters", "transforms", or also "selects" certain characteristics in the second (Black 1962, 42). What is decisive here is that in such an understanding of metaphor as a dynamic interaction, a visual-perceptual principle of figurative thinking is outlined that is not based on given relations of similarity, but produces these (cf. also Schmitt, Greifenstein, and Kappelhoff 2014).

Metaphors in Black's sense can thus not be traced back to previously existing concepts, which are fixed and given as "image-giving domains" and "image-receiving domains",(Müller 2008a, Weinrich 1983 [1963]) or as source and target domains of metaphors (Lakoff and Johnson 1980b). Metaphors are to be seen as products of a dynamic interaction between as-if perceptual scenarios, which include schemas of everyday perception, a wide variety of movement and sensorial qualities, and the perceptual sensations, affects, and feelings associated with them. The medium of this interaction is always the empathy of an understanding subject, who acquires the specific perspective of another subjectivity in those relations between distinct perceptual scenarios (or experiential realms). By bringing together separate experiential domains in a (dynamic) metaphorical interaction, a prototypical agent thus constructs metaphors as experiences of another subjectivity (Kappelhoff and Greifenstein 2016).

## 4.4 The 'Other I'

Put differently, Black's interaction theory of metaphor is, indeed, a formula for the intersubjectivity of metaphorical meaning-making. In 'doing' cinematic metaphors, the spectator is affectively involved in the unfolding of the film; in that process the experiences of viewers' bodies interact with the experiential modalities of other subject positions. We describe this process as the interplay of cinematic expressivity and the formation of cinematic metaphor. This puts the focus on the dynamic production of metaphors, in which perceptual schemata, symbolic concepts, and expressive qualities of audiovisual images are configured as modes of experience at the level of concrete film staging and are mutually related in their difference.

#### Cooperation

Seen from this angle, it is not that two statically linked objects, domains, or facts are related to one another by metaphor; rather metaphor itself is the product of a dynamically developing interaction of different realms of experience, which can function in this connection as an interface between diverse, distinct, subjective scopes of experience. Instead of assuming the duality of a more or less 'single-meaning' projection between two experiential domains, we must reconstruct the network of figurative projections. Or, to formulate it in Cameron's terms (here with regard to everyday discourse): metaphors often arise when to close a gap in mutual understanding or otherness, 'alterity' (Cameron 2003, 31). Metaphors thus appear to facilitate understanding where there is no unproblematically shared experience, no self-evident understanding. If they indeed fulfill such a function in conversations then they must be considered as jointly produced (Cameron 2011).

The theoretical position developed in this book connects with two metaphor theoretical concepts in which the dynamics of discourses in a linguistic sense – concrete dialogs, texts, and conversations – are the object of concern.

The first refers to metaphors that arise and develop in concrete dialogs. Lynne Cameron has investigated the performance of metaphorizing, on the one hand, in communication between teachers and pupils – thus in a communication situation, characterized by a massive imbalance in the positions of the agents; and, on the other hand, in the context of so-called "reconciliation processes" between a former IRA militant and the daughter of a victim of an IRA assassination (Cameron 2007, 2011). In each case, she describes a dynamics of discourse processes that is structured by the emergence and elaboration of metaphors.

It appears, therefore, that precisely in the attempt to relate with a perspective opposing or incomprehensible to one's own, metaphor formation matters decisively. Metaphor in Cameron's sense is thus precisely *not* understood as a pre-hoc given entity that is applied intentionally like an instrument.

Another level of investigation integrated in our framework concerns research on gesture in interaction and the activation of metaphoricity (Müller 2008a). Analysis of metaphor usage in gestural interactions has shown that the activation of 'sleeping' metaphors goes hand in hand with concrete processes of mimetic-gestural embodiment: when, for instance, the gesture of a speaker calls up a significant trait of a fictive perceptual event that illuminates the source domain of a metaphor, which then, through the verbally articulated metaphor, relates to a target domain. What becomes apparent with this gestural interaction in concrete conversations is that processes of metaphorizing contribute basic affective vectors to a dialog that embed the local act of communication in a jointly shared imaginary perceptual scene, which can also then function as a sensory-affective common ground, even if none of the conversational partners is aware of it.

What is manifested in the dynamics of gestural interaction, as much as in the dynamics of discourse, is that metaphors are both co-productions of actors in an interaction and function as structuring factors of those interactions. No matter whether fully conventional, sleeping metaphors are called upon or if entirely new transfers arise: "Metaphor is not a part of a system that is put to use; from a dynamic perspective there is only use." (Cameron et al. 2009, 67)[1]

The activity of metaphorizing is often deeply involved in structuring conversation as an interaffective event between discourse participants – their reciprocal lack of understanding, their differences, and their striving for mutual understanding – and that embeds the conversation in a jointly shared horizon. In the 'space between' that reflects the "inevitability of difference" in understanding between people (Cameron 2003, 31), metaphors give rise to a jointly shared ground, from which, the difference of the separated horizons of experience is gradually disclosed.[2]

1 Our theoretical position has been developed in close cooperation with Lynne Cameron and following her work.

2 "The alternative is to take up a construct from Bakhtin – 'alterity' or 'otherness'. In doing so, we reject the possibility of a perfect convergence of understanding by participants in discourse and focus on the inevitability of difference. Alterity, as differences in understanding and perspective, is not merely to be lamented, but to be understood and worked with. I suggest that alterity, the somewhat neglected, dialogic counterpart of intersubjectivity, offers a key construct for analyzing metaphor in educational discourse at several levels." (Cameron 2003, 31)

Gibbs' 'doing' metaphor (Gibbs 2018b, cf. Jensen 2017a) is thus not to be understood as a solipsistic cognitive process, but as a co-production of different agents that encounter each other's subjective scopes of experience that do not meet in complete congruence (cf. Cameron's notion of "alterity", Cameron 2003). This brings up once more a fundamental difference between the cognitive and the phenomenological notions of embodiment. The concept of experience in Lakoff and Johnson's formula "The essence of metaphor is understanding and experiencing one kind of thing in terms of another" (Lakoff and Johnson 1980b, 5) is the critical point at which cognitive metaphor theories and phenomenological film theories find themselves in fundamental contradiction.

Following neo-phenomenological film theory, cinematic movement-images are structured through a doubled and mutually-referencing perspectivism: the expression of an experience in the projection of another subjective experience. This is what Sobchack characterizes as "cinema as life expressing life, as experience expressing experience" (Sobchack 1992, 5).

While the definition of conceptual metaphor theory takes the metaphor to be a mapping between a clearly outlined and concrete experience and a diffuse or abstract experience as content of a homogenous thinking process, the cinematic image builds up an interaction between heterogeneous subjective perspectives. In the expressivity of the cinematic image, the spectator therefore always already confronts another 'I', which is related to reality in a specific way and gives expression as a subjective experiencing; it confronts me, as spectator, as something that I sense as an experience of reality, as a perceiving and thinking that differs from my own way of experiencing reality, although I reflect it as my own physical sense experience.

From this perspective, the screen is a sensitive retina that only becomes a seeing eye in the affective coupling with attentive, focused bodies of spectators that surrender to perception. The cinematic movement-image is a kind of blueprint of an experience of reality that requires the bodies of spectators to be realized[3]. Perceiving a way of experiencing as an experience would then mean that a basic temporal logic is inscribed in the cinematic movement-image which structures the constellations of plot and character, first and above all as configurations perceived and experienced from a specific subjective viewpoint. The cinematic image presents its world to spectators as a certain way of seeing and hearing, from a specific subjective experiential perspective, which they have to turn into their own physical sensory experience.

**3** See also Voss' notion of 'surrogate body' [*Leihkörper*] (Voss 2011, 2013).

## 4.5 The Spectator as Agent

Black's model of an active subject carrying out metaphorical interaction corresponds with our film studies' assumption that the 'meaning' of audiovisual images can only be reconstructed in terms of an interaction between a perceiving body and the audiovisual image, that is, as an activity of the spectator intrinsically entangled with the unfolding of cinematic movement-images.

It could be argued that our position only takes the perspective of the viewer and excludes the point of view of media production, and, further, that our analysis of cinematic movement-image is not framed in terms of media communication structured through clearly defined positions of agency. In fact, our position, as we discussed earlier, assumes that the process of meaning-making with audiovisual images, provided that we do not reduce them to isolated audiovisual representations, is not graspable within a frame of the duality of the producer and recipient, i.e., a code model of communication. Heterogeneous positions of agency have to be derived from analysis of the cinematic image in the first place.

Cinematic movement-images must therefore always be described and analyzed as a perceptual event structured through the reflexive multiplying of modes and perspectives of experience; they can neither be detached as text, nor as image, from the living bodies in which they occur in the process of perceiving, feeling, thinking. When we talk about audiovisual images, we refer to neither textual nor narrative structures that objectively exist for themselves. This is why, as we have argued above, we reconstruct audiovisual images as cinematic movement-images, that is, as a kind of audiovisual script that, following a temporal logic, shapes perceptual sensations, affects, cognitive concepts, and ways of understanding. By expressing another subjectivity, cinematic movement-images orient the spectator towards the perceptual position of another subject. Meaning-making is thus not a matter of an audiovisual representation which depicts some content 'that moves', but happens in the activity of a perceiving, sensing, feeling spectator. The spectator is thus the agent of meaning-making and it is in the spectator's understanding of film that meaning-making takes place.

## 4.6 Multi-Perspectival Embodiment

Poiesis of film-viewing then means an act of experience, in which the experiencing of another 'I' is introspectively conceived as one's own subjective bodily experience. It is thus quite possible to describe this as an act of empathy; admittedly, it would be necessary to distinguish between an (individual) psychological and a phenomenological understanding of introspection. After all, phenomenology conceives of empathy as an intersubjective structure, which is inherent to the embodied processes of meaning construction. The embodied experience of audiovisual images refers thus to the manner in which another subject experiences the world, an unfamiliar subjective manner of experiencing the world; notably, what is being conceptualized here is the difference between other- and self-perception. This brings up once again the as-if mode concerning metaphor and audiovisual images.

I realize this other world-view as-if it were my own physical perceptual sensation, my own feeling for the wholeness of the locally situated world – as 'unity of experience'. It is just this as-if of film experience that forms the entry point for a fictionalization and for which the process of metaphorical meaning-making may serve as an exemplary case. Indeed, this is the point at which the phenomenological definition of the cinematic mode of experience (as the "expression of experience by experience", Sobchack 1992, 3) and Lakoff and Johnson's definition of conceptual metaphor ("The essence of metaphor is understanding and experiencing on thing in terms of another", Lakoff and Johnson 1980b, 5) are directly related to one another. However, we must still take care not to lose sight of the crucial difference.

Fictionalization, in this sense, means the conceiving of a feeling for the whole of a perceived world. In DER KRIEGER UND DIE KAISERIN, this involves a feeling for love as orchestrated by Tykwer's car-crash scene, which unites heterogenous perspectives into one "experiential gestalt" a multidimensional, yet structured (Lakoff and Johnson 1980b, 81). This "whole", however is always a fiction – something spectators create in their process of film-viewing and that finds its place in a shared world (of film viewers). This holds for documentary descriptions as much as for cinematic narrating.

Both are based on perceptual scenarios. Cinematic metaphor is, in that sense, a form of fictionalization, structured by and grounded in embodied scenarios of perception that involve a clear-cut difference between everyday modes of perception and the as-if of 'another I's' manner of perceiving the world (Kappelhoff and Greifenstein 2016).

## 4.7 Embodiment in Neo-Phenomenological Film Theory and Conceptual Metaphor Theory

It is, precisely here, where a fundamental antinomy between the cognitive and the phenomenological understanding of embodiment shows. For the phenomenological understanding of embodiment, as taken over by film theory, the difference between self- and other perception is constitutive; indeed this is why the as-if of experiencing the audiovisual image concerns the interaction of separate and opposing subjective perspectives of experience. The metaphorical structure of audiovisual images is grounded in the interaction of heterogeneous perspectives. It refers to the interrelation of two clearly distinct modes of experiencing the world: one that is expressed in the composition of movement-images and another which is the ordinary mode of experience of the viewer.

The experience of viewing films in the phenomenological sense refers to the interrelations of clearly distinguished, heterogeneous modes of experiencing the world – the way of experiencing, particular in each case, that is expressed as the cinematic movement-image and the viewer's own way of experiencing. The film image articulates acts of perception in which an alternative perspective on experience – a perceptual operation externalized in the film image (for instance, the camera's gaze) – is coupled with the spectator's own physical experience.

When, on the other hand, conceptual metaphor theory, refers to two different domains of experience: one, concrete and clearly delineated; the other, abstract and diffuse: "we conceptualize the less clearly delineated in terms of the more clearly delineated" (Lakoff and Johnson 1980b, 59), this includes an assumption of experiential domains as cognitive entities of a homogeneous individual mind. A metaphorical mapping is basically described as cognitive operation between source and target domain of such an individual mind. Embodiment concerns a process of interaction between an individual organism and a homogenous environment: primary metaphors and image schemas then appear as anthropological universals grounded in a monadic concept of human beings. This position assumes a homogeneity of human thinking, which, however, appears to be quite problematic from a phenomenological point of view.

Metaphor, in the strict interpretation of conceptual metaphor theory, involves the relation between two separate conceptual domains of experience, which are held to be identical to *our* thinking, *our* perception, and *our* language. The implied 'we' here contains the claim of a seamless unity of human thinking: It is in this sense that the title itself of Lakoff and Johnson's famous book *Metaphors We Live By* indicates such a seamless homogeneity of human thought. The identity and consistency of this 'we' is, however, thoroughly problematic. In consequence, the uncritical positing of such a homogeneous 'we' has blocked out the cultural-historical dimensions of human thinking from conceptual metaphor theory.

This points once more to the importance of being clear as to how the notion of embodiment is characterized in the context of a theory of metaphor. On the one hand, embodiment is conceived of as referring to a physiologically grounded, shared, meaningful reality which is assumed to exist prior to any communicative situation. On the other, embodied experience is always an experience for someone, that is, a subjective and particular perspective on reality.

# 5 Cinematic Metaphor as Commonly Shared Reality

This chapter discusses the notion of a commonly shared reality in relation to cinematic metaphor and finds it wanting in several respects. The scope of a commonly shared reality is itself always precarious. It cannot be presumed as a constantly given fact, but is always to be unlocked anew in respect of the cultural and social situatedness of given subjective perspectives. Even seemingly evident schemata such as the "Moving Observer Metaphor" and "Moving Time Metaphor" that Johnson offers (Johnson 2007, 29–30) only describe a commonly shared reality concerning space and time until an alternative metaphor is found that spatializes time in a different manner. In particular with regard to conceptual schemas of space and time it is to be expected that they will be falsified as yet unknown future experiences. And indeed audiovisual images expose us on a daily basis to such different experiences – the multi-perspectival perceiving that spectators experience in the viewing of Tykwer's car-crash scene is such an example. It produces new experiences of time and space in the form of a multidimensional experiential gestalt.

Every ground that we pull into our argumentation is ultimately dependent on what gets addressed as common reality. Sweetser's works on perspectivized referencing through linguistic and gestural means clearly shows how much our everyday forms of communication are marked by an awareness of the heterogeneity of perspectives toward reality (cf. Sweetser 2012, Ferrari and Sweetser 2012). Here is exactly where a dynamic comes in that belongs equally to metaphor and to the cinematic movement-image: its historicity. And this brings us back to Max Black, who described metaphor, not only as a medium of cognitive operations, but also as the agent of historically changing, heterogeneous patterns and perspectives of experience (cf. Winkler 1989): "some metaphors enable us to see aspects of reality that the metaphor's production helps to constitute" (Black 1993 [1977], 38). The ideas of Black, together with those of Dewey, Blumenberg, and Nietzsche, help set out a more adequate notion of what is happening when cinematic metaphor emerges from encounters with film.

## 5.1 Reflexivity

In Black's perspective, metaphor also includes differentiating and establishing of different subject positions; it concerns an act of subjectification, by transferring, re-constituting, or varying given descriptions of reality. It is exactly here that the

https://doi.org/10.1515/9783110580785-006

fundamental difference between phenomenological and cognitive-theory concepts of embodiment comes to bear. Ultimately this comes down to the possibility of an awareness of a difference between self- and other perception, i.e., the irreducible reflexivity of human thinking.

### Fully embodied meaning

When Johnson, in an attempt to sketch out his understanding of experience, returns to Dewey, he formulates a highly instructive theoretical speculation: "For nonhuman animals, meaning is fully embodied" (Johnson 2007, 135). The theoretical construct marks the limiting case of the cognitive-theory model of embodiment: it conceives a body that, in its metabolic coupling with the surrounding world, produces a fully automatized meaning-making; it develops the idea of a meaning-making, a sense-making that directly derives from a continuum of stimulus-response couplings of an organism with a given surrounding that is not interrupted by any reflexive work of the mind (for Plessner 1981 [1928], this only applies to non-animal bodies, e.g., plants). The body of this meaning knows nothing of the difference of its own corporeality in relation to the bodies surrounding it, and with which it interacts. It lacks the reflexive feeling for its own being-involved in the situation, a feeling that spans the entirety of its reflexes and reactions.

The interesting point of this metaphorical concept – which conceiving of the animal body as fully embodied maker of meaning supposedly is – is that embodiment itself becomes the differential anthropological criterion of human thinking. Now, obviously it does not make sense to conceive of cognition as non-fully embodied meaning-making, because this would reduce the human contribution to purely logical, disembodied operations in the realm of semiotic systems, conventions, and cultures. It is obvious that such a dichotomy in the concept of experience that Johnson seeks to define would not make any sense. In fact, his reflections relate to those processes of embodiment that cannot be explained by physiological mechanisms. Dewey – to whom Johnson is referring here – develops the dichotomy, however, not as differentiating anthropological criterion, but as difference between automatized perception and experience. For Dewey, the feeling for the entirety of a situation, that 'I', the perceiving subject, embrace in my own processes of sensation is the critical criterion to be met in order to speak of 'experience' in the first place (Dewey 1980). The body of a 'fully embodied meaning' does not know anything about the difference between its own corporeality with regard to other bodies by which it is surrounded and with which it interacts. It lacks the reflexive feeling for its own entanglement in the situation, it lacks a feeling that embraces the entirety of its reflexes and reactions.[1]

The reflexivity of feeling, i.e., the perceiving of one's own perceptual and affective process, distinguishes 'experience' from 'perception' that does not become aware of itself, that is automatized. Viewed in this light, the theoretical fiction of a fully embodied meaning is nothing else but the difference between reflexive and non-reflexive embodiment, between an automatized and a consciousness-generating interaction between organism and environment; none of which is, admittedly, to be thought of less embodied than the other one.

## Consciousness

The theoretical speculation of a 'fully embodied meaning' brings into play a difference that has been notoriously worked over in the history of Western philosophy: consciousness. Even if this issue raises sometimes massive problems, we cannot get rid of the question of a reflexive consciousness by treating all sense-producing processes of human interaction as an interplay of physiological or conventionalized schematizations. Johnson's model assumes such a seamless intertwining of automatized schemas and conventionalized patterns, a continuum of cooperating action, reaction, and environment; such a model, however, only works if one excludes any subjective awareness, any feeling for one's own entanglement in a given situation; put differently, this model depends upon understanding the intertwining of physiological and conventionalized automatism as 'fully embodied meaning of nonhuman animals'. If conceptual metaphor theory traces metaphors directly back to universal cognitive patterns, it takes this position. Their introduction of the term 'primary metaphor' (based on Grady's work) illustrates this:

> Primary metaphors are part of the cognitive unconscious. We acquire them automatically and unconsciously via the normal process of neural learning and may be unaware that we have them. We have no choice in this process. When the embodied experiences in the world are universal, then the corresponding primary metaphors are universally acquired. This explains the widespread occurrence around the world of a great many primary metaphors. (Lakoff and Johnson 1999, 57)

---

1 The term 'feeling' therefore does not refer to bodily states and reactions, but to a reflexive sensation of the relation between my particular body and the other bodies surrounding me, it means a "being-of-the-world" (Ratcliffe 2008), which is not to be thought of differently than a being-in-community.

Phenomenology takes the opposite direction: with its distinction of the term 'body' [*Körper*] and 'body proper' [*Leib*] it posits the constitutive reflexivity of human perception. 'Body proper' means the awareness of the entirety of my sensory perceptions and affective tensions as 'I am this body proper' (this is more or less what Damasio calls 'feeling', cf. Damasio 2000); in contrast to the 'body' that I possess as an object and that I locate in a commonly shared reality.

The awareness of one's own corporeality [*Leiblichkeit*] (Plessner 1981 [1928], 1982 [1957]) is the basic form of reflexive feeling; it is awareness of the dynamic continuum of my sensory perceptions as a feeling for the wholeness of continuously changing situations, in which I am entangled. This also applies in reverse: the awareness of my own bodily mode of existence – the awareness of 'I am this sensing body' – is owed to the reflexive feeling for the entanglement with the surrounding reality; it is the experience of this being-entangled. Experience, if we follow Dewey, always refers to the experience of one's own sensed perception. Experience ultimately refers to the interface of subjective and commonly shared realities.

But then, the reflexive feeling for the corporeal [*leiblich*] being entangled with the world that is surrounding me means not so much a differential anthropological criterion, but the distance that opens up between an 'I' and a 'We' perspective; a distance between an unquestioned shared common reality, in which we as a 'We' are completely bodily integrated [*eingekörpert*] and the awareness of an entirely idiosyncratic corporeality [*Leiblichkeit*].

### Lifeworld

Blumenberg has this difference in mind, when he captures the unquestioned shared common reality with the term 'lifeworld' [*Lebenswelt*]. However, his understanding of the term results from a unique reconstruction of the Husserlian concept of lifeworld (Blumenberg 1986, 63, 309). Blumenberg has explicitly formulated his reading of the term as a critique of the traditional understanding of the term. Lifeworld, in Blumenberg's sense, does not mean the unquestioned given, everyday life-context. Instead, the term targets a purely theoretical limiting value [*Grenzwert*], with respect to which the conditions of general meaning-making [*Sinnbildung*] are to be specified in the first place. Also Blumenberg's notion of lifeworld is thus a purely theoretical construct which designates the limiting case of a unquestioned given reality. This is why he speaks of limiting term [*Grenzbegriff*] (Blumenberg 2010, 65). Lifeworld designates a world that is completely accessible without any rational contemplation in each of its traits to everybody who belongs to it. Thus far, Blumenberg's reading of 'lifeworld' corresponds to the theoretical fiction of a 'fully embodied meaning', only with the difference that lifeworld designates precisely the very facet which is given to every meaning-making [*Sinngebung*] as reference to an unproblematically given, shared reality; while meaning-making itself is a response to the absence of a self-evident commonly shared reality (Blumenberg 1987 [1981]).

In any case, this holds for Blumenberg's view of metaphor. It follows that metaphors mark (as does every rhetorical figure) a breach with an unquestioningly given reality. Further, they result from the experience with such a disruption (Blumenberg 1987 [1981]). Metaphors are necessary if something happens to shatter the automatisms or conventions of a fully embodied, that is, unconscious, unquestioned meaning. Looked at it in that light, Lakoff and Johnson's thesis, quoted above, reads like a confirmation of this argument: "The metaphors come out of our clearly delineated and concrete experiences and allow us to construct highly abstract and elaborate concepts [...]" (Lakoff and Johnson 1980b, 105).

In this sense, metaphor emerges as a break with what is generally intelligible (Gehring 2014). Even if the attempt to bridge such a breach simply and concretely reacts to a respective lack of understanding in a conversation, the inconsistency of a theoretical argument in a text, or a break with a poetic tradition, ultimately metaphor points to the fragility of a commonly shared reality.

If the title *Metaphors We Live By* (Lakoff and Johnson 1980b) is not metaphorical in itself, then it treats metaphorical concepts as forms of experience in which we not only reproduce the conceptual systems that constitute our reality, but also develop, form, model, construct, and transform them. First and foremost, this assumes creating reality as a commonly shared scope of different experiential perspectives. 'Doing' metaphor is then primarily the production of such a 'we' of commonly shared experience. Film and media studies are interested in the relationship between metaphorical concepts and film images, first and foremost in view of the production of such a 'we' of the shared scope of experience.

Metaphors produce a commonly shared meaning of what counts as 'real' when a self-evident reality is not available. In the acknowledged symbolic form the relation between linguistic expression and reality is fixed, and with it a piece of unquestioned commonly shared reality has emerged.

## 5.2 The Rhetorical Nature of Commonly Shared Reality

Blumenberg has developed his idea of lifeworld as a theoretical construction (a limiting term [*Grenzbegriff*]) of a pre-reflexive form of existence (i.e., a fully embodied meaning), precisely to get a grasp on the rupture that constitutes the reflexivity of human thinking. From the break with the pre-reflexive lifeworld come endless re-descriptions of a heterogeneous reality. Commonly shared reality is rhetorical to the extent that it is generally valid, i.e., that it can claim a natural, self-evident truth.

This is why, for Blumenberg, metaphor is the paradigmatic object to ground rhetoric anthropologically (Blumenberg 1981, 108–110, 1987 [1981], 433–435). Rhetoric appears where no commonly shared and mandatory truth, concerning what we describe as our reality, exists. It aims at creating a commonly shared reference to reality, a common ground, precisely at those points where it is fragile or not existing. Metaphors allow areas of reality to emerge over and over again through automatization and conventionalization: zones of non-reflexive life-world-ness [*Lebensweltlichkeit*] of automatized understanding that correspond to a fully embodied meaning.

Meaning-making [*Sinnbildung*] then is per se defined as connecting separated subjectivities, as connecting idiosyncratic, separated bodies proper [*Körper-Bewußtseine*] in the medium of gesture, reading, speaking, watching images, listening and watching (cf. also Krämer 2004, Schmitt forthcoming/2019). Consequently, meaning does not arise from a congruence between cognitive, semiotic or linguistic systems and the phenomenological world; rather meaning is to be understood as a branching dynamic network of affects, percepts and concepts, in which human actors, media and semiotic systems are equally included (cf. also Larsen-Freeman and Cameron 2008b). Blumenberg's metaphorology traces back to a radical revaluation of metaphor, where truth itself became a question of rhetorical creation of commonly shared scopes of reality.

### Conceptual metaphor theory and Nietzsche's theory of metaphor

In Friedrich Nietzsche's founding text of modern metaphor theory *On Truth and Lie in the Extra-Moral Sense* (Nietzsche 1989 [1873]), metaphor has become the paradigm of a radical perspectivism; it becomes the incarnation of a heterogeneous reality that was only ever perspectivally constructed and that knows no other ground than human forms of meaning-making [*Sinnproduktion*]. Truth then resides in the perspective of those who describe their views of reality. Metaphors are thus the result of ever new descriptions of shared realities (Rorty 1989). When Max Black says that some metaphors constitute new aspects of our reality, he is following exactly this idea:

> For such reasons as this, I still wish to contend that some metaphors enable us to see aspects of reality that the metaphor's production helps constitute. But that is no longer surprising if one believes that the world is necessarily a world under a certain description – or a world seen from certain perspective. Some metaphors can create such a perspective. (Black 1993 [1977], 38)

In relation to the history of human forms of experience, certain metaphorical concepts can therefore create new realities, which have not been part of our shared reality beforehand.

At this point, it also becomes clear that even conceptual metaphor theory is inseparably linked with Nietzsche's radical perspectivism. In a stroke, *Metaphors We Live By* (Lakoff and Johnson 1980b) liberates metaphor from the tight restrictions of definitions which characterize metaphor as a regularly occurring flaw within a structural model of regular meaning-making. In this regard, conceptual metaphor theory – actually, much more radically than many of its critics in philosophy – makes a turn that had already been anticipated by Nietzsche.

Conceptual metaphors – understood as "multidimensional structures" that organize "experiences into structured wholes" (Lakoff and Johnson 1980b, 81) – can thus not only provide access to meaning-making and audiovisual images; they establish a new understanding of language, one that relates to the interaction of perceptual scenarios in concrete acts of communication – instead of closed systems.

Metaphor is conceived of, put pointedly, as a form of ongoing language evolution, an inner dynamic within language itself. In Blumenberg, a similar idea of metaphor is formulated, when he writes: "[I]f the limiting case of judgment is identity, the limiting case of metaphor is symbol." (Blumenberg 1987 [1981], 439–440). By symbol, he means the generally accepted form of description of a commonly shared reality.

Seen from this angle, metaphor is always on the way to becoming symbol – on the path towards appreciation as recognized denotation (one might also say: to conventionalization). Here, another constitutive aspect of conceptual metaphor theory comes to bear, in which so-called 'dead' metaphors are held to indicate vital metaphorical projections (Müller 2003, 2008a). Put differently, from a historical perspective, they are nothing more than rhetorical formulae that have become self-evident. Viewed in this way, presumed dead metaphors are only a form of an unquestioned construction of reality, an index for sound common sense. In the recognized symbolic form, the relation between linguistic expression and reality is fixed – and with it, a slice of indisputable, commonly shared reality has emerged.

### Historicity and awareness of time

Only by situating conceptual metaphor theory in the lineage of the modern understanding of rhetoric is it possible to relate metaphorical concepts to the history of their elaboration, transformation, and cultural differentiation in all dimensions of human interaction that Mark Johnson recommends:

> [...] to explore more concretely how forceful bodily experiences give rise to image-schematic structures of meaning that can be transformed, extended, and elaborated into domains of meaning that are not strictly tied to the body (such as social interactions, rational argument, and moral deliberation). (Johnson 1987, 44–45)

In such a perspective, even the history of poetics and rhetoric can be read as a cultural differentiation of basic cognitive schemata. As soon as we speak of literature, visual arts, or visual media and film art, metaphorical concepts come up for discussion that are per se aimed at grasping or negating reality as a transformable and precarious, commonly shared scope of experience. This is why our questions on the relationship between metaphorical concepts and film images address both, the one and the other, as part of a history of humanly created 'tools of thought'– be they metaphors, media displays, or other semiotic systems; this means the history of the media of thinking is the ideal way to their understanding.

It is therefore more than just an anecdotal detail that the perceptual forms of film images serve Black as an obvious example by which such a change of our world can be grasped through new descriptions, through new perspectives. Black writes:

> Here the 'view' is necessarily mediated by a man-made instrument (though this might cease to be true if some mutant children were born with the power to see 'slow motion' with one eye). And yet what is seen in a slow-motion film becomes part of the world once it is seen. (Black 1993 [1977], 37)

The modes of our experience would then be no less, and in a variety of ways, entangled in a history of cultural production, such as media, meaning systems, and languages, in which we give them expression. This is exactly what Black is referring to when he "believes that the world is necessarily a world under a certain description – or a world seen from a certain perspective". (Black 1993 [1977], 38)

Relating Black's reflections once again to the poiesis of film-viewing, we suggest that: cinematic metaphor should be conceived as an interaction that operates at the level of spectators' film-viewing; of a viewing that allows for a fictional scenario to emerge in the interplay with cultural conventions and patterns of ordinary perception. The scenario emerges in the process of perception itself, which renders a meaningful gestalt to the "images, patterns, qualities, colors, and perceptual rhythms" (Johnson 2007, 234) of a film – that is, to its expressivity. Cinematic metaphors, as metaphors in audiovisual moving images, are, following the understanding outlined here, dynamic connections between different experiential domains, which are constituted in the aesthetic arrangement of film expressivity as one's own physical experience, and at the same time as distinct from a mode of experience of another subjectivity. In this sense, cinematic images generate an understanding and a thinking that is in no way exhausted in the reproduction of existing cognitive schemas of movement, space, and time, but that gives rise to new differences and modalities. It is the spectators who produce, in the act of viewing films, new metaphors, new links between different modes of experience as they allow fictional worlds to emerge from film images. Correspondingly, interaction as the basis of metaphor (in Black's sense) should be examined as a basic form of film experience, which is realized across the various genres and media formats of audiovisual images, and emerges from empathic and affective-embodied processes.

## Résumé

Part I has developed a framework for cinematic metaphor as performative action, as sense-making, grounded in the dynamics of viewer's embodied intersubjective experiences with the film and entangled affectively with cinematic movement-images, temporally orchestrated on every level. Metaphoricity emerges with the movement experience of film-viewing. Considering cinematic metaphor as poiesis of film-viewing replaces the idea of a spectator as information-processing computer as in cognitive approaches to film and heals the break with rhetoric established by conceptual metaphor theory.

Having posed critical questions concerning the media specificity of audiovisual images, we have proposed a framework rooted in the history of film theory. By putting the concept of movement-image center stage, we have shown how the model of cinematic metaphor as poiesis of film-viewing goes beyond conceptual metaphor and cognitive film studies. The idea of cinematic metaphor differs profoundly from the later applications of conceptual metaphor theory to audiovisual media. Rather than conceiving of metaphors as instantiations of image-schemas or primary metaphors, we consider metaphoricity to be emerging locally from the spectator's experiencing of movement-images in the moment of film-viewing.

The model of cinematic metaphor adopts Black's idea of metaphors as cognitive instruments, and Lakoff and Johnson's early formulation of metaphors as multidimensional experiential gestalts that create fragile realities. We suggest that cinematic metaphors are 'done' by the spectators and, like metaphors in discourse and face-to-face communication, are dynamic, emergent, always changing. Obviously, this 'doing' of metaphor is not a deliberate process, it happens as viewers are perceiving and sensing the film; it happens as they are entangled affectively with the unfolding of cinematic movement-images. Cinematic metaphors thus evolve from perceptual sensations, from the viewer's engagement with what we describe as 'cinematic expressive movements'.

Meaning-making in cinematic metaphor thus becomes the joint sharing of an always changing reality. Embodied experience is taken to be intersubjective, reflexive, and dynamic, and integral to cinematic meaning-making. We show how this phenomenological concept of embodiment differs from the universalist and individual model of embodiment advocated by cognitive film and metaphor theories. 'Doing' cinematic metaphor is a co-production of two agents: the viewer and the film.

With reference to Blumenberg's metaphorology, Nietzsche's philosophy of rhetoric and Black's reality-constructing power of metaphor and of film, we have argued for a return to rhetoric and poetics in metaphor theory – a plea that affects not only audiovisual media.

Having set out in Part I to illustrate what it means to start from film images as a specific media experience and to explore its consequences for metaphors in audiovisual media, we now proceed to apply these ideas and illustrate three cornerstones of cinematic metaphor: experience, affectivity, and temporality.

# Part II: **Cinematic Experience and Audiovisual Figurativity**

# Introduction

In the second part of the book, we examine the interrelation between the media mode of perception of audiovisual images and metaphorical forms of expression. It offers a close consideration of a key characteristic of cinematic metaphors: they emerge within the interaction between spectator and audiovisual image, which we have described in Part I as film-viewing, a process in which the temporal structure of the audiovisual composition is embodied in viewers as a temporal gestalt of perceiving, thinking, and feeling, produced in that process. In film-viewing, spectators are 'doing' metaphors, creating fictive realities, and connecting them with everyday reality. We have described this process as an artistic production, a poiesis of film-viewing that defines the specific character of the media mode of experience of audiovisual images, i.e., cinematic experience. This experience is embodied; it presupposes reflexive awareness, intersubjectivity, and temporality of meaning-making.

With the temporal flow of film-viewing, fluid connections within a web of different experiential domains evolve and are altered and changed constantly over the course of a scene or an entire movie. These domains emerge as multidimensional experiential gestalts (Lakoff and Johnson 1980b, 81, cf. Section 2.3) from the process of film-viewing. They are modulated by the temporal structures of the compositional forms of cinematic expressivity and are realized by spectators as perceptual and audiovisual figurations of a cinematic movement-image. Alongside metaphorical meaning-making as a prominent aspect of cinematic experience, these dynamic, perceptual, audiovisual figurations very often lead the way into the creation of another extremely widespread figurative mode: that is, metonymy. Although boundaries between metonymy and metaphor are often blurred, the basic principle of metonymy is described as contiguity, that of metaphor as similarity and difference (see Croft 1993, Jakobson 1990 [1956], 1987 [1965], Mittelberg 2010, Peirce 1960). While metaphors establish interactions between different realms of experience, metonymy establishes new connections within one experiential realm. Lakoff and Johnson (1980b, 39) characterize metonymy as "more basic and natural", and Günther Radden, arguing along similar lines, says that "metonymy provides an associative and motivated link between the two conceptual domains involved in metaphor" (Radden 2000, 93). Metonymy thus operates within the same experiential domain (e.g., Barcelona 2009) or semantic frame (Fillmore 1982); the connection is either an inner contiguity relation (e.g., part for whole) or an outer contiguity relation (i.e., a pragmatic link) (see Mittelberg 2006, 2010, 2013 for the differentiation of internal and external metonymy in verbo-gestural contexts of use).

https://doi.org/10.1515/9783110580785-partII

From webs of metonymies, metaphorical meanings may emerge and very often form intertwined metonymical and metaphorical scenarios (Mittelberg and Waugh 2009). Considering metonymy in connection with cinematic metaphor allows for a more encompassing account of how viewers are creating 'as-if realities' through cinematic experience. Cinematic metonymies share with metaphor the grounding in a specific mode of perceiving, that is, they are modulated media-aesthetically. Both figurative modes are based on and created from the process of film-viewing – that albeit individually perceived – creates a commonly shared horizon of experienced experiences (in terms of Sobchack's intersubjective understanding of cinema, cf. Chapter 5).

Against the backdrop of the theoretical discussion of embodied experience that is vital for our understanding of cinematic metaphor offered in the first part of the book, the second part now sets out to illustrate the consequences of our understanding of cinematic experience for analyses of figurativity (i.e., metaphor and metonymy). For this purpose, we start from a comparative analysis of multimodal interaction and film-viewing. We begin with two case studies that illustrate how embodied experiences ground metaphorical meaning-making in a ballet class (Section 6.1) and in a scene from a Hollywood classic (Section 6.2). They illustrate how embodiment, reflexivity, intersubjectivity, and temporality structure metaphorical meaning-making and we suggest that this is precisely what multimodal face-to-face interaction shares with the poiesis of film-viewing. Subsequently, a series of case studies, ranging from a TV news feature (Section 7.1), to classical Hollywood cinema (Section 7.2), music video (Section 7.3), and election campaign commercial (Section 7.4), document how cinematic experience constitutes a media specific mode of perception which grounds cinematic metaphor and metonymy.

# 6 Experiencing Metaphoricity

The analyses in this chapter zoom in on the characteristic traits of cinematic experience. They illustrate what it means for experience to be bound to the reflexivity of human thinking as an awareness of the difference between self- and other perception. They show what it means for an analysis of metaphor to follow Dewey's position of experience as being bound to a feeling for the entirety of a situation that differentiates automatized perception from experience. They also document how the intersubjectivity of embodiment and the temporal dynamics of meaning-making characterize the 'doing' of metaphor.

In short, the chapter illustrates how the phenomenological concept of embodiment that continues to inform film studies, allows us to understand how metaphorical meaning emerges from embodied experiences. The interactive processes of meaning-making that we can observe in a multimodal interaction, and which involve full body movements, hand gestures, and speech (e.g., Goodwin 2000, Mondada 2011, 2013, Streeck, Goodwin, and LeBaron 2011), can be considered a role model for the interaction that viewers engage in when they are viewing a film. Cinematic metaphors share the characteristic of embodied meaning-making with multimodal metaphors in gesture and speech. In the following, this theoretical parallelism is illustrated with a metaphor analysis of multimodal interaction in a ballet class and of a film scene.

## 6.1 Feeling the Feeling: Embodied Metaphor in a Ballet Class

Dance teachers often face the challenge of communicating highly subjective bodily sensations.[1] The awareness of one's own body as different from other bodies in the class appears trivial, but this difference between self- and other awareness of felt sensations is what constitutes reflexivity of embodied experience generally. This difference is clearly constitutive for teaching dance classes in general and it is the prerequisite of reaching this particular teacher's goal of leading students to the point where they feel the feeling that she is seeking to describe. This is what makes this embodied discourse a process of achieving

1 Analysis by Cornelia Müller, Silva H. Ladewig, and Lena Hotze (Mittelberg 2013). Data was gathered for the research project "Body Language of Movement and Dance: Emergence of Meaning, 'Languageing' and Therapeutical Application", sub-project 'languaging of body-movement' and supported by a grant from the German Ministry of Education (BMBF) (cf. Kolter et al. 2012). The version for this book was prepared by Cornelia Müller.

https://doi.org/10.1515/9783110580785-007

intersubjectivity – or, simply said, of reaching mutual understanding. Here is where metaphor comes in. Dance instructors regularly employ metaphors in their body work. Sometimes they use established scenarios such as imagining closing a zipper of a bodysuit or the shape of a silk thread that extends vertically from the head or the chest. Sometimes they create new ones. In this latter case dance classes become a masterpiece for studying how metaphorical meaning emerges from embodied experiences. They can be looked upon as a role model for the more abstract idea of embodied experiences that film viewers engage in when experiencing a film. This connects with Sobchack's neo-phenomenological position towards film as an "expression of experience by experience" (Merleau-Ponty 1968 [1964], 155, quoted in Sobchack 1992, 3). The embodied experiences of spectators are in the same way reflexive, intersubjective and temporally orchestrated as is the process of achieving a shared meaning concerning a particular subject matter in a ballet class (such as, in the following example, a feeling of balance and erect posture). Metaphorical meaning then emerges, evolves, changes between these interacting bodies – it is never owned by one person – although there are moments of explicitly shared intercorporeal understanding.

Sarah, the teacher of a ballet workshop on balance and posture that we video-recorded, discovers a new metaphor during the class:[2] the idea of a horizontal silk thread. She uses it to guide her students towards finding a similar bodily feeling. This means, her feeling of balance is reflexively bound to her students and vice versa. The process of working out a shared understanding of how balance is best achieved, and how it feels when it happens in one's own body, is subject of an extended back and forth, in which metaphoricity is altered, changed, adjusted from conversational move to conversational move.

The process begins relatively early in the lesson and continues all through the workshop. In fact, it constitutes a metaphorical axis that returns again and again during the class. Metaphoricity is multimodal from the beginning, i.e., it

2 This data was gathered for the research project "Body Language of Movement and Dance: Emergence of Meaning, 'Languageing' and Therapeutical Application" (see Footnote 1, this chapter) and particularly for the sub-project 'languaging of body-movement' (Cornelia Müller and Silva H. Ladewig). Workshops on 'Balance and Posture', 'Walking and Turning' and 'Sharing dance space' were held in four different dance traditions: ballet, Laban movement studies, ballroom waltz, tango argentino. The settings for the workshops was fixed: they begin with warming up, then explaining and practicing alternate for an hour. After that, the experiences with the first hour are discussed in the group. Then, class resumes again, and explaining and practicing alternate. At the end of the workshops, participants were interviewed individually.

is articulated in words and in gestures: in the warming-up phase of the class, Sarah asks her students to stand upright, and lean with their backs against the mirror-wall. Shortly before, she had talked about and enacted the metaphorical idea of a silk thread that pulls the body upwards from the head, as if the dance is hanging on a string, like a puppet. Subsequently, she shifts focus from the head to the center of the body. A stable center is essential for a proper balance. But it is not only the stability of the center, it is the position of the hip that matters very much in ballet because it has to be in an upright position, too. To achieve that position, a small tilting motion of the hip is necessary, and this is where Sarah begins to create a metaphorical scenario guiding her students towards doing and feeling this movement. While leaning against the wall and pointing to her navel, she describes her sensation of an imaginary horizontal silk thread pulling the navel toward the spine: "The feeling is a silk thread" [*Das Gefühl ist ein Seidenfaden*]. Then she turns to the student next to her and while touching her lap, she continues "from the navel" [*von dem Bauchnabel*] and restarts the whole sentence: "a silk thread from the navel to the spine" [*ein Seidenfaden vom Bauchnabel zur Wirbelsäule*] (Figure 6.1, the first three drawings).

By touching the body of the student standing next to her and pointing to her navel, Sarah locates the metaphorical experience that she is trying to explain. Her metaphorical pointing gesture (she points at an imagined silk thread, attached to the navel within the body) shows the student, standing next to her, where she is supposed to have the experience that the metaphorical scenario describes. Put differently, Sarah gestures with the body of the student next to her. This becomes her teaching model for this exercise. Giving up her position at the mirror, she then walks around and shows the other students, where the respective feeling, for the suspension point of the metaphorical silk thread, is located in their own bodies (Figure 6.1, the last three drawings). In this way, she actively inscribes the metaphorical meaning, a silk thread pulling the navel to the spine, into the bodies of her students.

This is not a one-way activity, as we can witness little later when a variation of this hip-tilt exercise is done. The students are asked to lie down on the floor, to feel the contact with the floor as a result of the hip-tilt that is motivated by the metaphorical scenario within the body. Sarah continues to work with the bodies of the students, and touching the lap of another student she says: "Then really light and now think light, think of the silk thread that goes backwards to the spine" [*und dann ganz leicht, und jetzt wirklich leicht denken, leicht denken an den Seidenfaden, der hier nach hinten zur Wirbelsäule geht*] (Figure 6.2, first drawing). Students are performing the exercise, and Sarah, passing around and between them, describes the hip movement as a "really smooth movement" [*eine ganz sanfte Bewegung*]. A moment later, one of the students articulates her

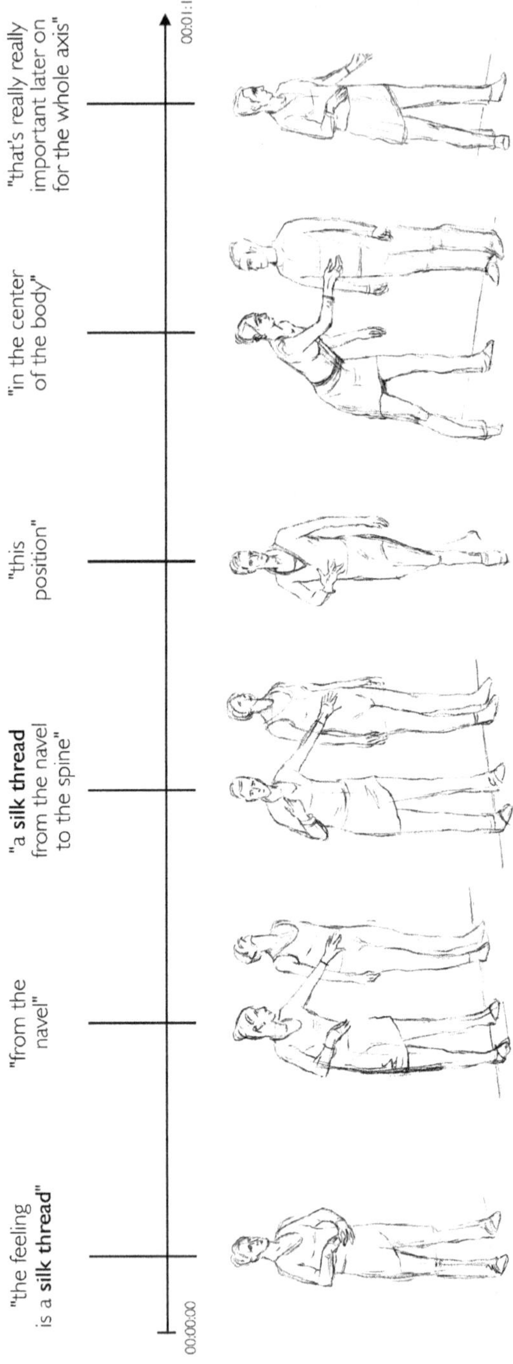


**Figure 6.1:** Touching and feeling metaphorical meaning in a ballet class: “The feeling is a silk thread”

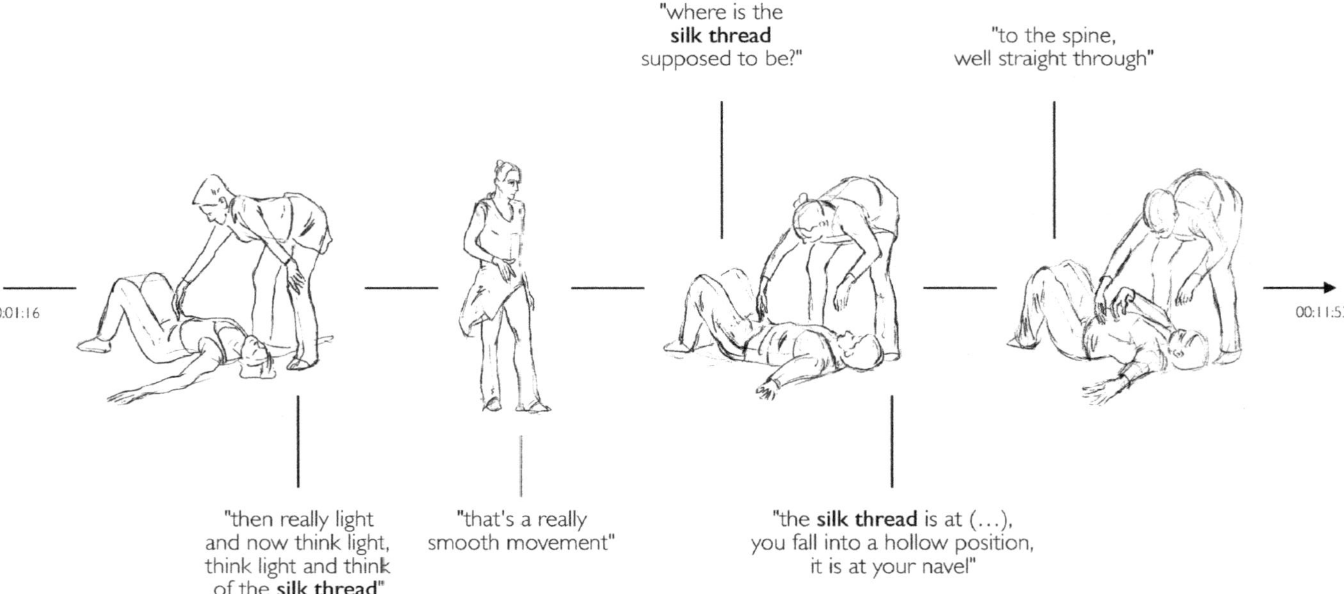


**Figure 6.2:** Intersubjectivity and reflexivity at work in a ballet class: "Think light"

difficulties with finding the right location of the starting point for the silk thread and asks: "Where is the silk thread supposed to be?" [*Wo soll der Seidenfaden sein?*] Again, Sarah indicates the location with her hand by touching the student's stomach and verbally describing the location for the metaphorical scenario that is supposed to be evoked as a feeling in the student's bodies: "The silk thread is at [...], you fall into a hollow position, it is at your navel" [*Der Seidenfaden ist [...], mach mal Hohlkreuz, der ist an deinem Bauchnabel*] (Figure 6.2, third drawing). The student confirms Sarah's description multimodally: she continues Sarah's sentence "[...] to the spine, well straight through" [*[...] zur Wirbelsäule, also so quer durch*] and joins Sarah's pointing gesture to her stomach. In so doing, for a moment, they actually point together (Figure 6.2, fourth drawing). A moment of shared understanding has emerged, in which words and gestures of both speakers work together in achieving an intersubjective moment of "I feel what you feel in the light of my own bodily experience". The metaphorical meaning that helps to find this feeling is thus a shared one, it is co-constructed, and involves the reflexive awareness of the distinction between self- and other body.

Figure 6.3 illustrates some moments of this dynamic interactive process of working out a shared understanding, a shared metaphorical meaning. It shows that metaphoricity is not reducible to different vehicles (in the words or in the gestures) but emerges between and from them; it is a process, it is dynamic, it is always in flow, reflexively bound to the other participants' presence and the specific context of this class. What we see in the single instances depicted below are temporal stabilizations in the flow of metaphorical meaning-making.

In conclusion: in a process of talking, touching, and feeling emerges metaphorical meaning that is reflexive, intersubjective, and dynamic. It is not in the words or in any one of the gestures, it is procedural, always changing, stabilizing in a word, a movement, a gesture only to be revised, changed, and altered as the discourse moves on. It involves embodied experiences that are inspired by a metaphorical scenario of a silk thread that pulls the navel towards the spine. However, these embodied experiences are no solipsistic sensations, no automatized perceptions (cf. Dewey, Section 5.1). They are reflexive, in that there is an awareness of one's own perceiving activity. This becomes evident in the extracts from the dance lesson when the dance students and the teacher make their bodily experiences explicit. Speaking about them, their bodily experiences become shared, they become reflexive – they become meaningful in and through the mutual cooperation between the participants: in the light of another 'I', of another subjective experience, emerges a feeling of the feeling of balance.

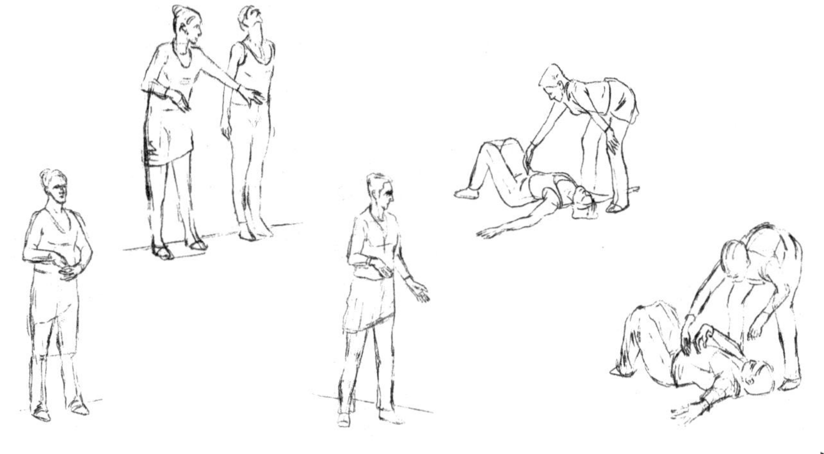


**Figure 6.3:** Finding balance is feeling a silk thread pulling the navel towards the spine in a ballet class

## 6.2 Film-Viewing and Successive Metaphorization: MAGNIFICENT OBSESSION

'Feeling the feeling': what we have just described with regard to the dance class interactions as reflexive and intersubjective embodiment, this experiencing in the light of another subjective experience, is a cornerstone of contemporary film theory (see Part I, Section 5.1). From the point of view of neo-phenomenological film theory, this constellation characterizes the specificity of cinematic experience. Film-viewing, from this perspective, is a perceptual activity of the viewer, it is the experiencing of the film in a spectator's body. This experience is reflexive in that it engages with movement-images as an expression of another subjectivity. The film comes to life in the bodies of the viewers. Reconsidering a fragment from Vivian Sobchack's *The Address of Eye*, discussed earlier (cf. Section 4.1), this reads as follows:

> In a search for rules and principles governing cinematic expression, most of the descriptions and reflections of classical and contemporary film theory have not fully addressed the cinema as life expressing life, as experience expressing experience. Nor have they explored the mutual possession of this experience of perception and its expression by filmmaker, film, and spectator [...] Indeed, it is this mutual capacity for and possession of experience through common structures of embodied existence, through similar modes of being-in-the-world, that provide the intersubjective basis of objective cinematic communication. (Sobchack 1992, 5)

This is what we described in the dance lesson interactions as 'feeling one's own body in the light of another body's feeling', and this is what we consider, with reference to Sobchack, an intersubjective view of embodiment. In the process of perceiving a film, a viewer becomes as much entangled with the flow of unfolding cinematic movement-images as the dance teacher and her students in their interactions. The film emerges through the embodied experiences of the viewer and from this specific mode of perception cinematic metaphor evolves. It is in that sense that metaphors are based in the spectator's embodied experiences of cinematic movement-images and their temporal orchestration (Chapter 2; Part IV). In the following analysis of a scene from Douglas Sirk's 1953 melodrama MAGNIFICENT OBSESSION (USA), we describe the unfolding of the film as arising from this kind of embodied perceptual experience of the viewer.[3] Note, that when we speak of the spectator or the film viewer here, we do not address the psychology of film-reception. Instead we describe a theoretical position of agency that might be taken by an empirical subject. We reconstruct how metaphorical meaning emerges from a perceptual mode that can be described as the viewer's process of experiencing the film as another subjective experience.

MAGNIFICENT OBSESSION is about a woman, Helen Phillips (Jane Wyman), who loses first her husband and then her eyesight, caused by the actions of a young man that she falls madly (blindly) in love with: Bob Merrick (Rock Hudson), a rich playboy, who, over the course of the film, transforms into the virtuous hero. The plot can be read as a crude version of the Oedipus myth. A mythical sign of guilty desire – blindness – is transferred to the woman, from which she is then freed, literally in an operation, by the man, who in the meantime has become a doctor.

The sequence that we are focusing on presents a stereotypical melodramatic scene: the woman alone in her room is a standard dramaturgical formula, which refers to the basic melodramatic constellation, even beyond the cinema. The heroine finds herself abandoned by her lover, and plummets from the illusion of love into the awareness of radical abandonment. It is evening in a Swiss hotel room. In the first shots, we see living room furniture, a large window, balcony doors, the décor is washed in moody reddish-brown tones. The step-by-step darkening of the image as the night falls, resonates with Helen's blindness. It is evening and it is getting darker, and soon it will not be possible to see anything anymore. This is true for the situation described here (the evening in

3 Analysis by Hermann Kappelhoff (Kappelhoff 2004a, 156–172, cf. also Greifenstein and Kappelhoff 2014). The English version for this book was prepared by Hermann Kappelhoff, Cornelia Müller, and Sarah Greifenstein.

the hotel room) and for the spectator (the too dark image), but not for Helen, who is already blind. Here, a metaphorical experiencing of one thing in terms of another has begun to develop and the dark image relates different realms of experience within the scene. In the process of viewing, the scene evolves in a double structure: on the one hand, we see a 'woman alone in her hotel room', and on the other, we gradually grasp the orchestration of the image space, in its unfolding and increasing darkening, as the expression of a feeling, as an 'I sense' that we ascribe to Helen. This emergence of metaphorical meaning can be described as a transformation of the represented room into an expression of a subjective feeling over time. It is a dynamic metaphor of the 'I sense' of the character Helen, which is grounded in the viewer's experience of an increasing darkness staged in this scene.

### The emerging sense of darkness

As we gradually experience a range of facets of darkness, darkness becomes increasingly connected with the feelings of the character Helen. The naïve postcard idyll of a Swiss mountain village, that shows in a view from the hotel window, reinforces the basic tone of warmth. The dramatic lighting of the scene is in sharp contrast to this harmonic atmosphere. We see Joyce Phillips (Helen's stepdaughter) closing the French doors to the balcony, Helen enters the room, then lingers for a while in a very dark part of the image. A conspicuous sidelight, falling in through the window, divides the visual surface: two bright stripes in the middle, thick fields of shadow on the upper and lower edges of the image. The two characters, Joyce and Helen, are increasingly moving into backlight, so that by the end of the dialog, we can hardly see much more of their faces than silhouettes (Figure 6.4). A visual scenario of increasing darkness is unfolding, which is paralleled by a scenario created on the level of the dialog, and which also emphasizes the darkness and the evening hour (Figure 6.4).

They speak of the looming night and the agonies of sleeplessness, and finally, of the desperate hour, in which the knowledge becomes unbearable that the night will no longer be brightened by any light. Helen says: "The night time is the worst time. It does get darker you know. And then, when I finally do get to sleep, I know that when I wake up in the morning, there won't be any dawn." When Joyce begins weeping next to her, Helen adds: "[...] I didn't mean to parade my emotions." The dialog spans an arc from the evening hour, through the darkness of the blind person, and into the night of death, and combines this all with the "emotions" of Helen. Together, the dialog and the visual staging (the dark silhouettes of Helen and Joyce) articulate a metaphorical interaction in time: they create a connection

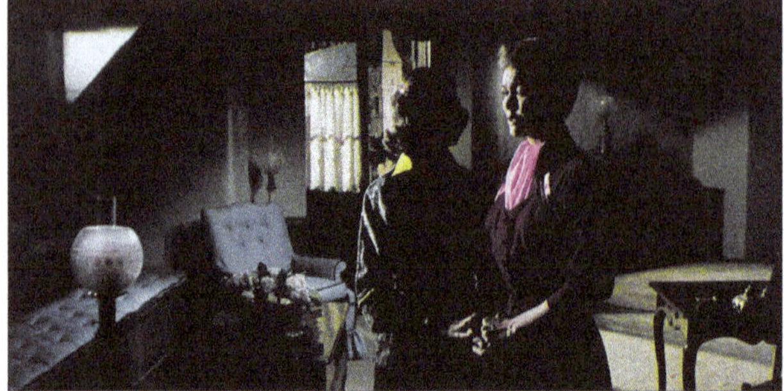

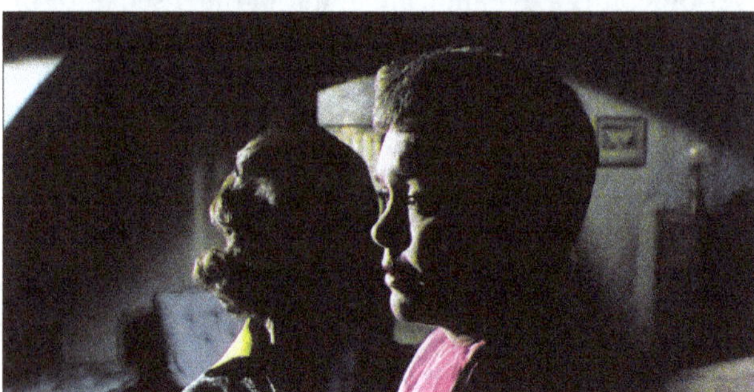

Helen:

The night time is the worst time.

It does get darker, you know.

And then, when I finally do get to sleep, I ... I know that when I wake up in the morning, there won't be any dawn.

(*Joyce starts crying.*)

Joyce, Joyce, forgive me!

I didn't mean to parade my emotions.

**Figure 6.4:** "It does get darker you know": an emerging metaphor for Helen's emotions in MAGNIFICENT OBSESSION

between darkness and emotions. The audiovisually staged darkness is emphasized by the dialog, connecting what we see and what we hear the two women saying. This speaking of darkness thus becomes meaningful in several ways: on the one hand, it literally designates the approaching night, which we see on the depicted level as the darkening room. But it also designates the darkness of the blind woman, as well as a metaphorical connection in which not-seeing and sleeping are interwoven. When Helen responds to the weeping Joyce by saying "I didn't mean to parade my emotions" the linguistic imagery refers through contrast to the darkness of a hidden emotional life. The phrase "there won't be any dawn" indicates something lying in the future, in which the not-getting-brighter is already associated with grief.

### Experiencing darkening as increasing desperation

The dialog lays out the process that is set up in the staging that follows. It can be read almost like a script of the scene as it unfolds. As expressed in the words:

"it does get darker", "my emotions", "there won't be any dawn", the staging of the scene orchestrates a development: from a dawning darkness to an increasing nightly darkness that finally develops to a shadowed brightness. This staging, here particularly strongly articulated through the composition of light, is what viewers feel as they are watching the scene. What they are doing is then ascribing their subjective feeling of this process to the character on the screen. It is with this dynamic ascribing that metaphoricity emerges. From these embodied experiences emerges a seeing-as, an experiencing of desperation as a successive darkening, which is grounded in the subjective experience of the aesthetic orchestration. It is in that sense that we consider cinematic experience as a specific perceptual mode from which metaphorical meaning dynamically emerges in the process of film-viewing.

But let us reconsider the beginning of the scene. From the moment that the verbal and audiovisually staged expressive elements are combined, the darkness is no longer a characteristic of the represented location alone – a hotel room in the evening – but has already started transforming into metaphorical meaning. As the scene unfolds, this becomes more and more an audiovisual metaphorical scenario of an 'internal darkness'. For the viewer, the unfolding of the scenario orchestrates Helen's increasing desperation. The internal darkness is, thus, not to be understood abstractly, it is primarily constituted in the play of how light and color are configured, also encompassing the actors' gestures.

Before leaving the room, Joyce turns on two table lamps; one of them is located right next to Helen, who is now sitting in an armchair, and the other is in the background of the image. This continues the motif of increasing darkness. For a short moment there is indeed literally more light, but the dim bulbs hardly shed any brightness. Helen remains stuck in her darkness, and this solitude is the room, which for the viewer – but not for the character of the blind woman – is illuminated by the faint sources of light. Like the opening dialog, like the standing-in-the-shadows of Joyce and Helen, the prominently exhibited action, when Joyce switches on the two lamps, and the contrast-rich dramaturgy of the lighting, become a repeated emphasis of light in the staging.

Helen gets up, it is her empty gaze that this shot inserts into the image; it strays off into the uncertain outside, into the off-screen space. She disappears from the frame; the next shot shows her in the middle of the image. A bright light comes in from the balcony, it makes a wide diagonal swath that divides the image into sharply contrasted areas of shadows. Another sidelight – placed somewhat higher and broken by the pattern of the curtains – casts a turbulent network of shadowy lines across the surface of the image. Helen takes a step toward a lathed wooden post, leans on it and slumps down slightly. Her form is turned away from the light, from the dark post, increasingly submerging her in shadows; finally, her face disappears entirely in the darkness. The lighting thus underscores the uncertain movements of the blind woman; it orchestrates, as it were, the action of the actress.

The creeping shadows gradually unfold a sinister undertone. They are pragmatically defined by the time of day; but the source of the sidelight – the French doors of the balcony – is emphasized more and more from shot to shot. The accentuated light from the imaginary outside world takes this moment into the uncanny, as the coming night here is contrasted with its opposite, that of a growing, indeterminate light: a gleaming light that casts the oversized shadows of the cross made by the window panes and the lace curtains into the interior of the room. In this way, the signs of the time of day become associated with the symbolism of death. The music is arranged with similarly sharp contrasts, choirs sing in high tones, violins and a piano also plays a high-pitched melody, then deeper sounds from the piano accompany the high voices. The darkness, depth, and the high brightness of the sound are built up from the beginning as a sharp musical contrast.

We are tempted to ascribe to the actress what is in fact essentially an effect of the staging: over the time of the viewing, the room as a whole has become an expression, a moving image of her inner world (Figure 6.5). A multidimensional experiential gestalt: this room *is* her existential feeling.

Starting from the evening hour and passing through the darkness of blindness, night begins to fall and the desperation starts to grow. For the spectator, it is the time in which one's own feelings are ascribed to the visible movements of the actors, thus constituting a world of sensation and feeling of the character. The desperation of the character is revealed to the spectator as a transformation of the cinematic image. The composition of the scene thus expresses another subjective experience, which, in turn, is experienced by the viewer.

The scene establishes a mode of embodied perception, in which all elements of the staging appear as figure-ground-constellation. It is as if Helen's movements were connected with all the other visual elements: Helen's getting up causes the music to get louder; her groping around makes the image darker; her turning around accelerates the shadowing.

Through all these sensory congruences, which the audiovisual composition has created, the feeling of having no way out is connected with the moving actress. An aesthetic-audiovisual figuration, in which all the visual and auditory elements work together, allows for the subjective sensation of a character to emerge, which should not be conceived as separated from the film experience, since the ascribed feelings are the embodied experiences of the viewer in the first place. Over the course of the viewer's process of viewing, all the objects of the diegetic exterior space are transformed into a subjective interior space. In this process metaphorical meaning emerges successively. Two realms of experience

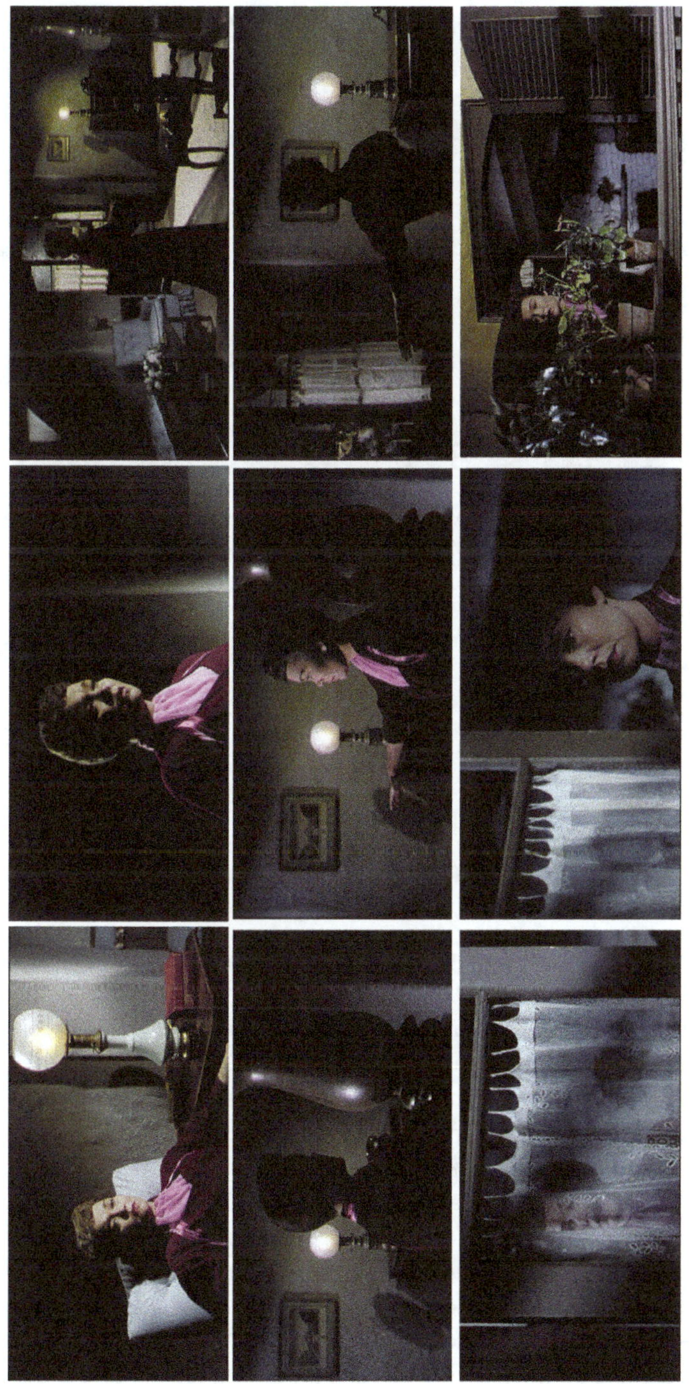

**Figure 6.5:** Experiencing successive darkening as increasing desperation in MAGNIFICENT OBSESSION

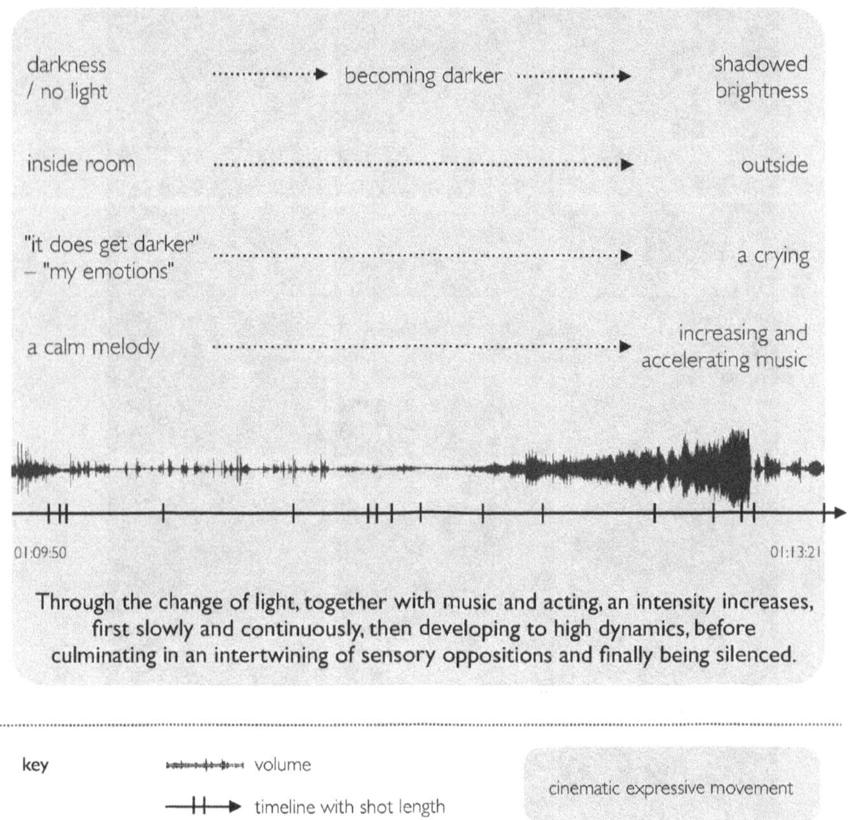


**Figure 6.6:** The room becoming a felt interiority, in MAGNIFICENT OBSESSION

interact: at the beginning we see a room with a woman from alternating/changing viewpoints. But as the scene unfolds, we cease seeing it as a description of a situation in an outer world; through the mise-en-scène, we see it becoming an interior world. External objects become the interior objects of the drama, light and darkness become nuances of feeling, color values become an image of mood, the room becomes a space of feeling, an absolute interior (Figure 6.6).

The diagram in Figure 6.6 illustrates the temporal unfolding of the staging's dominant levels: lighting, mise-en-scène, acting and dialog, music, which all together create the expression of a subjective experience that the spectators of the film experience bodily and ascribe it to the character on-screen.

Only through the aesthetics of the cinematic staging does what is represented – a hotel room, in which a woman is alone, gets up, and goes to the window – become an interiority over time, a world of feeling that is absolutely visible and audible. The successive filling up of the image space by color, music, light, and gestures is the expressive movement of the staging, which, at the same time, is the unfolding emergence of the image as an expression of experience by experience. Only the time in which the movement-image unfolds, the altered lighting, the shift of the music, which goes along with the changes in the acting, make a transformation possible, placing the two arrangements of the image in a metaphorical connection for the viewer as concretely experienced realms of being-in-the-world in Sobchack's above mentioned sense.

The first level of arrangement in this scene concerns the film's expressivity – it is tied to the scene's temporal staging, which is congruent with the time of the viewer's experiencing of it. The scene's second level of arrangement only becomes possible and perceivable due to the first realm of experience. This second realm of experience can be characterized as the level of what is represented: a woman, her movements, and an interior space of a room. And it is through the temporal unfolding of the scene that both arrangements are integrated in such a way that viewers are inclined to understand what they sense in their own bodies as the sensation of a fictional character. The metaphorical meaning that emerges from this experience is thus itself processual; it describes a process of transformation and defines the formation of meaning over the course of the scene. It is in this experiential process that viewers successively and actively connect an exterior darkness with an interior feeling of desperation. Put differently, in the process of viewing this scene, spectators are gradually experiencing an outer darkness as an internal feeling of desperation. Referring to Sobchack's characterization of film, we can describe this as a cinematic staging of experiencing the experience (or feeling the feeling) of an increasing desperation. This is what characterizes the reflexive embodied experience, the specific mode of cinematic perception from which metaphorical meaning emerges.

# 7 Audiovisual Figurativity Emerging from Cinematic Experience

We have argued above that cinematic metaphors are grounded in intersubjective, reflexive, and temporally orchestrated experiences of film viewers. However, cinematic experience not only characterizes the interaction between films and their spectators, it is a specific perceptual mode that applies to audiovisual forms in general. What we have described above, as intersubjective sharing of embodied experiences that provides the basis for meaning to emerge, holds basically for any form of audiovisual communication. While it is true that the staging of cinematic expressivity will most certainly not be comparable to an aesthetic masterpiece such as a feature film directed by Douglas Sirk, even television news or political reports create cinematic experiences that are essential for the meaning-making processes they stage. To underline this point, the following four case studies illustrate how figurative meaning emerges from cinematic experience in non-fictional as well as in fictional audiovisual formats.

The term figurative meaning indicates that in audiovisual forms metaphorical and metonymical modes often interact. However, most cognitive-linguistic research on figurativity "has traditionally been overshadowed by the study of metaphor" (Catalano and Waugh 2013, 32), and only a fairly limited set of studies consider metonymy as primary topic of investigation (especially Mittelberg 2006, 2008, 2010, 2013, Mittelberg and Waugh 2009, 2014, see also Catalano and Waugh 2013, Urios-Aparisi 2014, Yu 2009, and more recently Littlemore 2015). This holds even though cognitive theories of metaphor and metonymy conceive of them as indispensable elements of ordinary language, thought, and understanding, which are both based on experiencing and understanding one kind of thing in terms of another (cf. Radden and Kövecses 1999, 18). Yet metaphor differs from metonymy because it connects two *different* experiential domains and creates similarity between them. Metonymy, on the other hand, establishes links within the *same* experiential domain through the semiotic principle of contiguity (see Croft 1993, Jakobson 1990 [1956], 1987 [1965], Mittelberg 2010, Peirce 1960). Put differently, in metonymy "one thing is used to refer to something else, to which it is closely related in some way" (Littlemore 2015, 5), be it factual or pragmatic linkages (cf. Barcelona 2000, Croft 1993, Gibbs 1999, Mittelberg and Waugh 2014, Radden 2000). Given the fundamental distinctness of both figurative modes, metaphor and metonymy can nevertheless intertwine in meaning-making (cf. Goossens' (1990) notion of 'metaphtonomy'). Taking a cognitive-semiotic perspective, Mittelberg (2006, 2008, Mittelberg and Waugh 2009) has underlined that, in the process of understanding gestures, metonymy leads the way into metaphor. It thus seems

https://doi.org/10.1515/9783110580785-008

worthwhile not to focus exclusively on cinematic metaphor, but to take metonymy into consideration, too. Although an encompassing analysis of how different figurative modes play together in audiovisual compositions extends the scope of this book, the analyses presented in this chapter serve to indicate that the media mode of cinematic experience grounds not only metaphorical meaning, but audiovisual figurativity more generally speaking (cf. Horst forthcoming/2018).

## 7.1 Feeling Losing and Winning: REPORT MAINZ (TV News Feature)

REPORT MAINZ is a monthly political magazine on German national television that contains a set of critical reports on current political topics.[1] The report we are focusing on discusses the consequences of the financial crisis of 2008. It sets up a strong contrast between the effects crashing banks exert on bankers compared to middle class people who invested their small amounts of money. In the analysis presented here, only two scenes of the report are considered; a full analysis of the feature is provided in Part IV.

In the beginning, outplacement consultants are featured as winners of the banking crisis. We see a group of them standing together, celebrating successful business with a champagne reception in their office space (Figure 7.1., the upper six stills). After some statements, a voice-over sums up their outplacement business concept. The scene ends with a statement of the head consultant (Figure 7.1., the still below) highlighting the suitability of outplacement as a rescue strategy for bankers who have lost their jobs in the crisis. The report thus sets off with an ironic twist, since, obviously, it is not the bankers that first come to mind when the losers of a banking crisis are at stake. This audiovisual irony is supported by the fact that what we are witnessing is a happy event, a champagne reception, celebrating the positive development of the outplacement business: we see groups of people, gathering around tables, forming a kind of closed circle. The camera approaches them again and again, highlighting a rather static quality of the circular formations, showing 'closed circles' from different perspectives. This first

1 Gottlob Schober and Steffen Hudemann in the six-and-a-half minutes report in the German political broadcast REPORT MAINZ (shown on German national TV, ARD, October 20, 2008). The analysis of this broadcast was developed in the context of the research project "Multimodal Metaphor and Expressive Movement" and has been further worked on within the Cinepoetics' research focus 'Metaphor – Film Images, Cinematic Thinking, and Cognition' (Müller and Schmitt 2015). For an extended version see Schmitt (forthcoming/2019). The version for this book was prepared by Cornelia Müller and Christina Schmitt.

scene ends with a shift in the action space and a cut to the office of Eberhard von Rundstedt (the head of consultancy), changing from the liveliness of the reception to a calm atmosphere. With a static and fairly long take, the camera rests on the sitting von Rundstedt, emphasizing his voluminous body with a low angle shot. This second interior space is highlighted by von Rundstedt's reverberating and deep voice that creates a strong feeling of his physical presence. Together, mise-en-scène, camera, and sound quality stage the impression of a physical presence in a closed space.

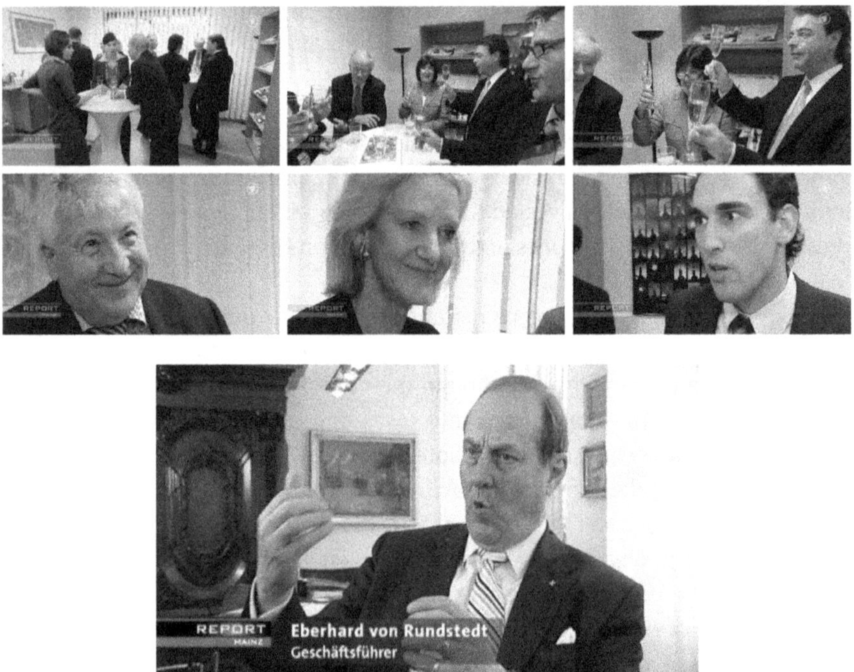


**Figure 7.1**: Experiencing winning as being inside and socially included, from REPORT MAINZ (20 October 2008) on the global financial crisis

As viewers follow the aesthetic course of the composition of this scene, they experience different kinds of interiority, of being inside celebrating, or of being inside in a representative office, which are all metonymically connected with belonging to a group of successful people. From the perceptual experience of this closed interior, a metaphor emerges that connects being inside with the group of winners. This aesthetic modulation of the viewer's process of viewing as a specific media mode of experience is what we consider to be the experiential grounding of a cinematic metaphor, which connects winning in the economic crisis with being inside and being socially included.

In the next scene of the report, the viewers are exposed to a very different experience. Now, losers of the crisis come into play metonymically: small investors, staged as ordinary people that have lost their lifetime savings with the crash of the banking system. We see a group of them, out in the streets, walking towards a building of the bank that is responsible for their losses. Standing in front of the door of the Frankfurt branch office of the Kaupthing Bank, which had blocked their bank accounts, a voice from the intercom refuses to let them in (Figure 7.2).

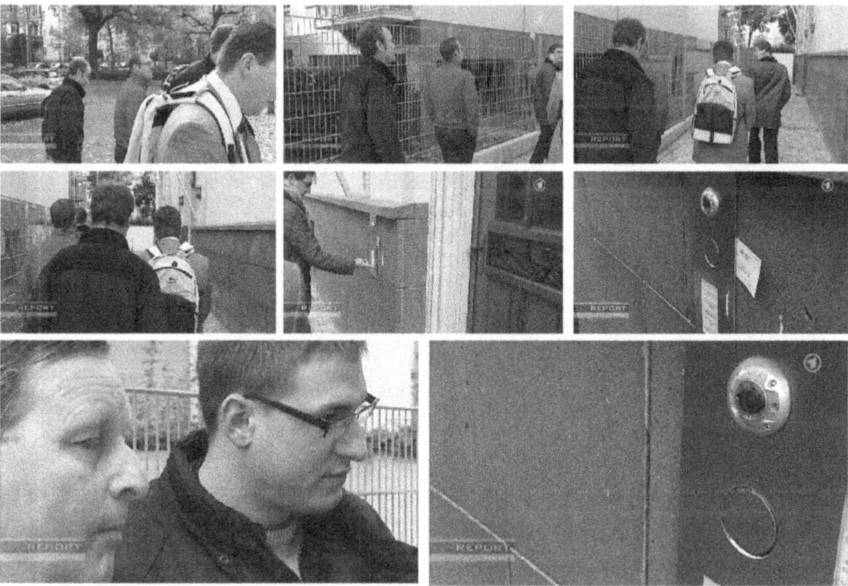

**Figure 7.2**: Experiencing losing as being outside and excluded, from REPORT MAINZ (20 October 2008) on the global financial crisis

With a long tracking shot, the camera follows the group. Camera movement and framing successively transform the group movement into a kind of tunnel-shaped goal oriented forward motion. The length of this shot underlines the duration and continuity of the movement. A shot reverse shot montage cuts off this continuous movement, creating the feeling of a harsh stop. We now see faces staring at an intercom in the wall of the bank building that alternate with close-up shots of the intercom. At the same time, one hears a disembodied voice coming from the intercom system.

In this way, the viewers now experience a steady goal-directed movement of a group of people, which is harshly stopped. This movement experience does, however, not primarily refer to the movement of the people seen on the screen, *it is the way in which their walk is being filmed that creates the feeling of moving towards something and of being abruptly stopped.* Camera and montage are the dominant staging strategies here. The audiovisual composition transforms the represented outside space (the people walking along the street) into the cinematic image of an excluded exterior. From this kind of experiencing of being outside, of being refused entry to a bank, not allowed to come inside, a feeling of exclusion emerges that becomes metaphorically connected with the losers of the crisis.

With this second scene, an experience of being outside and excluded is staged that establishes an experiential contrast with the 'winner' scene. It connects the experience of losing a lot of money with being out in the streets, excluded from the office space of the banks, while the winners of the crisis are shown inside in some representative office space. In this way, profiting from a crisis as opposed to losing money is turned into a media-specific perceptual experience of physical inclusion versus exclusion, through which, in turn, metaphorical inclusion is connected with being a winner, and metaphorical exclusion is connected with being a loser.

The report thus offers a particular mode of perception in which inclusion and exclusion are staged: viewers entangle with the expression of this specific experience. And in this embodied process of cinematic perception, even only over the first two scenes of the report, metaphoricity emerges. This is what grounding metaphoricity in the media mode of experience means in this political news feature: it stages inclusion/inside and exclusion/outside and creates a metaphorical scenario in which this perceptual experience becomes connected with belonging to the group of winners or losers of the banking crisis.

Watching a news report on television, indeed involves different aesthetic experiences than viewing a feature film. However, the basic media-setting, the embodied perceptual mode that the term cinematic experience captures, Sobchack's expressing an experience by experience, remains the same. In the next section, another classical Hollywood feature film illustrates how the cinematic movement-image as a specific mode of experience grounds metaphoricity. The analysis of a scene from Hitchcock's film noir SUSPICION describes how the feeling of suspicion emerges in the process of film-viewing, more specifically, from a particular movement experience and as a metaphorical process.

## 7.2 Movement Experience and Metaphorical Process: SUSPICION

At first sight, Alfred Hitchcock's SUSPICION (USA 1941) appears as a simple crime story of a young woman's increasing suspicion that the man she just married might not only have committed a murder in the past, but is intending to murder her as well.[2] But more importantly, it turns out to be an aesthetic orchestration of the very feeling of 'suspicion'. At one point, the young wife's emerging suspicion is staged as a loss of consciousness, an increasing and overwhelming insight, eventually causing a break-down. Her process of successive revelation is composed as a cinematic movement experience, grounding an emergent metaphorical meaning: an accelerating rhythm culminating in a sudden break-off and a rapid downward movement stages a media-specific experience of fading and falling down, which is becoming the vehicle for a metaphorical topic, the woman's thinking process, or her emerging suspicion.

The corresponding scene shows Lina (Joan Fontaine), engaged in a word game with her recently married husband John (Cary Grant) and Beaky, a friend of theirs (Nigel Bruce). What starts with a leisurely atmosphere successively transforms into an increasing suspicion that John is a murderer. This transformation of affective moods is modulated by a specific pattern of cinematic movement, in which the pleasurable relaxed atmosphere changes into a scenario of a terrifying insight. It stages the thought processes of Lina and eventually causes Lina to faint.

In the beginning of the scene, montage establishes a pattern of three alternating images: the face of Joan Fontaine, a word game, and the talking men (Figure 7.3). The alternation becomes a repetitive rhythm of three cinematic images, a slow and leisurely pace, whose triadic alternation suggests a waltz.

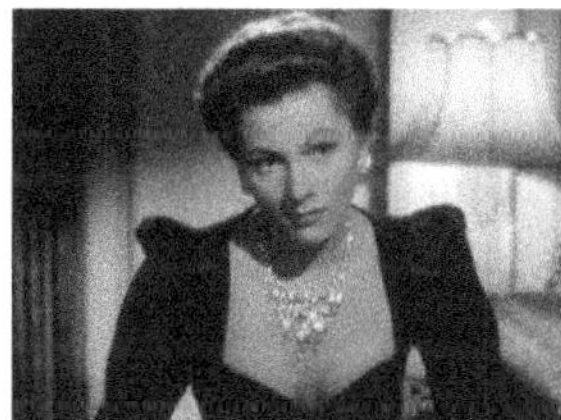
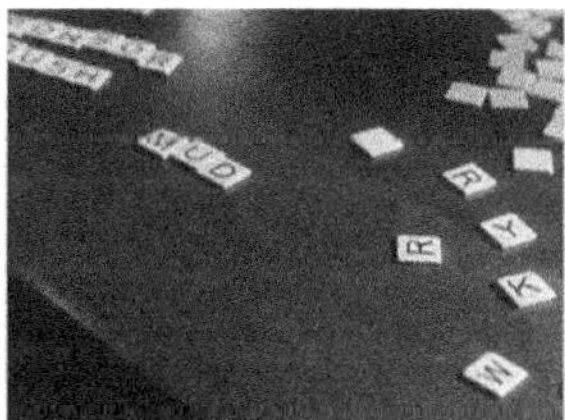
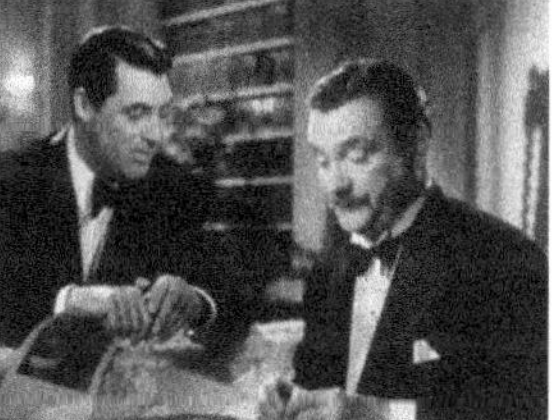

**Figure 7.3:** The pattern of three alternating shots staged in a waltz rhythm in SUSPICION

The three alternating images each develop in their own way. Beginning with an establishing shot that shows the three protagonists gathered around a living room table and engaged in a board game, the camera approaches the face of Joan

2 The analysis was carried out in the context of the research project "Multimodal Metaphor and Expressive Movement" and was further developed within the Cinepoetics' research focus 'Metaphor – Film Images, Cinematic Thinking, and Cognition' by Sarah Greifenstein. The version for this book was prepared by Cornelia Müller and Sarah Greifenstein.

Fontaine step-by-step until it becomes the center of a close-up shot (Figure 7.4). Through the accumulation of the cinematic images and also through the visual power of the face this centering dominates this part of the tripartite cinematic movement. Every word spoken and everything else that is shown in the other alternating shots becomes emphasized and related to her. The waltz rhythm has here a decisive accent here. Or, as Ejchenbaum (1974 [1927]) puts it: the close-up perspective accentuates the flow of the surrounding shots. The consequence is that all other elements of the unfolding cinematic movement are related to the questioning, observing and then skeptical gaze of Lina.

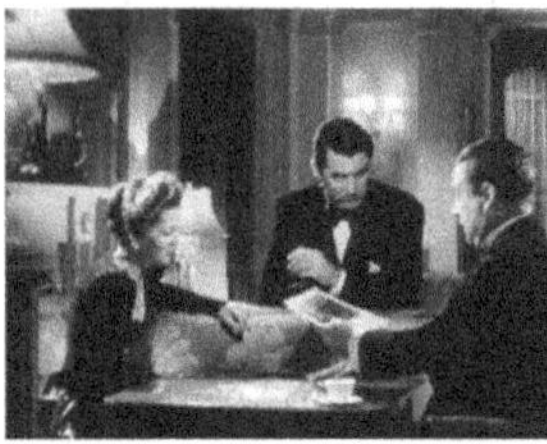
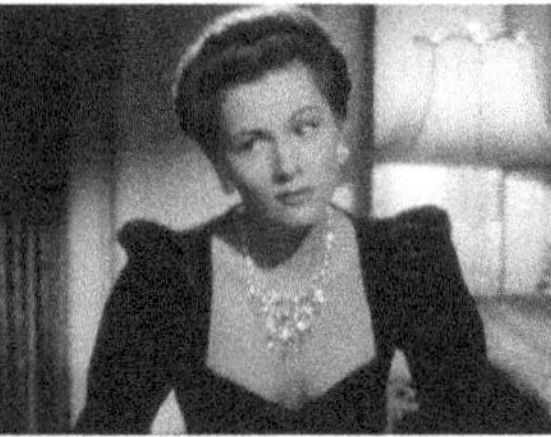
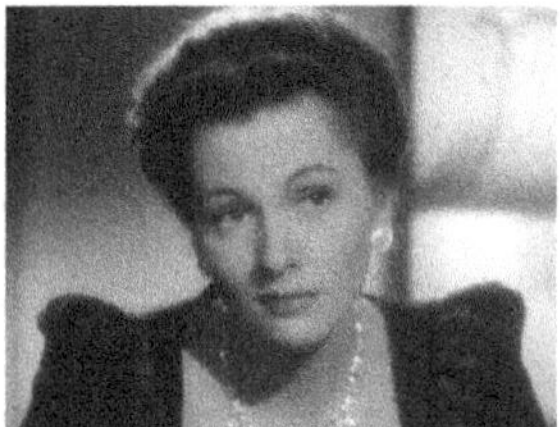

**Figure 7.4:** The set of first images in the waltz pattern: Lina becoming the center of a close-up shot (SUSPICION)

A centering camera movement establishes Fontaine as reference point. Rhythmically interlocked with the focusing of Joan Fontaine's face, the two other cinematic images also stage the idea of something developing: for one thing, there is the temporal orchestration of the word game. We see the hands of Joan Fontaine playing, and we follow the casual moving around of loose letters step by step leading to a combination of the word "MURDER" (Figure 7.5).

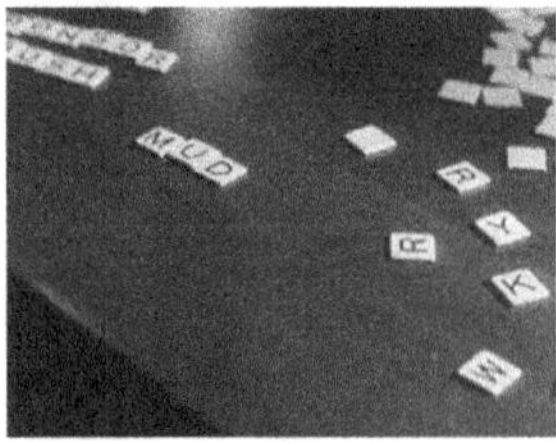
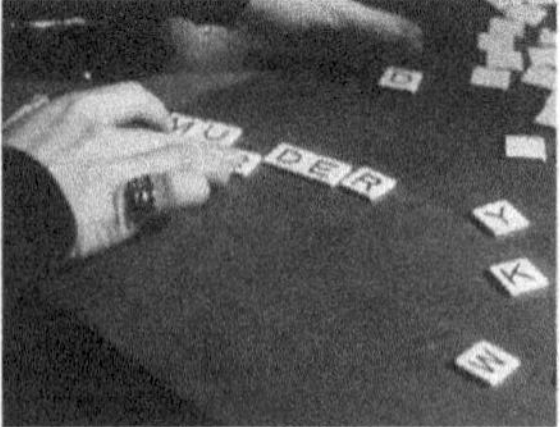
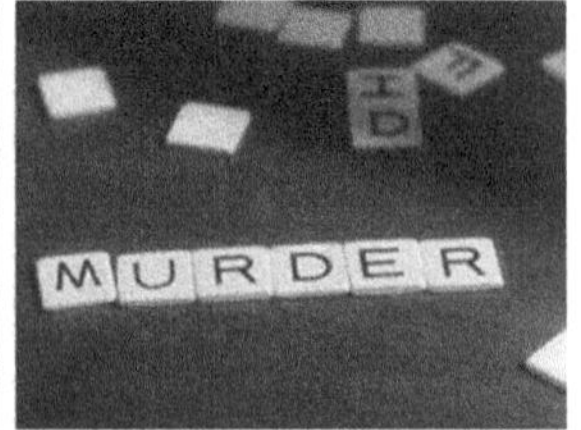


**Figure 7.5:** The set of second images in the waltz pattern: combining letters and "murder" appears (SUSPICION)

For another thing, the third cinematic image develops in a movement of successive isolation. Something crystallizes step by step: from seeing the three players together sitting around the table to a zooming in on the two men and ending in a close-up of Cary Grant's face (Figure 7.6).

All these three cinematic images, each staging a different kind of development, are interwoven through the scene's montage. Combination and isolation are both related to the center, the face of Joan Fontaine. Her face is shown so often and seems to attract and incorporate the other two movement-images.

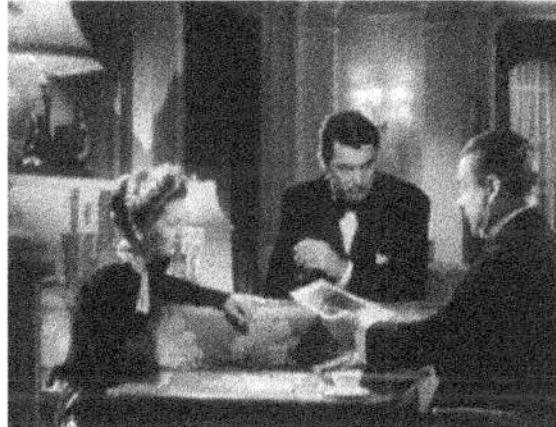
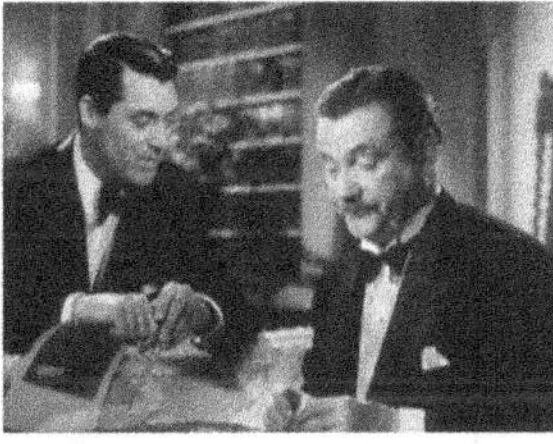
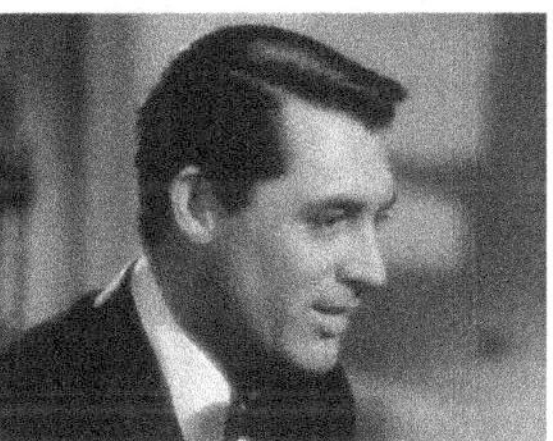

**Figure 7.6:** The set of third images in the waltz pattern: successive isolation (SUSPICION)

This temporal ensemble illustrates nicely how a trivial understanding of the scene is arranged: she thinks that he is the murderer. What is less banal though, is the way, in which this is actually realized. What we see in the unfolding flow of images is, in fact, our thinking as film viewers, modulated through the specific perceptual experience of the temporal composition. It is only in the viewer's perceptual activity that combining and isolating (the second and third image of the waltz) are done, and it is the viewer's experience of viewing that is ascribed to the actor's body (through the first image of the waltz), as-if we were participating in the heroine's thinking and feeling.

Along with the waltz rhythm, metaphoricity slowly appears as a dynamic form of embodied cinematic meaning. It is the media mode of experience from which metaphoricity emerges and through which suspicion successively and increasingly appears as being experienced and understood in terms of a dance rhythm that playfully structures a thinking process in which the combination and isolation of seemingly random aspects of a situation successively crystallize in a terrifying doubt (Figure 7.7).

It is this cinematic experiencing of an experience that viewers ascribe to the characters on the screen; in this way the process of the viewer's perceptual experience, orchestrated by a kind of visual waltz rhythm, becomes the experiential grounding for cinematic metaphorical meaning.

In the second part of the scene, the staging of the cinematic movement changes to two alternating shots. Again the face of Joan Fontaine is the center, she remains the constant, but the other image changes: we see a black and white photo of a steep coast, a falling man, and the foaming sea (Figure 7.8).

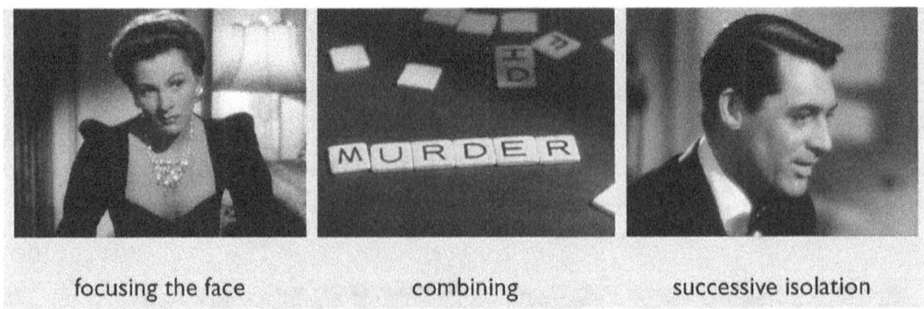


**Figure 7.7:** A metaphor for suspicion emerging. Suspicion as Lina's thinking process orchestrated by a visual waltz rhythm (SUSPICION)

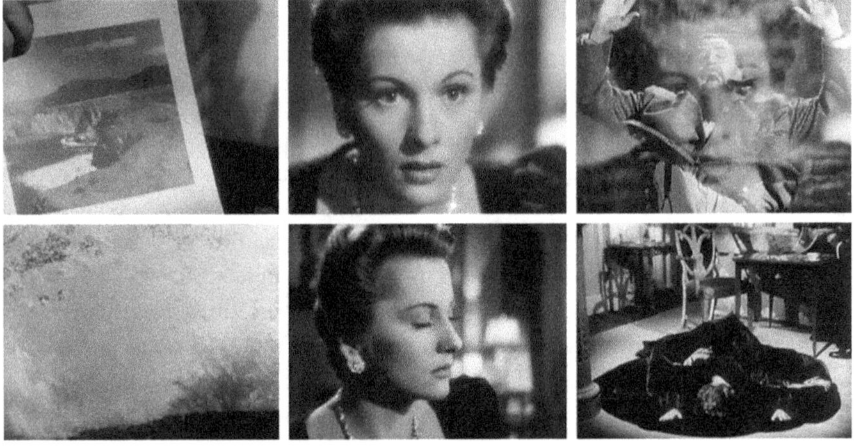

**Figure 7.8:** Dissolve montage orchestrating subjective imagination as a metaphorical scenario (SUSPICION)

In contrast to the beginning of the scene, it is the alternation of the two cinematic images that emphasizes a process of perception, rather than the characters. Hearing the reverberating laughter of Beaky, Lina's face with eyes wide-open and Beaky's falling off the cliff are staged as a rapid oscillation (on the level of sound) and a cross-fade, merging into an almost white image (foaming water) and silence. Then the camera moves back from Lina's face with closed eyes and we see Lina falling from her chair, fainting. In the montage, the fainting of the woman is connected with its preceding movement: the falling of the man (Figure 7.8).

The aesthetic orchestration of this second part of the scene creates a change in movement experience: the oscillation of laughter and the cross-fade images become an expression of Lina's process of perception. As viewers, we perceive her perception as a temporal process of cinematic composition, it becomes a movement-image in the Deleuzian sense (Deleuze 2008 [1983]).

It is through the staging that viewers participate in something that they project onto the character of Lina. We do not see an action from the outside (the falling of a man) but we experience it as an action of an interiority. We experience the quality of a disturbing thought and its consequences (the fainting) as a quality of the cinematic movement composition. In the process of watching this part of the scene, viewers feel the falling and fainting in their own bodies. This subjectivization is connected with the close-up of Joan Fontaine's face, but it is primarily motivated by montage, which creates a cinematic experience of vertigo and fainting, which is then projected onto the actor's body.

Along with this second part of this scene and its changing pattern of cinematic movement comes a change of metaphorical expressivity: Lina's subjective imagination is experienced in terms of fast oscillations on the level of sound, and the dissolving of her face with Beaky's falling off the cliff.

Going through this parcours of movement experiences changes the narrative of the scene. While, in the beginning, we see three people gathered around a table and playing a word-game in a relaxed leisurely atmosphere of a living room, in the end, this relaxed friendly situation turns into Lina's horrifying hallucination.

The emergent metaphoricity motivates the construction of a new narrative setting. Viewers construct these actions as elements of a thought-guided and emotional hypothesizing of the woman figure Lina (and not as a series of events happening in the external diegesis of the film), because the cinematic composition modulates this specific perceptual movement experience, which, in turn grounds the metaphorical process just described.

Metaphorical meaning thus emerges from the media mode of experiencing the aesthetic composition as an expression of another experience, another subjectivity. It is bound to the concrete specific staging of cinematic images, grounded in the temporal parcours of cinematic movement and emerges in the process of film-viewing. It is *not* 'contained' in the film, it does not exist outside of the experience of viewing the film.

This perspective also involves a different take on cinematic narrativity and the question of how it is possible to reconstruct a narrative level. It asks for how an audiovisual 'representation' is constructed without taking what is represented, without taking a narrative level of the film for granted, and as starting point of film analysis. On the contrast, a non-representationalist view offers a way of understanding of how it is possible to come to a statement such as "the protagonist Lina thinks that her husband could be capable of murder". It assumes, that viewers' cinematic experiences are projected onto the actor's bodies on screen.

Their feelings and thoughts become the feelings and thoughts of the protagonists. Metaphoricity is one dimension of this emergent narrativity (Kappelhoff and Greifenstein 2016), but often metonymical processes intertwine in this process with metaphorical ones. The following sections consider this more closely.

## 7.3 Metonymies in Metaphorical Worlds: HER MORNING ELEGANCE (Music Video)

Metonymy in audiovisual forms is as much grounded in the media mode of cinematic experience as metaphor. Both figurative modes emerge from the perceptual experience expressed by cinematic staging; they play hand in hand in creating a narrative, but operate differently regarding the experiential realms they construct: while metaphor establishes connections between different domains of experiences, metonymy operates within the same experiential domain (cf. Barcelona 2009, Croft 1993, Gibbs 1999, Mittelberg and Waugh 2009, Radden 2000). The following analysis of a music video shows how closely metonymy and metaphor intertwine in the process of meaning-making.

The music video HER MORNING ELEGANCE (Oren Lavie, Yuval & Merav Nathan ISR 2009) not only offers an interesting case to study how figurativity emerges from the embodied experience of audiovisual images in this very specific media form, but it also shows how metonymies may be vital in creating metaphorical worlds.[3] It illustrates and extends a characteristic of metaphor to the interaction between metaphor and metonymy that Black has described as "some metaphors enable us to see aspects of reality that the metaphor's production helps to constitute" (Black 1993 [1977], 38).

In Lavie's music video a sleeping woman transforms into a dreaming woman. Her bed becomes the stage of her inner world, of her dreaming. As viewers watch the video, they experience sleeping as dreaming, or, put differently, they witness her dreaming at the same time as they see her sleeping.

At first sight, the realms of sleep and dream appear closely connected. In the aesthetic logic of the video, however, they are established as different with an ever-shifting experience of the staging: without a change in camera perspective, the realm of sleep is experienced from a bird's-eye view of the bed (i.e., looking at the

3 The analysis was developed within the Cinepoetics' research focus 'Metaphor – Film Images, Cinematic Thinking, and Cognition' by Sarah Greifenstein. The version for this book was prepared by Cornelia Müller, Sarah Greifenstein, and Dorothea Horst.

bed from above and perceiving a woman lying in it with her eyes closed); dreaming, on the other hand, is set with an eye-level experience (i.e., perceiving a woman with closed eyes on eye-level moving through a world of dreams). The stop-motion technique underlines this experiential shift in perspective further, because it seems to set the sleeping woman in dream motion. When she, for instance, 'starts walking' in the bed, the viewer's perspective shifts from a bird's-eye view to eye-level position, i.e., instead of looking down on her bed, we now face her as if she would be walking in front of us. As a consequence, rather than lying and sleeping, she is seen and experienced as wandering about her dream world (Figure 7.9). With this oscillating experience of the staging, metaphoricity begins to emerge: besides seeing a sleeping woman, viewers start experiencing her dream world.

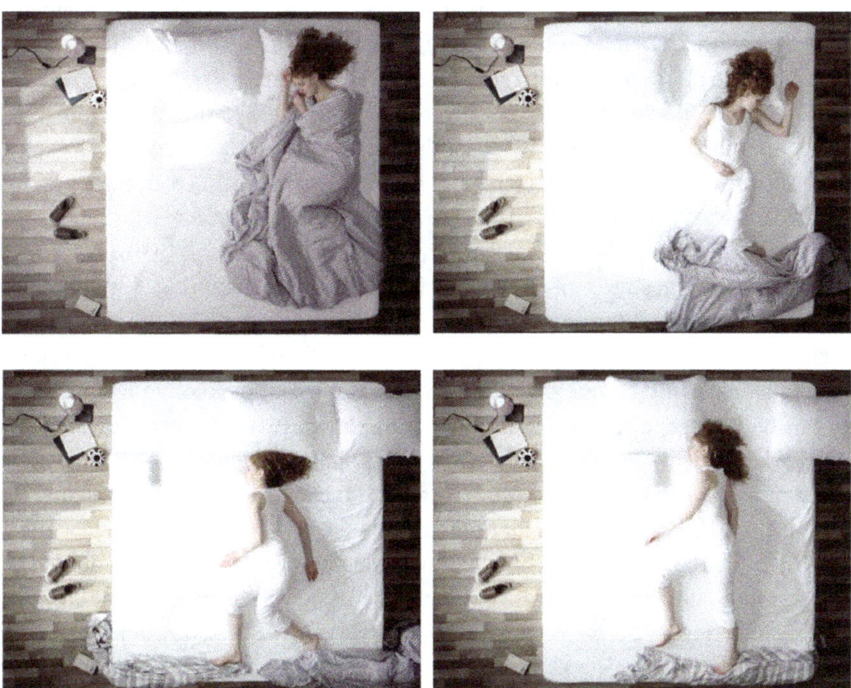

**Figure 7.9:** Shifting from the experience of bird's eye to the experience of eye-level perspective: sleeping becomes dreaming (HER MORNING ELEGANCE)

Within this metaphorical scenario, the dream world itself emerges from a web of metonymies and metaphors. Accordingly, the objects surrounding the woman are always both: concrete, visible objects and imaginations within a dream. For instance, towels, scarfs, sheets in different colors and patterns on the bed are suddenly transforming into metonymical parts of the interior of a tramway. The sleeping posture becomes a hand-gesture that metonymically stands for holding onto the rails in a tramway (Figure 7.10).

The clip unfolds the different dream worlds in a series of fluid, always changing metaphorical scenarios. For example, when a child's sock next to the sleeper seems to oscillate between actual and imagined object. The fish-like movements change the perception of the sock to seeing a small fish. The movement qualities metonymically call up an underwater scenario that further unfolds the metaphorical dream world. In this light, viewers experience the woman's subsequent movements on her navy blue bedsheet not in terms of a sleeper changing her sleeping position, but as a metonymical vehicle for a diver, drifting through a lively populated, increasingly unfolding underwater world (Figure 7.11): groups of socks/fishes surround her, she interacts with a single sock/fish that is moving around her and when a fluffed up scarf appears, we only recognize it as a jellyfish, because of its contracting metonymical movements.

Watching the video clip, the viewer is thus seeing two things at a time: the concrete and the imagined object. Both objects call up their respective experiential realm: bed or clothes on the one hand, diving or riding a tramway on the other. This way, the music video makes the essence of metaphor – the seeing and experiencing one thing in terms of another (Lakoff and Johnson 1980b) – its main subject and a vital source of experience for the realm of dreaming. Metaphoricity emerges mainly from the media-specific perceptual experience of the stop-motion technique. It is an ambivalent seeing that constantly oscillates between seeing a concrete object and an imagined one (evoked through the metonymical principle of contiguity; see, e.g., Jakobson 1990 [1956], Peirce 1960). In fact, the imagined objects keep their metaphorical form only for a short moment, they are constantly in motion: for a short moment they merge into the dreamt object, only to quickly dissolve or to change into another dreamt object.

The viewing of those fluidly changing metaphorical scenarios is guided by the framing action of a sleeping woman in her bed that turns into a white or black projection screen, a cinematic image that can transform a staircase into a train within seconds, or quickly change a cloudy autumn sky into an underwater landscape. In the process, in which the cinematic images unfold, it is primarily metonymy that calls up the metaphorical scenarios. For instance, in a sequence that makes one believing to see the sleeping woman in cold and windy autumn weather, the scenario is produced by emerging and constantly changing grouping of metaphorical elements: when the sleeper is all of a sudden not only surrounded by white, but also by grey cushions and socks in warm yellow, brown (autumn like colors) are moving around her (Figure 7.12), all metonymically calling up the experiential realm of the autumn season.

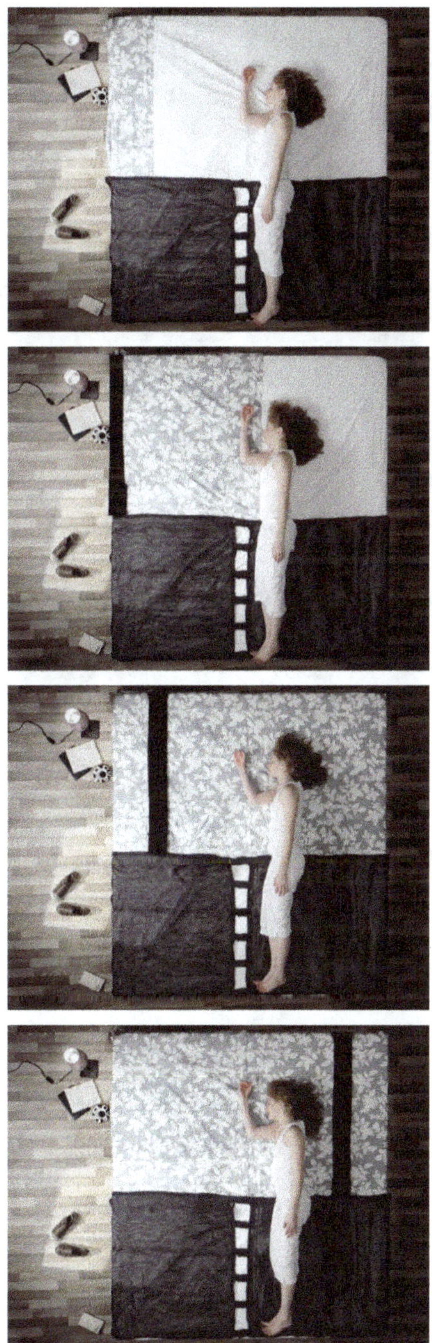

**Figure 7.10:** Metaphorical and metonymical dream worlds emerge (HER MORNING ELEGANCE)

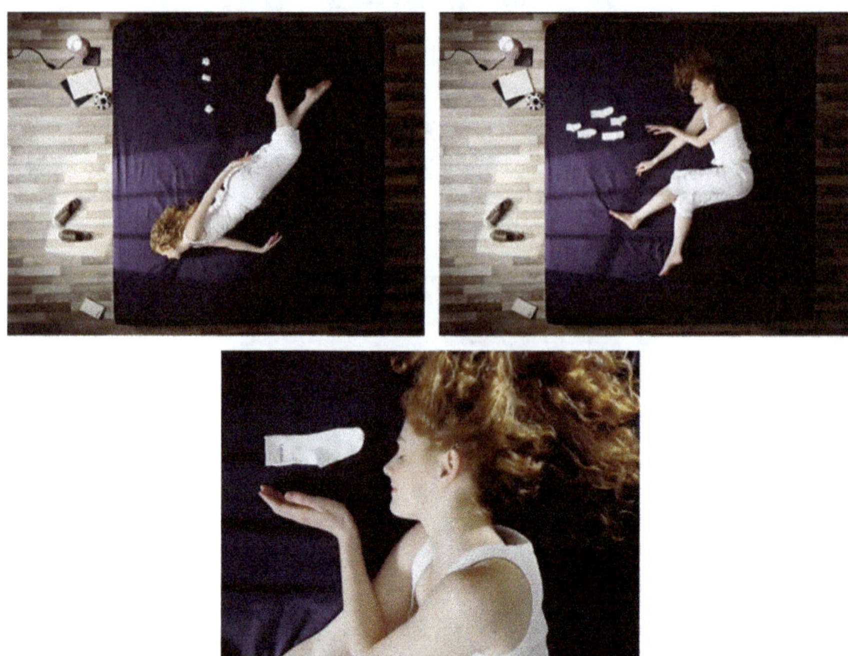

**Figure 7.11:** Underwater scenario in HER MORNING ELEGANCE

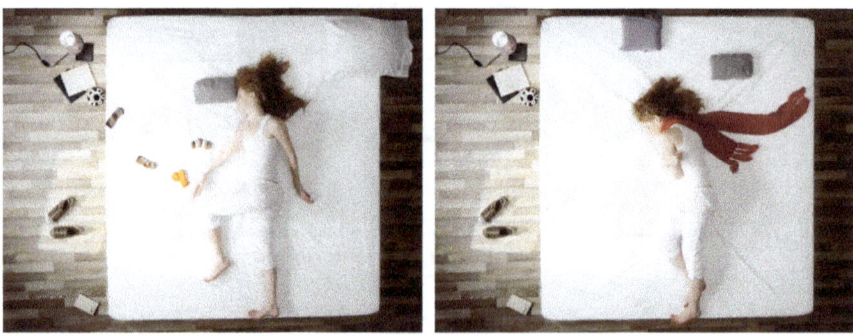

**Figure 7.12:** "Cloud of steam" – metaphorical scenarios with metonymical elements (HER MORNING ELEGANCE)

The metonymical dimension of the metaphorical objects is reinforced by the song lyrics: "cloud of steam", verbally calls up the semantic domain of autumn weather. In conjunction with the words and the character of their cinematic motion, the grey cushions, the yellow-brown socks, the red scarf, and the shivering posture of the woman's body all are becoming metonymical vehicles for cold autumn weather.

The aesthetic logic of the music video thus employs metonymical references to call up metaphorical scenarios: concrete objects become parts of the metaphorical dream world – a baby shirt whose sleeves morph into wings, when they start flapping – and they refer metonymically to the experiential realm of a summer breeze and birds flying high in the sky. These visible objects call up stereotypical situations: the scarf alludes to autumn or winter, swimming postures connect with the idea of water, sea or diving.

Verbal elements synchronize in their dynamics with visual elements, but also with acoustic and rhythmic ones. If we consider metaphor as well as metonymy as perceptual and experiential processes in which elements are highlighted (cf. Lakoff and Johnson 1980b, 10–13, Croft 1993, 348), we can specify the dynamic metaphoricity of the music video once more: the metaphorical seeing and experiencing is not abstract, it is subjected to the cinematic temporality and the staging of the clip with a stop-motion technique. Viewers experience different perspectives simultaneously, they experience a multidimensional gestalt in which the sleeping and the dreaming woman merge: the sleeping woman is also walking; the bed is also a screen; her movements are sleeping postures as well as walking ones; everyday objects – socks, covers, all kinds of clothes – suddenly become animated objects of the dream world.

The aesthetic orchestration concerns this multidimensional gestalt in which the single metonymies temporally compose to a constantly transforming ensemble of cinematic expressivity. It is this cinematic experience of constant oscillation and transformation that makes viewers of the music video see dreaming as if a body was set in motion, wandering through worlds of imagination.

The analysis of the music video has demonstrated that it is worthwhile to consider the intertwining of cinematic metaphor and metonymy in meaning-making. Following Mittelberg (2006, 2008, Mittelberg and Waugh 2009) metonymy has turned out to lead the way into metaphor not only in multimodal face-to-face interaction, but also in audiovisual forms.

## 7.4 Experiencing Transformations: ANGELA MERKEL (Campaign Commercial)

The concluding example of how audiovisual figurativity emerges from the specific mode of cinematic experience addresses yet another media format: a political campaign commercial (cf. Horst forthcoming/2018).[4] The commercial of the Christian Democratic Union (CDU) was produced for the German federal election in 2009 (TV-Spot II ANGELA MERKEL, advertising agency Kolle Rebbe, GER 2009). The strategy of the campaign was to focus uniquely on the renowned reputation of one of the most powerful women in the world: German Chancellor Angela Merkel. The campaign commercial is a small 'masterpiece' of orchestrating cinematic experience, since in the process of viewing it, a shared feeling emerges, a sense of commonality that includes Merkel in the "we" of the people. The clip thus stages cinematic experience with a clear political goal: viewers experience Merkel as part of the German people. However, this is not a simple 'pars pro toto' metonymy. The feeling of 'we' emerges from the embodied perception of movement-images in viewing the campaign commercial; it is a temporal experience from which gradual changes on the level of metonymical and metaphorical meaning evolve.

### Feeling the past, present, and future with the German Chancellor

The tone of the commercial is set, with the first shot: soft baroque-style music playing and Chancellor Merkel in a dissolve montage with a high-angle shot of the German Reichstag in Berlin behind her, staged as the current and the future sovereign of the German people (Figure 7.13). As she is standing at and gazing out the window of her chancellery, a series of partial dissolves appear on a kind of window-pane. Viewers see her thinking and feel her grandeur already in the first seconds of the clip. What they see, of course, is not a representation of the person Angela Merkel, it is the feeling created by its aesthetic composition that viewers experience and that they attribute to the current Chancellor. In that respect, the basic condition of cinematic experience applies to a campaign commercial as much as to a feature film.

The commercial designs an inner world of Angela Merkel, her thoughts and feelings, projecting them in a dissolve technique onto different screens. As viewers, we are taken to the 'back-stage' world of Angela Merkel, we witness her personal thoughts by ascribing the outer world of the projections to her, thus creating an inner world of her as an effect of the cinematic experience that the campaign commercial takes the viewers through: the outer world becomes an image

---

4 The analysis was carried out within the research project "Multimodal Metaphor and Expressive Movement" and further developed within the Cinepoetics' research focus 'Metaphor – Film Images, Cinematic Thinking, and Cognition' by Dorothea Horst. An extended version can be found in Dorothea Horst's dissertation (Horst forthcoming/2018). Dorothea Horst and Cornelia Müller prepared the version for this book.

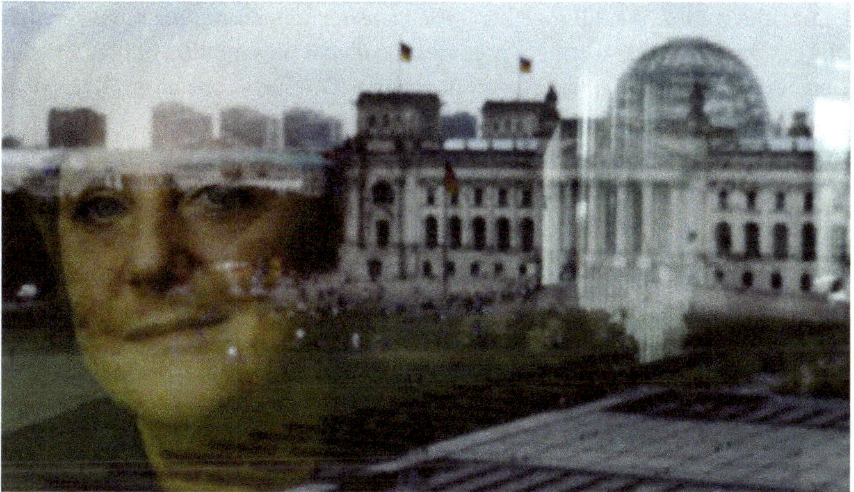

**Figure 7.13:** Merkel in a dissolve montage with a high-angle shot of the German Reichstag in Berlin behind her, staged as the current and the future sovereign of the German people (ANGELA MERKEL)

of Merkel's inner world. It is this cinematic experience that the clip modulates with a clear rhetorical strategy: to create a feeling that makes viewers appreciate Merkel and that influences their vote accordingly, or, to put it very simple, to make viewers vote for Merkel.

In the beginning, Merkel is presented alone with a pondering gaze, looking out of the semi-reflecting windows of her chancellery, on which recollections of moments of the recent German history as well as of her personal and professional history are projected (Figure 7.14, first still). In a voice over she comments on the thoughts that the viewers see quietly appearing and disappearing as ephemeral projections on a transparent window. In the second part of the commercial, Merkel is shown in a walk through different rooms of the chancellery, now interacting with different people passing by. The thoughts that continue to be projected as picture-in-picture fade-ins appear in different parts of the cinematic image, and together with her voice over, articulate her vision of the future (Figure 7.14, still in the middle). At the end of the commercial, Merkel walks straight up to the camera, and now, for the first time, directly addressing the viewer and, also for the first time, shown as she speaks, thus creates a feeling of the here and now: she is looking directly into the camera, and as we perceive her approaching the camera (i.e., 'us, the viewers'), she formulates her central message: "Together we can achieve a lot. We, all together." [*Gemeinsam können wir viel erreichen. Wir, alle zusammen.*] This statement prepares the visual presentation of the Christian Democratic Union's election slogan in writing: "We have the power" [*Wir haben die Kraft*] (Figure 7.14, last still).

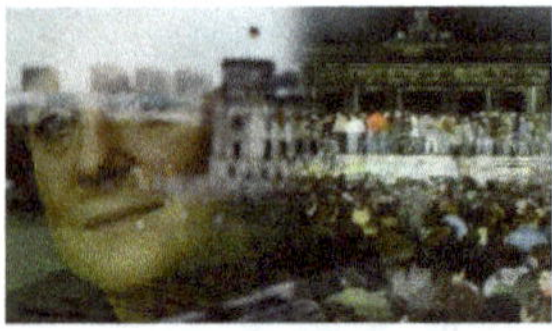
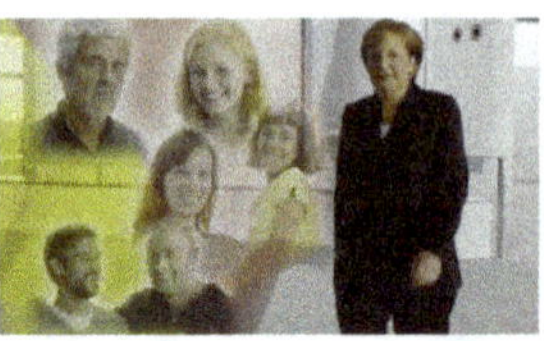
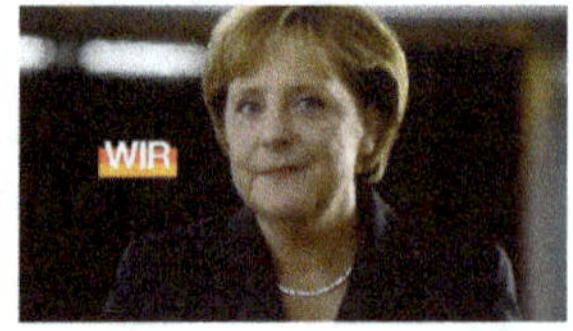


**Figure 7.14:** Past, future, present feel different: the aesthetic orchestration of a straightforward thematic structure, ANGELA MERKEL

The commercial runs at a solemn pace throughout, particularly orchestrated through many slow-motion shots, a generally rather low cutting rate and the slow pace of the musical score which becomes more dynamic in the second part of the clip. However, viewers perceive a difference between the first part dealing with the past, and the second part dealing with the future from the perspective of the present not because they are explicitly labeled, but because they are staged differently and thus express a different kind of experience. The past feels different from the future. The past part stages an extremely quiet atmosphere; the camera moves slow and cautiously. Together with long takes this supports a dream-like 'slow motion feeling'. This staging rhythm also coalesces with the long shots that arrange the mise-en-scène in a kind of static, grave tableaus that entail a quiet succession of dissolves. Merkel is the center and vanishing point of each cinematic image. Lighting supports this prominence: Merkel's silhouette appears darker, sharper, and clearer. Everything in the cinematic image is visually related to her. The underlying baroque court music is an important facet of the grave, thoughtful, and careful rhythm of the visual movement qualities just described. An interplay of rhythmic and cheerful violin notes in the background, overlaid with a slow legato piano and violin notes in the foreground expresses cheerfulness and gravitas at the same time (Figure 7.15).

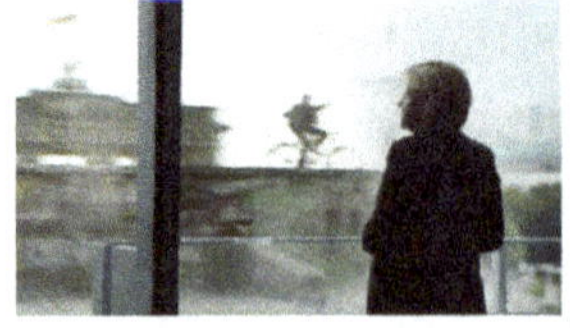
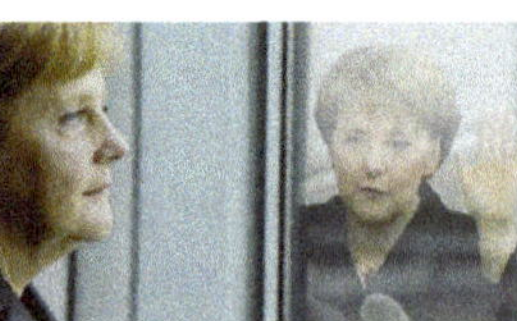
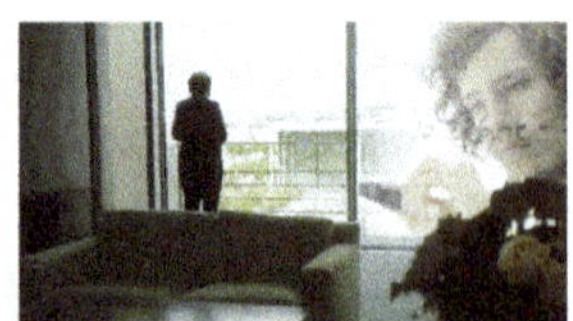

**Figure 7.15:** How the past feels, ANGELA MERKEL

With a change in the audiovisual rhythm, the future part of the commercial is set in scene. Faster camera movements and a slightly accelerating musical rhythm 'set Merkel in motion' in the second part describing the future. Now, we see her walking, 'doing her job', working for Germany's future in the chancellery. Other protagonists are now involved, but Merkel remains the center of the visual composition throughout, until, in the last sequence of the commercial, she is set in a face-to-face position with the viewer.

Cinematic experience changes along the commercial. The future comes with cautious and determined dynamization which increases steadily and leads up to showing Merkel in a frontal perspective, in clear, contrast-rich colors that stage her walking towards the camera, until (literally) facing the viewer, as clear-cut and determined. This is how the future feels. From that vantage point, she addresses the spectators of the campaign commercial directly (Figure 7.16).

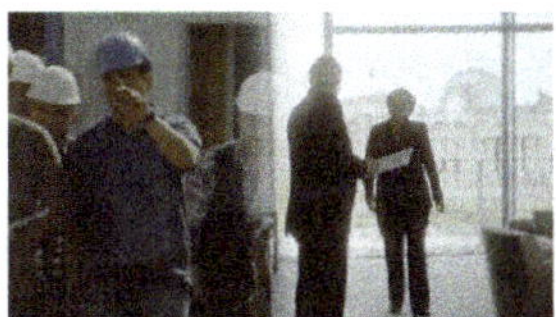
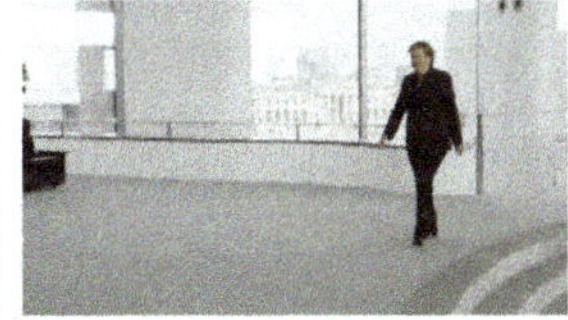
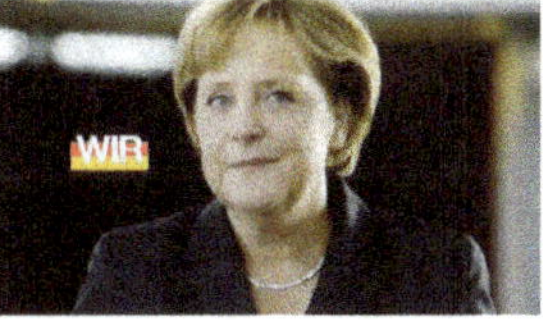


**Figure 7.16:** Moving from the past to the future – how the future feels, ANGELA MERKEL

For the viewers of the commercial, this rhythmic transition creates a feeling of careful consideration, which they experience bodily: over the course of the clip, one feels gravitas, determination, and caution as movement qualities of the two parts. These qualities are attributed to Merkel, and it is through them that we as viewers experience and see her as a sovereign in the center of power, who is compassionate with the people.

### Merkel is 'WE': How the chancellor becomes part of the German people

This link with the people is where metonymy comes in as a major staging principle. Already in the first 20 seconds of the clip the connection between Merkel and the German people is established. It brings together Merkel's political career with the most important moment in recent German history, the reunification. Merkel and the Berlin Reichstag are visually correlated: either the Reichstag is her background or it is staged as her view. This image composition forms the ground against which we perceive faded-over images cover different parts of it. Metonymy as a figurative principle connects Angela Merkel with the flow of cinematic images: listening to the voice over "I was not born a chancellor", the Reichstag, the seat of the government, is shown: the government's venue is thus metonymically connected with its head (Figure 7.17).

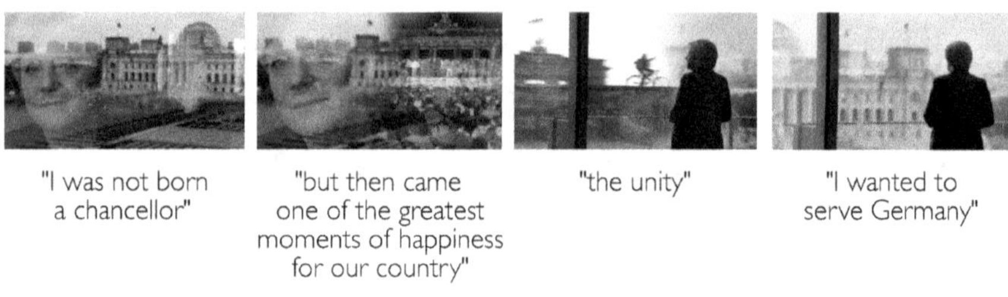


Angela Merkel stands for the people

**Figure 7.17**: Successive metonymical links that connect Merkel with the people, ANGELA MERKEL

A moment later, Merkel's voice over describes the German reunification as one of the "greatest moments of happiness for our country – the unity". Using 'unity' instead of the more formal German expression for reunification [*Wiedervereinigung*] underlines a feeling of "we" that was already created by showing (East) German citizens, shouting what became the icon and the motor of the peaceful revolution in East Germany: "We are the people". Merkel being staged in a fade-over with these celebrating crowds climbing the wall at the Brandenburg gate is metonymically linked with these happy crowds that, in turn, metonymically link with all East German people. When Merkel's voice over speaks of "the unity" she is metonymically linked with this historical event, with the people that made this event happen, but also with every single member of the people. Contemplating a view from her chancellery, a dissolve montage of the Brandenburg gate and the Berlin wall shows Merkel following the course of a cyclist passing by on the Berlin wall and in front of the Brandenburg gate as if happily connecting this historical site with another one that the viewers will perceive immediately after, the Reichstag, and that in the next montage appears as we listen to Merkel's voice saying "I wanted to serve the German people". In the montage, the cyclist's path comes to be metaphorically related with the political path of Merkel. She is thus perceived as one of the celebrating people from East Germany whose political path leads directly from the German reunification to becoming the head of all German people, metonymically depicted with the Reichstag.

It is noteworthy that this passage from one moment in the history of Germany to another one is the expression of a subjective experience that we are set to ascribe to Merkel's as an authentic one. The views we see as we are following the commercial are aesthetic arrangements that are not connected with any 'objective' representational element. Merkel does not have the view on the Reichstag from her chancellery that we see, she does not see the Brandenburg Gate the way it is shown, the cyclist cycles in the 'wrong' direction if he were to cycle from the Brandenburg Gate to the Reichstag. The interesting fact is that this does not matter at all. What does matter is the aesthetic orchestration of a feeling that connects Merkel with the unity and the people of a reunified Germany. Viewers of the clip experience this feeling, ascribe it to Merkel and by metonymically linking Merkel with the people they ascribe it reflexively onto themselves again. The viewers are the people. The commercial thus operates on staging this "we" of the people. It creates a common sense of this "we".

Multimodal metonymies of the kind just described, pervade the entire campaign commercial. Merkel's oath of office stands for her becoming Chancellor ("I finally became chancellor"), a dissolve of a baby stands for the strengthening of families ("we have shown that we can empower families"), a student writing math formula on a window screen metonymically relates to higher education and scientific research ("We have shown [...] that we can advance education and scientific research") as well as with Merkel's own continuous learning process ("everyday I learn something new"); a jubilating crowd stands for the agitation expressed verbally ("not joining in every agitation"), and when she is shown raising her arms to celebrate a goal scored by the German soccer team among the football crowds in a stadium, this scene metonymically displays her as being able to join in a commonly shared moment of excitement (Figure 7.18). She becomes "we" in the soccer stadium and the scene metonymically stands for "us", the people of Germany.

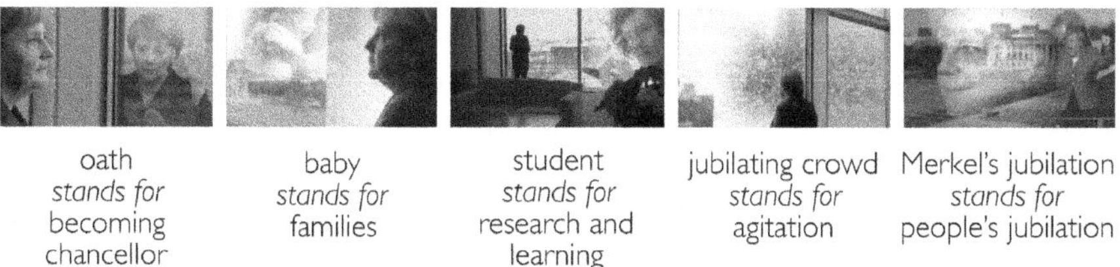

| oath *stands for* becoming chancellor | baby *stands for* families | student *stands for* research and learning | jubilating crowd *stands for* agitation | Merkel's jubilation *stands for* people's jubilation |
|---|---|---|---|---|

**Figure 7.18:** Multimodal metonymical pattern: Merkel becomes the people, ANGELA MERKEL

Altogether, these multimodal metonymies unfold a pattern that goes beyond their respective local meaning. Their continuous occurrence is a central element of the staging principle of the entire commercial: the aesthetic orchestration of a contiguity relation between Merkel and the German people which is present without being explicitly formulated.

In the second part of the commercial, this pattern continues in a more dynamic staging evoking a feeling of doing, of activity and a world in movement: when we listen to Merkel's voice over mentioning the challenges of the world, we see her together with her staff; she is shown walking towards us, joining faded-in construction workers that also walk towards the camera. Audiovisual representations and Merkel's verbal comment combine to multimodal metonymies (Figure 7.19): for example, the faded-in workers stand for the needed employment Merkel's voice over is mentioning; a little girl smiling and waving at Merkel alludes metonymically to the verbally mentioned "our children deserve the best future" and to the idea of a prospective "republic of education"; couples of different ages blended with the German flag stand for the "most important" cohesion in the country; and finally, Merkel stands for the verbally mentioned "we" who can achieve a lot – and the "WE" showing up on a German flag stands for the German people.

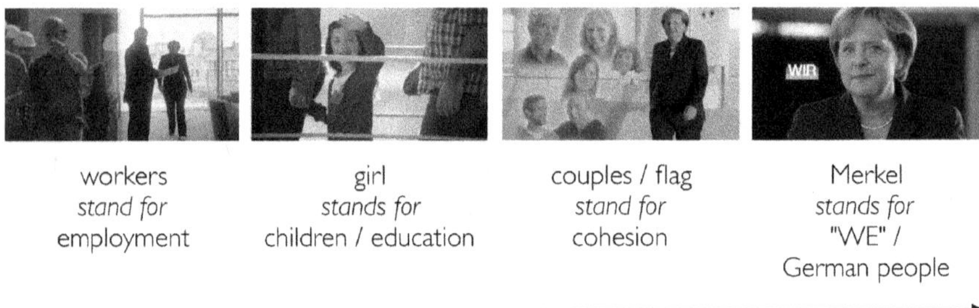


**Figure 7.19**: "Merkel is WE": Viewers experience her as the German people, ANGELA MERKEL

With the last shot of the commercial Merkel has become the "we" of the German people. As she is approaching the spectator, this is a change in perspective. So far, we only heard her talking, now we see her talking to 'us', the spectators. As she is walking towards the camera, she is using various expressions that refer to the community of people ('we', 'all', 'together'): "Together we can achieve a lot. We, all together." At the end of the clip, Merkel has become the WE of the German people: a civil sovereign.

The commercial thus creates the experience of a remarkable synthesis: the image of a powerful sovereign who – at the same time – is presented as somebody with civil roots standing for the people. This emergent personification of a collective 'we' is grounded in the media mode of cinematic experience. It is dynamically produced in the poiesis of film-viewing.

## Résumé

We have reconsidered the core facets of the neo-phenomenological and film-theoretical concept of embodiment introduced in Part I: cinematic metaphor has been conceived as a 'doing' that resides in intersubjective, reflexive, and temporally-structured experience. This cinematic experience, accordingly, defines a media specific mode of perception.

To illustrate the consequences of a theoretical perspective that starts from such a basic constellation of embodied interaction, this second part of the book has offered a series of case studies on audiovisual figurativity covering a broad range of different media formats. The analysis of the ballet lesson and of a scene from MAGNIFICENT OBSESSION served to describe the phenomenological concept of embodiment as a fundamental facet of metaphorical meaning-making (and of meaning-making more generally). The metaphorical meaning that develops within and from such a flow of embodied interaction (be it with gestural and body movements, or with audiovisual movement-images) is intersubjective, reflexive, perspectivized, and locally anchored in the here and now of a communicative encounter. This is the sense in which we consider it as embodied. Gallagher's characterization of social cognition as embodied formulates a similar position:

> On the embodied view of social cognition, the mind of the other person is not something that is hidden away and inaccessible. In perceiving the actions and expressive movements of the other person in the interactive contexts of the surrounding world, one already grasps their meaning; no inference to a hidden set of mental states (beliefs, desires, etc.) is necessary. When I see the other's action or gesture, I see (I immediately perceive) the meaning in the action or gesture; and when I am in a process of interacting with the other, my own actions and reactions help to constitute that meaning. (Gallagher 2008, 449)

With such a concept of embodiment, the notion of cinematic metaphor differs from the common cognitive-science understanding. A phenomenological perspective considers embodiment as inseparable from concrete moments of experience (Gallagher 2008, Sheets-Johnstone 2011 [1999], Wilson 2002). It involves intersubjectivity, reflexive awareness of another subject position, another 'I', and of a situated context. It includes a particular perspective, the taking of a specific, subjective viewpoint, as well as the historicity of interaction, with its anchoring of meaning in a given moment of time.

The term *cinematic* metaphor reflects our focus on the media specificity of experience. It applies to metaphors in feature film as much as to metaphors in televised and streamed audiovisual formats such as news coverage, campaign commercials, and music videos. All these forms, apart from their functional differences, share a fundamental mode of perceptual experience that Sobchack has characterized as "an expression of experience by experience" (Merleau-Ponty 1968 [1964], 155, quoted in Sobchack 1992, 3). For all of them, the perceptual mode of the viewers is an embodied experience, an experience that is intersubjective and reflexive. In the light of such a phenomenological understanding of embodied experience, metaphoricity is not statically instantiated but dynamically created. It is 'done' by the film viewers.

With the ensuing case studies of audiovisual figurativity, we have particularly underlined the case that meaning-making is based on this specific perceptual mode that characterizes cinematic experience. This perceptual mode accounts for media formats ranging beyond cinema. Although, clearly, a feature film differs in many respects from a television magazine or a campaign commercial, they all share a fundamental property: meaning emerges from a poetic doing in the process of film-viewing, it is created through the temporal experiences that viewers have when attending audiovisual movement-images – the flow of movements of colors and shapes, of voices, music and sounds. In this sense, including different media formats in the analyses reflects the theoretical perspective developed in this book: a reflection of the specifics of audiovisual media as 'media' and accounting for metaphor and metonymy as figurative modes of meaning-making against this backdrop.

For the analysis of audiovisual figurative modes of expression, the temporality of cinematic experience is central (cf. Part IV). Rather than appearing as clearly delineated concepts, metaphors are open, fluid, and constantly changing, sometimes forming metaphorical scenarios as we have seen, for instance, in Oren Lavie's music video. Vague and ambivalent meanings stabilize only shortly, by merging only for a short moment of time into the specific metaphorical ensemble of a dream world. Often, the figurative as-if is verbally established retrospectively, when the objects have already passed and transformed, further highlighting the ephemeral and fluent character of dreaming.

The aesthetic orchestration of the unfolding movement-images intertwines with the affective experiences of viewers, and grounds figurative meaning (cf. Part III). Be it the feeling of being included or excluded staged in the news feature from REPORT MAINZ, or the orchestration of suspicion as an affective movement experience in Hitchcock's film noir, figurative meaning emerges from the felt sensations of an attending spectator. This media-specific perceptual experience involves metaphorical as well as metonymical meaning and grounds dynamically emerging webs of cinematic metaphor and metonymy. Shifts of metaphorical and metonymical meaning that make tangible how losing feels in contrast to winning in the financial crisis, or that merge the perception of chancellor Merkel as a sovereign and as a member of the German people equally, do not exist prior to the aesthetic experience of viewing this specific news feature or that campaign commercial. They only emerge in the poiesis of film-viewing.

These metonymical and metaphorical scenarios are grounded in the specific media mode of perception: modulated aesthetically, multidimensional gestalts of experience are created that, albeit individually perceived, nevertheless constitutes a horizon of experience that we share with other spectators in the cinema or viewers of television shows. Cinematic perception is thus an inherently reflexive one that is shaped by the cinematic expression of an experience, as much as by the viewer as an individual, historical body of perception.

# Part III: **Cinematic Expressive Movement: Affectivity and Metaphor**

# Introduction

The immediate 'understanding' of other subjects through the expressivity of their mode of behavior and their styles of movement, of which Gallagher (2008, 449) speaks, has been developed theoretically by classical phenomenology under the notion of 'expressive movement' [*Ausdrucksbewegung*]. For us, the notion of expressive movement is especially important because it allows us to describe the process of film-viewing in its affective dynamics. If – as we explained in Part I – we seek to capture the poiesis of film-viewing as a process of 'doing' metaphors, then this poiesis is always interwoven with the affective dynamics of an emerging, shifting feeling for the whole of a cinematic movement-image. We have attempted to illustrate this in the analysis of MAGNIFICENT OBSESSION (Section 6.2).

Cinematic expressive movement is the theoretical concept and the methodological anchoring point to capture the affectivity of cinematic experience. It is a touchstone for cinematic metaphor. In Part III we delve deeper into the notion of expressive movement in order to work out its relevance as a key concept in analyzing the affective dimension of cinematic metaphor. Cinematic expressive movements shape the process of film-viewing affectively. It is in this process that metaphorical meaning emerges.

In Chapter 8, three short example analyses are offered. They serve to introduce expressive movement as a form of cinematic composition that modulates affective experiences of film viewers, and that characterizes feature films as well as television news features. While all analyses illustrate the notion of expressive movement, each has a slightly different focus: LOLA RENNT (Tom Tykwer, RUN LOLA RUN, GER 1998) introduces the idea of 'moving spectators' by means of cinematic staging, BATAAN highlights 'temporal unfolding as affect modulation', and the German news feature illustrates how viewers are 'touched by news'.

In Chapter 9, we introduce the film-theoretical frame against which the notion of cinematic expressive movement has been developed. The chapter includes theoretical reflections and an illustrative case study of expressive movements in face-to-face interaction. It begins with a short sketch on the idea of body movements as expressive, as discussed in philosophical anthropology, psychology, and linguistics (Section 9.1), illustrates how metaphoricity emerges in a small group discussion within an interaffective dynamics of gesture, speech, and body-movements in interaction (Section 9.2), and then describes the parallelism between body movement and cinematic movement expressed by the notion of movement-image (Section 9.3). A historical perspective shows the rooting of this idea in the aesthetic strategies of affect modulation, developed within the concept of melodrama in theatre and film (Kappelhoff 2004a, Greifenstein and

https://doi.org/10.1515/9783110580785-partIII

Kappelhoff 2014, Kappelhoff and Bakels 2011, Kappelhoff and Greifenstein 2016, Scherer, Greifenstein, and Kappelhoff 2014). With these historical, theoretical, and empirical reflections in place, the grounds are provided for applying the notion of cinematic expressive movement to an analysis of metaphors in film and television.

Chapter 10 illustrates the affective dimension of metaphor with case studies of two different media formats, showing how cinematic metaphors emerge with the affective qualities of cinematic expressive movements: classical Hollywood cinema (Section 10.1) and a television news feature (Section 10.2).

# 8 Cinematic Expressive Movement and the Poetics of Affect: Three Examples

Films move their spectators. The aesthetic composition of a film modulates the bodily sensations of its spectators. With their temporally orchestrated audiovisual expressivity, cinematic expressive movements affect spectators as immediately as a laughing person affects her conversational counterpart who cannot help but laugh, too. So, when we say that films move their spectators, this is not meant metaphorically at all: film images develop as movement patterns, combining different staging tools like sound composition, montage rhythm, camera movements, and acting into one temporal gestalt. They move spectators because they organize their perception processes over the temporal course of film-viewing. The aesthetic composition of an entire film can thus be described as an artful orchestration of those dynamic patterns which, on the level of a scene or of other forms of shorter segments, we consider as cinematic expressive movements.

To introduce the film-theoretical concept of 'cinematic expressive movement', we have selected three examples including different genres, different media formats, and different cultures. Cinematic expressive movement being a theoretical but also an analytical category, each case study not only documents the empirical shape of expressive movements as form of cinematic staging but also indicates how the specific and variable aesthetic orchestration of all the facets of audiovisual composition merges into a movement gestalt that involves spectators in a temporal movement experience. Understanding cinematic expressive movements, both as a theoretical and analytical concept, is the pathway we are offering to explain how moving images become temporally-structured affective experiences.

The first example discusses a sequence from the German feature film LOLA RENNT, directed by Tom Tykwer in 1998; the second analyzes a sequence from the Hollywood war movie BATAAN, directed by Tay Garnett in 1943; and the third analysis addresses a television news feature from Germany's national broadcast in 2008. Each analysis has a slightly different focus, but all address the connection between cinematic movement (i.e., temporality) and being moved.

## 8.1 Moving Spectators: LOLA RENNT

Movement in film happens on very different levels and in various dimensions. Movements of actors or objects happen within single shots; on the level of editing, movement occurs as change of different shots as rhythm or tempo change;

https://doi.org/10.1515/9783110580785-009

dynamic changes in light, color, and visual composition happen over seconds or even minutes. It is the interplay of these different scales and forms of movement that characterizes the affective quality of cinematic expressivity. For example, in a sequence from the German feature film LOLA RENNT (Tom Tykwer, RUN LOLA RUN, GER 1998)[1] movement is very prominent on the level of the montage, and the quality of the montage, its rhythm, incorporates a certain affective flow, 'moving' the viewer by creating a specific temporal affective experience.[2] Put differently, the qualities of the cinematic movement shape the affective flow experienced by the spectator.

The sequence shows the main character Manni (Moritz Bleibtreu) in a subway station, realizing that he has left a plastic bag with a huge amount of money in the subway train whose doors are about to close. The staging of this sequence orchestrates the process of his terrible insight as a feeling of stress and of increasing dismay. The way spectators see, hear and feel the realizing of the loss and how they experience the stress of this moment is created through the specific composition of movement of the scene (Figure 8.1). What evolves into one movement gestalt, one cinematic expressive movement, begins with a longer shot showing Manni leaving the train (in black and white), followed by an abrupt change of speed, a staccato of alternating shots (now in color) of Manni and his girlfriend Lola (Franka Potente) talking to each other on the phone, shown from different perspectives. As shots of them talking on the telephone repeat, what they say is repeated as well, very rapidly: "the bag – the bag" [*die Tasche – die Tasche*]. In the last part of the movement gestalt, we see the subway station (again in black and white) and Manni, now detained by two ticket inspectors and held firmly. At that moment, we hear a siren and techno-music becoming louder and louder which increases the strong dynamics of the middle part of the movement even more.

The movement gestalt is opened and closed by longer shots in black and white. It begins with a calm movement modulating a subjective sensation of time, in which a terrifying moment feels stretched, extended, in an unnatural manner, like a slow-motion picture. In the middle part of the expressive movement, repeated close-up shots contrast with the framing shots in terms of color, montage, and framing creating a sensation of hectic, stress, and panic. The cinematic movement closes by returning to the black and white staging, a longer static

---

1 For a cognitive perspective on metaphor in LOLA RENNT see Kathrin Fahlenbrach's (2018) chapter "Moving Metaphors. Affects, Movements, and Embodied Metaphors in Cinema" in *Cinematic Metaphor in Perspective. Reflections on a Transdisciplinary Framework.*

2 The analysis was developed in the context of the research project "Multimodal Metaphor and Expressive Movement" and further worked on within the Cinepoetics' research focus 'Metaphor – Film Images, Cinematic Thinking, and Cognition' by Sarah Greifenstein and Dorothea Horst. Cornelia Müller prepared the version for this book.

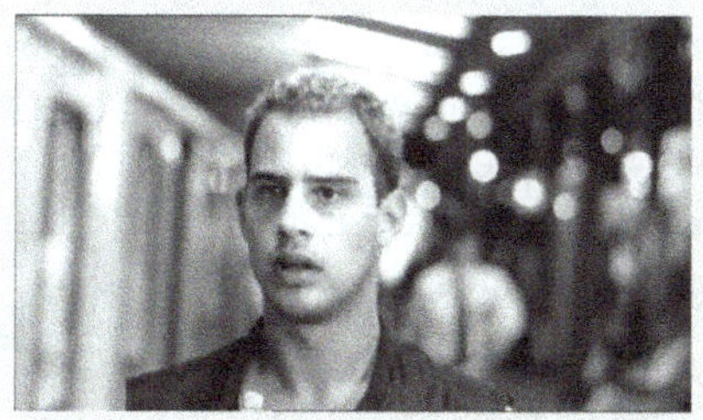


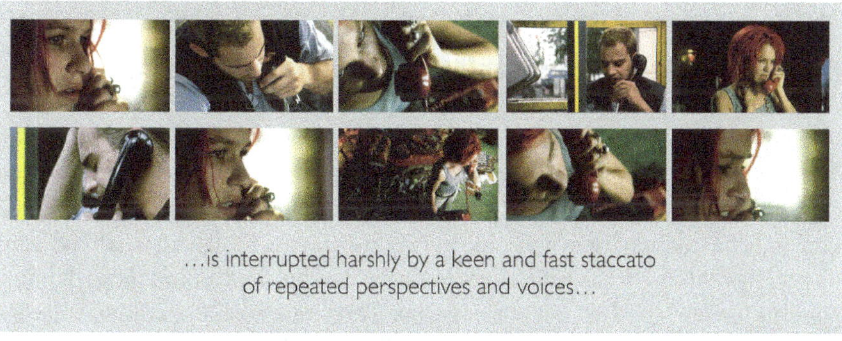


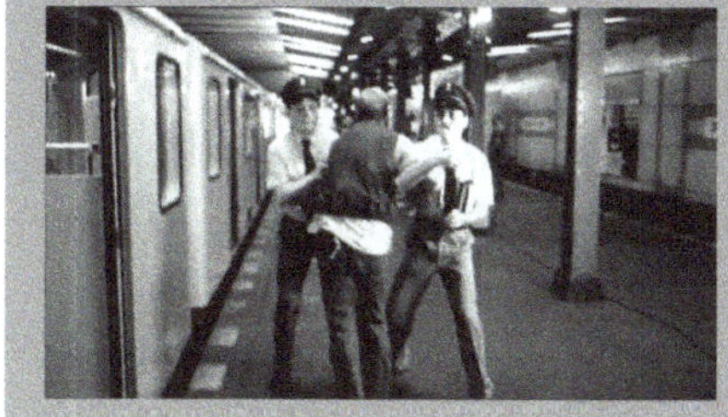


**Figure 8.1:** Movement qualities and temporal structure of a cinematic expressive movement (LOLA RENNT)

shot again showing Manni on the subway platform. Now, the slow-motion terror of the insight changes into the shrill sound of panic brought in by the audio: the increasing volume of two parallel sounds, i.e., a siren and techno music.

What goes along with this aesthetic orchestration of cinematic movement is an affective flow moving from horror to increasing stress, that is modulated through the montage movement and through the changing of movement qualities: *a slow and calm movement is interrupted harshly by a keen and fast staccato of repeated perspectives and voices, culminating in an increasing and extended loud and shrill sound staging.* This composition of movement-images is what affects the viewers. It is the temporal orchestration of the cinematic movement gestalt that is experienced as an immediate affectivity by viewers.

From the point of view of empirical analysis, we consider audiovisual compositions as expressive movements when dynamics on various levels come to form a distinct gestalt: those aesthetic orchestrations structurally resemble an unfolding melody, where the beginning is still present at the end, or a dynamic structure of a hand gesture in face-to-face communication, which is prepared, culminates in a stroke, and finally retracts (Kendon 2004). It is the very dynamic gestalt that makes an audiovisual movement expressive and that, quite literally, affects or moves the spectators.

## 8.2 Temporal Unfolding as Affect Modulation: BATAAN

Over the course of a film, audiovisual images unfold in a dynamic way, creating different periods of time, layers, and spans of audiovisual composition. Cinematic expressive movements establish different forms of temporality, such as prolongation and compaction, or synchronic versus succeeding forms of visual and auditory orchestration. In their development over the course of a film, those dynamic patterns create specific temporal gestalts and movement qualities: intense, abrupt patterns creating short-term tension and stress for spectators, or a gradually increasing expectation through an extended pattern.

The following analysis of a scene from the classical Hollywood war film BATAAN (Tay Garnett, USA 1943) focuses specifically on the temporality of cinematic expressive movements and their affective qualities.[3] Entrenched in the jungle, a US army squad commander gives an order to one of his soldiers to climb up a palm tree to look out for Japanese enemies. Shortly after reaching the top, the soldier on lookout gets shot from off-screen and drops down dead in front of his comrades. Obviously, this is a rather dramatic and sad scene. On the other hand, a reconstruction of how spectators understand the narrative structure of a sad story tells very little about how their sadness emerges as a specific affective experience. It is through the distinct movement qualities, created through the particular ways in which different articulatory modalities – such as montage patterns, camera movements, framing, sound, and mise-en-scène as well as acting figurations – come

3 The analysis was developed in the context of the research project "Multimodal Metaphor and Expressive Movement" and further worked on within the Cinepoetics' research focus 'Metaphor – Film Images, Cinematic Thinking, and Cognition' by Thomas Scherer, Sarah Greifenstein, and Hermann Kappelhoff (Scherer, Greifenstein, and Kappelhoff 2014). Thomas Scherer and Cornelia Müller prepared the version for this book. For a video clip of the scene and a detailed description see: www.empirische-medienaesthetik.fu-berlin.de/en/emaex-system/affektdatenmatrix/filme/bataan/10_tod_auf_der_palme/index.html (Kappelhoff 2010–2014).

together and form an unfolding temporal gestalt, that sadness becomes an affective experience in the scene. As a consequence, we suggest that it is not primarily a cognitive process of identifying with characters on the screen that creates the sadness, but the temporality of the cinematic form in which they are presented.

Considering the BATAAN scene from the point of view of its temporal orchestration, it turns out that the scene is arranged along two fairly distinct movement patterns (see Figures 8.2 and 8.3): while the first one is composed as a continuous

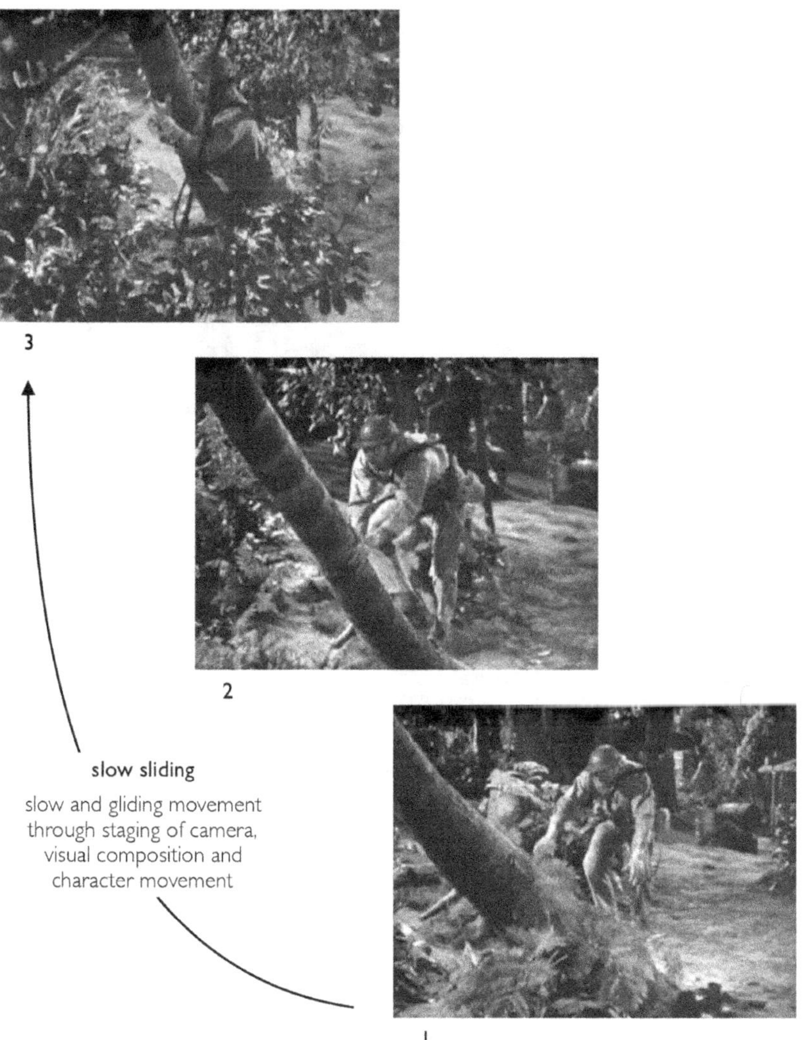


**Figure 8.2:** First movement pattern from BATAAN: *slow sliding*

and slow movement, the second is staged in a staccato rhythm. The first movement pattern (Figure 8.2) ends with the arrival of the soldier at the top of the tree and is orchestrated in a slow and gliding rhythm: in long takes we see the soldier receiving the command and approaching the tree slowly, preparing for the climb. After the order is spoken, only quiet sounds interrupt the silence. When the soldier starts climbing silently up the tall, bent trunk of the palm tree, the camera follows him with a soft and sliding movement. This upward movement, which slowly develops, is staged in an intertwining of various different modalities of filmic articulation: the camera movement, the visual composition, and the actor's movement merge into

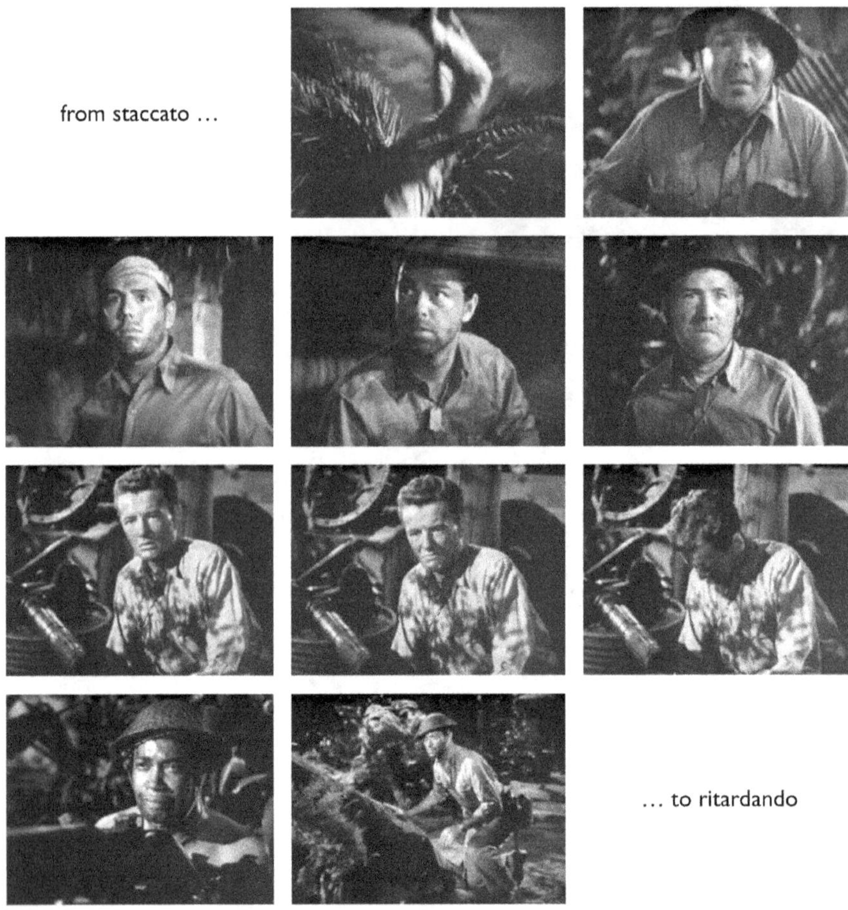


an abrupt increasing of shot frequency and volume
turns into static calmness by slowing down (of music, editing and acting)

**Figure 8.3:** Second movement pattern from BATAAN: *from staccato to ritardando*

a continuous gliding, accompanied by silence on the soundtrack. Together, these articulatory modalities of audiovisual staging temporally merge and create one distinctive movement quality: a slow and silent sliding. It is by means of this staging of a temporal gestalt, this quality of cinematic movement in which all the audiovisual means play together, that a specific affective experience on the side of a spectator is audiovisually orchestrated. Such an experience of 'calm tension' emerges from the aesthetic composition of the cinematic movement gestalt.

The second movement pattern (Figure 8.3) comes with a change of articulatory qualities, moving from a staccato rhythm to ritardando or slowing down. It begins with a static long shot of the soldier who is keeping watch at the top of the palm tree. All of a sudden this is interrupted by the sound of a gunshot and the falling and screaming of the soldier. A series of close-ups follows, showing, in a fast montage and with a high cutting rate, the shocked faces of the dying soldier's comrades. Along with the slowing down of the cutting rate, we see how one of the soldier's face (again in close-up) changes from surprise to grief. In this series of close-ups, the different faces merge into one cohesive figure: a surprised and shocked face, a multiplied expression of fear that, in the slowing down of the montage, transforms as if it were one moving facial expression. Music sets in dramatically after the shot noise and changes tempo and volume, turning into a melancholic tune.

Taken together, this second movement pattern (predominantly staged by montage, sound, and acting) is orchestrated as a contrast between a quiet, extended, enduring tempo, contrasting sharply with a staccato rhythm that then increasingly slows down. With the staccato montage and the high frequency of shots of several faces, an experience of shock is modulated which then turns into a sad alleviation of tension, modulated by the slowing down of the montage, the subtle changes in the soldiers' faces, and the change of the music.

The diagram (Figure 8.4)[4] visualizes the two movement patterns that form the temporal parcours of the cinematic expressive movement in this scene. It highlights the focal aspects of the expressive movement, showing specifically the temporal dynamics of the movement-images and how they create an affective parcours: the temporal dynamics, specifically the flow of the movement-images, is modulated in this scene particularly through an interweaving of sound volume and the rhythm of the shot montage. Of course, spectators do not perceive the two modalities separately; in processes of synesthetic perception they are always merged in a temporally orchestrated gestalt, an affective parcours. The increasing

4 For further explanation of the figure see "Appendix: Cinematic Metaphor – A methodological outline", Section A.3.2.

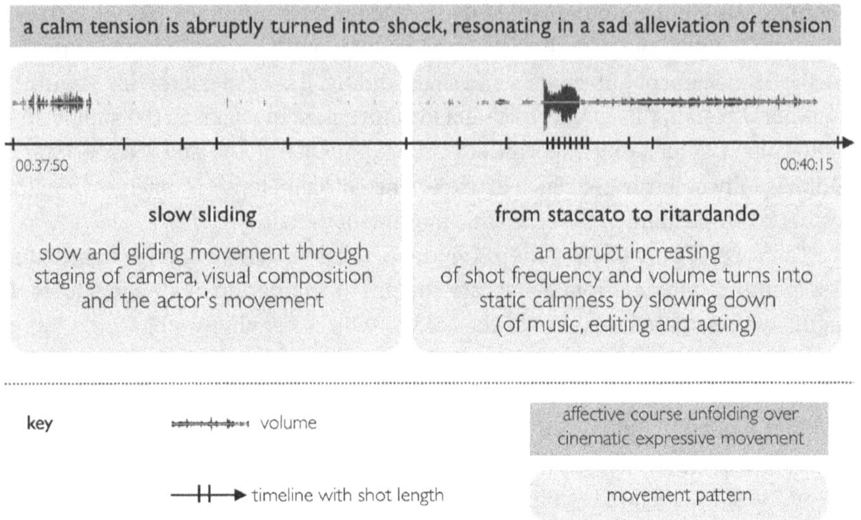


**Figure 8.4:** The temporal parcours of a cinematic expressive movement in BATAAN

tension of the first movement pattern and the staccato rhythm of the second one shape a temporal course which is in fact an affective movement, a movement with an affective quality, much like bodily expressions of surprise, shock or grief.

Such movement patterns are not isolated temporal units; they interact dynamically with each other and they are interwoven, connected in the perceptual processes of the viewer. The two patterns form a larger unit of cinematic expressivity: a cinematic expressive movement. As they are viewing this scene, spectators experience a temporal parcours of movement (from slow, to staccato, to ritardando) that becomes an affective parcours. Put differently, the expressive quality of the scene changes from a slow, stretched pattern in the beginning (movement pattern 1) to an abrupt staccato in the later part (movement pattern 2). The temporal orchestration of these movement patterns modulates an affective course on the side of spectators that can be described as a calm tension that is abruptly turned into shock and resonates in a sad alleviation of tension.

Cinematic expressive movements are such temporally-structured audiovisual forms that shape the affective perception of the viewers as an inherently temporal experience. They concern a specific dimension of movement: an experiential quality or rhythm, a temporally organized perceiving of a dynamic whole. It is in this sense that we conceive of film as staging the affective course of spectators through a complex temporal aesthetic orchestration. An analysis which addresses the film only on the level of its narrative fails to explain the difference in the ways people are touched by reading a novel and by viewing the same story set as a film. With the concept of cinematic expressive movement we are addressing the specific media character of moving images, their dynamic multimodality, in contrast to, e.g., written texts. The difference resembles the change in perspective that we have witnessed in linguistics and that was caused by a move from written language to the dynamics of multimodal spoken language. Indeed, we assume that the temporal unfolding of cinematic images is affecting their spectators in similar immediate ways as multimodal expression does in face-to-face communication. We believe that the perceivable and aesthetic dimension of expressive movements is essentially relevant to what spectators experience when watching a scene. In brief, we regard the composition and temporal unfolding of a cinematic expressive movement as mainly responsible for what spectators feel and understand when they go through the film.

However, the fact that cinematic expressive movements can be described as units of cinematic expressivity on the level of the composition does not imply that they actually exist outside of any process of perception through and by a spectator. They only emerge in a process of seeing, hearing, experiencing the movement-images as a synesthetic experience. This means that the dynamic patterns that we have described (like the slowly increasing tension of the first and the staccato rhythm of the second movement pattern) emerge over time. Sound volume, montage shots, and the acting in the second movement pattern are not additive means of cinematic articulation; they are intricately intertwined to create a synesthetic, holistic experience that we only analytically dissect in our attempt to reconstruct a unified temporally orchestrated experience. It is a technical term that allows us to grasp rhythm and beat of audiovisual figurations (cf. Bakels 2017, 60–61).

This specific understanding of audiovisual images is not, however, limited to the realm of feature films. On the contrary, the insights gained in film research along the lines of this chapter are largely transferable to other media-use settings. Furthermore, as outlined in the following section, we suggest that results from research on cinematic expressive movement and the dynamic forms of affect dramaturgy in film can offer fundamental insights for cross media observations.

## 8.3 Being Touched by News? TAGESSCHAU (TV News Feature)

Other media formats screened outside the cinema, such as television news programs work with techniques of cinematic staging of the kinds we have just described. Camera movements, montage, sound, acting, mise-en-scène, framing are orchestrated to form cinematic expressive movements producing a temporal course of affective experiences which shape the feelings of viewers

[*Zuschauergefühl*] (Kappelhoff and Bakels 2011, 78–95). On the other hand, each audiovisual format does have its own character. Music videos, for instance, emphasize the sound, which results in highly dynamic movement patterns. In television news features, on the contrary, spoken language is extremely prominent and constantly accompanies the flow of images. Music or other very distinct sounds are rarely highlighted in news formats.

Clearly, televised news is normally not as dramatic and pointed as the scenes we have discussed from BATAAN or LOLA RENNT. But it is worth mentioning that they do use the temporal orchestration of audiovisual staging to create specific moods and feelings to engage the viewer affectively. The audiovisual composition provides the form in which the news information is organized, and this form has a significant influence on the meaning-making processes. This holds for mass media but also for serious journalistic formats and is particularly present in reports on crises of all different kinds. Cinematic metaphors orchestrate news features of war scenarios as well as reports of natural disasters. However, they are particularly prominent in economic news. Maybe the abstraction and complexity of topics such as market dynamics, stock market developments, or currency rates do not lend themselves to visualization per se. In economic news, most of the movement patterns are created by the camera and on the editing table. An example in which this cinematic staging is used in a fairly elaborate way is a German news report of 2008 on the global financial crisis[5]. In a two-minute segment titled *Kurseinbruch* ('slump in the market') on the 8pm TAGESSCHAU[6] from January 21st in 2008, the crash of the global financial markets is thematized. In this segment, audiovisual staging creates a perceptual scenario that frames the verbal message of the report and produces a nonverbal affective undercurrent. To describe the staging of the news feature as a cinematic expressive movement (as an affective undercurrent) our analysis will not go into the details of the verbal part of the staging.

After the introductory statement by presenter Ellen Arnold, the report begins with a pronounced camera movement: a diagonal downward movement takes the viewer down onto the trading floor of the Frankfurt stock exchange. The downward-orientation continues in the following two shots in a different form, when the camera shows a close up and a medium-range shot of the falling graph on the main display of the trading floor indicating the negative development of the DAX on that

5 The analysis was developed in the context of the research project "Multimodal Metaphor and Expressive Movement" and further worked on within the Cinepoetics' research focus 'Metaphor – Film Images, Cinematic Thinking, and Cognition' by Thomas Scherer. Cornelia Müller and Thomas Scherer prepared the version for this book.

6 TAGESSCHAU is the most renowned news broadcast in Germany. It is produced by the public broadcast ARD.

day. On the acoustic level, a repetitive *pling* sound sets in and remains during the subsequent interview with a broker, interrupting his statement repeatedly, thereby creating an atmosphere of restlessness. This pattern of the camera moving down to the trading floor with close up and medium shots of the display board is then repeated with the Chinese stock market. By staging the two stock markets in such similar manner, Germany and China are aesthetically framed in a parallel way. After a statement from yet another expert, who is shot in close up, a series of static shots with a distinctive image composition and content starts (Figure 8.5).

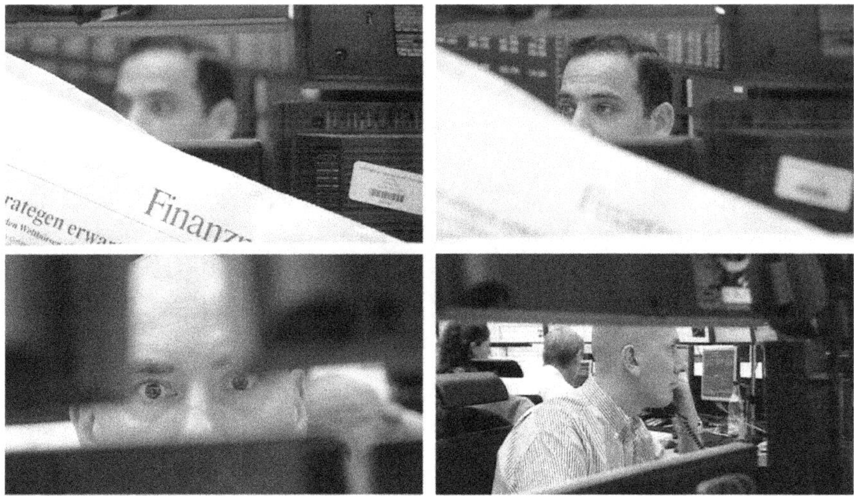

**Figure 8.5:** Framing of actors creating a feeling of constriction (TAGESSCHAU, 21 January, 2008)

A series of brokers' faces are presented in rapid succession with a special focus on their eye area and framed by monitors and newspapers. The first shot echoes the falling graph of the stock market with a diagonally positioned newspaper in the foreground. Through a shift in focus, the eyes of the broker in the background are emphasized. When the man turns his head towards the camera, the report cuts to another broker with eyes wide open, also framed by monitors facing the camera. Through this match-cut, the different men melt into one movement-image creating a feeling of constriction. After a third and last expert interview and a brief shot of a stock ticker, the camera returns to the trading floor in Frankfurt, this time moving diagonally upwards and focusing on the bright white ceiling of the room, and thus reversing the movement with which the clip began.

With this staging of a temporal course, a cinematic movement is created that involves the viewers via its temporality in an affective experience. Even before taking the cognitive processing of the verbal content and the symbolic use of images into account, we can thus reconstruct on a very basic level an affective course of the report. This is what we consider a cinematic expressive movement: with a downward movement on different staging levels, the camera brings the viewers onto the trading floor in Frankfurt. This downward orientation of the camera movement is echoed in the report of the Chinese stock market. A feeling of being constricted and of unrest is then created acoustically and visually. With an upward movement in the last shot, the report ends by inverting the initial downward movement and providing a sense of closure by means of this symmetric structure (Figure 8.6).

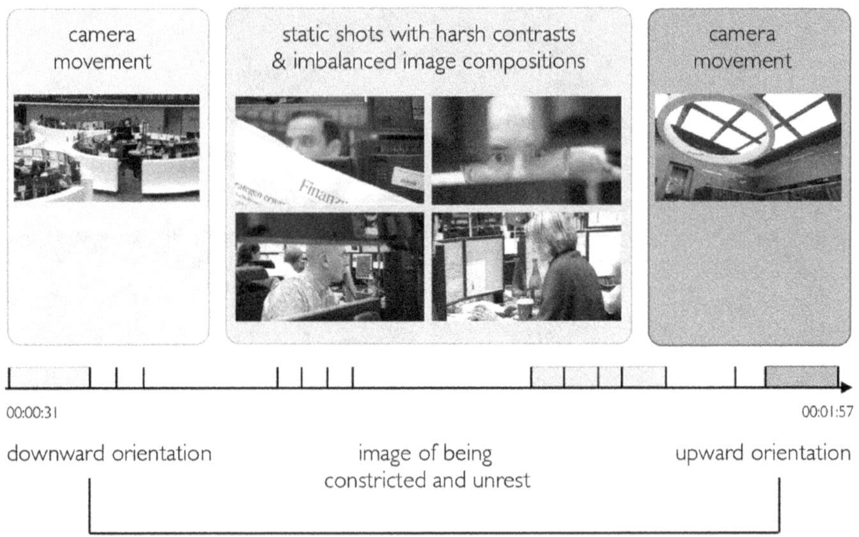


**Figure 8.6:** The temporal parcours of the cinematic expressive movement (TAGESSCHAU, 21 January 2008)

In conclusion, we have seen how television news features can also affect their viewers through the temporal orchestration of audiovisual modalities; they do it, however, and they have to, in a much more condensed manner than a feature film, just because news reports are much shorter. Whereas expressive movements in most feature films have a length of two to five minutes, the movement gestalts in news tend to be under a minute. Another important difference concerns the role of speech in the staging. Whereas most films have episodes with no or few spoken words, mostly as dialog, news offers a constant stream of verbal information in monologs, either from a presenter in the studio, a voice-over, or an interviewee who is shown in close-up. This constant flow of verbal information changes the way viewers perceive the image: verbal expressions and image elements are much more closely tied together. But even when the viewer watches news in a language she does not understand, a specific affective stance is created through cinematic expressive movements of the moving images and their embodied perception as movement-images.[7] How these affective undercurrents generated by the staging of the report are connected to the dominant semantics of the voice-over, creating cinematic metaphors, is explored in Chapter 10. For now, the point we want to make is how, via the orchestration of cinematic expressive movements, viewers can be touched even by a news feature.

## 8.4 Discussion

We regard cinematic expressive movements as temporally-structured forms of cinematic expressivity (as movement-images) that shape the spectators' perceptual, affective, and embodied activity over the course of their unfolding. They concern a specific movement dimension: an experiential quality or rhythm, a temporally organized perceiving of a dynamic whole.

Feature films and other presentational forms of audiovisual culture have developed sophisticated means of telling stories and constructing impressive architectures of fictive and diegetic worlds. What they do in the first place, however, is to shape the feelings of their spectators. People go to the movies to be amused, shocked or thrilled. Some films amuse spectators, others leave them outraged, shocked, melancholic or contemplative. They promise specific affective experiences: being moved is one main expectation of moviegoers that is reflected in the decision whether to see a comedy, a romance, a horror film, or a thriller. But how do films address the feelings of their spectators? What basic aspects of film are relevant for these processes, and on what levels do audiovisual images interact with viewers? How can affective resonances be related to the very concrete and situated act of sitting in a movie theater and experiencing light projections and sound reproductions?

We believe that a concept of distinct emotions cannot provide a convincing answer to these questions. It appears rather problematic to link static emotional categories with dynamic audiovisual images. A major problem here is what we might tentatively characterize as the representational fallacy (cf. Chapter 1). In such an approach, the characters on the screen are analyzed as if they were re-presentations of reality, while, in fact, we have to first and foremost explain how, for spectators, a diegetic world can emerge as-if it were a reality.

7 For an overview of experimental research on the embodied perception of audiovisual images, see Bakels (2014).

Secondly, even in the case of actual human beings, emotions are never static (Scherer 1993, 2009a, b). Also, facial expressions of emotions are movements with a temporal gestalt and distinctive movement qualities. The idea of distinct emotions freezes them to the statics of a photographed facial expression and ignores cinematic dynamics.

By highlighting the inherently temporal character of all expressive movements we take a counter position to such an idea of distinct and static emotions in the cinema. Affect in film (we deliberately avoid the term emotion)[8] is a consequence of film aesthetics, of the temporal staging of all its expressive means. This staging is what shapes an affective parcours for the film viewers (Kappelhoff 2004a, Kappelhoff and Bakels 2011). And it does so in a very similar way to how bodily expressivity affect people engaged in a conversation.

Film images organize the perceptual processes of spectators dynamically, as they are unfolding over the course of seeing the film. While, for example, one scene might be staged throughout in terms of strong tensions and clear attentional foci, in a subsequent one, suspense might be relieved after a few minutes. From such a perspective (we have discussed this in Section 1.2), film as much as television is to be analyzed in terms of an affective dramaturgy, in other words, as a temporal course that the spectators go through. Such an aesthetic addressing of the perceptual, affective, and understanding activity of the spectator is what we consider as cinematic expressive movement (Kappelhoff 2004a).

Ever since the invention of moving images, film theory has intensively discussed how films arouse emotions and shape the affective experiences of their audience. We have mentioned earlier that several current approaches consider narrative settings, actions of characters, and plot developments as decisive means of evoking emotions in feature films (Grodal 2009, Plantinga 2009, Tan 1996). These cognitively-oriented theories conceptualize a spectator's reactions to a film predominantly as a conscious activity, controlled by mental operations of hypothesizing and constructing schemata. Whether a spectator finds characters on screen likeable or not, feels with them or not, is assumed to be dependent on the cognitive evaluation of a narrative situation. Briefly, these theories regard the narration as predominant, while film aesthetics appears as more subsidiary facet of cinema. Although, for instance, Ed Tan (1996) distinguishes between emotions evoked by fiction and those which are stimulated by evaluating the aesthetics of a film, he primarily considers the spectators' conscious and cognitive activity to account for an emotional 'response' to a film. In short, such approaches tend to regard film aesthetics either as supporting means, as a secondary stylistic or

8 For a detailed discussion of the terms emotion, affect, feeling see Kappelhoff (2018a).

technical tool, or as cognitively-evaluated aesthetic moments that stand out from the narration. What remains mainly unconsidered by them is the way spectators experience film images affectively, bodily, and also unconsciously. This is and was, however, of major interest to a philosophical tradition within humanities research on cinema. From this point of view, the aesthetics of film is considered the relevant vantage point: films themselves are considered as offering an imagination as well as complex reflections, and interpretations (Cavell 1979). Affect is conceived of as being intrinsically bound to the aesthetic and poetic forms of audiovisual images (Deleuze 2008 [1983]). For film theorist and psychologist Hugo Münsterberg (2002 [1916]), film images were congruent with mental and emotional activities: he conceived of a camera's movement that is focusing on an object as structurally congruent to the way humans draw mentally attention towards an object. To address the question of how films move their spectators, neo-phenomenological film theory puts the body of the viewers into the limelight. Films are considered as bodily modulating affective experiences (in terms of embodiment; e.g., Sobchack 1992, 2004, Bakels 2014, Schmitt and Greifenstein 2014). In Raymond Gibbs' psychological terms, those bodily experiences can be described as embodied simulations (see Gibbs 2018b).

Films involve spectators bodily and affectively by creating, for example, media-specific forms of distance towards a scenario or by bringing them very close to a face. A rapid montage of action and fight might make spectators feel agitated or troubled, while a long, slow, gliding camera movement above a city or landscape might orchestrate sensations of relaxation. The concept of cinematic expressive movement captures this embodied engagement that reflexively connects the films with their viewers. Theories on expressive movement and the expression of affect relate to this concept by focusing on the aesthetic and temporal organization of audiovisual images as a way to address the feelings of viewers [*Zuschauergefühl*]. The following chapter considers audiovisual images and gestures as movement-images.

# 9 Movement-Image: From Body Movement to Cinematic Expressivity

Metaphors in audiovisual media are grounded in the perception of movement-images. It is the modulation of affective experiences in the process of viewing a film or a television newscast that frames the emergence of cinematic metaphorical meaning. Such a perspective on metaphors in audiovisual formats starts from the media specifics of audiovision. This chapter describes expressive movement as a fundamental trait of both film and human gestures. With a focus on the aesthetics of movement, we address the movement qualities of gestures as a form of human expressivity to empirically underpin a theoretical discussion that was vital in the early days of film theory and which affected the full range of scholarly debates in the beginning of the twentieth century. To say that films are movement-images (not 'moving images') appears tautological, but addresses a central parallel between gestural movements, as we observe them in everyday situations of people talking to each other, and films. 'Expressive movement' as the concept which makes this connection clear was coined in a rich philosophical debate. To lay out its empirical and theoretical richness both for gesture studies and for film analysis is paramount for the understanding of cinematic metaphor that we advocate in this book.

## 9.1 Hand Gestures as Expressive Movements

In his theory of expression, the German psychologist and linguist Karl Bühler considers gesture as functionally equivalent to language (Bühler 1968 [1933], Horst et al. 2014, Müller 1998b). An important assumption of his functional model of language is that all three functions – expression, appeal, and representation – are simultaneously present in each communicative act (Bühler 1990 [1934], 39). Employed as partners of speech, gestures are "used to express inner states, to appeal to somebody [...], and to represent objects and events in the world" (Müller 2013, 204). Moreover, they are always expression, appeal, and representation *at the same time* (Müller 2013). It is the quality of the gestural movement which embodies the expressive quality of gestures (Müller 1998b). In addition to the movement quality, the mere fact that somebody is employing gestures (instead of not gesturing) is an increased communicative effort and expresses a higher affective involvement in a conversation (Müller and Tag 2010). Gestures thus display how engaged speakers are in conversation and qualify this circumstance affectively – all this being intertwined with the 'representational', the depictive function of gestures. For Bühler (1933, 39) this affective expressivity is a vital facet of any depictive

https://doi.org/10.1515/9783110580785-010

gesture. Giving the example of a drawing gesture, he says that it can be performed in many different ways: "Once it might be performed in a cheerful, another time in an angry, yet another time in a frightened and hesitant manner. In each case, the moving hands imitate an action, appeal to an interlocutor, and express an inner state." The different movement qualities express "our affective stance towards the object we are depicting" (Müller 2013, 202). This means, it is not only the '*what*' of a gestural performance which is meaningful, but also the '*how*'. However, considering hand gestures as expressive movements of the body does not mean that they are regarded as symbols for inner states. On the contrary, when we see a gesture we immediately comprehend the other's expression of affect without any decipherment and interpretation of inner motivations. Merleau-Ponty describes such an intertwining of gestural expression and affective experience:

> Faced with an angry or threatening gesture, I have no need, in order to understand it, to recall the feelings which I myself experienced when I used these gestures on my own account. [...] I do not see anger or a threatening attitude as a psychic fact hidden behind the gesture, I read anger in it. The gesture does not make me think of anger, it is anger itself. (Merleau-Ponty 2005 [1945], 184)

With this position, Merleau-Ponty distances himself from the widely discussed concept of 'empathy' (German '*Einfühlung*') according to which a person would be able to recognize and understand the emotions of another because he or she projects his or her own recalled emotional and affective experience onto the other. Taking a counter position to the empathy model which assumes a gap between inner feeling and outer expression, Merleau-Ponty argues: "The meaning of a gesture thus 'understood' is not behind it, it is intermingled with the structure of the world outlined by the gesture, and which I take up on my own account" (Merleau-Ponty 2005 [1945]). Beyond rejecting an arbitrary relation between expression and experience, what is important here is Merleau-Ponty's notion of structure with regard to behavior. Subscribing to a gestalt-psychological view on gesture, he proposes "to designate specifically how a Gestalt is organized" (Embree 1980, Merleau-Ponty 1963 [1942]). A gesture's direct intelligibility with regard to affect is hence grounded in its specific course of movement, i.e., its particular structure (what we just have called the '*how*' of gestural performance). As a consequence, the temporal gestalt of body movement and affective experience is assumed to be structurally congruent. Gestalt psychologist Max Wertheimer puts it as follows: "When a man is timid, afraid or energetic, happy or sad, [...] the course of his physical processes is Gestalt-identical with the course pursued by the mental processes." (Wertheimer 1997 [1925]). Merleau-Ponty also assumes a congruency of movement and affect. In his view, comprehending a gesture is inherently tied to a body which perceives the structure of the other's gesturing.

It is within and through this gestalt structure that the expressing and perceiving of a gesture intertwines. To put it very simply: interaffectivity emerges through the body.

In this light, the specific way of performing a gesture *is* the expression of an affective stance. Affect in such a perspective is dynamic and differs strongly, for instance, from Ekman's (Ekman 1972, 2006, Ekman and Rosenberg 1997) idea of discrete emotions expressed in the face, which assumes a static, frozen configuration of facial muscles as the 'expressive configuration' of what are considered basic emotions. In the counter position that we are formulating, a speaker's affective attitude is not a succession of a series of static facial expressions, it is fully embodied in the dynamics of body movements. It is intimately tied to the interaction with interlocutors to whom a speaker reacts and who in turn react to him: "It would be a mistake to subjectivize these experiences of qualities of motion, as if they were locked up within some private inner world of feelings." (Johnson 2007, 25). On the contrary, "emotions are processes of organism-environment interactions. They involve perceptions and assessments of situations in the continual process of transforming those situations" (Johnson 2007, 66–67). This means that multimodal interaction is permeated with affective experience in terms of a bodily, inter-subjective, and dynamic phenomenon: "[A]ffects are not enclosed in an inner mental sphere to be deciphered from outside but come into existence, change and circulate between self and other in the inter-corporeal dialogue" (Fuchs and De Jaegher 2009, 479).

We speak of gestures as expressive movements, that is, the expression of affect in the movement of the hands. Gestures are intersubjective acts of expression and perception. Thus, we perceive of them as direct, unmediated expression, and we think of interaffectivity, rather than of affect expression of an individual speaker. From such a point of view, the expressivity of gestures calls up bodily resonances in the perceiving interlocutor (Kappelhoff and Müller 2011). Accordingly, what happens during a conversation is that, with their gestures and body movements, interlocutors establish a structure of constant affective exchange. Regarding gestures as interactive expressive movements as we will do in the next section thus sets affectivity center stage. It is on this 'stage' that metaphorical meaning emerges, permeated by interaffectivity.

## 9.2 Interaffectivity and the Emergence of Metaphor in a Group Discussion

In the following, we particularly focus on how the dynamics of interactively shared and shaped affectivity grounds metaphorical meaning of gestural body movements.[1] By taking into consideration the interactive and temporal process in which multimodal metaphors in speech and gestures are embedded, we illustrate how metaphoricity emerges from interacting partners engaged in a dialog. We thus expand our perspective, from looking at the expressive movement qualities of one gestural movement (i.e., Bühler's drawing gesture that can be performed cheerfully, in a hesitant or an angry manner), to the flow of gestures and speech across conversational partners, i.e., to the flow of multimodal interaction. The interactive dimension of expressive movement, along with the interaffectivity involved in the enacting and perceiving of expressive body movements, functions as a 'role' model for the film-theoretical model that we are advocating. With an empirical study of metaphorical gestures, we illustrate some theoretical assumptions of theorists of "expressive movement". We assume that the process of viewing films is one in which viewers are interactively and reflexively engaged with the course of the cinematic expressive movements that form the aesthetic composition of a film or of the staging of a television news broadcast.

In the following analysis of a three-party group discussion (depicted in Figure 9.1), we describe how interaffectivity 'happens' in speech and gestures and across the co-participants, here called Anna, Berta, Charlotte.[2] We focus on how it contributes to the emergence of metaphorical meaning in speech and gesture.[3] The conversation of approximately thirty minutes comes from a corpus of video-recorded group discussions and was initiated by a thematic stimulus: a newspaper article commenting critically on academic education as exerting too much pressure on students and therefore restricting their freedom to engage in processes of self-realization.

Early on in the discussion, it becomes clear that the three students have quite different opinions about and also very different experiences with self-realization. After about thirteen minutes of the conversation, two conflicting positions are worked out and the discussion revolves around these two opposing points of view: self-realization as something arising from within oneself, or

1 The analysis was developed in the context of the research project "Multimodal Metaphor and Expressive Movement" and further worked on within the Cinepoetics' research focus 'Metaphor – Film Images, Cinematic Thinking, and Cognition' by Dorothea Horst (Horst et al. 2014). Dorothea Horst, Lynne Cameron, and Cornelia Müller prepared the version for this book.

2 We use Daniel Stern's notion of interaffectivity (Stern 1985, 132–133).

3 The discussion comes from a data corpus that consists of ten argumentations (five about the public debate on Thilo Sarrazin's comments on immigration and five about personal problems during one's studies) and ten narrations (five about one's first semester experiences and five about self-realization).

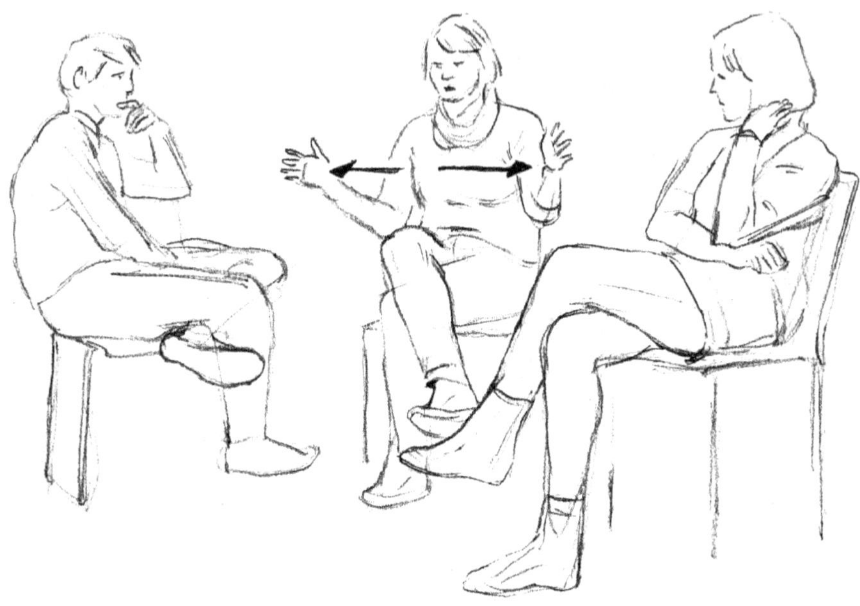

**Figure 9.1:** Three-party group discussion between Anna, Berta, and Charlotte (from left to right)

something imposed from the outside. While Anna and Charlotte agree on the first perspective, Berta advocates the second. The controversy evolves into a two-and-a-half-minute sequence of confrontation, including an angry outburst from Charlotte and an emphatic reply from Berta. In this increasingly heated negotiation process, in which all three speakers engage affectively and intensively, metaphoricity emerges, formulating and escalating the controversial positions. In a cynical reply to Berta's argument that fulfilling one's duties (imposed from the outside) would contribute to one's self-realization, Charlotte brings up the metaphorical idea of a 'whip'. Quoting an idiom saying that "Just because you are not seeing a whip doesn't mean it's not there" [*Nur weil du die Peitsche nicht siehst, heißt es nicht, dass sie [nicht] da ist*], she tries to show that the 'rules' mentioned by Berta are just a fantasy of self-realization and actually something alien imposed from the outside. Charlotte continues, "Well, making somebody believe that there is something like self-realization but actually it doesn't exist anywhere. That's really cool" [*Also vorgaukeln, dass es so was wie Selbstverwirklichung gibt, aber dann gibt es sie doch in keinem Bereich. Das ist echt geil*]. She turns the idea of an invisible whip into a metaphorical critique of a deluded self-realization. In contrast, proper self-realization for her and Anna is something arising from within oneself.

Berta again tries to make herself understood. Charlotte, however, refuses to agree with Berta's "Yes, but you are saying yourself that there has to be a whip" [*Ja, aber du sagst ja selber, dass 'ne Peitsche da sein muss*] and emphasizes her refusal with a loud and energetic right-hand slap on her thigh. This gesture is a prime example of an expressive movement. It reveals a significant communicative effort from Charlotte expressing her individual involvement at this point and what she does not consider to be self-realization: "I think it's mean that somebody gives me an idea of self-realization, to which I should aspire, according to which I should, like a puppet, like yeah, looking for happiness, but behind it, there is actually only 'Hopp Hopp, do that and that and that'" while performing a metaphorical whipping gesture (Figure 9.2 left) *[Ich find's nur gemein, dass man mir so'n Begriff wie Selbstverwirklichung gibt, nach dem ich streben soll, nach dem ich, wie so 'ne Marionette so, yeah, Glück suchen soll und eigentlich steckt dahinter aber nur: 'Hopp, Hopp, mach mal das und das und das'].* The movement quality of her gestures expresses her attitude towards what is being discussed and responds to the interactive situation of mutual confrontation. As such, Charlotte's emphatic slapping gesture does not stand by itself, it did not emerge out of the blue, but is a consequence of previous utterances and a motivation for subsequent communicative actions. With its accentuated slapping movement, the gesture is part of and orchestrates an intensive affective phase of the conversation that can be described as follows: many repetitions of gestures and gestural sequences, overlapping gesturing of different speakers, increasing speed and a marked accentuation of the gestural movement quality.

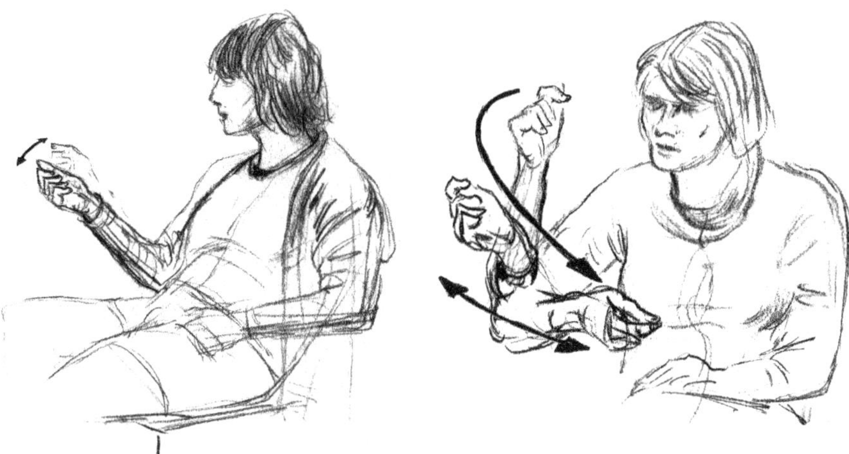

**Figure 9.2**: Embodied metaphors of "whipping" from Charlotte and Berta

Defending her idea of self-realization in order to finally get ratification from her interlocutors, Berta takes up this vital idea of the whip. She explains that she needs it both from outside and from inside, but objects "But I don't want to live in a dictatorship, where somebody is whipping me" [*Also, ich will nicht in irgend 'ner Diktatur leben, wo dann einer immer so mir hinterherpeitscht*] with an accompanying metaphorical whipping gesture towards her own body (Figure 9.2 right).

These gesture performances constitute a mutually perceptible and interactive communicative effort. In this phase of confrontation, the women participate actively in the conversation: while Berta is constantly trying to make herself understood as to why she regards the following of determined rules, a kind of metaphorical whip, as an essential aspect of her self-realization, her interlocutors refuse to agree. Lacking ratification, she reformulates her argument and again encounters disapproval. There is a constant shifting between positions, which is expressed and achieved by the manner of gesturing, including the movement qualities. Berta's gestures are interrupted by the gestures of the other participants in the discussion. Berta interrupts them again, repeating her respective gestures, i.e., the "internal whip", and performing large gestures in an accentuated and vigorous manner right in the center of the interactively shared visual focus of attention. Her interlocutors join in this intensification multimodally (Oben and Brône 2015, 2016) As this dynamic "interplay of affective exchanges of intensity" (Kappelhoff and Müller 2011) temporally unfolds in the multimodal performance of the three participants engaged in the discussion, an interactive movement pattern evolves.[4] In a continuous increase of tension and mutual anger, the discussion unfolds in a choppy rhythm of repeated starts and harsh interruption.

With this jointly created dialogic rhythm and shaping of shared affect (interaffectivity), a gestalt emerges that we consider to be an interactive expressive movement. Such a movement gestalt, which may encompass several minutes (in our example, two and a half), unfolds a particular affective quality. Its particular affective intensity not only shows up in gesturing, but also in speech and bodily interaction.

The rhythm of anger is articulated interactively and in multiple modalities. On the level of speech, Berta is interrupted by the others who speak with a raised pitch and a high volume. Berta interrupts the others, and she also raises her

4 For instance, Schmidt/Richardson's (2008) and Shockley/Richardson/Dale's (2009) research on the coordination of body movements, postures, and gazes in interpersonal interaction alludes to a similar phenomenon.

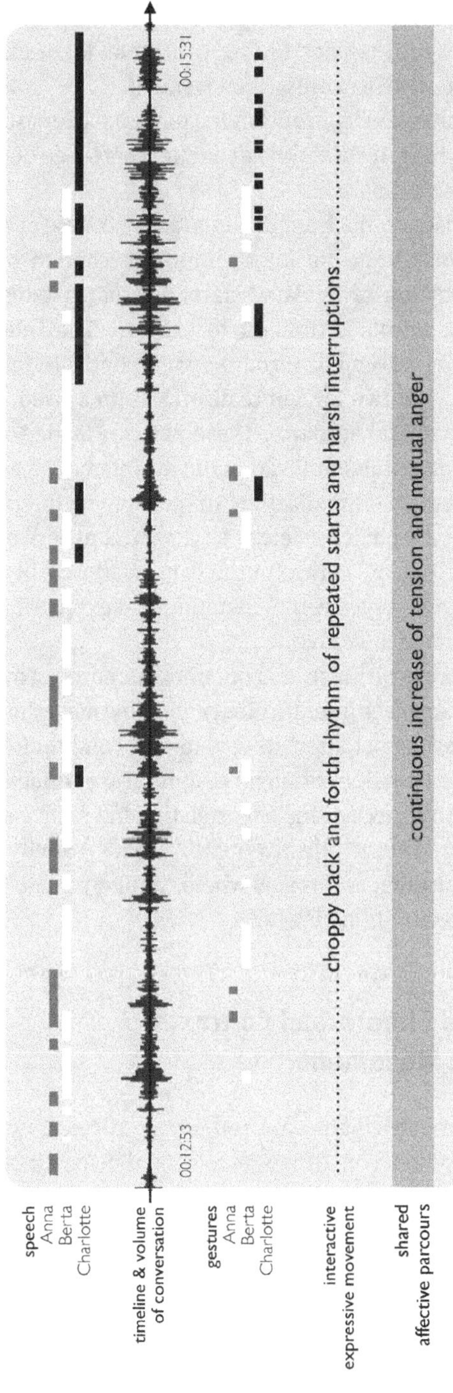


**Figure 9.3:** The temporal course of interaffectivity in the group discussion

voice and pitch. The constant back and forth of turns, the increased tempo of speech, and the rate of turn-takings further contribute to an increasing tension and compose to the interactive expressive movement.

Figure 9.3[5] shows an intensity profile of the temporal course of interaffectivity that we have just described. It shows the dynamic emergence of affective intensities as they evolve along a timeline.

Metaphoricity is inseparable from this interactive course of affective engagement. In fact, it emerges from the interlocutors' perception of the increasing tension and choppy rhythm of repeated starts and harsh interruption, and as mutual understanding becomes difficult to achieve. The interaffective experience of the expressive movement turns the metaphorical idea of a whip as a negative or a positive incentive for self-realization into a lived, shared, interactively embodied metaphorical scenario. These two contrasting multimodal metaphors are emerging temporal stabilizations in an interactive and interaffective negotiation process around self-realization. In the ongoing interactive exchanges of the discussion, interaffectivity emerges as a shared experience of expressive movements unfolding over the course of the conversation. Affectivity is shared, negated, fought over and merges verbal metaphorical expressions with prosodic and gestural enactments of metaphor.

With this analysis we have illustrated our understanding of interactive expressive movement, how it involves interaffectivity and how metaphoricity emerges in this process. This emergence of affect in face-to-face communication transcends the expressive movement qualities of single gestures. Face-to-face interactions can be seen as sequences and successions of correlating interactive expressive movements, each with their specific affective quality. Metaphoricity emerges within this interaffectivity over time, and this is where we find parallels with cinematic metaphor and the process of film-viewing.

## 9.3 Historical and Theoretical Contexts of Expressive Movement

The ways in which co-participants are reflexively affected by their bodies in motion and their speaking constitutes a role model for cinematic expressivity that has informed film theory from its very beginning. While in face-to-face interactions expressive multimodal gestalts emerge on the level of hands, head,

5 For further explanation of the figure see "Appendix: Cinematic Metaphor – A methodological outline", Section A.3.2.

legs, arms, trunk movements together with the prosodic contours of speech, in audiovisual media the expressive modalities from which those temporal gestalts emerge include camera movement, sound design, framing, mise-en-scène, montage, and the acting. As in face-to-face communication, such movement gestalts only emerge in and from an interaction. Interactive movement as reflexive affection is a key element from which the gestural as well as the cinematic gestalts ultimately emanate. Conceiving of multimodal face-to-face communication as temporally orchestrated and as inherently interaffective is what connects gestures and spoken language with film.

In the following section, we present a survey of how this connection between the expressivity of gestural behavior and media generated expressivity developed into a theory of the melodramatic mode of modern entertainment culture and address the question of how audiences can be moved by a theater play or a film. Cinematic metaphors are always embedded in and ultimately emergent from the affective experiences of the process of viewing films. This is why such an understanding of aesthetic strategies as modulating spectator's affective experiences is of central importance for cinematic metaphor.

### Poetics of affect and the melodramatic mode of theater and film

The intersection of affect and expression was already a topic of lively discussion in film theory back in the 1920s. In this regard, the concept of *cinematic expressive movement* provides a theoretical framework through the cultural-historical examination of melodramatic theater, film, and musical theater (Kappelhoff 2004a).[6] From the perspective elaborated there, the aesthetic concepts of the first melodramas and the late eighteenth-century theater of sensibility are considered as the original constellation of the modern entertainment arts. They develop media and art forms (the stage, the play, dance, film), aesthetic operations, and a poetics of affect, which focus on activating and forming the emotions of a broad and anonymous audience. An analytical comparison with the melodramas of Hollywood cinema showed that these fundamental affective poetical concepts of sentimental entertainment have maintained their validity up to the present day (Kappelhoff 2004a).

6 See also Greifenstein and Kappelhoff 2014, Kappelhoff 2013, Kappelhoff and Bakels 2011, Kappelhoff and Greifenstein 2016, Kappelhoff, Grotkopp, and Gaertner 2016, Kappelhoff and Müller 2011, Scherer, Greifenstein, and Kappelhoff 2014, Schmitt, Greifenstein, and Kappelhoff 2014.

The objectives associated with these cultural practices of aesthetically forming emotional experiences are, in fact, different in each case. This is also true of how these practices are tied to other media, artistic operations, and materials. It is possible, however, to determine certain fundamental patterns of affective formation through media across the history of sentimental art and entertainment (Kappelhoff 2006). One of the significant operations through which this can be observed is the shaping of figurations of time and movement as a specific form of expressivity: the expressive movement. This can mean the gestural formation of the performance of acting, but also the stage set as an image, changeable within itself; it can mean the performance of dance or pantomime, or even the interplay of declamation and musical composition. In the concepts of the sentimental arts of entertainment, expressive movement characterizes forms of artistic performance that do not merely express moods, atmospheres, and feelings in an intentional manner, but can call these up in spectators as an affective reaction – and that means, as bodily response.

In the sentimental and entertainment arts, expressive movements have always assumed an empathetic mode of perception on the part of the audience as the strategic aim of various aesthetic operations. In the eighteenth century, the relevant strategies of aesthetic effect were still put to the service of a pedagogical program aiming at cultivating an individual's capacity for compassion. In current entertainment culture, the experience of intense affective reaction as the sensation of one's own corporeality has become an end in itself, and is received as aesthetic pleasure. Thrill, horror, and sentimental sadness are qualities of sensation in the self-perception of one's own corporeality, which in the modern arts of entertainment have become primary factors of content. What has remained the same is the condition that an anonymous audience, mediated by the representation of compositional figurations of time and movement, passes through a focused process of changing and increasing emotional content.

Accordingly, our argument starts from the premise that the compositional formation of patterns of movement in audiovisual images produces affective resonances on the part of the viewers. These affective resonances are not identical with the feelings being represented or those of the characters represented. Instead, we are dealing with a complex atmospheric network of mood, extended over time, which only matches up with represented emotions in exceptional cases. It is thus primarily a matter of broad-based affective operations and episodic structures, which are called up and shaped on the part of the spectator through the staging strategies and compositional patterns of audiovisual images. It is in this sense that we speak of *poetics of affect* in the ways audiovisual images are presented.

### The modern concept of expression in film theory

The theoretical framework in which the modern concept of expression developed also entered aesthetic-philosophical and art theoretical reflections (cf. Fiedler 1991 [1881], 1991 [1887], Simmel 1959 [1901], 1993 [1905]). It has become one of the central points of reference in classical film theory.

In the context of the founding of modern psychology, Wilhelm Wundt foregrounds precisely that dimension of expressive movement that has defined the history of the term since the Late Enlightenment, and which formed the basis for its astonishing career. Indeed, expressive movement is situated here as the source of language evolution:

> The psycho-physical expressions of life, of which language can be considered a particularly singularly developed form, we denote according to their general terms as 'expressive movement'. Every language consists of vocalizations or other signs perceptible to the senses, which use muscle effects to announce inner states, ideas, feelings, affects to the outside. (Wundt 1900–1920, 31, translation by CM & HK)

Wundt speaks of expressive movement as a physical activity that characterizes all linguistic and non-linguistic forms of expression. However, this already sets up a distinction that will be significant over the historical course of the discussion: the formulations "signs perceptible to the senses" and "announcing to the outside" suggest that expressive movement is at least as much a question of perception as it is one of intentional utterance. Karl Bühler dwells exactly on this point when he distinguishes between the "announcement" of an affective attunement in expressive movement and intentional notification (Bühler 1968 [1933]). Expressive movement in Bühler's sense is not based on the intentional imparting of information, but indicates a more or less involuntary utterance that is, however, taken and understood as a meaningful whole from the outside. Bühler reconstructs the term expressive movement as a theoretical discourse that originated in the aesthetic psychology of the Late Enlightenment. He ties his reflections to the search for the aesthetic strategies of the arts and entertainment media to guide the emotions of the spectator. The affect poetics of the late eighteenth century formed a consciousness of expressive movement as an experiential modality that could not be traced back to any purely information function of expressivity.

What these modern approaches to expressive movement have in common is that they no longer understand expression, as the traditional teaching on expression has since the eighteenth century, as intentional or involuntary proof of the inner orientation of a human subject. Rather, they assume an expressive behavior on the part of all living beings, conceived as an interplay of affective exchanges of intensity. Expressive movement comes about as a direct matching of affective alignments between individualized bodies. This idea was developed particularly clearly by Helmuth Plessner (Plessner 1982 [1925]). For him, expressive movement is a physical action that is not focused on any goal of action, but leans to an image of the entirety of the interaction between an organism and its environment.[7] It quasi denotes the figurative in an action, a kind of gestural shape of organic movement (Plessner 1982 [1925], 82).

> Wherever movements appear in the realm of the organic, they proceed according to a unified rhythm, they show a dynamic, even also experimentally verifiable, shape. They do not unwind piece by piece, as if the phases of their succession could be associated from individual elements; they do not form any temporal mosaic, but a certain wholeness is provided, within which the individual movement curves are variable.[8]
>
> [*Wo immer im Reich des Organischen Bewegungen erscheinen, verlaufen sie nach einheitlichem Rhythmus, zeigen sie eine, wohl auch experimentell nachweisbare, dynamische Gestalt. Sie rollen nicht stückhaft ab, als ob ihre Phasenfolge aus einzelnen Elementen assoziiert worden wäre, bilden kein Zeitmosaik, sondern eine gewisse Ganzheit ist vorgegeben, innerhalb derer die einzelnen Bewegungskurven variierbar sind.*] (Plessner 1982 [1925], 77–78)

Plessner takes expressive movement to be a level of behavior that synchronizes the organism with its surroundings – that is, not as a human faculty. From this original perspective, expressive movement is presented as a temporal shape, a dynamic pattern. Movement, successively running in time, is perceived as the wholeness of an unfolding, complex affective attunement. While the action runs successively in time, and thus can be broken down and analyzed, expressive movement refers to the time of the unfolding of a dynamic relation of exchange between organism and environment as a visual whole. Plessner describes this dynamic shape with the term "movement-image".[9]

> These wholenesses belong to the organism through its relation to the environment, its morphology, its specific instincts as motor categories [...] As a result, the movement shapes are pictorial, even stretched out over a certain duration of time, are co-present with the observer [...] Grasping, fleeing, repelling, seeking, but also the "affectless" forms such as walking, flying, swimming [...] represent such movement-images.[10]

---

**7** "In the expression, an entirety is manifest, and within this manifestation rests the living bearer of the expression." (English translation by Daniel Hendricks) [*Im Ausdruck wird ein Ganzes manifest und in dieser Manifestation ruht der lebendige Träger des Ausdrucks.*] (Plessner 1982 [1925], 94).
**8** English translation by Daniel Hendricks.
**9** Notwithstanding the fundamental differences between an anthropological and a constructivist approach, Plessner's understanding compares quite well with the film theoretical term movement-image in Deleuze' sense. Both terminologies are based on the same philosophical source, namely Henri Bergson.
**10** English translation by Daniel Hendricks.

> [*Diese Ganzheiten gehören zum Organismus durch sein Verhältnis zur Umwelt, seine Morphologie, seine artspezifischen Instinkte als motorische Kategorien [...]. Infolgedessen sind die Bewegungsgestalten bildhaft, wenn auch auch über eine gewisse Zeitdauer erstreckt, dem Beobachter gegenwärtig. [...] Greifen, Fliehen, Abwehren, Suchen, aber auch schon die "affektlosen" Formen wie Gehen, Fliegen, Schwimmen [...] stellen solche Bewegungsbilder dar.*] (Plessner 1982 [1925], 78)

Expressive movement refers here to a specific mode of experience or perception. Plessner speaks of a direct perception of the psyche, of a becoming-aware without closure, of a direct internalizing of expressive movement as a movement of sensations.

> The fact that the cat is walking away from me can also be objectively represented in mere movements: moreover, the fact that she is fearfully running away from me is also expressed in these movements as a unified character. The fact that the dog jumps up on me can be objectively stated; the fact that he is joyfully greeting me is clear to me in his behavior as a form of direction.[11]
>
> [*Daß die Katze mir davonläuft, läßt sich auch objektiv in bloßen Bewegungen darstellen: daß sie mich ängstlich flieht, ist mir überdies in diesen Bewegungen als einheitlicher Charakter gegeben. Daß der Hund an mir emporspringt, ist objektiv konstatierbar; daß er mich freudig begrüßt, ist mir in seinem Gebaren als Richtungsform deutlich.*] (Plessner 1982 [1925], 82)

At another point Plessner writes:

> Could joy develop as joy without a pressure upward and outward, rage as rage without a savage tendency to thrust forward, dread as dread without a tendency to shrink and flee downward and backward? (Plessner 1970 [1941], 55)
>
> [*Könnte sich Freude als Freude entfalten ohne den Drang nach oben und außen; Wut als Wut ohne die verbissene Stoßrichtung nach vorn; Angst als Angst ohne die Schrumpfungs- und Fluchttendenz nach unten und hinten?*] (Plessner 1982 [1941], 261)

What Plessner is trying to get at with the term "movement-image" does not conform to the idea of coding and decoding an intentional notification. Expressive movement is no symbolic image of an inner process of feeling, which has to be deciphered. Instead, it is the behavior that proclaims itself as a dynamic form-pattern of a movement-image. It corresponds to a specific mode of experience, a sensorium of perception, to which such movement-images are directly deployed as dynamic affective operations.

Plessner suggests that this experiential modality is based on mimetic reaction patterns, and that the sensory-visual aspect of the perceived movement of the other is realized in the reflection of one's own bodily sensation. He assumes that elements of the sensory-visual are subordinate to a form-function relation, which

**11** English translation by Daniel Hendricks.

belongs to the realm of the psychic as much as it does to the physical. Expressive movement, as the dynamic pattern of a self-unfolding affect, is directly embodied by the perceiving being as affective response.

> As soon as we cut the organism away from its relation to the environment, even if this is only in thought, what remains in movement is simply a living body [...]. The dog with its head held out in front of it on the ground, anxiously running back and forth, stopping sometimes here, then suddenly there, sniffing, then returning again to its starting point, rushed, strongly accentuating the flow of movement in its interruptions, offers us the typical image of seeking.[12]
>
> [*Sobald wir freilich den Organismus aus seiner Beziehung zur Umgebung, und sei es nur in Gedanken herausschneiden, bleibt bloß ein lebendiger Körper zurück [...]. Der Hund mit vorgestrecktem am Boden gehaltenen Kopf, der unruhig hin und her läuft, bald hier, bald dort plötzlich stehen bleibt, bietet uns das typische Bild des Suchens.*] (Plessner 1982 [1925], 79)
>
> As soon as the observer switches over to disassembling the images into their component parts and investigating their kinematic connections, which do not seem given to us, he abandons the course of direct or indirect understanding and begins to explain causally.[13]
>
> [*Sobald aber der Beobachter dazu übergeht, die Bilder in ihre Aufbauteile zu zerlegen, und deren kinematografischen Zusammenhang erforscht, der uns nicht gegeben erscheint, verläßt er die Schicht des unmittelbaren oder mittelbaren Verstehens und fängt an, kausal zu erklären.*] (Plessner 1982 [1925], 78)

Expressive movement should thus be defined as a specific mode of experience, as the sensory-affective embodiment of a perceived dynamic shape, without assuming a conscious act of understanding. Nonetheless – and in this respect Plessner develops the expressive concept as an anthropological system of relations – it is the specificity of human perception that it grasps movement-images as the expression of an intentional and mental individuality.

Within human communication, Plessner's concept of expressive movement characterizes the perception of dynamic patterns of movement as a structure of suspense that unfolds between more or less involuntarily occurring affective-bodily reactions and complex sensory interpretations of behavior as intuitively unlocked intentionality. Like classical film theory, the artistic avant-garde in the twenties shifted this relation of tension or suspense to the center. Poetic concepts as diverse as German Expressionism, the French film avant-garde, and the Russian school of montage shared the idea that it was possible for cinema, in a quite special way, to deploy a dimension of movement in which feeling and thinking, sensation and understanding coincide.

---

**12** English translation by Daniel Hendricks.

**13** English translation by Daniel Hendricks.

The decisive historical link between this theoretical position of expressive movement and movement-image is formed by two classic authors of film theory: Béla Balázs and Sergej Eisenstein. In his book *Visible Man*, Béla Balázs celebrates the movement dimension of the film image as a cultural revolution initiated in media. He emphatically welcomes film as a return to "physiognomic thinking".

Like Plessner, Balázs links this experiential mode to a specific experience of the image's temporal structure: it is the movement of facial expression that this temporal structure exemplifies. Balázs emphasizes the fact that the close-up of a face does not bring out the symbolic character of facial expression, but the dynamic unfolding of a complex expressive movement. And as such, as the shape of a successively unfolding movement, the face in close-up becomes the paradigm for the movement-image.

> There is a film in which Asta Nielsen is looking out of the window and sees someone coming. A mortal fear, a petrified horror, appears on her face. But she gradually realizes that she is mistaken and that the man who is approaching, far from spelling disaster, is the answer to her prayers. The expression of horror on her face is gradually modulated through the entire scale of feelings from hesitant doubt, anxious hope and cautious joy, right through to exultant happiness. We watch her face in close up for some twenty meters of film. We see every hint of expression around her eyes and mouth and watch them relax one by one and slowly change. For minutes on end we witness the organic development of her feelings, and nothing beyond. (Balázs 2010 [1924, 1930], 34)

This means neither the symbolic gesture nor the facial rhetoric of the actor. Instead, the technical term "twenty meters of film" relates the time of the transformation of the face directly to the spectator's perception: "We watch...; We see...; For minutes on end we witness...". Only in the image of the camera does the facial movement get collected into a unit, is it framed as a dynamic form of expression. Only in the framing by the camera does the facial movement become the entirety of an expressive movement. "Twenty meters of film", that means the time in which the transformations of the camera's image structure the process of the unfolding sensation of perception on the part of the spectator. It means the duration of a movement-image, which, for the spectator, takes place as the history of the development of his or her sensation. (Kappelhoff 2004b)

"Béla forgot the scissors!" (Eisenstein 2010 [1926]) was Eisenstein's reply to *'Visible Man'*, when the book was first published. And yet it is precisely the expressivity of film, so emphatically stressed by Balázs, that Eisenstein will come back to time and again. Eisenstein resorts to the term expressive movement – be it in view of Wundt's *Völkerpsychologie* (1900–1920), be it in view of contemporary art theory. Indeed, for Eisenstein, expressive movement refers to an almost naturally given, psycho-physical fabric between the movement represented in the film and the reaction of the spectator. What for Plessner is inherent as the temporal shape of the succession of movement, and for Balázs is framed through the duration of the camera's shot, is for Eisenstein fractured in a rhythmic sequence of isolated and thoroughly static frames. Expressive movement here itself becomes the object of the construction of movement-images (here primarily) through montage.

Montage brings these immediate reactions into an intelligible structure. It allows, according to Eisenstein, for collective thinking processes to arise from the active interweaving of sensation, of emotion. This assumes that the compositional interplay of edited movement-images synchronizes the spectators in their bodily self-sensation with the staged process of perception and thinking. This synchronization can be seen as similar to what happens in social interaction through the mutual perception of body postures and gestures (Kappelhoff 2008, Kappelhoff and Müller 2011).

In contemporary film and media theory, these classical film-theoretical concepts of Balázs and Eisenstein are present in the notions of *time-image* and *affect-image* (Bellour 2002 [2002], Deleuze 2008 [1983], Kappelhoff 1998, 2000, 2004a, b, 2006, Löffler 2004, Rodowick 1997); and, as we have illustrated earlier, they are also present in approaches to embodiment in film and media studies (Marks 2002, Robnik 2007, Shaviro 1993, Sobchack 1992, 2004).

## 9.4 Discussion

With the line of argument we have presented in this chapter, we have sought to reconstruct our understanding of cinematic expressivity, of its aesthetics as a temporal form of affecting viewers in their process of viewing a film. The historical 'role model' for such a theory of film is the expressivity of body movement. This expressivity, however, is not understood as a relation between an inner state and its externalization. The expressivity of a smile or a dismissive wave of the hand lies in their temporal unfolding, in their temporal orchestration as movement. A smile is not a static facial expression as for instance Ekman's work suggests; it involves movement. A frozen smile is a mask, not a smile. In the process of smiling or waving the hands, movement gestalts emerge that have a distinct temporal orchestration, a distinct affective quality. As expressive movements they form movement-images (movement gestalts) and they affect observers immediately. They engage with interlocutors reflexively in an interactive exchange of bodily affectivity. One can even say they only come into being in and through this interaction. Starting from the aesthetics of movement, from its expressivity and interactivity, formulates a counter position to the idea of a sender-receiver model of communication. In contrast to this code model, the anthropological model, which sees affectivity as an exchange of intensities, rhythms, and shapes in the pattern of movement, is what we consider as paradigmatic for how audiovisual compositions engage with their spectators.

Against such a theoretical frame, the film image is regarded in a similar way to a facial expression or an unfolding hand gesture in its temporal dynamics. This, and we have mentioned it already, includes all levels of the shaping of the film image as elements of a dynamic figuration of expression: acting but also color, lighting, set design, music, montage, etc. Our film analysis reconstructs this cinematic expressivity in the temporal orchestration and the interweaving of these different articulatory modalities, forming movement gestalts in terms of cinematic expressive movements. Resonating with Merleau-Ponty's formulation, cinematic expressive movements as much as body gestures *are* the affect; in short, the affect is the movement. The modulation of affect is, thus, given in the mode of experience that characterizes our seeing of films even before a represented action. It is given in the cinematic expressive movements, from which and in which metaphorical meaning emerges.

Our concept of cinematic metaphor takes these theories of expressive movement as point of reference and follows them in considering gesture and facial expression as a paradigmatic form of movement, that extends to explain how viewers engage with a film they are seeing.

# 10 The Affective Dimension: Expressive Movements and Cinematic Metaphor

Having developed the film-theoretical concept of expressive movement from the philosophical and anthropological idea of expressive movement, we are now in a position to describe more precisely its relation to cinematic metaphor. Cinematic expressive movements in film and television ground the emergence of metaphorical meaning in the temporal shapings of affect modulation: this is what we consider the aesthetic side of metaphor.

In the following, we illustrate this position further. With a case study from a Hollywood classic and a German television news feature, we describe how the aesthetic orchestration of cinematic expressive movements may form the experiential and affective grounds on which metaphor emerges. In so doing we are addressing fundamental characteristics of audiovision as a medium of expression. Parallels between film and television reside on the level of mediality, differences on the level of staging.

## 10.1 Dynamic Forces and Static Structures: JEZEBEL

William Wyler's melodrama JEZEBEL (USA 1938) stages the breakup of the traditional white society of the American South in terms of the counter-positions of dynamic forces and static structures.[1] Watching the film, viewers are affected by its staging of these antagonistic forces. They feel the dynamics as much as the static, and metaphorical meaning emerges from this affective course that merges the experience of the dynamic with the new world, the changes it brings, and the breaking up of the old established world. Viewing the film comes with an experience of the static and how it is challenged by the dynamic forces bringing about change. Over the course of the film, metaphorical meaning emerges from the flow of viewing, sensing, hearing the film: white society appears as a static structure that is challenged by dynamics of change, of breaking loose the old bonds, of destroying the old world. This dynamic is metonymically and metaphorically embodied in the persona of the main character: Bette Davis as Julie.

We begin with an analysis of four successive expressive movements that form a scene from near the beginning of the movie. In a second step of the analysis

---

1 Analysis by Hermann Kappelhoff (Kappelhoff 2004a, 210–220). The English version for this book was prepared by Cornelia Müller (Kappelhoff and Müller 2011).

https://doi.org/10.1515/9783110580785-011

we focus on the emergence of metaphoricity from the affective course staged in those four cinematic expressive movements. There we illustrate how a metaphorical axis begins to unfold from the staging of cinematic expressivity that later on develops throughout the full movie.

In this scene, a woman enters on horseback at a quick gallop, causing the waiting coachmen and grooms to scurry about looking for cover. It is the leading lady: Bette Davis in the role of the protagonist Julie. She jumps down from her horse, laying her riding crop over her shoulder. The animal is so wild that the groom, to whom she has tossed the reins, has to struggle considerably. She sweeps around, shouldering her draping skirt with the crop, strides up to the entryway of the house, turns around again in her own tracks, calling out one last directive to the groom, then enters the house. Keeping her stride, expansively spinning and turning, she crosses the entryway of the house in a straight line, past the servants, who react nervously to her inappropriate entrance, until she reaches the threshold of the ballroom and stands before her guests. Once she has crossed through the door frame, the space expands. We see the large group of guests, their loose groupings forming a diagonal line and thus creating a scale of depth. Like a continuous wave movement, the guests turn to her group by group. This has the effect that they coalesce in a coordinated movement on screen, like the slats of Venetian blinds, forming a wall encompassing Julie.

The description of Julie's short passage shows how the film metaphorically establishes its main character as a dynamic force contrasted with static structures: Julie is introduced as a character who moves nimbly, who can run and walk, spin and turn around. She is staged in strict opposition to the guests, whose arrival had been shown immediately beforehand. The radius of their movement is as restricted as Julie's is expansive – creating a metonymical opposition that evolves into a metaphorical axis for the entire film. For the spectator, this metonymical opposition is not graspable at the level of the action, but at the level of the mise-en-scène. It is only through the composition of cinematic expressive movements that we grasp this opposition as an interplay of affective efforts and attitudes which grounds metaphoricity. This becomes clear if we envision the entire course of the scene as a composition of four expressive movements. Here is a schematic sketch of the scene's overall composition (of which the above description already has touched the first two movements).

The scene's first expressive movement is initially emphasized at the level of sound; we hear only the galloping of the horse, while previously and immediately afterwards, in the interior of the house, we hear music being played. The powerful movement of the horse and its rider are contrasted with the helpless attempts of the young groom to tame this power. Julie seamlessly transfers the dynamic of the galloping rider into a complex pattern of movement including jumps, steps, and turns; as if a continual line of movement led from the galloping of the horse, through the spinning and turning woman on the stairs, and into the interior of the house (Figure 10.1).

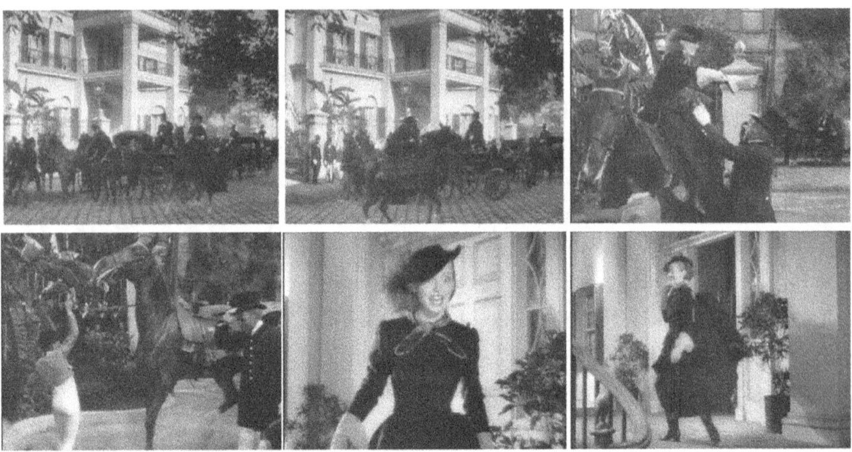

**Figure 10.1:** First cinematic expressive movement: *Julie's elegant, powerful and dynamic arrival* (JEZEBEL)

The second expressive movement, the walk through the entryway of the house, is accompanied by music (Figure 10.2). Julie's movement is now direct and focused on a target; her intensity is soon brought down. She quickly crosses the entryway, only to be stopped for the first time at the threshold to the ballroom by this wall that continuously builds up as the guests turn towards her. Their literal stopping of Julie's dynamic walk brings up the metaphorical theme of two contrasting forces: the dynamics of change encountering the stasis of the traditional society.

All levels of what is represented on the screen have become elements of the composition of a movement-image, a cinematic expressive movement. The members of the cast, in their period costumes, form a variable arrangement, turning the surfaces and depths, the plasticity of foreground, middle ground, and background of the images into parts of a dynamic composition of movement. The women's light, full-skirted dresses and the consistently black and white silhouettes of the men form the basic elements of a metaphorical space moving within itself.

The third cinematic expressive movement is introduced with a change in the music (Figure 10.3). A new pattern of movement is established, a dance with the camera and the butler, snaking through the ballroom as in an obstacle course. The positioning of the actors forms a network of lines, gaps, niches, and blocks

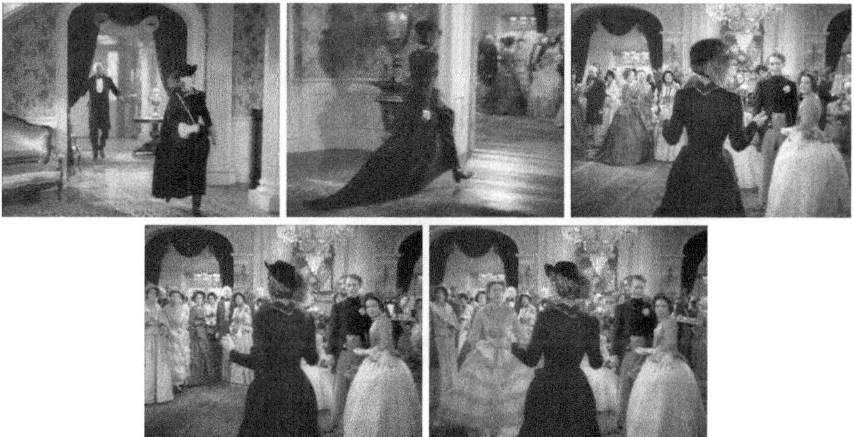

**Figure 10.2:** Second expressive movement: *Julie's focused, direct, and energetic walk into the house* (JEZEBEL)

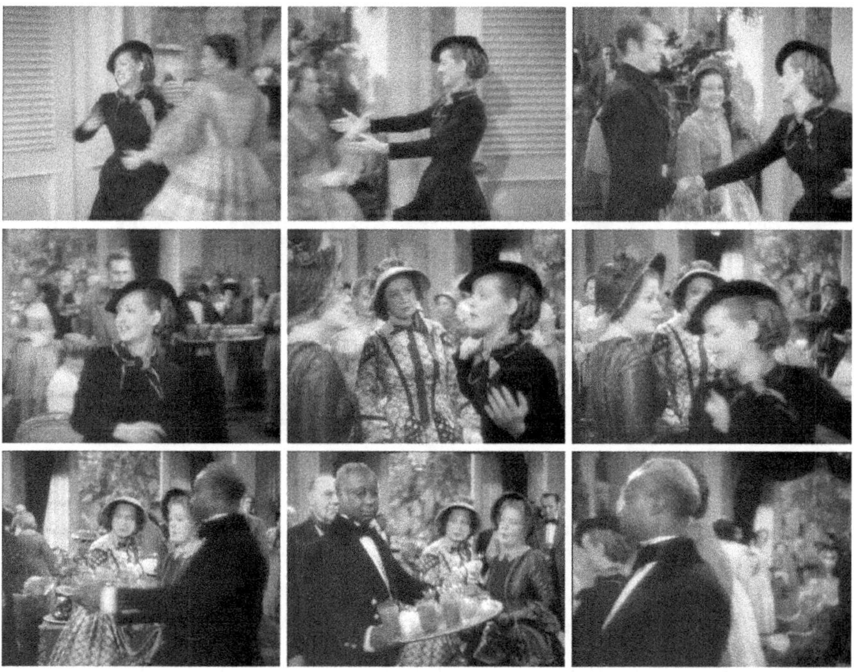

**Figure 10.3:** Third cinematic expressive movement: *Julie's dance with the camera and the butler* (JEZEBEL)

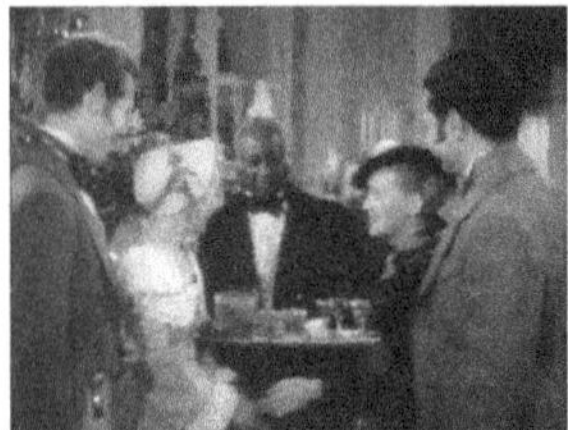 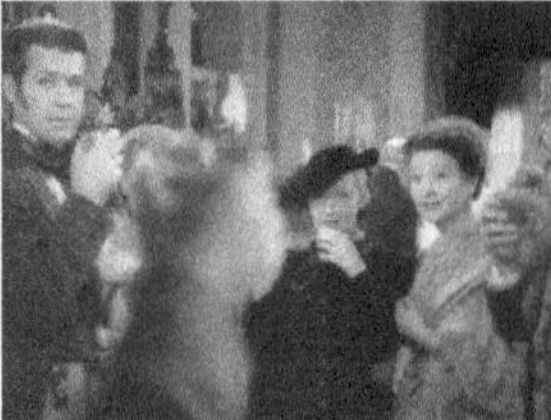 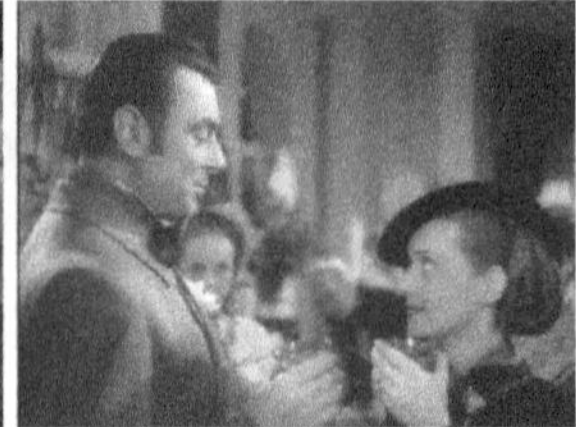

**Figure 10.4:** Fourth cinematic expressive movement: *Julie's movement is interrupted and stopped* (JEZEBEL)

through which Julie then winds her way. She alone crosses this space; holding the hem of her riding dress she greets her guests – spinning and turning from group to group as if she were following a line snaking through the room. The camera follows Julie. We see a very long sequence shot which begins when Julie enters the room and ends with the cut at the end of the scene. The interplay of the flowing camera, moving between the guests, the servants, and the protagonist is organized in a kind of choreography. In the continual reframing of the sequence shot, the movement coalesces into a movement-image in Plessner's sense, an expressive movement. Staging the affective experience of a dynamic energetic moving that is being stopped over and over again in a choreographed metaphoricity.

The scene closes with a fourth expressive movement that in its static quality sharply contrasts the dynamics of the previous ones (Figure 10.4). The impact of this unexpected counter-movement affects the composition of the image as much as the spectator. The movement ends abruptly with the sudden appearance of a hand (Figure 10.4, middle image), stretched out to counter Julie. Once again, a metaphorical stopping of dynamic by static is staged. The dance is over. The ensuing dialog shows Julie trapped in a conversation in which the movement – in ever decreasing potency – finally comes to rest.

We can describe the unfolding of this scene – and of the metaphorical meaning – as four steps of transformation, as forming an overarching movement pattern of a dynamic parcours with a rigid stop. That is to say, the overall scene is a composition of:

1. the powerful movement, connecting the rider with the powerful dynamics of her horse;
2. the continuation of this dynamic pattern in her targeted movement, up to the first stop at the threshold of the ballroom;
3. a new pattern of movement in the form of an obstacle course through the ballroom;
4. the outstretched hand and the ensuing end of movement.

For the viewers, this figuration of cinematic expressive movements becomes an obstacle course of affective mood alterations, which they literally realize as a sequence of perceptual sensations taken as bodily experience and from which metaphorical meaning emerges successively. If the camera's movement becomes wrapped up in the protagonist's dance, this could also be said of the spectator's gaze. And if the hand that is stretched out frontally to Julie brings the dance to an end that is as sudden as it is disharmonious, then the impact of this unexpected counter-movement affects the composition of the image as much as it does the spectator. This is the sense in which we understand expressive movement as a compositional form of cinematic images, whose function is to shape the affect of the spectator and from which metaphoricity emerges in the process of viewing this movie.

### An emerging metaphorical axis

The connection between the untamed power of the horse and Julie's dynamic movement forms one element of a central metaphorical axis in this scene (and notably not only of this particular scene, but of the film as a whole). It is activated verbally, when Julie speaks of the problems of training young horses a short while later. And the hand that brings the dance to an end resumes the opposition that was staged at the beginning of the scene. The helpless attempt by the young groom to control the rearing horse finds its counterpart in the man who tries to curb Julie's dance. In her riding outfit, her feathered hat, her gait, accelerated by spins and turns, Julie is – as we have said – introduced from her first appearance as the dynamic center of force, which is directly associated with the wildness of the horse. In contrast to this, the groups of women among the partygoers with their space-taking crinolines, their hats and bonnets, exhibit the world of proper femininity as a kind of plant-like immobility, while the groups of men – the slim, black-and-white silhouettes of suits, shirts, and top hats – underscore this immobility. Julie, however, rejecting the static position of the festively clad women, claims the field of movement and activity for herself. She dances to a different drummer as she snakes through the crowd, cutting against the direction of the dance. The force of the galloping horse, revolting against being led by the stable boy, and the dynamic mobility of the woman, who snakes between the statically positioned groups of partygoers like in an obstacle course, form a first metaphorical transfer. It shows us, the viewers, the desire of a woman for freedom as the dynamic-forceful struggle for unrestricted mobility. This is contoured on the one hand by the static arrangement in the room, by which the other members of the society are represented; on the other hand by the staging of the slaves and house servants.

Over the course of the whole film, it becomes highly prominent that the protagonists of the white society are defined by their status, their position in the space, and their outer stature; they are defined by the space they take up: a forest of looming top hats, a black-and-white line pressing forward, and a sea of unloading crinolines in billowy grey tones. Even the restricted radius of their motion follows an external mechanics, given in their gazes, their movements and gestures within the spatial axes as a strictly choreographed schema. In the recurring statuesque group arrangements in the space, the slightest shift of position and gait in the strictly calculated movement palpably creates an enormous tension, as if the group's formation could suddenly burst apart in the next moment. The way of staging a group, fixed in place but full of suspense, stands for the paralyzed order of a social entity that is on the verge of breaking apart from its inner paralysis. In the variation of these scenes over the course of the film, this metaphor as well will be extended and reworked.

Obviously, the metaphorical connection figures not only in the scenes that position the honor code of the Old South against the dynamic development of the modern North. This becomes even more palpable in the way in which the slaves are represented. Radically excluded from the party and from proper society, they nonetheless form the moving elements that, down to the last detail, provide for the vital necessities of a community that remains largely passive. Movement seems to belong entirely to the slaves, who drive the guests up in carriages, lead them through doors, give them their food, clothe them, and even fan the air that they breathe. And it is just this movement – the movement of the domestic slaves and carriage drivers, the pages and servant girls – that Julie participates in when she crosses through the spaces together with the servants, which the others occupy with their gazes and their positioning as a group. While the men in the society move with deliberate steps in calculated courses, Julie follows an impulse of movement that disturbs, deforms, and oversteps these courses.

These cinematic metaphors can be described from the point of view of the film viewers as a process of metaphor emergence that stretches out over the entire film. So that, seen from the end, we can reconstruct a metaphor that cannot be defined through any singular mapping. Instead, what makes up a cinematic metaphor is that it unfolds over the course of the film in ever new variations, as a dynamic process, temporally divided into segments, of ever new metaphorical transferals and shifts. This process structures the process of understanding as an interplay of optical-acoustic expressive movement, of linguistic signification in the dialog, and of the action represented.

The most important stages by which the film, over its first forty minutes, unfolds this through a dense network of intermingling metaphorical mappings from which a complex cinematic metaphor arises, can be summarized as follows: the force of the woman, her affective type, can be sensorily experienced by the spectators as the force of a young, tempestuous horse, rearing against the hand that would tame it. This force is sensed as a dancer who has no desire to join the pre-set courses of the society at the party, but who, in the end, can be sedated after all. The Southern slave society is staged as a statuesque group structure, with only one very limited kind of movement; the slaves' activity is the movement that maintains this group structure. This antagonism will be developed further in the conflict between Julie and her fiancé Pres. Since she opts during the preparations for the Olympus ball for the red dress of the prostitute rather than the white one of the virginal bride, the spectators understand the force of the woman as sexual desire. When, conversely, her fiancé arms himself with a cane to chastise Julie, he is presented as the representative of social order (acting on behalf of the family), who meets this desire with oppressive violence. (The cane is understood as instructional and constraining violence, equally used on horses, slaves, and women). This culminates within the ball scene, where Julie and Pres are shut out of the circle of the many dancing couples due to the provocation of her red dress – she is avoided like a leper. In the epidemic that marks the second part of the film, the social order unravels in an accelerating process of anarchic collapse. The epidemic, like the force of the woman, of the horses, and of the slaves, can be sensed as a nature that threatens and finally demolishes the social order.

For the viewers, a world arises over the course of the film that is characterized by the opposition between the static society, which procures and allocates positions – master, servant, man, woman, slave, citizen – and the movement of the slaves, who keep this society alive. For the viewers, the character of Julie can be experienced as a manifestation of a force that, in the bustling of the slaves, the wildness of the horse, and finally the devastating epidemic, characterizes an oppressed and excluded life within this community. The static arrangement of the white, rich Southern society, represented by the men's honor code, is contrasted with a dynamic, disorderly life, associated with the desire of a woman for freedom, the force of horses, and the activity of slaves. In Julie's mobility, like that of the slaves and the horses, the spectator experiences an excluded and oppressed vitality, to which the society maintains a parasitic relationship. The film develops its drama by allowing the catastrophe to arise out of the matrix of a world disclosed in terms of sense and affect.

The construction of (metaphorical) meaning only becomes possible by going through the successively unfolding perceptual situations. In the framings of the staged perceptual constellations, the rearing horse, the dance against the flow, the statuesque party society, and the assiduous servitude of the domestic slaves are disclosed as configurations of expressive movements that are realized on one's own body as concrete corporal-affective valence. They are realized as the perception of another person's ways of sensing as one's own bodily experience. This intertwining of embodiment and the construction of meaning, of expressive movements and the activation of metaphor, structures the time in which the film, through alternating ways of perceiving and various perspectives, reveals itself as a world that follows a logic quite of its own, that is, *a poetic logic* – and not that of our everyday life. Over the course of the film, a world of perception unfolds in which sensation and the manner of sensation cannot only be fundamentally distinguished from how they are sensed and perceived in the everyday world, but which is folded back into itself and splits. Vivian Sobchack characterizes this dimension of film in the following way:

> The film lives its perception without the volition – if within the vision – of the spectator. It visibly acts visually and, therefore, expresses and embodies intentionality in existence and at work in a world. The film is not, therefore, merely an object for perception and expression; it is also the subject of perception and expression. (Sobchack 1992, 167)

This narrative attribution of ways of perceiving and sensing is disclosed at the level of activated metaphors. Using them, the spectators carry out the attributions of their own corporeal experience of sensation on intentionally directed, individually shaped relations to the world and affective attunements: Julie's expansive drive, her resignation at failing in the face of opposition, her renewed desire when she gets her strength back; the shared emotional world when she sings with the slaves' children. The narrative that arises in the process is thoroughly and completely something other than the represented action. For there is no action disclosed to the spectators in an objectively given world, rather there is a subjective world of experience, experienced in concrete ways of perception and forms of sensation. The obstacle course that the protagonist of the film crosses unfolds this world as a subjective perceptual figuration [*subjektives Welterleben*], which is literally realized by the spectators in the seeing and hearing of their own bodies: realized as a specific way of physically-sensorily being-in-the-world. Over the duration of the film, their own perceptual experience is disclosed to them as the feeling for a world, to which the characters are subject in their bodies. It is a world that in every element is a thought-out and sensed reality. Cinematic metaphors emerge from the affective parcours that viewers go through, they emerge from experiencing the aesthetics of cinematic expressivity.

## 10.2 Sand in the Gears of the Economic Cycle: TAGESSCHAU (TV News Feature)

Compared to a classical Hollywood melodrama such as William Wyler's JEZEBEL, a short televised news report obviously does not compete in terms of the aesthetics of cinematic composition. However, when it comes to its fundamental characteristics as audiovisual media, news coverage, like feature film, is first and foremost temporally orchestrated audiovisual composition. That is to say, TV spectators also experience a temporal flow of audiovisual composition; they too go through an affective parcours, when watching a television news feature. The watching of the daily TV news show is much more an affective experience than a simple gathering of facts. Of course, one can examine television news from the point of view of rhetoric strategies, such as addressing, attracting attention, informing, convincing, and so on (Ulrich 2012), or in terms of its emotional impact (Detenber and Lang 2011, Unz 2011). We, however, consider the temporal orchestration of the cinematic staging as primary, and, with this, we place the affective experiences of the viewer center stage. Affectively, spectators may feel concerned or even shocked when watching coverage of the political situation in Afghanistan; or they may feel amused by the ways in which daily developments on the stock market are presented.

Connecting news and emotions seems counterintuitive, since journalism handbooks recommend producers of news coverage to base their work on the idea of informing the audiences rather than entertaining them (Harcup 2009). At the same time, media research of mass communication has recurrently highlighted the emotional implications of news coverage (Milburn and McGrail 1992, Unz, Schwab, and Winterhoff-Spurk 2008, Uribe and Gunter 2007, Winterhoff-Spurk 1998). Research on the relationship of image and speech in television news (see Holly 2010 for a linguistic perspective) has, however, not analyzed audiovisual images in their temporal orchestration. As a consequence, the fundamental affective character of news that resides specifically in the temporal staging escaped scholarly attention. This means, that techniques of cinematic staging are also applied in TV news (e.g., camera movement, montage, sound etc.), and are perceived and realized by spectators as cinematic expressive movements, i.e., as affective experiences that shape their feelings (Kappelhoff and Bakels 2011). Such an aesthetic modulation of an essentially affective temporal course goes hand in hand with the emergence of metaphorical meaning. In other words: cinematic metaphors may emerge also in television news in a perceptual process that engages the viewer affectively.

The first thirteen seconds of a German television newscast TAGESSCHAU, reporting on the financial crisis of 2008[2], form such a cinematic expressive movement.[3] Specifically through a montage of three shots, a temporal course is

---

2 TAGESSCHAU, ARD, 20.10.2008, 8:00–8:15 pm.

3 The analysis was developed in the context of the research project "Multimodal Metaphor and Expressive Movement" and has been further worked on within the Cinepoetics' research focus 'Metaphor – Film Images, Cinematic Thinking, and Cognition' by Cornelia Müller (cf. also Kappelhoff and Greifenstein 2016, Schmitt, Greifenstein, and Kappelhoff 2014).

established that evokes a metaphorical transition from a powerful smooth movement to a heavy drifting mass out of control (Figure 10.5). In the first close up shot, viewers see pistons of a huge engine moving up and down smoothly. The second shot changes in framing to a medium distance and slower movement, showing a worker in an engine room, wiping the tubes of a large engine with a cloth. In the third shot, again changing the framing to a medium long shot and a slow camera movement away from the ship, underlines the heaviness and slow movement of the ship. Viewers see how a big container ship drifts slowly to the side, generating a sense of a massive object drifting out of control. With this staging, a sensation of something powerful, smoothly running on its own, is gradually transformed into something that needs care, that is hard to keep under control, a massive object drifting on its own whose direction, once in motion, is extremely difficult to change. Note that this overall slowing down is not a movement of objects or persons depicted in a single shot, but a movement that is articulated aesthetically through the rhythm of the montage.

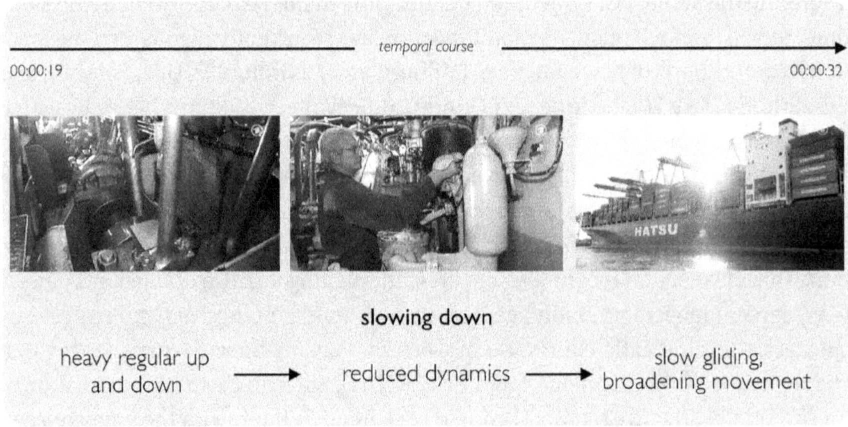


**Figure 10.5:** Cinematic expressive movement: *slowing down* (TAGESSCHAU, 20 October 2008)

In its dynamic unfolding, the audiovisual staging (specifically camera movement and montage) creates this course of changing movement patterns and forms an affective parcours, an experiencing of an intense and heavy spiraling up-and-down movement that transforms into a more restricted movement and turns finally into a slow, gliding, broadening horizontal movement.

Viewing this cinematic expressive movement of only 13 seconds in length, creates an affective ground for the voice-over commentary with which the metaphor vehicles in speech resonate. Discussing the probable impact of the financial crisis of

2008 on the German economy, the voice-over commentary uses several verbal metaphors (metaphor vehicles according to Cameron and Maslen 2010 are highlighted in the following transcript through italics [and vice versa in the German original]):

> The economic *cycle* is not *running as smoothly* as it has been anymore; and the financial crisis may soon continue *to throw sand in the gears*. The German economy expects a significant *weakening* next year. Therefore the federal government wants *to steer in the opposite direction*.
>
> [*Die Konjunktur* läuft nicht mehr wie geschmiert, *und die Finanzmarktkrise könnte bald weiteren* Sand ins Getriebe streuen. *Die deutsche Wirtschaft rechnet mit einer deutlichen* Abschwächung *im nächsten Jahr. Deshalb will die Bundesregierung* gegensteuern.]

The succession of metaphor vehicles in the voice-over begins with an economic cycle that does not "run as smoothly" anymore, continues with the financial crisis that "throw(s) sand in the gears (of the German economy)", moves on to the German economy expecting "a significant weakening", and concludes with a federal government wanting "to steer (German economy) in the opposite direction". This trajectory of metaphor vehicles is paralleled by the slowing down pattern of the expressive movement described above and shown in Figure 10.6.

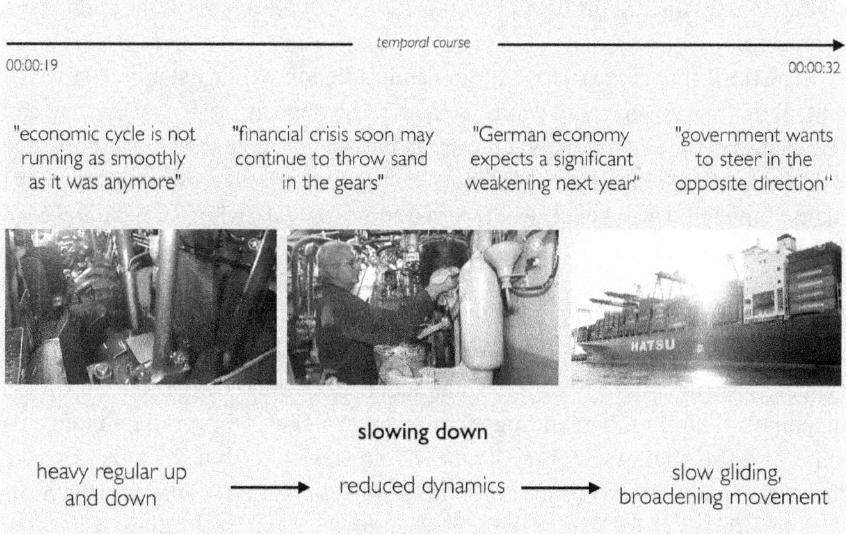


**Figure 10.6**: Cinematic expressive movement interacting with metaphors in voice-over commentary (TAGESSCHAU, 20 October 2008)

Let us consider the interaction between the staging and the metaphorical meaning in the voice-over: what viewers see, when they hear "The economic cycle is not running as smoothly as it was anymore", are gleaming, well-oiled, smoothly running pistons, moving powerfully up and down. The smoothly running pistons of a huge engine appear to go well with the idiomatic expression ("running as smoothly"). In fact, however, this first shot stages an experiential contrast or paradox including a double negation: what is said is synchronized ('running smoothly' is presented verbally and visually), while the negating verbal statement ("is not running") is simultaneously countered by the visual image (running).

The next shot repeats this staging pattern. On the one hand, we hear the commentator saying: "the financial crisis soon may continue to throw sand in the gears" (of the German economy) and, on the other hand, we see a man in an overall standing in a large engine room doing maintenance work, as he is cautiously wiping a handle, and in the background we see a perfectly running smaller single piston. Again, the verbal metaphorical meaning contrasts with the sensorily induced audio: "Throwing sand in the gears" contrasts with the cleaning and a piston whose functions are not disturbed at all.

What is visually depicted (machines in motion, maintenance man in engine room) highlights metaphoricity. The coverage does not address the engineer as a person; it thematizes abstract agents such as "the economic cycle" or "the financial crisis". These noun phrases are not only grammatical subjects of the verbal phrases but are the overall protagonists: they are agents in the audiovisual composition.

The third shot comes with a further contradiction. While listening to the next metaphor, "the government wants to steer in the opposite direction", a long container ship is shown. Cadrage and camera movement stage the ship as a drifting, heavy mass. The ship seems to drift to the right, countering the camera's movement to the left. Once again, what we see contrasts with what we hear and highlights metaphoricity.

The verbal vehicles are part of an emergent metaphorical scenario unfolding in the (temporal) form of a cinematic expressive movement, which comes into being only in the process of seeing and hearing the news. Both verbal and visual articulations dynamically depict a nautical setting that is experienced through machines in motion, demanding maintenance to keep on running, to move the ship. And the ship, its engine, engineer, and steersman link with the topics of the verbal metaphors: 'economy', 'financial crisis', and 'government'. Along with this fluent unfolding of the scenario, an economic and political situation emerges that is experienced and understood as a nautical one and as a conflicting one.

Starting from smooth dynamics which is increasingly slowed down, the pattern of the cinematic movement interweaves with the temporal succession of the threefold contradiction. In going through the process of viewing and listening to this newscast, the complex issue of German economy is connected with a concrete contradictory scenario and a bodily experience of slowing down and drifting, creating a feeling of increasing uncertainty (of control over the economy) and a cinematic metaphor (Figure 10.7).

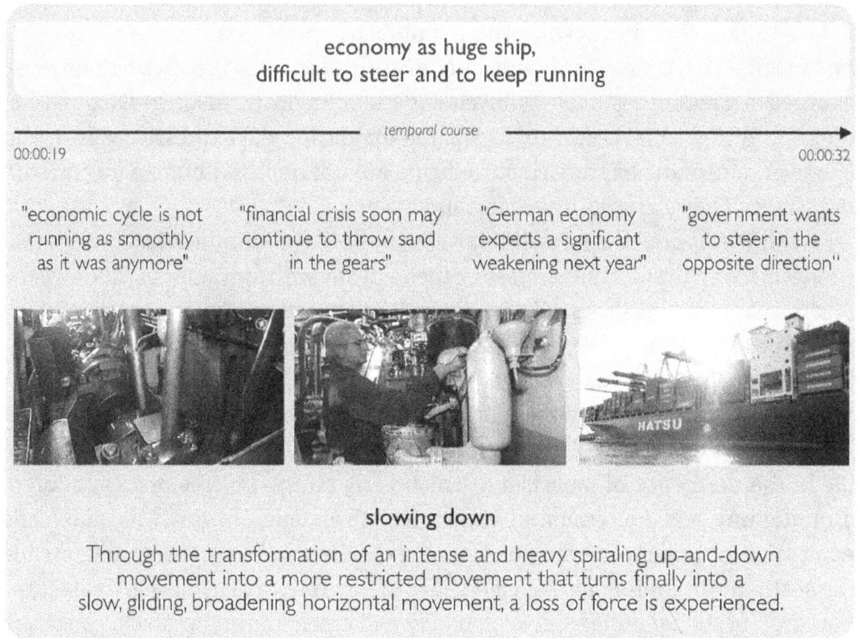


**Figure 10.7**: Emergence of a cinematic metaphor from a cinematic expressive movement (TAGESSCHAU, 20 October 2008)

The overall temporal orchestration of the expressive movement (across the three shots) and its quality of slowing down, or decreasing smoothness and control, goes hand in hand with an experience of alignment and contradiction on the level of the verbal metaphorical vehicles and their metaphorical visualizations. In this process, the words of the voice-over become a concrete affective experience: a feeling of worry concerning the potentially threatening effects of the financial crisis on Germany's economy emerges from the course of the expressive movement in which all the articulatory modalities merge to form a movement-image. It is in this sense that the metaphors in speech are grounded in the affective experiences of expressive movements. Cinematic metaphor emerges in the process of seeing, hearing, feeling, and sensing the temporal interweaving of all the articulatory modalities.

## Résumé

This part of the book has introduced the idea that metaphorical meaning in audiovisual media as well as in bodily gestures is grounded in the affective experiences of expressive movements. Affectivity is held to be incorporated in the embodied experiences of movement qualities. Metaphoricity emerges in speech and gesture in face-to-face encounters within an interaffective process which is similar to the process in which spectators of film or television engage in. Theories on film as an expressive medium assume – as psychological or linguistic theories of expression do – bodily and facial gesture to be a paradigmatic form of expressive movement. However, cinematic expressive movements are not depicted human gestures on the screen. They are units of moving audiovision.

With the notion of expressive movement, we have introduced a concept that connects the analysis of human gesture theoretically with film analysis. Audiovisual media share with gestures a basic property: they are movement gestalts which modulate affective experiences interactively. In both cases, affectivity is congruent with the qualities of the movements themselves.

Viewing a film or a news report is first and foremost an affective engagement with cinematic images. And the affective quality of cinematic images is graspable in the aesthetics of movement, which is manifested in the orchestration of an unfolding and succession of expressive movements. In this way, cinematic expressive movements modulate affective experiences of the viewers and provide the aesthetic grounding for the emergence of metaphorical meaning. Against the backdrop of such parallels between bodily and cinematic expressivity, conceived already in classical film theory, we have then argued that expressive movements modulate affective experiences in an immediate process of perceiving and that, in this process, metaphorical meaning emerges that is 'experientially based' in the most literal sense of the word.

It is noteworthy that such a concept of expressive movement resonates with contemporary embodiment theories. Shaun Gallagher and Dan Zahavi, for instance, also underline the intrinsic connection between expressive body movement and affective experience:

> Affective and emotional states are not simply qualities of subjective experience; rather, they are given in expressive phenomena, i.e. they are expressed in bodily gestures and actions, and they thereby become visible to others. (Gallagher and Zahavi 2007, 182)

What Gallagher and Zahavi refer to is the idea of expression as an intersubjective phenomenon, in which affective experiences are synchronized between co-participants through visible and audible forms of movement. They highlight the link between motion and emotion, respectively between aesthetic forms and affective responses (Gallagher 2008, Johnson 2007, Sheets-Johnstone 2008, Stern 2010).

It is in such a sense that we conceive of films as moving their spectators and more specifically of cinematic expressive movements as shaping the affective experiences of spectators. Cinematic expressive movements in film and television are aesthetic forms of addressing the spectators' perceptions. The ways in which a film or a news feature communicates with its audience is not in the first place a matter of narrated stories. The communicative act between spectators and the unfolding of audiovisual images resides on a more basic level: that of performed and perceived movements. Cinematic expressive movement can be understood as the aesthetic dimension of movement, addressing and shaping the way spectators feel. When we speak of expression or expressive movements, however, we do not mean that the director expresses his or her emotional states. Instead the film itself performs acts of expressivity that only come into being in a spectator experiencing the film over time.

The parallel between gestural and cinematic forms of expressivity is what we consider as paramount for the analysis and theorizing of cinematic metaphor (and also for metaphor in gesture and speech). Against the background of our exposition of expressive movements in conversational gestures and the historical outline of the film-theoretical concept as an aesthetic category, we have thus described how metaphor in films and in television emerge from the process of being affected by the orchestration of expressive movement gestalts over the course of a film. This kind of affective experience is central for our understanding of metaphor in audiovision: only when metaphoricity is grounded in this media-specific perceptual experience, can we speak of cinematic metaphors. Cinematic metaphors emerge in a process of affective perception of cinematic expressive movements. They are emergent, dynamic, temporally structured and grounded in the rhythms, intensities and other affective qualities of cinematic expressivity.

# Part IV: Temporality of Cinematic Metaphor: Intertwined Dynamics on Micro and Macro Levels

# Introduction

Cinematic metaphor is inherently temporal and its temporality affects all levels of cinematic staging: from small units of cinematic expressivity to the flow of an entire film. Moreover, it relates to film images as movement-images and thus emphasizes temporality as a fundamental characteristic of audiovisuality. In countering the idea of audiovisual media as a series of discrete depictions of action characterized as a narrative, as depicting 'contents that move', cinematic metaphor develops a theoretical perspective that starts from temporality as a core aspect of the poiesis of film-viewing.

The temporal dynamics of an unfolding film produces a specific mode of cinematic perception which characterizes all audiovisual forms, including film, television news, music videos, and political campaign commercials. Film-viewing involves an interactive dynamics which we have described as the viewer's entanglement with the audiovisual movement-image and as a specific form of dynamic embodiment, characterized in a phenomenological perspective as being reflexive, intersubjective, and temporal. Analyses from multimodal face-to-face interactions (for instance, the ballet class in Chapter 6 and the group discussion in Chapter 9) have shown that such an understanding of embodiment concerns a fundamental characteristic of human meaning-making more generally. Being entangled with the dynamics of speakers' body movements and/or audiovisual movement-images implies sharing their expressive quality through the body, experiencing them affectively (cf. Part II). These dynamic embodied experiences provide the ground for the emergence of figurative meaning in the process of multimodal interaction as well as of film-viewing (cf. Part I, Chapters 5, 6; Part II). In short, cinematic metaphor is always entangled with the dynamics of interaffective processes. In this light, temporality appears as common thread, as fundamental characteristic of face-to-face as well as of cinematic meaning-making, and it is a theme that runs through the entire book. None of the theoretical facets that characterize the poiesis of film-viewing can be conceived without recourse to the temporal structure of cinematic images, of audiovisual media and embodied experience in general.

Claiming that cinematic metaphor is temporal, then, is a rather obvious theoretical consequence of the temporality of audiovisual media more generally; however, such a position also resonates with linguistic positions on the dynamics of metaphorical meaning. Cameron's discourse dynamics approach to metaphor or Müller's dynamic view of metaphors both advocate the inherently dynamic, fluid, always changing threads of metaphoricity that evolve along with speaking and gesturing in interaction (Cameron 2010, Müller 2008a, 2017). Such a position challenges the idea of metaphors as static, fixed entities and advocates a

https://doi.org/10.1515/9783110580785-partIV

concept of metaphor as dynamic, procedural, and bound to the ongoing flow of talking and gesturing, of reflexive attending, of watching and listening. More generally speaking, metaphors are considered to go hand in hand with the temporal dynamics of meaning-making (cf. also Jensen 2017b). They emerge in processes of making sense, of striving for intersubjectivity, be it in face-to-face interaction or in the viewer's interaction with a film, a video-clip, or a television broadcast (Kappelhoff and Müller 2011).

This last part of the book places the dynamics, the temporality of cinematic metaphor center stage. It particularly highlights how temporal dynamics intertwine on different time-scales, how metaphors emerge on micro levels, how they successively unfold and develop, and how metaphorical scenarios emerge that sometimes evolve into metaphorical themes running through a feature film, a political report in television, or the face-to-face interaction in a tango workshop.

# 11 Emerging Metaphorical Scenarios

The detailed account of the temporality of cinematic metaphor begins with the interface between a micro level of emergent metaphoricity (body movement and speech, cinematic expressive movement) and unfolding metaphorical scenarios on a meso level of temporal orchestration. Two case studies document the commonality between the dynamics of discourse and the temporality of audiovisual images, and suggest that emergent metaphorical scenarios as forms of meaning-making (Müller 2008a) apply to processes of multimodal face-to-face interaction as well as to the cinematic mode of perceiving.

## 11.1 Face-to-Face Interaction: Tango Lesson

Observations that motivated this chapter were made during a larger research project on languaging of body movement that was driven by the question of how experts in teaching body movement make use of metaphors in their language and in their gestures.[1] Major insights were that new metaphors emerge from the interactive process of working out a shared understanding (of given subject matter) during dance classes, and that those metaphorical meanings are not isolated elements that are thrown in now and then in the discourse, but instead often initiate interactive processes of metaphorical meaning-making that unfold complete metaphorical scenarios and stories. Such scenarios typically develop in core moments of the workshops, while at the same time unfolding to a common metaphorical thread that ties together guiding themes of a workshop.

In fact, the following analysis reveals that a whole tango lesson can be described as successive and interlinked evolution of two metaphorical scenarios.[2]

---

1 The research was supported by a grant from the German Ministry of Education. The interdisciplinary project connected psychological (Sabine Koch), psychiatric, philosophical (Thomas Fuchs) and linguistic perspectives (Cornelia Müller, Silva H. Ladewig) on 'Movement and Dance' (cf. Kolter et al. 2012). The linguistic subproject focused on the 'languaging of body-movement'.

2 Analysis by Cornelia Müller, Silva H. Ladewig, and Lena Hotze (Müller & Ladewig 2013). The version for this book was prepared by Cornelia Müller. This data was gathered for the research project "Body Language of Movement and Dance: Emergence of Meaning, 'Languageing' and Therapeutical Application" and particularly for the sub-project 'languaging of body-movement' (Cornelia Müller and Silva H. Ladewig). Workshops on 'Balance and Posture', 'Walking and Turning' and 'Sharing Dance Space' were held in four different dance traditions: ballet, Laban movement studies, ballroom waltz, tango argentino. The settings for the workshops was fixed: They begin with warming up, then explaining and practicing alternate for an hour. After that the

https://doi.org/10.1515/9783110580785-012

Although the tone is set by the teacher and his ideas about how a balanced posture is best achieved and maintained for a tango dancer, it is only the shared engagement in practices that brings the metaphors about. The problems that he assumes and observes in the training of his dance students not only attract special attention from the teacher but trigger the creative recourse to metaphorical conceptualizations and unfolding scenarios in order to capture problems and overcome them. This recalls the functionality of metaphors in the process of creating mutual understanding raised earlier and of Lynne Cameron's observation from her work on post-conflict reconciliation discourse in the Northern Irish context. Metaphors often appear as a response to not-understanding and are an attempt to overcome it by 'building a bridge' towards (partial) understanding (Cameron 2011).

### Experiencing balanced posture as spatial axis

The lesson begins with what the teacher characterizes as a small exercise on balance, necessary to develop a feeling for a balanced posture and the specific way of walking in Argentine tango. In this exercise, dancers' attention is moved to finding their anchoring in the center by standing upright and swaying forward and backward, left and right, standing on both feet or on one foot. The teacher underlines that a sudden move of the arms in order to compensate a potential state of imbalance during the exercise is not a problem because "You should first of all experience it" [*Ihr sollt ja vor allem die Erfahrung machen*]. Saying so, he makes clear that it is the experience of what balance is and how it feels that is center stage here. In this process, the bodies successively become the center of a coordinate system with an imagined axis running through the body, through the pelvis anchoring the dancers in the ground ("I take the pelvis so to speak as a reference point for where front is" [*Ich nehm mal das Becken sozusagen als Referenzpunkt für wo vorne ist*]). Notably without ever explicitly saying something like 'imagine your body is anchored in a coordinate system', this idea emerges as the teacher pursues and describes his (and also the students') movement experiences in words and in descriptive hand gestures (e.g., "back to the middle" [*wieder bis in die Mitte*]; "a bit forwards" [*bisschen bis nach vorne*]; "backwards but get not into an insecure zone" [*nach hinten, aber ohne in die kritische Region zu kommen*]; "without getting into the extreme" [*ohne in das Extrem zu kommen*] (Figure 11.2, 188). By performing swaying movements along transversal (left-right) and sagittal (front-back) axes to the point where it is possible without falling over,

experiences with the first hour are discussed in the group. Then class resumes again and explaining & practicing alternate. At the end of the workshops, participants were interviewed individually.

the dancers' bodies become the center of a three-dimensional coordinate system (Figure 11.1). The distinction of sagittal, transversal, and vertical axes and planes is central to analyses of body movement, here specifically developed in Laban Movement Studies (Bartenieff and Lewis 1980, Hackney 2002, Laban 1966). Figure 11.1 shows these spatial dimensions of the human body in movement.

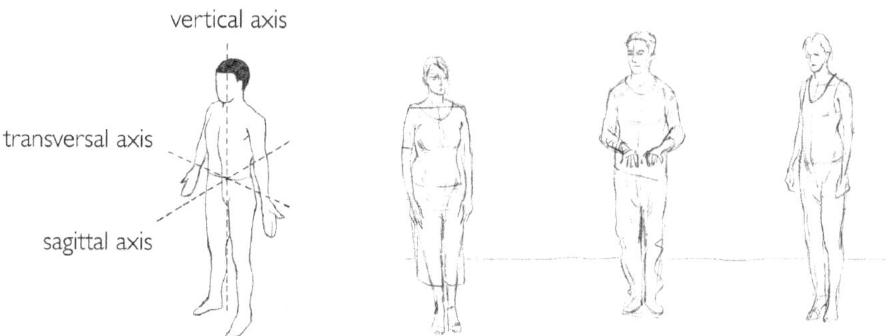


**Figure 11.1:** Moving along the three axes of the moving body (sagittal, transverse, vertical) in a tango class

With the 'swaying body' exercises the teacher guides the dancers towards feeling the center of their own bodily coordinate system. He raises the bodily awareness of their respective movement center and in doing so, a body-metaphor emerges which is never explicitly mentioned. A feeling of being anchored in the center of one's own moving body is the beginning of an emerging feeling for a balanced posture (Figure 11.2).

### Experiencing balanced posture in walking

The 'coordinate system' metaphor emerges from the subjective experiences of standing in an upright posture, feeling the weight of the body's center above the feet (on the vertical axis) and softly swaying backward, forward, sideward along the sagittal and the transversal axes. Once the metaphorical feeling of the body as being placed within this spatial coordinate system and anchored firmly in the ground, once a feeling for balance and posture is established, the next step in the class is introduced. It concerns bringing the body into motion. What is at stake now is the transfer from standing with a balanced posture to walking with a balanced posture. This new topic comes with the metaphorical idea of a 'heavy leg'. It enriches the just established metaphorical idea of a balanced body posture

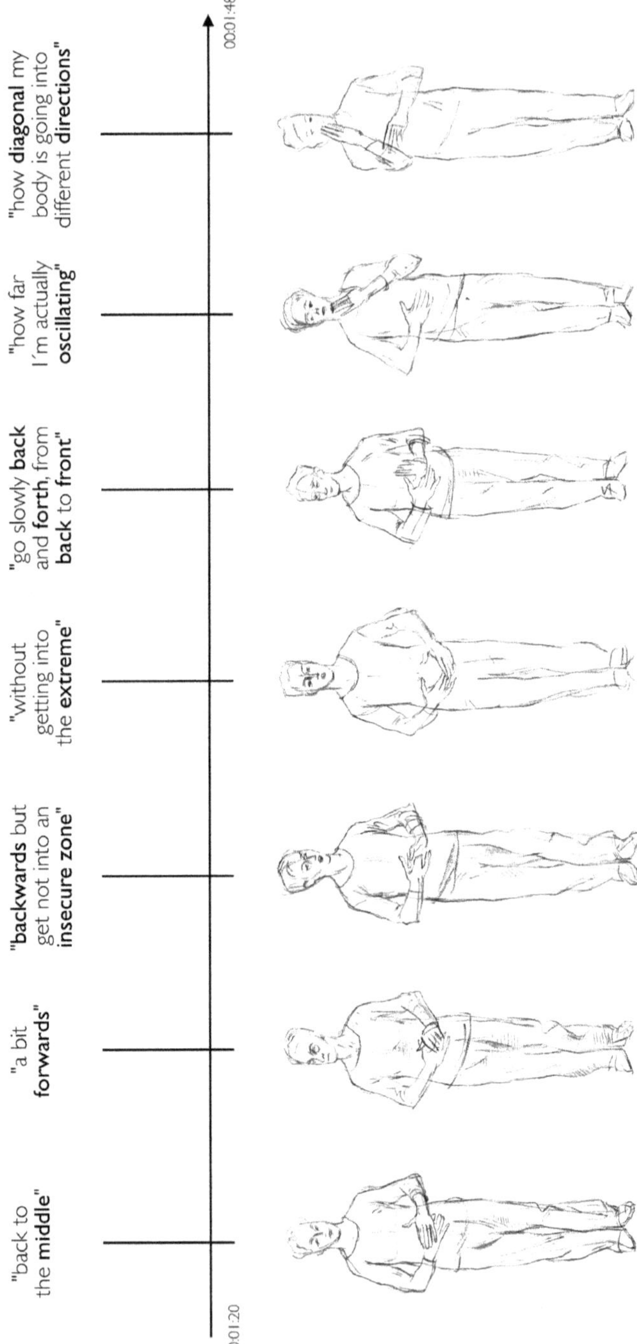


**Figure 11.2:** Balance and posture: establishing a feeling for a stable center of dancer's spatial movement system in a tango class

as firmly grounded axes of the coordinate system by setting the body as vertical axis in motion. How to stay anchored [*verankert*] in the ground and maintaining the balanced posture while walking, i.e., while shifting weight from one foot to another? How is it possible to stay balanced when walking (and eventually also turning)? In short, how to dance tango and stay balanced even when standing on one leg? The answer connects with the metaphorical idea of 'anchoring' the axis firmly in the ground: stability of the vertical axis evolves from the inertia of the leg stretched out behind, creating a feeling of heaviness (Müller and Ladewig 2013). Clearly, the long, free leg is not heavier than the other leg. But we can imagine it to be heavy, and it is this subjective experience that the dance instructor is working to invoke in his students. With a couple of exercises, he engages the students in playfully and cautiously experiencing their vertical and sagittal axis in motion, stabilized by a heavy leg.

At some point in this practicing sequence, the teacher interrupts a dance couple and begins to describe a problem he has observed: one of the dancers – instead of leaving a stretched leg behind – bends his knee too early. This observation makes clear that the idea of the stretched out heavy leg has not yet 'entered' the body of the dancer. In order to make clear what he considers to be 'wrong', the teacher imitates the walking with the knee bent while explaining that the student moves his full body weight (i.e., his axis) too early to the standing leg. The student responds with several weak 'okays' pronounced with a questioning intonational contour, which motivates the instructor to explain the 'lagging behind' principle of the 'heavy' leg with a story. Before, however, embarking on the story, he mentions that he will explain the same thing to the whole group later on. In this way, he transforms the problem of the dancer into a model relevant for all students. Here is where the new metaphorical scenario fully comes into being.

The instructor embarks on a long and vivid storytelling that at first seems far-fetched. He describes how he was always puzzled by how a ship's anchor works, how the anchor reaches the sea bed in very deep waters, and how to free an anchor that is stuck in rocks. And indeed, at first this conversational move towards seafaring seems really out of place in a dancing lesson and his two interlocutors appear rather puzzled, not sure why they have to listen to this kind of story. Subsequently, however, they understand that the story unfolds an experiential realm, explicitly mentioned by the verbal metaphor 'anchoring' that addresses precisely the problem just observed: the free leg that is bent too early in the step. The realm of embodied experiences that the teacher opens up for his interlocutors is the principle of anchoring a ship, transferred to the topic of maintaining balance in an Argentine tango style of walking. In a very vivid manner and by integrating a series of hand and full body gestures, he unfolds a metaphorical scenario that serves to illustrate metaphorically the principle of the heavy, stretched and lagging behind leg so characteristic of Argentine tango and so essential to stay balanced in walking while moving the body axes smoothly from one standing leg to another one. In this process, the metaphorical scenario that previously established the dancer's vertical (and sagittal) axes in a stable center of a spatial coordinate system connects with a different metaphorical scenario: the anchoring principle as a model for the smooth shifting of the dancer's axis in walking (Figure 11.3)[3].

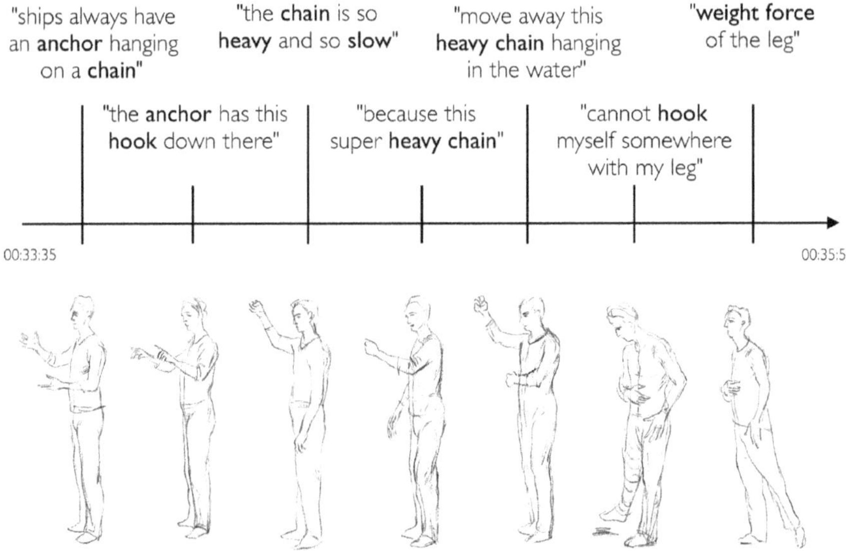


**Figure 11.3**: Balance and walking: an emerging metaphorical scenario in a tango class[4]

Further singular metaphorical expressions appear, such as the starting block of a sprinter for the pushing impulse of the step that becomes the long leg, or the idea of badly balanced "bodies as swaying Finnish fir trees" [*dann schwanken die Körper wie finnische Fichten*], but these are not developed into a scenario.

3 For further explanation of the figure see "Appendix: Cinematic Metaphor – A methodological outline", Section A.3.2.

4 [*Schiffe ham ja immer nen Anker, der an ner Kette hängt*]; [*der Anker hat doch unten diesen Haken*]; [*die Kette ist so schwer und so träge*]; [*weil diese superschwere Kette*]; [*diese im Wasser hängende, schwere Kette wegzubewegen*]; [*mich natürlich nicht mit dem Bein irgendwo unterhaken*]; [*Gewichtskraft des Beines*].

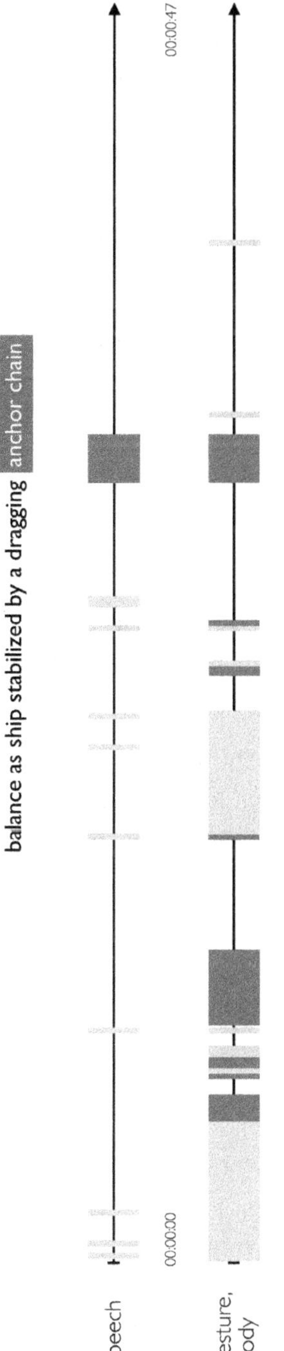


**Figure 11.4:** Two interwoven metaphorical scenarios developing over time in a tango class

On the other hand, the coordinate system and the anchoring metaphors both develop into experiential metaphorical realms. They become the experienced source domains of metaphors for finding a balanced posture and for maintaining balance in an Argentine style of dancing.

Figure 11.4[5] illustrates how the two metaphorical scenarios evolve over time: how the coordinate system structures the beginning of the lesson, how the anchoring system then co-occurs, how they intertwine and how the anchoring scenario emerges as a pattern in the second half of the workshop.

The two emerging metaphorical scenarios respond to the local problems of the dance students. They are dynamically emerging forms, temporally orchestrating a meso level of shared metaphorical meaning-making. As we see in the next section, a similar temporal structure of metaphorical meaning-making may emerge from processes of film-viewing.

## 11.2 Audiovisual Perception: SAT1 NACHRICHTEN (TV News Feature)

In October 2008, German private channel Sat1 broadcasted a news report on the deferred flotation of Deutsche Bahn in view of the then global financial crisis. It specifically raised the question of whether the postponement was actually a symptom of the crisis.[6]

The news feature opens with an introduction read by a presenter (Figure 11.5). The teaser image in the background already presents the metaphorical idea that will unfold as scenario over the course of the report. It shows a red stock market graph steeply declining and three bankers in front of it. The men, too, are visually arranged in a declining way. Moreover, one of them points his raised hand steeply downwards in a prominently positioned gesture, echoing the shape of the declining stock market graph in the background of the image (Figure 11.5). These three images of downwardness strongly foreground the idea of a steep decline as an experiential realm for the financial and economic crisis, and it is taken up in the opening sequence of the feature dealing with the postponed stock market launch of the Deutsche Bahn.

5 For further explanation of the figure see "Appendix: Cinematic Metaphor – A methodological outline", Section A.3.2.

6 The analysis was developed in the context of the research project 'Multimodal Metaphor and Expressive Movement' and further worked on within the Cinepoetics' research focus 'Metaphor – Film Images, Cinematic Thinking, and Cognition' by Dorothea Horst. Cornelia Müller and Dorothea Horst prepared the version for this book.

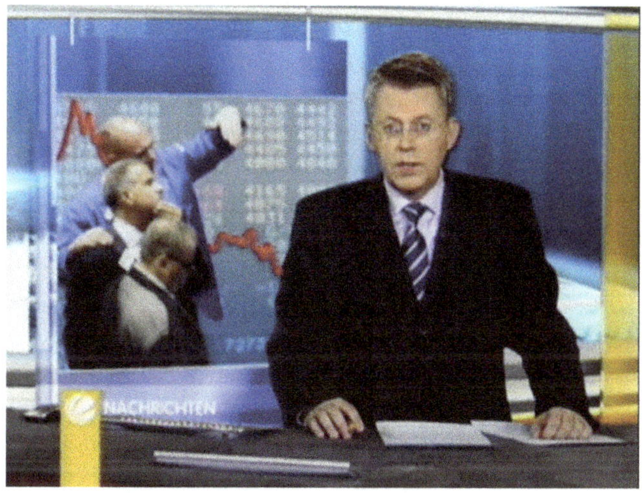


**Figure 11.5:** Teaser image activating the 'downwards' framing metaphor domain for the report (SAT1 NACHRICHTEN, 9 October 2008)

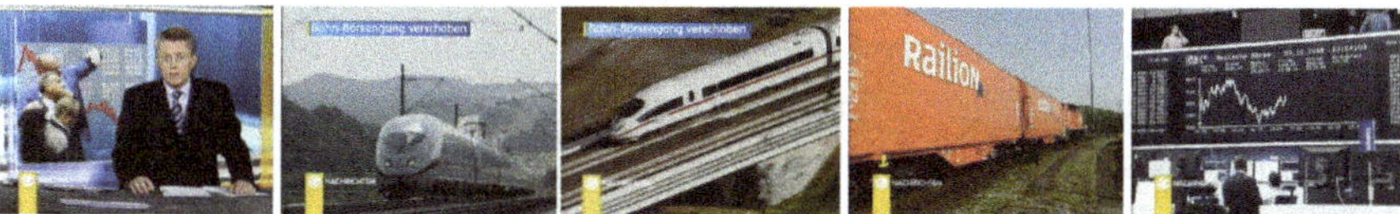


**Figure 11.6:** Disharmonious, unbalanced, tense, turbulent: a feeling of crisis is unfolding (SAT1 NACHRICHTEN, 9 October 2008)

The news feature begins with a close succession of shots with different trains of Deutsche Bahn criss-crossing the image-field. The first one shows a dynamic high-speed train which crosses the image from right to left in upward orientation. The next shot shows another high-speed train, but now it is filmed with a wide angle shot, rushing through the image from right to left in a downward orientation. The next cut, brings in yet another high-speed train and once again the direction of the train changes: now it moves from left to right in a slightly upward orientation. Note, that the three trains are all staged as rapidly moving and crossing in different directions. This is countered with the next shot in which this dynamics is contrasted with a slow goods train, red in color, which is braking and thus bringing the dynamics to a halt.

This audiovisual composition stages an expression of a disharmonious, unbalanced and rather tense dynamics, a turbulent change of directions that comes with an affective quality connecting with the feelings of disorientation, tension, even anxiety of a situation. In short, these felt qualities develop a feeling for the crisis which comes into view after the shot with the cargo train in the form of a board displaying the stock market graph moving up and down in steep angles (Figure 11.6). The imagery established through the teaser image in the introduction of the report is thus visually taken up and affectively enriched through the described sequence of unbalanced and turbulent dynamics. In other words, the cinematic experience of disorientation and tension elaborates the news feature's metaphorical topic, i.e., the crisis, over the first 16 seconds.

This temporal elaboration plays out verbally, too. While the different trains are shown, the voice-over comments that Deutsche Bahn wanted to "'roll' public" by the end of the month [*Ende des Monats wollte die Bahn an die Börse rollen*], i.e., Deutsche Bahn wanted to float on the stock exchange. The rolling trains function as a metonymy for Deutsche Bahn and they embody an experiential realm that connects with "rolling public" [*an die Börse rollen*] (a new mixed metaphor in German; see Gibbs 2016a, Müller 2008a, 2016b). In doing this, the trains activate the verbally expressed 'rolling' as a sensory-motor experience, and create a 'waking' metaphor (cf. Müller 2008a, 2017) that makes the enterprise's agenda of floating on the stock exchange into a vivid idea.

At the same time, however, this cinematic metaphor is contradictory: while the verbal metaphorical expression explicitly mentions a clear goal of the rolling movement ("roll public", i.e., to the stock market), what we see are trains moving in different directions. They create a counter-image to a united, clearly directed, smooth movement – of a metaphorical scenario in which the flotation of Deutsche Bahn would be experienced as moving ahead without problems. Instead, viewers experience the opposite: trains are not passing by smoothly, their entering the image from various steep angles expresses disharmony, contradiction, the opposite of a united clearly directed path towards the future as a public company. In this way, and without being ever explicitly expressed (as in the example of the tango workshop), a metaphorical scenario emerges over time and from the process of perceiving this temporally extended interplay between verbal and audiovisual imagery as an embodied experiential flow. In this way, the consequences of the financial crisis become tangible as turbulent movement throwing economic plans off course.

Such an audiovisual staging of the activation of verbal metaphorical expressions is as temporally orchestrated as the sensory qualities of cinematic expressive movements are. In fact, activated metaphoricity is an inseparable element of cinematic expressivity. It develops over the time of attending to the news feature and it is structured by this affective experience. What holds for cinematic metaphors, applies to metaphorical scenarios as well. They are 'done' by the spectators in an embodied process of creating an as-if perceptual scenario. It is the audiovisual composition that provides the experiential basis for single metaphors (e.g., the waking metaphor of “rolling public”) as well as for the metaphorical scenario (e.g., the crisis as a turbulent movement). As viewers are watching the news feature, they feel the affective qualities as a temporal parcours of embodied experiences as much as the dancers attending the tango workshop feel being balanced and losing balance. Based on these felt bodily experiences, the metaphorical scenarios unfold in film viewers’ meaning-making just as they do for participants in a face-to-face interaction.

# 12 Intertwining Metaphorical Themes in a TV News Feature: REPORT MAINZ

The temporal orchestration of a cinematic metaphor may not only run through an entire television news feature, it may even constitute the 'backbone' of its aesthetic and rhetorical composition. The feature from the German political TV-magazine REPORT MAINZ (ARD, GER 20 October 2008) on the financial crisis in 2008 is such a case. It unfolds its theme ('its message') through two emergent metaphorical scenarios, forming a complex metaphoric thread. The analysis of the report offered in Section 7.1 focused on how cinematic experience grounds a feeling for being a loser or a winner in that financial crisis and therefore zoomed in on the micro level of cinematic metaphor. Now, the focus is shifted to the macro level. While the earlier analysis concentrated on the first two scenes, the scope now extends to the news feature as a whole.

## 12.1 Cinematic Expressive Movements as Temporal Macro-Structure

As a specific articulation of cinematic experience, the concept of cinematic expressive movement opens a pathway to reconstructing the ways in which metaphoricity emerges from the experience of watching a film. It concerns the orchestration of perceptual and affective journeys of spectators through an aesthetic movement form. It is important to recall that this theoretical position does not presume a notion of a psychological subject; although it could be characterized as describing potential psychological processes which unfold as individual embodied simulation of a given viewer, the assumption does not presume a position of a psychological subject. In fact, it offers a theoretical counter position to cognitive models of cinematic understanding by grounding cinematic meaning in the locally emerging temporal experience of cinematic expressivity.

Very roughly speaking, cinematic expressive movements operate on the level of scenes or below and are characterized by an internal temporal-affective structure. The analysis of Wyler's JEZEBEL (Section 10.1) has already indicated that, besides modulating affectivity on the micro level of single units of cinematic expressivity, these cinematic expressive movements form larger experiential gestalts. For the macroanalysis of the political report, we are focusing on those

https://doi.org/10.1515/9783110580785-013

cinematic expressive movement units that stage the two metaphorical scenarios of winners and losers throughout the entire feature. In Figure 12.1 below, these units are positioned as boxes sequentially positioned along a timeline that represents the entire feature, including the introduction and some closing remarks by the magazine's presenter, Fritz Frey.

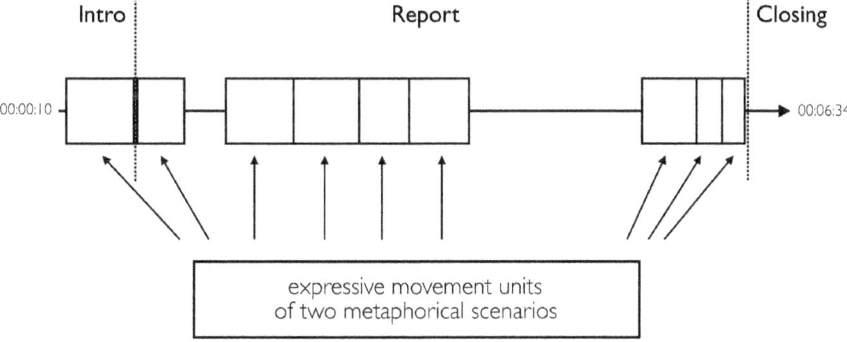


**Figure 12.1:** Cinematic expressive movement units as temporal macro-structure (REPORT MAINZ, 20 October 2008)

Within and along with the temporal unfolding of these expressive movement units, two metaphorical scenarios emerge: 'being a winner is being up and in a closed interior' and 'being a loser is being down and in an excluded exterior'.

## 12.2 Cinematic Metaphor as Temporal Parcours

Cinematic metaphors create a temporal parcours of cinematic experience as they unfold. This holds even for the mundane formats of a television feature of a monthly political magazine. We have seen that, in the feature on the financial crisis, two metaphorical scenarios emerge from experiencing the temporal succession of cinematic expressive movement units. To illustrate the dynamic unfolding, microanalyses of four cinematic expressive movement units are presented (Figure 12.2): the introduction by the presenter; a champagne reception of consultants; bankers as losers; and small investors locked out of a bank.

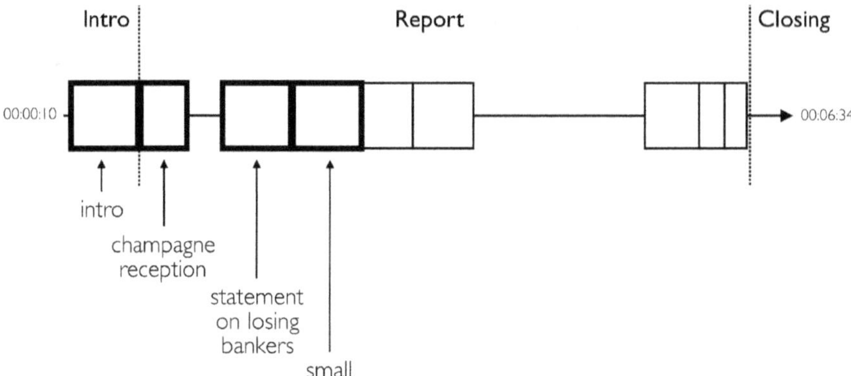


**Figure 12.2:** Temporal parcours of cinematic expressivity and metaphorical meaning (REPORT MAINZ, 20 October 2008)

## The introduction

The feature provides a critical commentary on the negative effects of the 2008 financial crisis. It sets up a strong contrast between the impact that failing banks have on their directors and on ordinary citizens who invested their small savings with those banks. Right at the beginning of the presenter's statement, two guiding lines of metaphoricity are introduced. They form an opposition that will be developed and further elaborated.

The introduction opens with a sharp criticism formulating the responsibility of bankers for the financial crisis with a concrete example. Josef Ackermann, chairman of the management board of Deutsche Bank from 2006 to 2012, is characterized as being part of a (literally) "lifted monetary caste" [*abgehobenen Geldkaste*]: "What is true is that Mister Ackermann's million-waiver [of his annual bonus, CM & HK] 'for the benefit of deserving employees' is a sign of loss of reality of a completely lifted monetary caste." [*Richtig ist, dass der Millionenverzicht des Herrn Ackermann 'zugunsten verdienter Mitarbeiter' ein weiteres Indiz für den Realitätsverlust einer völlig abgehobenen Geldkaste ist.*] (Figure 12.3)

Through the verbal metaphorical expression "lifted monetary caste", the employed group of bankers is metaphorically connected with being up. At the same time, the presenter is speaking against the background of a photography showing Josef Ackermann performing a victory gesture. Bankers are thus not only introduced as being up, but also as being winners. The metaphor "being a winner is being up" is thus already established in the introduction.

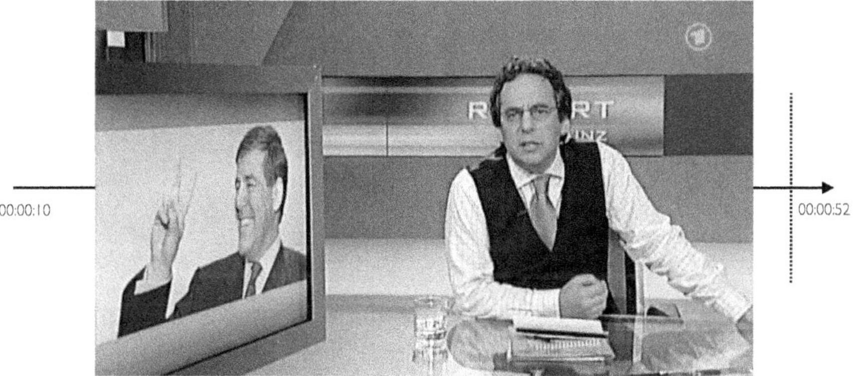


**Figure 12.3:** The introduction establishes the metaphorical opposition (REPORT MAINZ, 20 October 2008)

On the other hand, the introduction to the report closes by presenting a surprising counter position: (fired) bankers are now described as losers in the financial crisis, but as losers whose 'falling' is softened. "Some people may take comfort in the fact that many a banker has to leave his executive chair now. But don't cheer too soon: many fired bankers will fall gently if they fall." [*Da mag sich der eine oder andere freuen, dass so mancher Banker den Chefsessel nun räumen muss. Doch nicht zu früh gefreut: viele der gefeuerten Banker werden, wenn sie fallen, weich fallen.*] Elaborating on the metaphorical vertical axis, the losing bankers are metaphorically described as 'fallen' bankers. Being a loser in the financial crisis is thus metaphorically connected with a downward movement.

By setting up a metaphorical opposition of winners as being up and losers as being down – initially applied to the occupation group of the bankers – the introduction establishes the metaphorical frame for the report as a whole.

### A champagne reception

The actual feature begins with an expressive movement unit that stages winners of the banking crisis as having a champagne reception and celebrating. These 'winners' are so-called outplacement consultants, specialized in finding new jobs for fired bankers.

feeling being a winner is
a closed interior and sensing upwardness

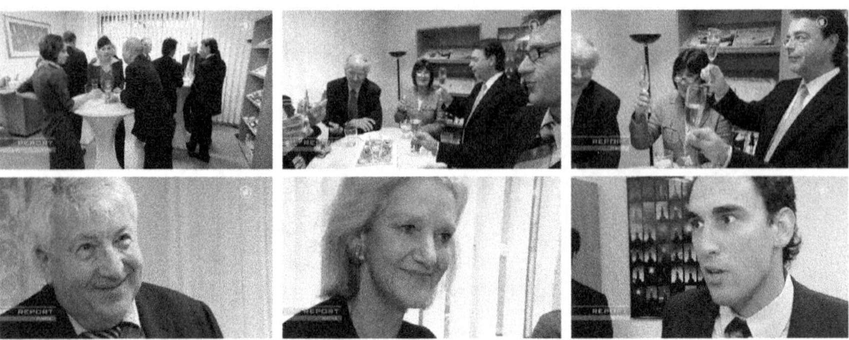

**Figure 12.4:** Multidimensional experiential gestalt: experiencing being a winner in the banking crisis (REPORT MAINZ, 20 October 2008)

Visual composition and camera orchestrate a feeling of cohesion and of a closed rather welcoming and comfortable interior. We see groups of people gathering around tables, all directed towards a shared center, an interior, forming a kind of 'closed circle'. The camera approaches them again and again, contrasting and highlighting the rather static quality of the circular formations. Then, a calm medium-close-shot montage of smiling faces follows, varying the circular group formations. Through the montage, the camera perspective becomes part of the closed circle (Figure 12.4).

The emerging comfortable feeling of being inside and celebrating is explicitly connected to being a winner through a voice-over at the beginning of the temporal unit that characterizes the outplacement consultants as follows: "They are part of the winners of the banking crisis: the consultants of the company Von Rundstedt Human Resources Partners." [*Sie gehören zu den Gewinnern der Bankenkrise: die Berater der Firma Von Rundstedt Human Resources Partners.*] At the same time, being a winner is audiovisually connected with different variations of experiencing 'upwardness'. Watching the reception, one sees accurately arranged canapés, followed by a camera move towards a group of business people drinking champagne. A close-up of a sparkling glass of champagne and a downward camera movement highlight the upward motion of the champagne bubbles. The next shot shows the consultants lifting their sparkling glasses to celebrate their success. A zoom-in camera movement intensifies the movement quality of the lifting of their glasses while the voice-over states: "business is doing brilliantly" [*die Geschäfte laufen glänzend*].

The expressive movement unit ends with a montage of three medium close shots of smiling consultants, the last one mentioning the company's strongly rising order situation while at the same time raising his head, eyes, and eyebrows (Figure 12.4). Here, yet another cinematic expression of upward experience goes along with a matching verbal expression.

As viewers follow this first temporal unit of cinematic expressivity, they thus not only experience a feeling for a closed and comfortable interior, but also a range of different feelings for upwardness. Within and through the expressive movement unit, a multidimensional gestalt emerges in which feeling an enclosed interior is experientially connected with the feeling of being a winner and with a sense for being up.

### The losing bankers

By shifting the action space, the smooth and rather relaxed dynamics of the previous unit of cinematic expressivity transforms into calmness and rest: with a static and fairly long take, the camera rests on the seated founder of the outplacement company, Eberhard von Rundstedt, emphasizing his voluminous body through a low angle shot (Figure 12.5). The sound quality, which had previously been fairly dry, parallels this by reverberating von Rundstedt's deep voice, making it sound voluminous, thereby evoking the impression of a physical presence in a closed space. The composition of this unit brings about an experience of resting and being inside, another facet of an image of a closed interior.

The unit entails a longer statement of von Rundstedt – introduced as the "star of the branch" – on outplacement. Von Rundstedt – alone in his office – comments verbally and gesturally on the fired bankers his company is counseling and describes them with a metaphor of downward movement: (literal) "these people, who, in fact, high, from high above have fallen" [*diese Menschen, die ja hoch, von hoch oben gestürzt sind*]. This statement is accompanied by a downward gesture, highlighting the downward quality of the verbal metaphorical expression and activating the mentioned falling as a vivid sensory-motor experience (Figure 12.5).

Later in his statement, he describes the situation of the unemployed bankers once again with a verbal metaphorical expression that operates in the experiential realm of downward movement: "actually, they want to dive away and not to be seen" [*sie wollen eigentlich wegtauchen und nicht gesehen werden*]. While saying this, von Rundstedt stops gesturing and lets his hands fall. As a result of the framing, his hands are no longer visible. In fact, they appear as if they had fallen into the off-screen depths. In this way, viewers get a vivid idea of the former bankers disappearing into some invisible depths, embodied in the downward movement of the hands. The fired bankers are thus experienced as connected

feeling being a winner is
a closed interior and sensing upwardness

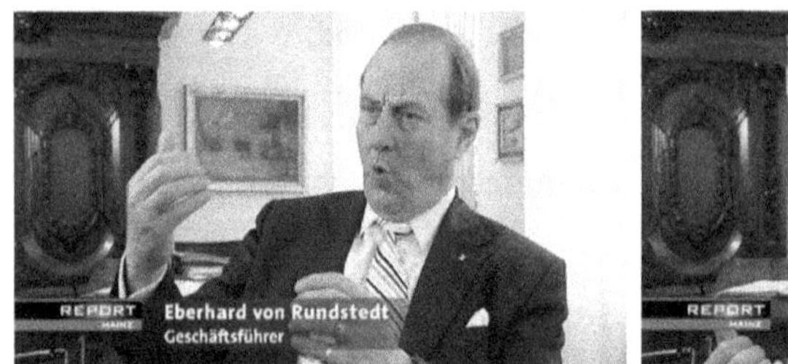


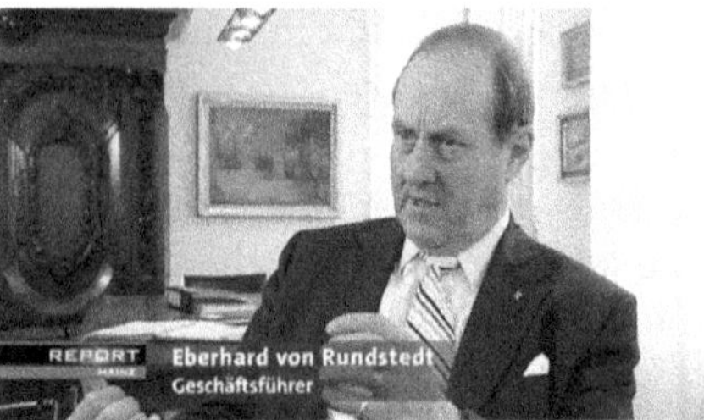


"these people, who, in fact, high, from high above have fallen (... )
actually, they want to dive away and not to be seen"

*[diese Menschen, die ja hoch, von hoch oben gestürzt sind (...)
sie wollen eigentlich wegtauchen und nicht gesehen werden]*

**Figure 12.5:** Multidimensional experiential gestalt: experiencing being a losing banker (REPORT MAINZ, 20 October 2008)

with downward movement, but they remain in the comfortable interior space just previously introduced as the winner's space. We next see how this changes in the cinematic expressive movement unit that orchestrates how the financial crisis affects ordinary citizens.

## The actual losers are the small investors

With a long tracking shot, the camera begins to move along with a group of people, all introduced as small investors, who have lost their savings in one of the insolvent banks, and are now on their way to a local branch of their bank (Figure 12.6). The camera movement establishes a sensation for walking as a group movement, which eventually transforms into a kind of tunnel-shaped goal-oriented forward motion. The length of this travelling-shot underlines the duration and continuity of the group movement. Then, a shot-reverse-shot montage cuts off this continuous movement. Next, one sees the wall of a house and hears a disembodied voice from an intercom system. This shot is contrasted several times with faces staring at the intercom in the wall. Through this montage, the previous ongoing and directed movement is brought to a sharp halt.

The walk of the group is accompanied by a voice-over, commenting that it is the fate of the small investors to pay for the faults of the banks. When reaching

feeling being an actual loser is
sensing an excluded exterior and a downward perspective

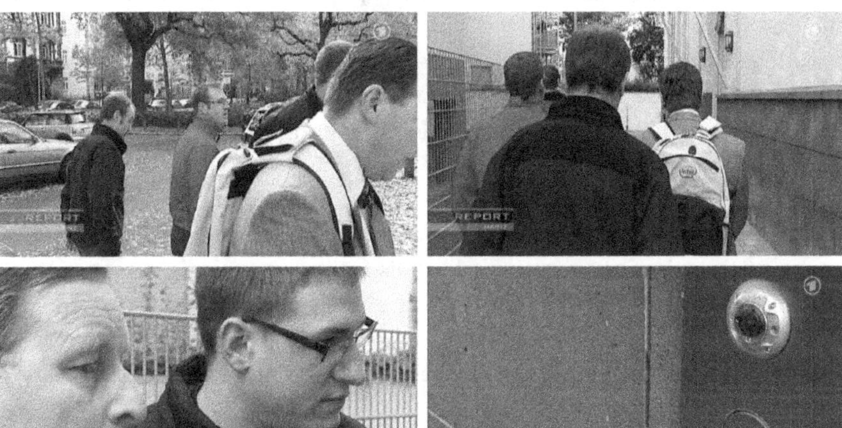

**Figure 12.6:** Multidimensional experiential gestalt: experiencing losing as a small investor (REPORT MAINZ, 20 October 2008)

the door of the bank that has frozen their savings accounts, everything is directed downwards: heads, eye gazes, camera perspective. This downward orientation continues in the following short montage, which stages a conversation between the voice from the intercom and the small investors. Their request for information and dialog fails. The voice just echoes their words:

*Small investor:*

> Yeah, for us, it is just important to know that everything humanly possible is being undertaken so that we can get back our hard-earned savings one day.
>
> [*Ja, wichtig ist uns natürlich einfach nur, dass alles Menschenmögliche versucht wird, damit wir unser sauer erspartes Geld wieder irgendwann bekommen können.*]

*Intercom:*

> Exactly. And this is exactly the case: everything humanly possible is being done.
>
> [*Ganz genau. Und genau das ist auch der Fall: Es wird alles Menschenmögliche getan.*]

In watching this feature, one successively connects losers of the crisis with these different ways of experiencing a sensation of 'down', while at the same time experiencing a temporal parcours in which a focused group-movement is harshly stopped. Note that the latter is not just the movement of the people we see on the screen: it is the way in which their walk is being filmed, which creates the feeling of moving towards something and being abruptly stopped. In this way, cinematic expressivity connects the small investors with an experience of being outside and excluded. Camera and montage are the dominant staging strategies here. The represented outside space, i.e., the small investors shown as they are walking down the street towards this bank building, is transformed into the cinematic image of an excluded exterior.

As viewers follow the temporal parcours of cinematic expressivity, they experience how it feels to be a small investor having lost their lifetime's savings. Emergent metaphoricity is grounded in this feeling expressed cinematically: an excluded exterior and a downward perspective. The losers of the crisis are thus metaphorically staged as being down, outside, and excluded: feeling being an actual loser (as against the losing bankers) is sensing an excluded exterior and a downward perspective (Figure 12.6).

## 12.3 Temporal Intertwining of Two Cinematic Metaphors

Summing up, the metaphorical opposition between an upward orientation of the winners and a downward perspective of the losers is embedded in another opposition, namely an "enclosed interior" and an "excluding exterior". Being a winner is not only staged as being up, but also as being in a closed interior. Being a loser, on the other hand, is not only staged as being down, but also being outside and in an excluded exterior. These embedded metaphors unfold in time, i.e., viewers experience a temporal parcours in which the embedded cinematic metaphors intertwine. Figure 12.7[1] shows that the two metaphorical oppositions forming two scenarios are temporally co-present and intertwined.

We would like to suggest that from relating such emergent trajectories of metaphorical meaning to each other across the feature, a kind of systematic metaphor in Lynne Cameron's sense emerges. Cameron describes "systematic metaphors (as) aggregated samples of actual use of language from a specific discourse event" (Cameron 2006) and as "dynamic mappings that reflect a temporary stabilisation in on-line language use" (Cameron 2006). She develops her concept of systematic metaphors from a point of view of applied linguistics. However, by conceptualizing the temporal dynamics of metaphorical meaning-making, she addresses a

1 For further explanation of the figure see "Appendix: Cinematic Metaphor – A methodological outline", Section A.3.2.

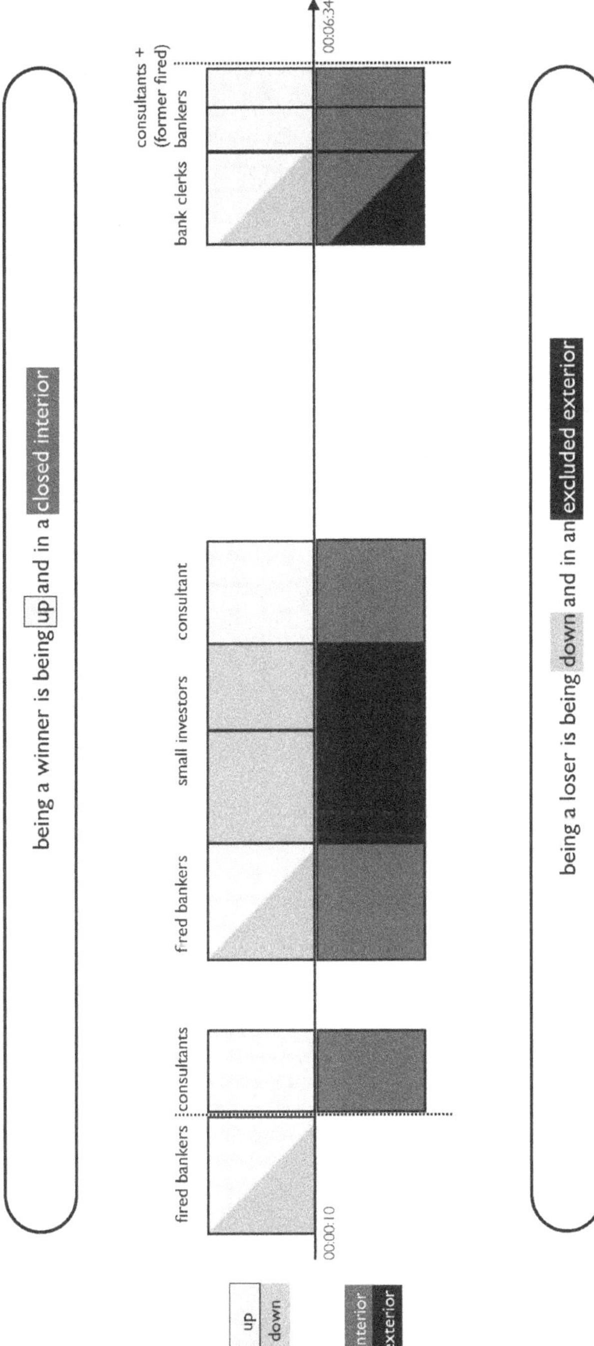


**Figure 12.7:** Intertwining of two cinematic metaphors (REPORT MAINZ, 20 October 2008)

metaphor phenomenon that applies to the interaction between the expressivity of a film and its viewer as much as to face-to-face interaction.

When we consider the feature as a whole, it turns out that it stages a temporal parcours of changing and relating metaphoricities, which begins by introducing the gentle falling of bankers who have lost their job. As the report develops, there emerges a rather broad variety as to who are the actual losers and winners of the financial crisis: outplacement consultants, small investors, fired bankers. But it is especially with the small investors that viewers are presented with how it feels to be really on the losing side: being down *and* outside in an excluded exterior. Through the elaboration on winning and losing related to varying groups of protagonists, what emerges over the course of the report is that the fired bankers, however, do fall gently. They find new jobs as bankers – or become consultants for fired bankers themselves.

This could be seen as narrative, but it does not emerge of its own accord. In fact, the metaphorical opposition staged in the report orchestrates an experiential parcours through the feelings and sensations of being a loser or a winner in this crisis. This temporally unfolding parcours of felt sensations is what grounds processes of fictionalization or metaphoric meaning-making more generally. The next chapter addresses such a temporal parcours of an evolving metaphorical theme along a feature film.

# 13 Unfolding Metaphoric Themes in a Feature Film: SPELLBOUND

Alfred Hitchcock's film noir SPELLBOUND (USA 1945) sets its metaphorical themes right at the beginning, entangling the viewer in a deliberate confusion.[1] Young psychoanalyst Dr. Constance Peterson (Ingrid Bergman) falls in love with her pretended new head of the psychiatry clinic 'Green Manors', Dr. Anthony Edwardes (Gregory Peck). However, the man posing as Edwardes is in actual fact John Ballantyne, who is suffering from severe amnesia and, not knowing who he is, believes he has killed the real Edwardes in order to steal his identity. When it becomes public that Ballantyne is an impostor, Peterson flees with him. Convinced that his amnesia is caused by a traumatic event in his childhood and that he is wrongly accused for murder, she seeks to recover his memory by applying her psychoanalytic method. In therapy with Constance, John slowly recovers his memory.

SPELLBOUND is a beautiful example of different forms and facets of the temporal orchestration of cinematic metaphor. Sometimes metaphor emerges within seconds, sometimes it takes a scene, sometimes the entire film, for cinematic metaphors to develop. The prolog to the film already establishes a metaphorical theme. Right here, we are presented with a text that introduces the principle of psychoanalysis and tells us what the film will be about. We see a text projected against a closed entrance door to a classicist mansion: "Our story deals with psychoanalysis, the method by which modern science treats the emotional problems of the sane", and subsequently, "The analyst seeks only to induce the patient to talk about his hidden problems to open the locked doors of his mind". In a static shot, the text begins to scroll up against the entrance of the residence named Green Manors (Figure 13.1). The doors look heavy and are closed. Together, the image of the entrance doors and the verbal metaphors, i.e., "the locked doors of a patient's mind" highlight the idea of psychoanalysis as the opening of doors to a patient's mind. By visually staging the experiential realm of the metaphor (its source domain), its imagery is vitalized, made prominent, and turned into a specific form of cinematic experience.

1 The analysis was developed in the context of the research project 'Multimodal Metaphor and Expressive Movement' and has been further worked on within the Cinepoetics' research focus 'Metaphor – Film Images, Cinematic Thinking, and Cognition' by Sarah Greifenstein, Hermann Kappelhoff, Cornelia Müller, and Christina Schmitt (cf. also, Kappelhoff & Greifenstein 2015). The version for this book was prepared by Cornelia Müller, Dorothea Horst, Sarah Greifenstein, Christina Schmitt, and Thomas Scherer. For a further perspective on metaphor in SPELLBOUND see Raymond W. Gibbs' (2018b) chapter "Our Metaphorical Experiences of Film" in *Cinematic Metaphor in Perspective. Reflections on a Transdisciplinary Framework.*

https://doi.org/10.1515/9783110580785-014

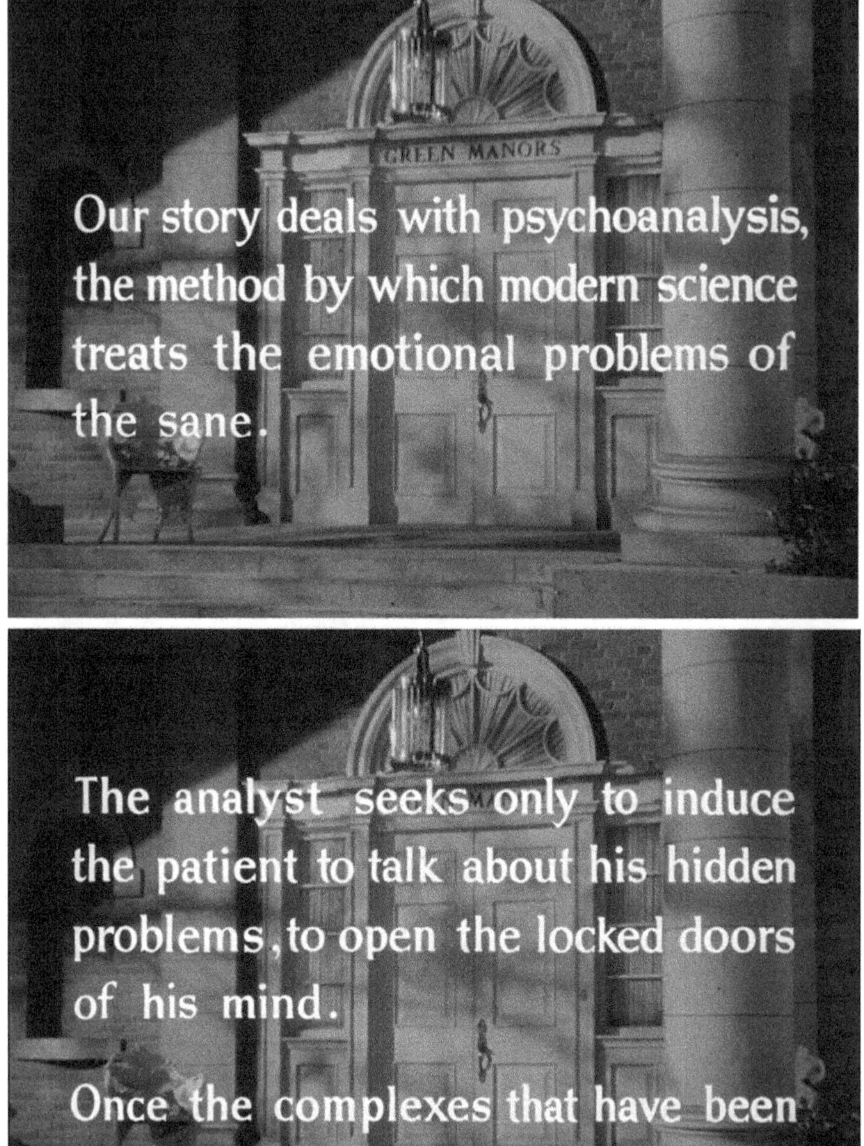


**Figure 13.1:** Explicit foregrounding of the metaphor: psychoanalysis is opening doors (SPELLBOUND)

"Psychoanalysis is opening doors" is thus very explicitly introduced as a metaphorical theme at the onset and it remains a theme throughout the film. However, there is another level of metaphoricity that is less obvious. It thematizes the experience of a psychoanalytic process as an affective process in which non-remembering of a traumatic event eventually turns into remembering (cf. also Kappelhoff and Greifenstein 2016). This is the temporally extended unfolding metaphorical theme that the next two sections consider.

## 13.1 How Non-Remembering Feels: A Cinematic Expressive Movement Unit

When the couple on the run enters into their bedroom, viewers see how Gregory Peck stares down and, in a point-of-view construction, see the object of his seeing (Figure 13.2)[2]: dark lines on a white bed cover staged as tracks by contrast lighting. The high-angle shot implies a downward perspective and highlights the immobility, the static character of the lines. Cut against this, and with an unsettling melody, one sees the frozen face of Gregory Peck from a downward camera position staring downwards.

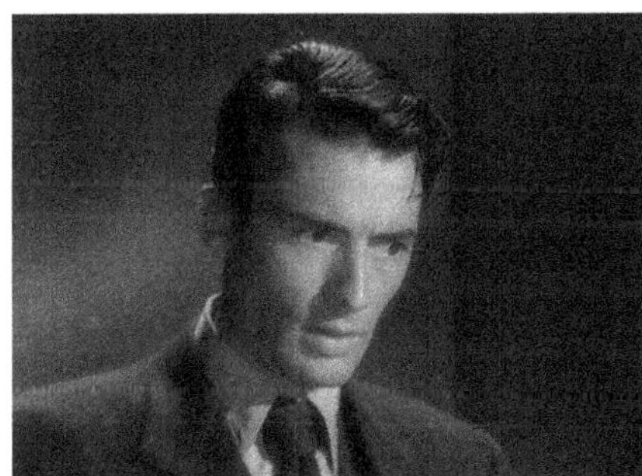

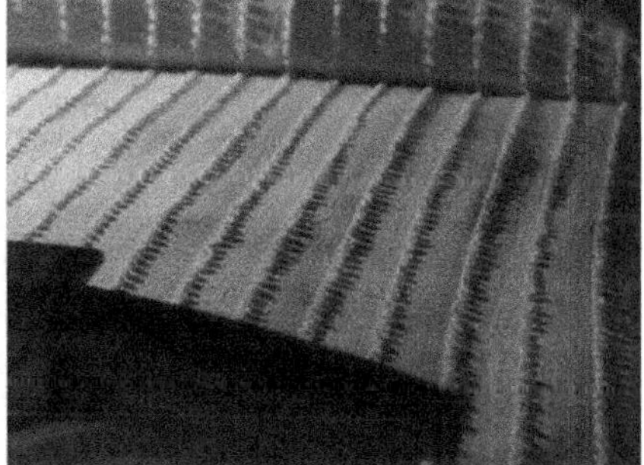

**Figure 13.2**: Feeling non-remembering: downward orientation as a static, immobile quality (SPELLBOUND)

Editing, camera position, and visual composition orchestrate the downward orientation as a static, immobile experience. The accompanying dialog connects the staging of the lines against the white bed cover with non-remembering: in response

2 For further explanation of the figure see "Appendix: Cinematic Metaphor – A methodological outline", Section A.3.1.

to Constance's "You remember something", John says "No". The sequence orchestrates a crescendo of tension staged in sustained shots, a slowly swelling and increasingly threatening music, the accelerating, pressing rhythm of Constance summarizing her analytic observations, and the commanding and desperate tone in which she eventually tells her patient "Look at it to remember", comes to a head and then breaks off. This is the moment of John's breakdown. He collapses, falls down, into the depth that he has fixated in panic, held and caressed by Constance.

The slow alternation of shots orchestrates the terrifying feeling of being stuck, from which there is no escape but collapse. It is a cinematic movement expression of how a breakdown feels and viewers live it through their own bodies. This montage sequence shapes a movement of cinematic expressivity that is recurring over the course of the film and thus unfolds a temporal pattern: *a sustained and slow alternation of shots is held in stasis* (by the insertion of core elements, the POV on tracks, lines, the swelling and threatening music, the numbed facial expression) *and suddenly breaks off.* This is how non-remembering feels, and this is what the viewer encounters again and again throughout the film. This feeling for the increasingly terrifying experiences is not an outcome of the world of depicted characters and objects; it is the staging of cinematic expressivity that exceeds the represented characters, objects, and sceneries and turns them into the expression of an inner life, which viewers then ascribe to the characters on the screen.

As in the analysis of the feature from the political TV-magazine REPORT MAINZ, the theoretical and methodological anchor point for reconstructing recurrent temporal patterns of emergent metaphoricity is cinematic expressivity on the level of expressive movement units. Created through forms of staging and audiovisual composition, cinematic expressive movement units modulate affectivity on the micro level of cinematic expressivity (see Appendix for more detail). At the same time, they form temporal structures of cinematic expressivity on larger levels of the composition. Their meaning emerges on the level of movement gestalts and from their position in the temporal development of the film. Figure 13.3[3] shows the position of those units that together stage the amnesic patient's suffering of non-remembering as a recurrent temporal pattern on the level of cinematic expressive movement units.

Over the course of the film, viewers are exposed to repeated variations of expressive movement units that orchestrate non-remembering as an intense bodily experience. The first time Gregory Peck is shown having a nervous outburst is when he stares at fork marks leaving parallel lines on a white table cloth; he breaks

3 For further explanation of the figure see "Appendix: Cinematic Metaphor – A methodological outline", Section A.3.1.

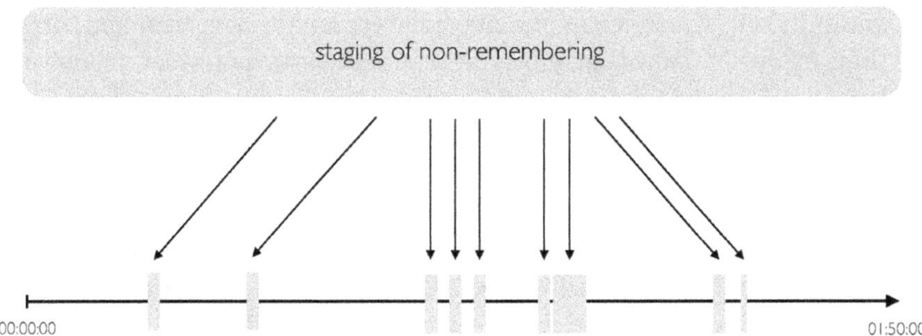


**Figure 13.3:** A feeling of non-remembering staged as temporal pattern of cinematic expressive movement units (SPELLBOUND)

down a second time, when he sees dark lines on Ingrid Bergmann's white night robe. Later in down the film, viewers face the dramatic breakdown just described, when Peck gazes at parallel lines on a white bed cover – and the series of breakdowns continues in further variations. The following section focuses on how these movement units unfold a recurrent pattern of cinematic metaphor that is orchestrated through the variations and contrasts within and between these units.

## 13.2 The Unfolding Metaphorical Theme

With recourse to Sobchack's characterization of cinema, this temporally extended unfolding metaphorical theme may be summarized as follows: "Non-remembering a traumatic event is experienced as expression of successively intensifying experiences of downward immobility." A series of nine units is orchestrated in a similar way. Framing is a prominent staging characteristic: the nearness of the camera to the actor, the acting itself, looking downward and the second shot/reverse shot of the camera positioned with a downward orientation. But most importantly, non-remembering is staged recurrently across the film through the quality of cinematic expressivity common to all the units: *a sustained and slow alternation of shots, held in stasis and suddenly breaking off.*

All the units stage moments of acute amnesia, instances of traumatic inability to remember, in a static manner, and they always involve a downward orientation, the camera establishing two aspects of downwardness: we see how Gregory Peck stares down, and we look down on the object of his seeing. Both perspectives recur in static shots. This immobility, the stasis, the downward orientation are forms of cinematic expressivity: what spectators see (a face, lines), is always already shaped by the way how it is orchestrated (in an immobile and downwardly staged manner) as one cinematic expressive movement unit. Across all these expressive movement units, the immobile staging provides not only the experiential ground against which different kinds of lines or tracks and the inability to remember a traumatic event are individually orchestrated. These units form multidimensional experiential gestalts of cinematic expressivity that, over the time of film-viewing, evolve into a larger temporal pattern.

In the first sequence of non-remembering ('lines on table cloth', Figure 13.4)[4], parallel lines on a table cloth and a counter-shot with the face of Gregory Peck staring downward, are staged in a static manner, including a baleful melody and an abrupt break-off. Another sequence ('lines on night robe', Figure 13.4) shows this point-of-view construction together with a similar movement pattern: long-lasting, steady shots in slow alternation, creating a mounting sense of stasis, of freezing terror, of rising tension, of stretching to a breaking-point, and a break on the level of acting.

Throughout the film, this repeats again and again and becomes a recurrent pattern emergent from the temporal process of film-viewing. Not only are the face and the lines as a kind of motif repeated, but the music, camera perspective, the editing, and visual forms also recur and become similar in the viewers' experience. It is thus not a series of represented objects, characters, or motifs that compose to a meaningful pattern, but the cinematic staging as expressive movement units that viewers realize in their own bodies. Strictly speaking, the temporal unfolding of the metaphorical theme 'runs' right through the bodies of the film viewers.

Similarity between the movement units (the lines traced by a fork, on a cloth, and on a blanket, Figure 13.4) is thus created by the spectators in the process of film-viewing. It is in this way that viewers make meaning of a development, that they sense as mounting tension and as increasingly disturbing. These bodily feelings are projected to the fictive characters on the screen.

Taken together, all expressive movements establish a metaphorical relation, in which a non-remembering is experienced and seen as immobility, as a downward orientation, and as tracks (Figure 13.5). This pattern is repeated again and again, increasingly evoking rising tension and growing panic. The music becomes more dramatic, Gregory Peck's face more frozen, the movement of the montage more articulated. Throughout the process of film-viewing, spectators thus not only repeatedly experience the inability to remember, and suffering from amnesia, bodily with all their senses. They moreover feel the mounting panic with every new cinematic expression of non-remembering. In this way, the temporal experiences of the micro levels of cinematic expressive movement units increase

---

4 For further explanation of the figure see "Appendix: Cinematic Metaphor – A methodological outline", Section A.3.1.

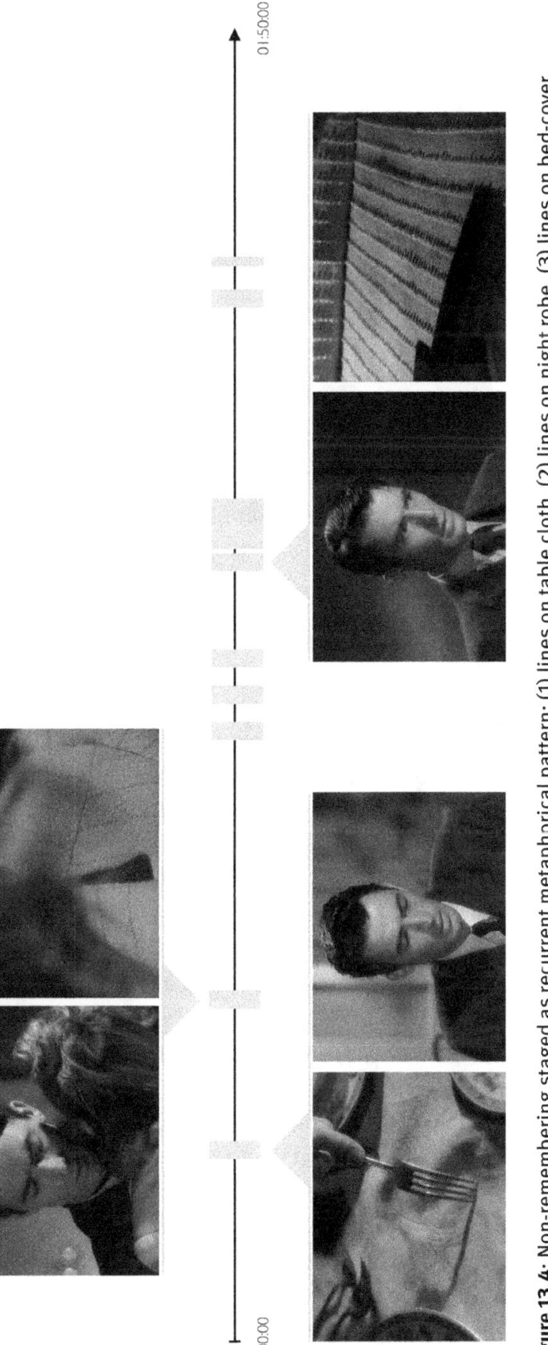


**Figure 13.4:** Non-remembering staged as recurrent metaphorical pattern: (1) lines on table cloth, (2) lines on night robe, (3) lines on bed-cover (SPELLBOUND)

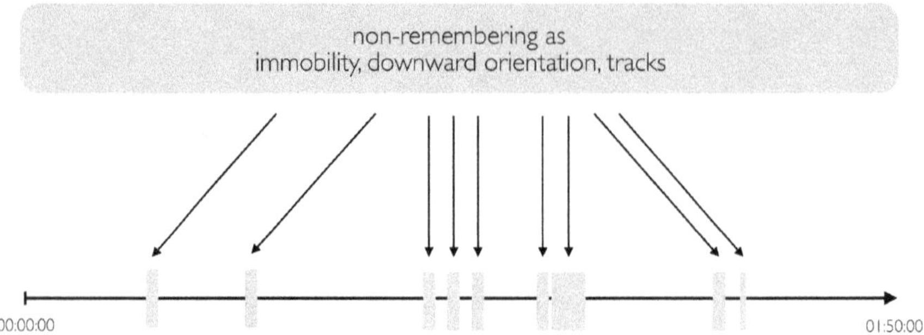


**Figure 13.5:** A feeling of non-remembering as an emergent metaphorical theme (SPELLBOUND)

affective pressure and tension. Within the temporal parcours of film-viewing, metaphoricity emerges with the felt sensations of the recurrent cinematic expressive movements, intertwining micro and macro levels of the film.

### Non-remembering turns into remembering

It is important to note that the recurrent pattern just described is not a simple repetition, but a series of *varying* cinematic expressions of how it feels to be blocked, to be stuck with the inability to remember one's own life and personal story. They are variations of a metaphorical theme that are temporally related. Their temporal development expresses the increasing tension, pressure, and panic, which forms a temporal parcours through which spectators go in their film-viewing, ascribing what they feel to the character played by Gregory Peck.

Furthermore, this emergent macro level of cinematic metaphor goes even further beyond the staging of non-remembering as a symptom of amnesia. It connects non-remembering with remembering on the level of cinematic expressivity (Figure 13.6).

It is in the last articulation of the recurring pattern just described that an important shift takes place. In this unit, a flashback to the childhood of Ballantyne is orchestrated. Although the pattern is repeated, it is also *varied* in a significant way. While point-of-view editing, camera position, and downward orientation remain the same, the parallel lines and the downward orientation are now staged as a forceful compelling dynamic experience: a montage of a long ski ride downhill and the traumatic childhood event. The breaking through of the traumatic memory is embedded in a scene staging a trip to the winter mountains. The couple follows a faint memory of Ballantyne/Peck that the location might be related to his

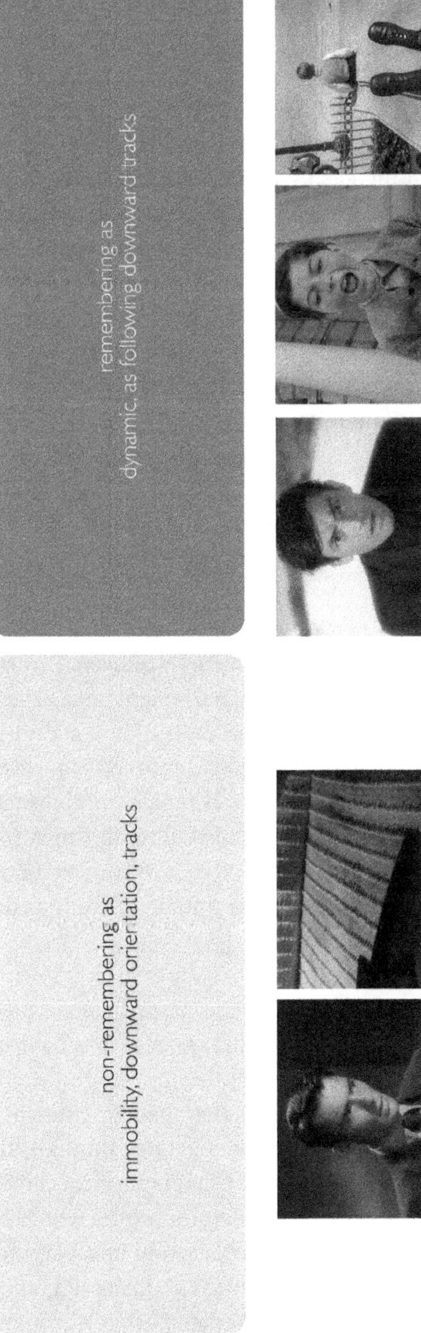


**Figure 13.6:** A shift in the recurrent pattern connects non-remembering and remembering (SPELLBOUND)

trauma. The protagonists are shown as black vertical 'structures' slowly trudging up the steep snowy hillside, forming traces on white ground. As they are reaching the top of the hill, the music reaches a dramatic peak. Starting the steep ski-run downhill, in long close-ups of the two faces, we see how they look down, we feel the great depth their gazes are facing, we hear the mountain wind and a rising, pressing music. In a long shot, with strongly swelling music, we see the two skiers descending downhill with increasing tempo and rapidly approaching a massive cliff. Here is where the flashback is edited in. In a montage sequence (Figure 13.6), we see Gregory Peck's face, then the face of young boy, and, in a counter-shot, the boy's point of view. We are with him as he slides down the broad handrail of a house entrance, dark pant legs against the light background of the stone rails sliding down fast towards the back of another boy, sitting at the end of the rail, and pushing him down onto the pointed pole of a wrought iron fence. Ballantyne killed his brother in an accident (Figure 13.6).

This scene transforms the stasis of the downward fixation into a downward dynamics. Visual composition turns the actors into elements of the evolving cinematic metaphor. They are facets of an aesthetic experience that stages the feeling of a transition from being blocked to an overwhelming dynamics of releasing a traumatic memory.

Along with the temporal perception of aesthetic similarities between movement units, non-remembering now becomes connected with remembering. Viewers experience the relation between all movement units as temporally orchestrated felt sensations of suffering from moments of acute amnesia: be it on the micro level of the single cinematic expressive movements, or on the emergent macro level of their temporal concatenation. Entangled with the temporal development of the film, viewers create a dynamic metaphor in which non-remembering is experienced and understood as immobility, downward orientation, dark lines against white surfaces, and remembering a traumatic event as dynamic, forceful downward motion along gliding rails.

## From non-remembering to remembering through metaphor shifting

Reconsidering the temporal structure of the specific cinematic metaphorical experience that Hitchcock's film takes its spectator through, this concerns on the one hand a specific temporal pattern of metaphorical movement units. On the other hand, there are the recurring temporal units which orchestrate non-remembering as immobility, downward orientation and varying experiences of perceiving lines against white ground (Figure 13.7, lower left box). The last movement unit of the recurrent pattern stages "remembering" through the contrasting experiential qualities: immobility becomes mobility, a freezing downward perception of tracks is turned into a downward movement along tracks, traumatic freezing becomes downward motion and results in the breaking loose of the memory (Figure 13.7, lower right box). This change in the staging of the recurrent pattern through contrasting experiential qualities that goes along with a change of metaphorical meaning, is a case of metaphor shifting in Cameron's sense (Cameron 2008c, Cameron and Maslen 2010). For Cameron, a change in the metaphorical vehicle in face-to-face communication is an emergent outcome of its interactive and temporal dynamics in the process of meaning-making. This applies equally to the emergent metaphorical theme in SPELLBOUND when immobility and stasis turn into mobility, when non-remembering shifts to remembering. However, SPELLBOUND stages the experience of the releasing of memory for an amnestic patient metaphorically not only in this isolated cinematic movement. Rather, this is the climax of a temporal experience of going through an affective process of raising tension and growing pressure connected with non-remembering to a point of break-off and break-through of memory. From this overall temporal experience, a metaphorical theme emerges (Figure 13.7, upper box): *remembering a traumatic event as increasing tension, as successive and varied experiences of downward oriented immobility, which abruptly shift to a breaking loose of a downward movement.*

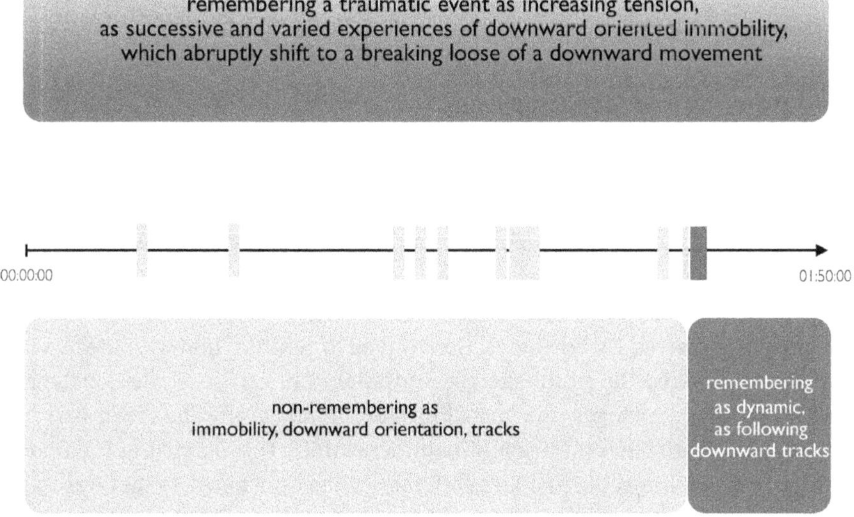


**Figure 13.7:** A metaphorical theme emerging through metaphor shifting (SPELLBOUND)

This metaphorical theme captures the process of changing experiences, it is about the transition from non-remembering, from being blocked, frozen of fear to moving, seeing movement and eventually feeling movement. The metaphor is not just a recurrent experiential pattern of movement units; it is about the changes between them.

## 13.3 90-Minute-Metaphors?

Thus far, we have described the temporal structures within cinematic expressive movements and how those metaphorically-structured units are related across the film. We have illustrated how they unfold a recurrent pattern of cinematic metaphor (a metaphorical theme) with an internal affective development that is orchestrated through the variations and contrasts within and between the movement units. As such a temporally organized form of metaphoricity, the described metaphorical theme in SPELLBOUND alludes to a systematic metaphor in Lynne Cameron's sense.

Along the film, two large trajectories of cinematic metaphors (i.e., metaphorical themes) evolve, change, intertwine, and alternate. One metaphorical theme is spelled out quite explicitly in the prolog and it also recurs as a temporal pattern across the film: psychoanalysis is opening doors to the patient's mind. In the same manner as in the prolog of the film, i.e., as explicit vitalization and foregrounding of the metaphor's imagery, expressive movement units that stage a sensation of opening doors reappear across different scenes: during the first kiss between John and Constance in the library, a series of doors down a seemingly endless corridor are opening one by one (Figure 13.8, top); or when the police officers finally send John to prison after apparently convicting him of murder, a prison gate is opening (Figure 13.8, center). Similar to the various expressive movement units staging non-remembering, the recurrences of opening doors are no simple repetitions, but variations of a metaphorical theme that are temporally related. Just as the metaphorical theme introduces the film (by being vitalized through the prominently staged doors of Green Manors), it concludes it: Constance ultimately figures out that her colleague Dr. Murchison is the man who really murdered Dr. Edwardes. Determined to confront him with the fact that she has discovered the truth, she goes upstairs to his office. From Constance's face, the camera changes to a travelling-shot, approaching the lower part of a closed door that shows a stretch of light beneath it. This staging of the door is related to the scene of the first kiss with John when Constance, on her way to the library, is going upstairs and sees the closed door to the office of Dr. Murchison. While she passed it then, now she opens it and enters (Figure 13.8, bottom). This

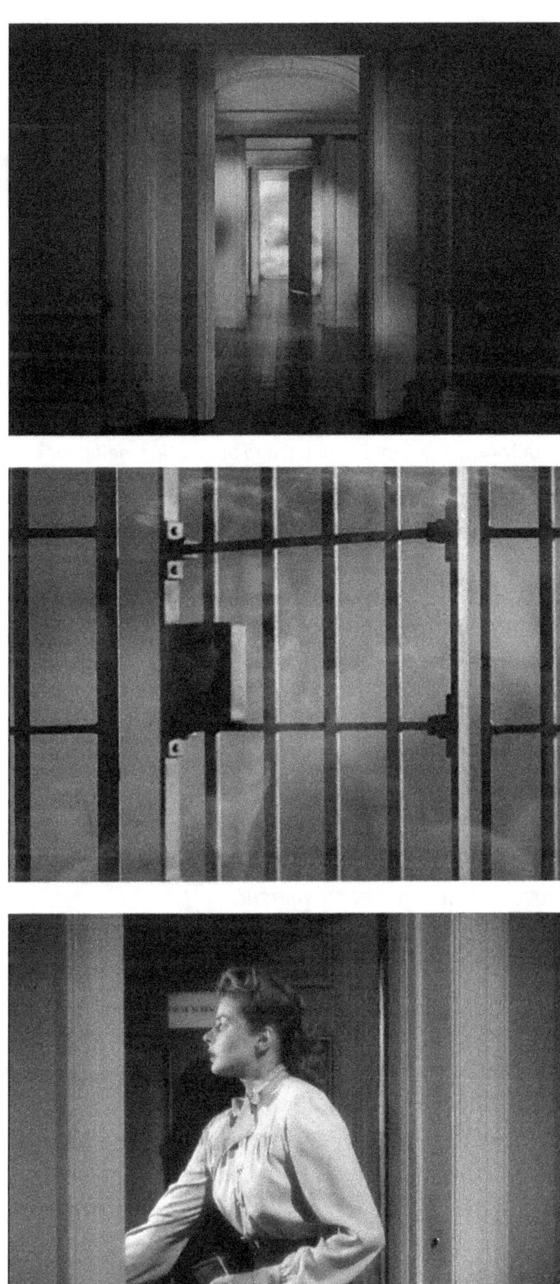

**Figure 13.8**: Cinematic expressive movement units staging a sensation of opening doors (SPELLBOUND)

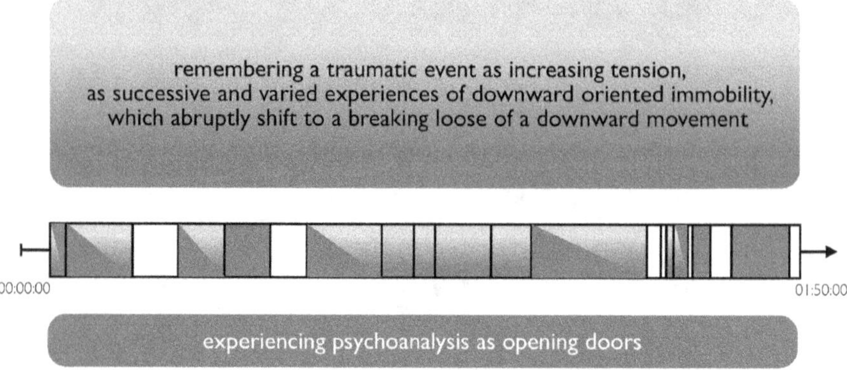


**Figure 13.9**: Temporally expanded, intertwining, and alternating metaphorical themes (SPELLBOUND)

orchestration of a sensation of an opening door concludes the recurrent pattern and the psychoanalytic process extending over the film.

The second metaphorical theme, revolving around the experience of acute amnesia is never spelled out explicitly; it only emerges along the temporal unfolding of the film and with experiencing the recurrent pattern of dynamic metaphoricity. Rather than describing the principle of psychoanalysis (as in the first metaphor), it stages the psychoanalytic process of becoming able to *remember a traumatic event as* a feeling, a felt sensation of *increasing tension, as successive and varied experiences of downward oriented immobility, which abruptly shift to a breaking loose of a downward movement.*

The two metaphorical themes are temporally extended both on the micro level of cinematic movements and on the macro level of the whole film. Over the film, both cinematic metaphors intertwine, sometimes they alternate; they describe per se a temporal form of more than one hour, shown below as a sequence of scenes (Figure 13.9)[5]. While the theme, 'psychoanalysis as opening doors', comes with experiences of transforming locked doors into opening ones, the second metaphorical theme makes spectators see and feel a raising haunting stasis becoming a movement. Each of them, i.e., in their unfolding and intertwining, forms a temporally organized systematic metaphor: the first, rather explicit systematic metaphor provides a sort of pointed imagistic definition of psychoanalysis, whereas

5 For further explanation of the figure see "Appendix: Cinematic Metaphor – A methodological outline", Section A.3.2.

the second, rather implicit, systematic metaphor makes a psychoanalytic process tangible as a vivid felt experience.

The two systematic cinematic metaphors emerge from the composition and unfolding of expressive movements, i.e., from the point of view of film viewers as a process that stretches out over the entire film. So that, seen from the end, we can reconstruct two systematic cinematic metaphors that cannot be defined through any singular mapping. Instead, what makes up systematic cinematic metaphor is that it unfolds over the course of the film in ever new variations, as a dynamic process, temporally divided into segments, of ever new metaphorical transferals and shifts. This process structures the process of understanding as an interaction of the dialog, of the action represented, and of cinematic expressive movement.

The temporal forms of metaphor revealed in the analysis of SPELLBOUND not only document the temporal emergence of cinematic metaphor on different time scales and on different layers of unfolding metaphorical themes; they exemplify cinematic meaning-making more generally.

## Résumé

Focusing on temporality reveals that it permeates all levels of cinematic metaphor. From the micro level of expressive movement units to the meso level of emergent metaphorical scenarios, and to metaphorical themes and systematic cinematic metaphors on the macro level of an entire film, the 'doing' of metaphorical meaning-making happens. Cinematic metaphors build complex dynamic networks of metaphorical meaning that are constantly changing along the procedural experience of film-viewing. This is another commonality with meaning-making in face-to-face discourse dynamics (cf. Larsen-Freeman and Cameron 2008a). Cinematic metaphors emerge from this temporal embodied process; they are not given, pre-hoc instantiations of universal schemas, but produced by the spectators in the poiesis of film-viewing.

And this holds across audiovisual forms (and beyond): cinematic metaphoricity concerns meaning-making and affect modulation as temporally-structured embodied experience.

# Beyond Cinematic Metaphor

Every facet of cinematic metaphor is dynamic, is flow, is movement experience, is feeling movement, is an affective, embodied form of meaning-making. Film-viewing implies a cinematic mode of experience that is permeated affectively and temporally. Experience, affectivity, and temporality, which were brought into focus one by one as the book progressed, are co-present and mutually dependent dimensions of cinematic metaphor. 'Our Metaphorical Experience of Films', as Gibbs characterizes it in his contribution in the companion volume *Cinematic Metaphor in Perspective. Reflections on a Transdisciplinary Framework* (2018b), are temporal experiences shaped by the temporality of movement-images, from the level of a scene to the unfolding of metaphorical themes in a film. As movement experiences they are inherently affective, the qualities of movement are affective qualities; in short, they are the affect. Bodily perceived as movements, they characterize processes of meaning-making that extend metaphors in audiovisual media. As our analyses of metaphorical meaning-making in gestures, body movements, and speech have indicated, experience (understood in terms of the reflexivity, intersubjectivity, and dynamics of embodiment), (inter) affectivity, and temporality also characterize metaphorical meaning beyond the cinema, television, and audiovisual media, and point to fundamental properties of multimodal face-to-face interaction, an interface between gesture studies and film studies beyond metaphor that deserves much future attention. Alan Cienki (2018), in the companion volume to this book, discusses some of the insights that linguistics and gesture studies may gain from engaging with film studies, including the multi-layering time-scales on which gestures and speech operate.

Cinematic metaphor also extends the study of metaphor beyond audiovisual media. It has vital implications for metaphor theory and the methods of their analyses, probably affecting all domains of metaphor usage in the social world. We have outlined some of the fundamental parallels between processes of metaphorical meaning-making in multimodal face-to-face interaction – none of them can be appropriated with an idea of metaphor usage as instantiating static, fixed schemas. Where conceptual metaphor theory has favored the idea of image schemas as stabilized universal experiential, cognitive patterns to be 'identified' on the level of filmic narrative and/or on the level of film as 'representation' of 'contents', we have suggested the notion of expressive movements to describe metaphors as dynamic, affective, and emerging within an interaffective parcours in an experience for participants in an interaction that parallels the experience of film viewers. Metaphors emerge in this process within an interaffective process, as multidimensional experiential gestalts of perceiving and feeling, they are 'done' by the film viewers much as people engaging in a conversation 'do' metaphors. This 'doing' is an interactive process in which metaphoricity emerges, develops, unfolds, changes, disappears, returns in ever changing transfers, *never* reaching a final state where *the* metaphor is to be identified. This, however, does not mean that there is no method to analyze such dynamic processes of 'doing' metaphors. We offer a sketch of our method in the appendix, and the analyses in the book can be read as a documentation for a systematic, but not schematic, process of analyzing metaphoricity as a dynamic form of meaning-making beyond the cinema. Obviously Lynne Cameron's discourse dynamic approach offers a methodology that powerfully illustrates an applied linguistic method of analyzing metaphors as a dynamic process rather than as a static feature (Cameron 2003, 2011, Cameron and Maslen 2010).

In her explorations of how the framework of cinematic metaphor opens up metaphor studies, Lynne Cameron speaking of metaphorizing, rather than of metaphor, indicates that dynamics is an inherent theoretical facet of metaphor across discourse types (including reading of texts). If, however, we are prepared to take this observation seriously, this insight affects metaphor analysis and metaphor identification to the point that the established 'A is B' formula demands replacement with a formula that captures the poetic process of creative metaphorizing. Arguing that talk flows as much as film does, Cameron advocates a replacement of the static 'A IS B' with a dynamic idea of metaphorizing, where 'vehicles' of potential metaphors are connected with potential 'topics' in a process of metaphorizing – captured in a formula '$V \sim T \rightarrow M_{ing}$'. The formula reflects the temporal primacy of Vehicles against Topics in the processes of Metaphorizing, the tilde represents the *simultaneous* equivalence and difference of vehicle and topic (Cameron 2018).

The term Cinematic Metaphor reflects the media character of audiovisual images. Starting from the concept of the cinematic movement-image we have formulated a theoretical framework that responds to the media specifics of film. Taking recourse to classical and contemporary film-theoretical positions it heals the break with rhetoric and poetics and goes beyond the representational fallacy and the static concepts of cognitive film theories as applied (not only) to metaphors in film and audiovisual media.

Our approach thus changes the emphasis on the ways films, and metaphors too, are understood by shifting focus from "represented narratives" to "film-viewing as a creative process" structured temporally and affectively by movement-images – the poiesis of film-viewing. From the point of view we have developed, film-viewing is not primarily a cognitive process of identifying with characters on the screen that creates sadness, joy, suspense, but a cinematic experiencing of the temporal form of how they are presented. What holds for film-viewing applies to the reception of audiovisual media more generally. Audiovisual images, in whatever form, set up their own space-time logic, because they are movement-images (not moving images). Cinematic perceiving engages with this cinematic space-time composition in the form of multidimensional experiential gestalts. Film viewers engage with this cinematic world in an as-if mode. It is this as-if which makes perception of film fundamentally different from everyday perception and, which involves, in fact, a complex process of fictionalizing, of creating a world of pretense (Kappelhoff and Greifenstein 2016, Voss 2009). From this process of fictionalizing, a narrative emerges. Fictionalizing may include metaphorical meaning-making on micro as well as on macro levels, but it does not equate to metaphorizing.

The 'narrative' thus does not exist prior/independently from the process of film-viewing. Rather it emerges within the flow of cinematic experience, as *film and film-viewing* progress in reciprocal entanglement. This holds for the narrative of a feature film as much as for the story of a television broadcast. It characterizes meaning-making with audiovisual media beyond the cinema.

This also implies that the 'doing' of metaphor, that metaphorizing is not to be understood as a solipsistic cognitive process, but as a co-production of different agents that encounter each other's subjective scopes of experience that do not meet in complete congruence. In her discussion of "alterity" Cameron suggests, with reference to Bakhtin, that rather than conceiving of meaning-making as a search for "a perfect convergence of understanding by participants in discourse [the] focus [should be] on the inevitability of difference. Alterity, as differences in understanding and perspective, is not merely to be lamented, but to be understood and worked with." (Cameron 2003, 31).

This points to a critical reflection of the model of communication that goes beyond cinematic metaphor and that affects metaphor research, face-to-face interaction as much as film and media studies, and which is particularly prominent in many applications of the concept of multimodal communication.

The notion of mode and of multiple modalities involved in communication all too often insinuates a sender-receiver model of communication which separates 'messages' from their mediality and rules out the active participation of both (or several) agents in the construction of meaning. Film viewers become 'receivers' of mediated 'messages', 'sent out' intentionally by a producer. They become the passive 'unpackers' of messages 'contained' in moving images, designed to be unpacked by a film-maker or the producer of a video clip. This reduces film-viewing to mere information processing, and film viewers to information processing 'machines' that process films as information.

Such a code model of communication cannot, however, explain the fascination of audiovisual media. People do not go to the cinema to be 'informed' and news shows are accidentally considered as ‘infotainment’. People go to the movies, they enjoy news shows, late night shows, campaign commercials, or video clips because they experience breaking news, suspense, love, sex, crime, and comedy through their bodies *as-if* they were reality. A fictional reality that they produce in their process of film-viewing. At least this is how film director Todd Haynes reflecting upon his film SUPERSTAR describes the mystery of film:

> I think there is something about having an unmoving face that makes the viewers HAVE to supplement and invest and complete the story visually for themselves. That’s maybe, that’s how your describing [as a viewer], or how you felt, something you summon yourself. I mean, I think, ALL movies at some level work that way. The emotional component of movies are things that WE create as viewers. And the movie is the setup, the conditions that evoke it. That’s the mystery of the power of film. It’s the spectator that’s making it come to life. (Haynes 2018, transcription by CM & HK)

We hope that this book has engaged you in a welcoming experience of exploring the mystery and the power of cinematic metaphor.

# Appendix: Cinematic Metaphor – A Methodological Outline

## Table of Content



https://doi.org/10.1515/9783110580785-015

## A.0 Introduction

Film-viewing and multimodal face-to-face interaction are both temporal forms of experiencing and interaffective engagement. The analysis of cinematic metaphor therefore starts from this temporality. The case studies presented in this book offer varied illustrations of our transdisciplinary method (CineMet) designed to capture dynamic structures specifically in relation to affective processes and the flow of metaphorical meaning-making. Film studies and linguistics have both contributed to its development. Note, that CineMet is not just a combination of two sets of methods coming from different disciplines, rather, it further develops and sometimes alters methods that were developed earlier. The method addresses the temporality of meaning-making as a specific mode of perceiving, sensing, and feeling, and offers different forms of visualizations of this temporal affectivity and the dynamics of metaphorical meaning. Our starting point is the temporality of experiencing which characterizes film-viewing as much as face-to-face interaction.

Analysis of temporal structures of unfolding metaphoricity, be it in audio-visual media or in face-to-face interaction, is flexible, creative, dynamic in itself. At the same time the analytical procedure is methodologically rigid in terms of accounting for temporality as producing an affective engagement that permeates processes of meaning-making (and of metaphor as a specific form of meaning-making) at any point of the analysis. The analytic process can, in short, be described as a dynamic engagement with the data, moving back and forth between different time scales, and zooming in on macro, meso, and micro levels of analysis whenever the process of analysis demands for it. For our methodological approach to metaphor analysis, this means that we do not search for single metaphors or instantiations of metaphors in films; we look at the emergence of metaphoricity from the affective experiences that people go through in the process of film-viewing or in multimodal face-to-face interaction. Our methodological entry point to analyzing these processes lies in the movement figurations that we have described as (cinematic) expressive movements.

The method builds, on the one hand, on the film-analytical method eMAEX (electronically based media analysis of expressive movement images) (Kappelhoff and Bakels 2011) and, on the other, on the cognitive-linguistic Methods of Gesture Analysis (MGA) (Müller, Bressem, and Ladewig in prep., Müller 2010) and Metaphor Foregrounding Analysis (MFA) (Müller and Tag 2010). It allows movement figurations to be related to verbal utterances as they unfold as multidimensional experiential gestalts. This affects all dimensions of temporal structures, from the micro level of expressive movement units to the macro level of unfolding themes. In this way, metaphors become describable in their temporality.

## A.1 Audiovisual media: eMAEX

The analysis of metaphors in audiovisual compositions starts from the media-specifics of audiovisual images as movement-images. Temporal structures are thus the entry point for the analysis on every level of audiovisual compositions. CineMet draws upon eMAEX as a standardized method for the analysis of audiovisual forms (Kappelhoff and Bakels 2011, Kappelhoff, Bakels, and Greifenstein forthcoming/2019).[1] The eMAEX system was specifically developed as an empirical method for describing the expressive qualities of audiovisual media. This includes research on cinematic expressive movement, on genre-specific poetics of affect, and on multimodality and embodiment as the basis of experiencing and understanding. Having been applied in several projects, eMAEX is continually being adapted and further developed.

eMAEX offers an analytical grasp beyond 'representations' of characters, places, or objects, and considers cinematic expressive movements as central methodological access to capture movement-images as a media-specific mode of composition and of experiencing. Audiovisual forms are examined in a step-by-step procedure. We look systematically at ever smaller temporal segments and at how they interact with one another temporally. Scenes are the building blocks for the films' dramaturgy of affect, and expressive movement units shape the dynamic form of each scene. The compositional elements produce the expressive movement. This basic structure also applies to other media formats.

## A.2 Multimodal face-to-face interaction: MGA and MFA

We have developed a set of methods that make it possible to determine metaphor activation in multimodal settings as an interactive phenomenon. They are designed to reconstruct processes of foregrounding as an interactive flow of attention in multimodal face-to-face communication (Müller 2008a, b). Metaphor Foregrounding Analysis (MFA) is designed to determine 'waking metaphors', i.e., metaphoricity that is attended to in an interaction. Foregrounding of metaphoricity in the flow of discourse is considered as indication of meaning that is made interactively relevant (Müller and Tag 2010). Based on converging expressions of metaphorical meaning in different modalities (here, speech and gestures), the flow of attention on metaphorical

1 For further information see: www.empirische-medienaesthetik.fu-berlin.de/en/index.html.

meaning over the course of an interaction is described. Metaphor analysis of waking metaphors only considers verbal metaphorical expressions when highlighted by audiovisual or gestural concretizations and/or elaborations of their experiential source domains. MFA makes it possible to document a temporal salience profile of activated metaphoricity established interactively with the flow of conversation/discourse.

MFA analysis may be complemented by a linguistic gesture analysis. Transcription as well as form-based analyses are conducted in ELAN (annotation software for audiovisual data, developed by the Max Planck Institute for Psycholinguistics, Nijmegen). Our 'Method of linguistic Gesture Analysis' (MGA) is a form-based two-step analysis of the semantics and pragmatics of hand gestures. MGA reconstructs the meaning of the gestural hand movement in terms of as-if actions (i.e., 'gestural modes of representation', 'gestural modes of mimesis', Müller 1998a, 2016a) and then looks at how this underspecified meaning form of the gestural form is specified within an actual context of use.

To visualize the temporal unfolding of interactive salience profiles, a Keynote-based Timeline Annotation (KeyTA, Müller and Ladewig 2013, Müller and Schmitt 2015) can be employed. This documents temporal metaphorical structures in terms of the repeated use of a particular metaphorical expression (verbal, gestural) on a timeline. In this way, it is possible to document visually how a particular waking metaphor (cf. Müller 2008a, 2013) is distributed across the discourse and across modalities (speech and gesture).

## A.3 The CinMet Procedure: Exemplary Analysis of a Film

However, CineMet as an analytical procedure does not simply combine film-analytical methods with cognitive linguistic ones (including gesture studies) that apply to the analysis of temporal structures, but has developed existing methods further. It offers a way to reconstruct temporal experiencing as a constitutive dimension for both audiovisual media and everyday face-to-face communication. Providing a descriptive and sequential method of analysis, it accounts for the specific temporal structures that characterize the interface of affectivity and metaphorical meaning-making.

CineMet addresses temporal structures on macro, meso, and micro levels, synthesizing the descriptive observations. Temporal macro-structures concern a discourse event (an entire film, a television show, or a dance class). While there are no fixed boundaries between levels, the micro level analysis mainly attends to expressive movements. Analyses of meso levels document how these movement figurations form larger compositional patterns, and how metaphorical meaning emerges with experiencing these patterns as multidimensional experiential gestalts. The synthesis then describes how the three levels work together, how a particular temporal arrangement of expressive movement units may create an interaffective parcours, and how metaphorical themes evolve along and within that experiential parcours.

### A.3.1 Hands-on Outline

The hands-on outline for the analytical procedure for Cinematic Metaphor Analysis entails analytic steps on macro, meso, and micro levels of temporality. Although the overall order of steps is flexible, we recommend starting with the macro level. Note that the steps need to be adapted to the demands of the audiovisual material under investigation.

**Macro Level (1)**

- View the whole film/audiovisual material. Describe prominent staging patterns across the film. Divide it into scenes/sequences
- Select scenes/sequences with candidates for metaphorical themes (foregrounding of metaphoricity)
- Choose some of the scenes/sequences that stage these themes

**Micro Level (2)**

- Take one scene/sequence and do a microanalysis
- Determine the expressive movement units within a scene/sequence
- Describe the affective quality/qualities of expressive movement unit/s
- Spell out metaphoricity as emerging from the affective quality/qualities of the expressive movement unit/s and as relating two experiential realms
- Consider verbal metaphoric expressions specifically when highlighted by audiovisual or gestural concretizations and/or elaborations of their experiential source domains

**Meso Level (3)**

- Describe a selection of expressive movement units in detail (film-analytically) with their movement qualities – as affective qualities
- See if they create a recurring pattern and/or experiential scenarios

– Describe the pattern/scenario with regard to continuities and variations as they develop along the full timescale

**Macro Level (4)**
– Describe the trajectory of expressive movement units that orchestrate a metaphorical theme or the temporal parcours of a cinematic metaphor
– Focus on the unfolding of affectivity and of metaphorical themes along the full audiovisual form/multimodal setting (movie, tv-show, dance class, conversation etc.)

Depending upon the research focus, meso or macro level analysis may be carried out. Micro level analysis is indispensable.

In the following, we first illustrate the analytical procedure with a recapitulation of the analytic steps involved in the analysis of cinematic metaphors in Hitchcock's SPELLBOUND and then zoom in on the three levels of analysis in more detail.

**Macro Level: SPELLBOUND (1)**
View the whole film and divide it into scenes. Describe prominent staging patterns across the film. Select scenes with candidates for metaphorical themes.

Figure A.1 shows all the scenes that stage the 'topic' of non-remembering in Hitchcock's SPELLBOUND. In Figure A.1 the boxes represent roughly the position of the scenes on a timeline for the film as a whole.

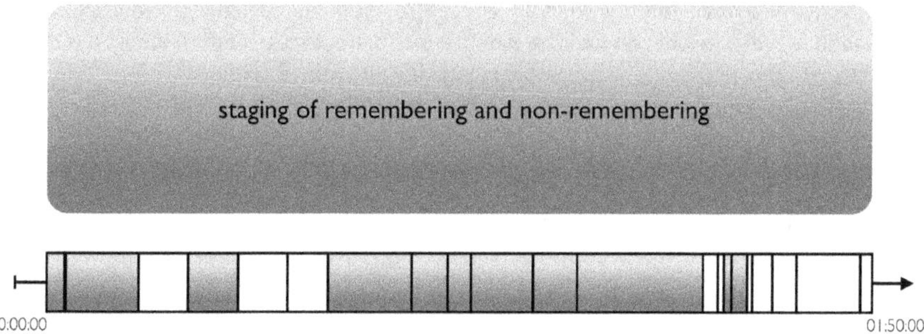


**Figure A.1:** Scenes staging remembering and non-remembering as temporal structure (SPELLBOUND)

To prepare the analysis on the micro-level, zoom in on the expressive movement units that stage a specific potential candidate for a metaphor.

In SPELLBOUND for instance, we looked at how non-remembering was staged on the level of cinematic expressive movement units. Figure A.2 below shows the pattern of expressive movement units that stage non-remembering along the full movie.

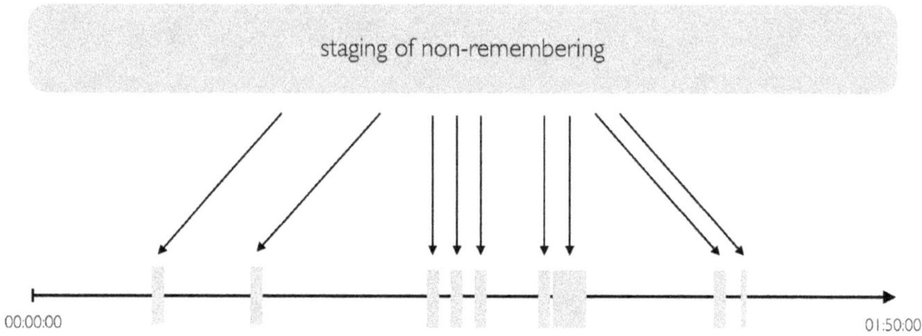


**Figure A.2:** Cinematic expressive movement units staging non-remembering (SPELLBOUND) (→ Figure 13.3)

### Micro Level: SPELLBOUND (2)

Take one scene/sequence and do a microanalysis. Determine the expressive movement units within the scenes/sequences that are relevant to a potential metaphorical theme. Describe the affective quality/qualities of expressive movement unit/s based on their cinematic staging:

> Expressive movements in film can consist of montage patterns as well as camera, sound, mise-en-scène, and acting figurations. Distinct movement qualities are created through the particular ways in which these different articulatory modalities come together and form an unfolding temporal gestalt. (Scherer, Greifenstein, and Kappelhoff 2014, 2085)

Spell out metaphoricity as emerging from the affective quality/qualities of the expressive movement unit/s and how they relate different experiential realms.

Figure A.3 illustrates the affective qualities of staging non-remembering as a cinematic expressive movement: downward orientation as a static immobile quality.

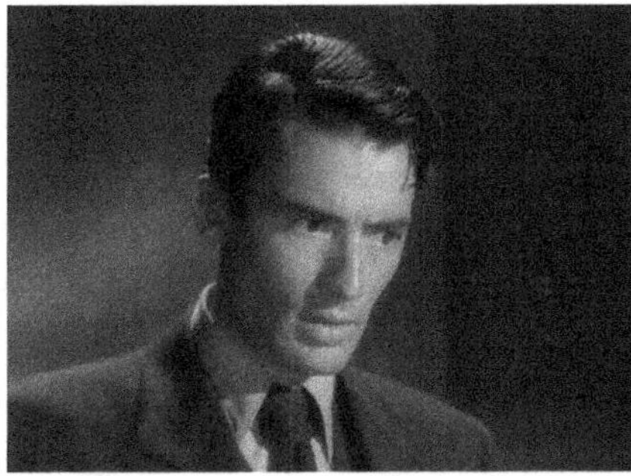
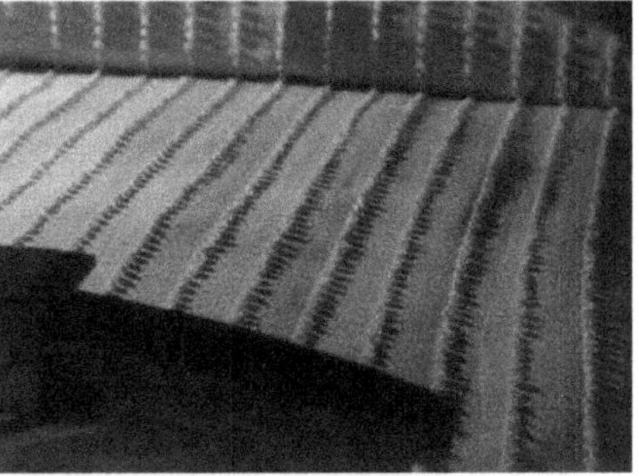

**Figure A.3:** Feeling non-remembering: downward orientation as a static, immobile quality (SPELLBOUND) (→ Figure 13.2)

This is how we described the affective qualities of this cinematic expressive movement unit:

> Editing, camera position, and visual composition orchestrate the downward orientation as a static, immobile experience. The accompanying dialog connects the staging of the lines against the white bed cover with non-remembering: in response to Constance's "You remember something", John says "No". The sequence orchestrates a crescendo of tension staged in sustained shots, a slowly swelling and increasingly threatening music, the accelerating, pressing rhythm of Constance summarizing her analytic observations, and the commanding and desperate tone in which she eventually tells her patient "Look at it to remember", comes to a head and then breaks off. This is the moment of John's breakdown. He collapses, falls down, into the depth that he has fixated in panic, held and caressed by Constance.
>
> The slow alternation of shots orchestrates the terrifying feeling of being stuck, from which there is no escape but collapse. It is a cinematic movement expression of how a breakdown feels and viewers live it through their own bodies. This montage sequence shapes a movement of cinematic expressivity that is recurring over the course of the film and thus unfolds a temporal pattern: *a sustained and slow alternation of shots is held in stasis* (by the insertion of core elements, the POV on tracks, lines, the swelling and threatening music, the numbed facial expression) *and suddenly breaks off*. This is how non-remembering feels, and this is what the viewer encounters again and again throughout the film. This feeling for the increasingly terrifying experiences is not an outcome of the world of depicted characters and objects; it is the staging of cinematic expressivity that exceeds the represented characters, objects, and sceneries and turns them into the expression of an inner life, which viewers then ascribe to the characters on the screen. (see page 209–210)

### Meso Level: SPELLBOUND (3)

Describe a selection of expressive movement units in detail (film-analytically) with their movement qualities – as affective qualities. See if they build a recurring pattern. Describe the pattern with regard to continuities and variations.

Figure A.4 shows in grey boxes all the scenes that stage non-remembering as feeling of freezing, terror, static, downwardness connecting with lines on white ground. Three pairs of stills show exemplary scenes and illustrate the staging of cinematic expressive movements as a freezing with a downward camera angle on Gregory Peck's face and its montage with lines against white surfaces.

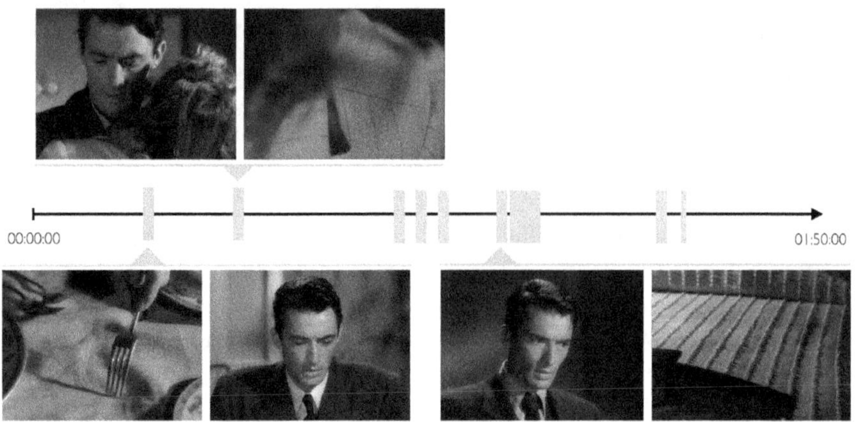


**Figure A.4**: Non-remembering staged as recurrent metaphorical pattern: (1) lines on table cloth, (2) lines on night robe, (3) lines on bed-cover (SPELLBOUND) (→ Figure 13.4)

Having carried out a microanalysis of a selection of scenes which stage non-remembering as a potential metaphorical theme we return to the macro level of temporal orchestration of the movie as a whole.

### Macro Level: SPELLBOUND (4)

Describe the affective temporal parcours along the complete audiovisual form/ multimodal setting (movie, tv-show, dance class, conversation etc.) Describe the trajectory of expressive movement units that orchestrate a metaphorical theme or the temporal parcours of cinematic metaphor. If there are other forms of staging a potential metaphorical theme then return to the micro level of analysis and carry out the same procedure for a second form of staging a given metaphorical theme. The same holds, if several metaphorical themes intertwine.

Figure A.5 shows how two metaphorical themes are staged on the level of scenes (grey boxes) roughly representing their position on a timeline. The dark grey boxes show the positions of the expressive movement units that stage 'experiencing psychoanalysis as opening doors'; the light grey boxes show all the units that stage 'remembering a traumatic event as increasing tension, as successive and varied experiences of downward oriented immobility, which abruptly shift to a breaking loose of a downward movement'. The big boxes below and above the timeline illustrate the metaphorical themes that emerge from the affective parcours that spectators and analysts experience in the process of film-viewing.

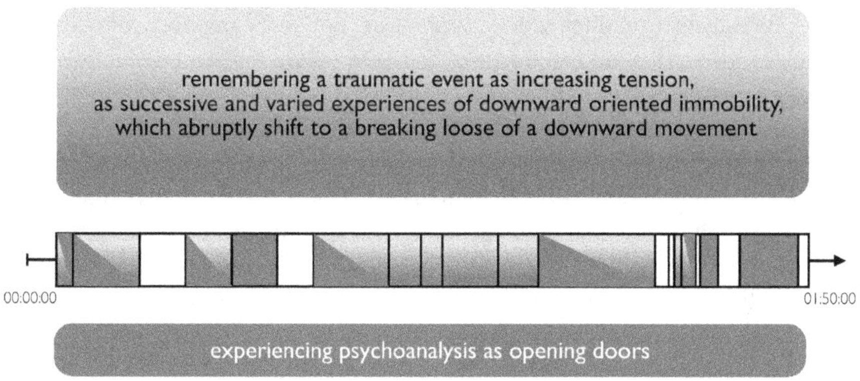


**Figure A.5:** Temporally expanded, intertwining, and alternating metaphorical themes (SPELLBOUND) (→ Figure 13.9)

Here is how we formulated the synthesis (here relating it with Cameron's notion of systematic metaphor, Cameron 2010, Cameron et al. 2009) in the context of our analysis:

> The two systematic cinematic metaphors emerge from the composition and unfolding of expressive movements, i.e., from the point of view of film viewers as a process that stretches out over the entire film. So that, seen from the end, we can reconstruct two systematic cinematic metaphors that cannot be defined through any singular mapping. Instead, what makes up systematic cinematic metaphor is that it unfolds over the course of the film in ever new variations, as a dynamic process, temporally divided into segments, of ever new metaphorical transferals and shifts. This process structures the process of understanding as an interaction of the dialog, of the action represented, and of cinematic expressive movement. (see page 221)

## A.3.2 Zooming In: Three levels of audiovisual and multimodal communication analysis

We now zoom in on the three levels of analysis separately in order to illustrate a) how they apply to the analysis of different audiovisual forms, b) how our film-analytical method offers a new perspective on the analysis of multimodal face-to-face communication and c) how different forms of visualization are employed to illustrate different aspects of the analysis.

#### Micro Level: Expressive Movements

The micro level of analysis addresses the cinematic expressivity of audiovisual forms. Be they feature films or television news, political campaign commercials, or music videos, they all can be described with regard to their cinematic-audiovisual expressivity. This expressivity, however is not identical with represented emotions (for instance the facial expressions of the protagonists on the screen), but is a matter of how all elements of cinematic staging (montage, sound, acting, framing etc.) are temporally orchestrated, how they merge into a temporal unit, a movement unit with a characteristic movement quality – a cinematic expressive movement unit.

Audiovisual compositions of single scenes are structured as an arrangement of temporal segments that unfold in a distinctive pattern (initiation, progression, closure). We define them as expressive movement units.

An expressive movement unit is a dynamic pattern that – in its simplest form – displays a tripartite temporal phase structure: initiation – progression – closure. This structure corresponds to the simplest phase structure of a hand gesture: preparation – stroke – retraction (Müller, Bressem, and Ladewig in prep. for an overview). The description of an expressive movement unit serves to reconstruct the affective quality of a movement-image. It seeks to describe the affective-sensory qualities that the dynamic pattern of the expressive movement unit stages.

Core aspects of aesthetic designing expressive movement units that may guide the analytic process are:

- Camera (camera movement and perspective, framing)
- Montage (of framing, rhythm of montage, shot transitions)
- Sound (music, sounds, voice, and their interrelation)
- Acting (gesture, facial expression, body movement)
- Mise-en-scène, choreography (constellation of characters and objects)
- Image composition (distribution of contrast and color, light values, visual patterns and fragmentation of image space, dynamics within and texture of the image)
- Dialog and written words

With reference to these forms of aesthetic orchestration, expressive movements are described. The qualities of the expressive movements are experienced bodily by the viewer as a specific affective flow, and we have developed several forms of visualizing the affective qualities of expressive movements. For example, in Figure A.6 the two big light grey boxes describe two movement patterns that together form an overarching pattern (depicted in the long dark grey box on the top of the diagram). The arrow shows the time length of the expressive movement unit; the vertical lines show the average shot length within the unit. Above the timeline, we have depicted the sound volume as it changes along the scene. We have chosen to do this here, because sound is a prominent staging pattern in this scene. Below the timeline the movement qualities of the two patterns are described ('slow sliding' and 'from staccato to ritardando') including their staging: 'slow and sliding movement through staging of camera, visual composition and actors movement', 'an abrupt increasing of shot frequency and volume turns into static calmness by slowing down (of music, editing, and acting)'.

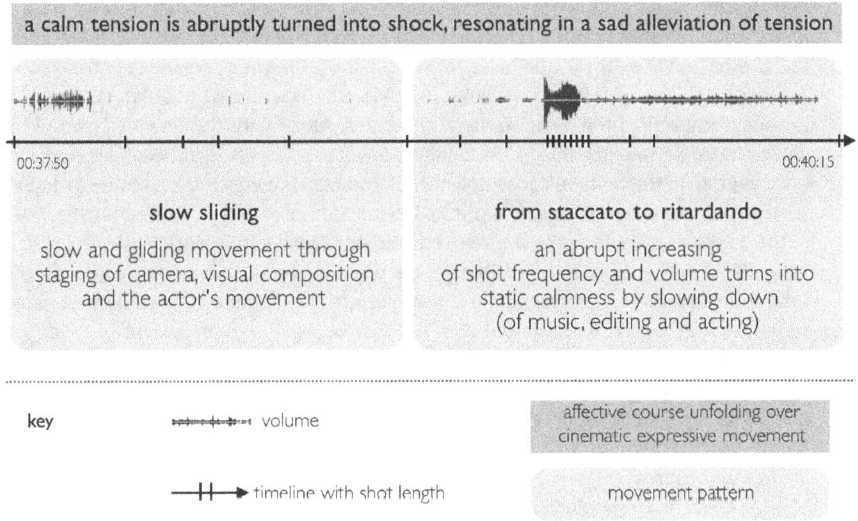


**Figure A.6:** Cinematic expressive movement (BATAAN) (→ Figure 8.4)

**BATAAN**

Here is how we described this complex staging of the cinematic expressive movement in the text:

> Considering the BATAAN scene from the point of view of its temporal orchestration, it turns out that the scene is arranged along two fairly distinct movement patterns ([see Figure A.6]): while the first one is composed as a continuous and slow movement, the second is staged in a staccato rhythm.

**The first movement pattern** [...] ends with the arrival of the soldier at the top of the tree and is orchestrated in a slow and gliding rhythm: in long takes we see the soldier receiving the command and approaching the tree slowly, preparing for the climb. After the order is spoken, only quiet sounds interrupt the silence. When the soldier starts climbing silently up the tall, bent trunk of the palm tree, the camera follows him with a soft and sliding movement. This upward movement, which slowly develops, is staged in an intertwining of various different modalities of filmic articulation: the camera movement, the visual composition, and the actor's movement merge into a continuous gliding, accompanied by silence on the soundtrack. Together, these articulatory modalities of audiovisual staging temporally merge and create one distinctive movement quality: a slow and silent sliding. It is by means of this staging of a temporal gestalt, this quality of cinematic movement in which all the audiovisual means play together, that a specific affective experience on the side of a spectator is audiovisually orchestrated. Such an experience of 'calm tension' emerges from the aesthetic composition of the cinematic movement gestalt.

**The second movement pattern** [...] comes with a change of articulatory qualities, moving from a staccato rhythm to ritardando or slowing down. It begins with a static long shot of the soldier who is keeping watch at the top of the palm tree. All of a sudden this is interrupted by the sound of a gunshot and the falling and screaming of the soldier. A series of close-ups follows, showing, in a fast montage and with a high cutting rate, the shocked faces of the dying soldier's comrades. Along with the slowing down of the cutting rate, we see how one of the soldier's face (again in close-up) changes from surprise to grief. In this series of close-ups, the different faces merge into one cohesive figure: a surprised and shocked face, a multiplied expression of fear that, in the slowing down of the montage, transforms as if it were one moving facial expression. Music sets in dramatically after the shot noise and changes tempo and volume, turning into a melancholic tune. Taken together, this second movement pattern (predominantly staged by montage, sound, and acting) is orchestrated as a contrast between a quiet, extended, enduring tempo, contrasting sharply with a staccato rhythm that then increasingly slows down. With the staccato montage and the high frequency of shots of several faces, an experience of shock is modulated which then turns into a sad alleviation of tension, modulated by the slowing down of the montage, the subtle changes in the soldiers' faces, and the change of the music.

[...] The increasing tension of the first movement pattern and the staccato rhythm of the second one shape a temporal course which is in fact an affective movement, a movement with an affective quality, much like bodily expressions of surprise, shock or grief. (see page 135–138)

## Face-to-Face Discussion

Since face-to-face communication is as much a temporally-orchestrated event as the process of film-viewing, and, as we have described above, multimodal interaction also unfolds as an affective parcours, we can use similar ways of describing the interaffective orchestration of an unfolding communicative interaction.

Figure A.7 shows an intensity profile of the temporal course of interaffectivity that characterizes the flow of affectivity merged across three speakers as they engage in an increasingly heated negotiation process. It documents the temporal unfolding of affective intensities along a timeline. Superimposed on that timeline, the diagram shows a visualization of the volume contour as jointly created by the three speakers along this segment of their discussion. Above the timeline, black, grey, and white boxes depict the segments of speech (turns) of the three speakers showing the rhythmic alternation of their respective turns. The boxes below the timeline show the interactive rhythm of the three women's gestures. Together, the gesture and the speech 'boxes' of the respective speakers visualize the choppy back and forth rhythm of repeated starts and harsh interruptions (dotted line) including a dynamic volume contour (the affective qualities of the interactive expressive movement unit) that is an expression of interaffective increase of tension and mutual anger (the shared affective parcours, the long darker box below). The big grey box represents the segment of the conversation that is structured as a shared expressive movement unit, a unit of interaffective expressivity.

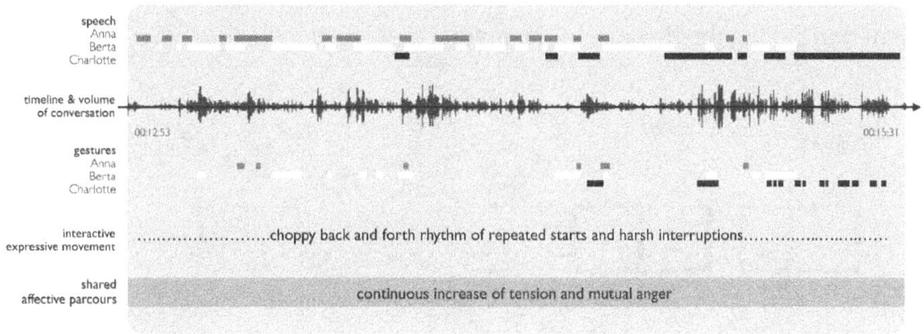


**Figure A.7:** Interactive expressive movement (face-to-face discussion) (→ Figure 9.3)

In the text we have described this parcours of interaffectivity and unfolding metaphoricity in the following way:

> In a continuous increase of tension and mutual anger, the discussion unfolds in a choppy rhythm of repeated starts and harsh interruption.
>
> With this jointly created dialogic rhythm and shaping of shared affect (interaffectivity), a gestalt emerges that we consider to be an interactive expressive movement. Such a movement gestalt, which may encompass several minutes (in our example, two and a half), unfolds a particular affective quality. Its particular affective intensity not only shows up in gesturing, but also in speech and bodily interaction.

The rhythm of anger is articulated interactively and in multiple modalities. On the level of speech, Berta is interrupted by the others who speak with a raised pitch and a high volume. Berta interrupts the others, and she also raises her voice and pitch. The constant back and forth of turns, the increased tempo of speech, and the rate of turn-takings further contribute to an increasing tension and compose to the interactive expressive movement. (see page 152–154)

## Meso Level: Patterns and/or Scenarios

On the meso level of temporality, expressive movements may recur forming temporal patterns or specific experiential scenarios. For the analytic procedure this means describing a chosen selection of expressive movement units in detail and carrying out microanalysis of their expressive movement units. See if they create a recurring pattern and/or an experiential scenario and describe the temporal contour along the full length of the audiovisual data. Describe the pattern/scenario with regard to continuities and variations as it develops along the time scale of the audiovisual material. The meso level example taken from SPELLBOUND above shows such a recurrent pattern. Sometimes, however, the recurrent patterns form an experiential scenario, as, for example, in the political feature REPORT MAINZ. Figure A.8 below shows the temporal arrangement of cinematic expressive movement units along the timeline of the report that form a metaphorical scenario.

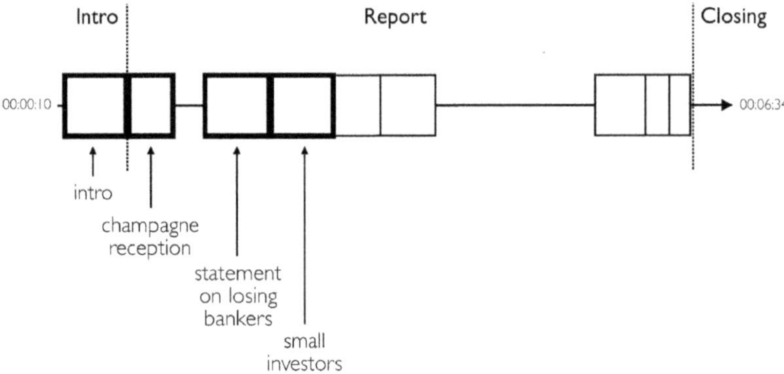


**Figure A.8:** Cinematic expressive movement units as temporal structures (REPORT MAINZ) (→ Figure 12.2)

### REPORT MAINZ

On the meso level of REPORT MAINZ, metaphorically-staged cinematic expressive movement units orchestrate an emerging scenario where being a loser in the financial crisis is staged as an experience of being down and in an excluded exterior. Figure A.9 shows the expressive movement units that stage losers in the financial crisis: grey boxes above the timeline depict units which orchestrate losing as being down, black boxes below the timeline show units in which experiencing of being in an excluded exterior is staged. Positions of boxes on the timeline roughly represent the temporal arrangement of the expressive movement units along the 6:34 minutes length of the report. The 'people' that are staged as losers are mentioned above the boxes (notably, small investors as well as bankers are presented as 'losers' of the crisis).

With their specific temporal arrangement, these expressive movement units orchestrate an affective parcours that connects losing with being down *and* in an excluded exterior. This metaphorical scenario emerges from the affective parcours that spectators experience in their process of film-viewing and it is paraphrased in the box above spanning the full length of the televised report captured in the diagram.

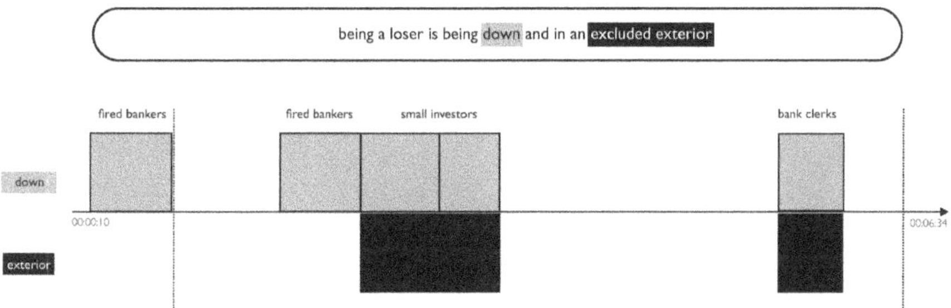


**Figure A.9**: Cinematic expressive movement units that stage losers of the financial crisis (REPORT MAINZ)

### Dance class

When considering multimodal face-to-face interaction as temporally orchestrated events that unfold beyond the micro level of words, turns, short exchanges of utterances, it turns out that rather often we observe that processes of interactive meaning-making unfold in forms of (metaphorical) scenarios (Müller 2008a).

The analysis of the tango dance class documents how applying our film-analytical perspective to multimodal face-to-face interaction reveals the temporal and interactive evolution of a metaphorical scenario as a temporal form of embodied meaning-making.

For the meso level analysis of multimodal face-to-face interaction this also implies to describe expressive movement units, to see if they create a recurring pattern and/or an experiential scenario, to describe the pattern/scenario with regard to continuities and variations as it develops temporally along the full length of the setting.

Figure A.10 shows a segment of 2:25 minutes length where the evolution of the multimodally embodied metaphorical scenario is particularly prominent. Timeline and vertical lines give an approximation of the temporal sequencing of those utterances that are vital in building the metaphorical scenario. The vertical lines furthermore connect sequences of talk (here only the teacher) with verbal metaphoric expressions building the metaphorical scenario, below the timeline drawings of the hand and full body gestures which contribute to the emerging scenario: we see several gestures molding and outlining the shape of an anchor (1, 2 from the left), then holding (3) and molding (4, 5) a massive vertical chain, then transforming into body gestures, where the stretched legs become the heavy chain and the upper body the ship that is stabilized by a dragging heavy chain. The diagram shows a detail of the evolving metaphorical scenario that emerges multimodally in speech, gesture, and body movement (a case of foregrounding metaphoricity).

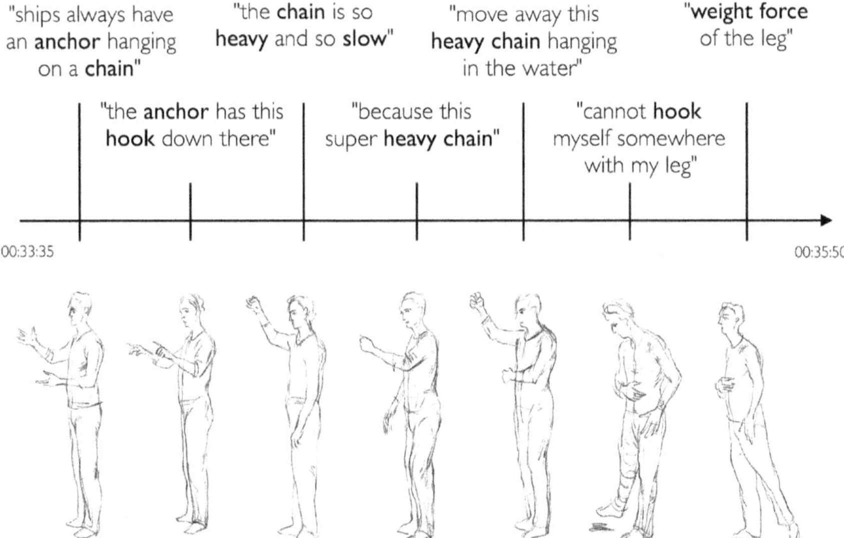


**Figure A.10:** An emerging metaphorical scenario in a tango class (→ Figure 11.3)

Figure A.11 then documents how the anchor chain scenario evolves along the 47 minutes of the temporal unfolding of the class. Speech, hand gestures, and body movements are depicted on separate timelines, the placement of the boxes showing the approximate position of moments that orchestrate the evolving metaphorical scenario. The metaphorical scenario is paraphrased above the timelines, employing possible metaphorical expressions used by the speaker.

balance as ship stabilized by a dragging anchor chain

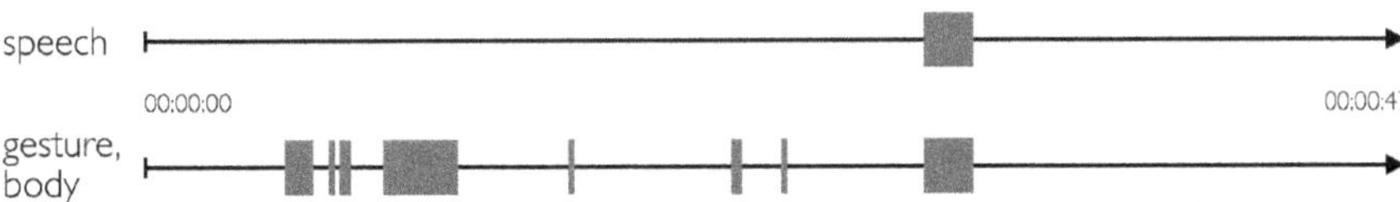


**Figure A.11:** One metaphorical scenario developing over time in a tango class

The diagram visualizes the scenario as a temporal structure (here only for the speaker) that emerges first on the level of the body (heaviness of the leg 'behind' as stabilizing 'walking' in tango) and that retrospectively becomes part of a temporally orchestrated metaphor. Note that this recalls the retrospectively orchestrated temporal structure that we have described for one of the metaphorical themes in Hitchcock's SPELLBOUND. Here, a process of remembering a traumatic event only retrospectively becomes connected with recurring and varied experiences of non-remembering that eventually break loose.

In the text we have described the scenario in the following way:

> The instructor embarks on a long and vivid storytelling that at first seems far-fetched. He describes how he was always puzzled by how a ship's anchor works, how the anchor reaches the sea bed in very deep waters, and how to free an anchor that is stuck in rocks. And indeed, at first this conversational move towards seafaring seems really out of place in a dancing lesson and his two interlocutors appear rather puzzled, not sure why they have to listen to this kind of story. Subsequently, however, they understand that the story unfolds an experiential realm, explicitly mentioned by the verbal metaphor 'anchoring' that addresses precisely the problem just observed: the free leg that is bent too early in the step. The realm of embodied experiences that the teacher opens up for his interlocutors is the principle of anchoring a ship, transferred to the topic of maintaining balance in an Argentine tango style of walking. In a very vivid manner and by integrating a series of hand and full body gestures, he unfolds a metaphorical scenario that serves to illustrate metaphorically the principle of the heavy, stretched and lagging behind leg so characteristic of Argentine tango and so essential to stay balanced in walking while moving the body axes smoothly from one standing leg to another one. In this process, [...] the anchoring principle [becomes] a model for the smooth shifting of the dancer's axis in walking. (see page 189–190)

**Macro Level: Metaphorical Themes**

On the macro level, we bring the analyses carried out on micro and meso levels together and formulate cinematic metaphors, i.e., metaphors as temporally unfolding forms of meaning-making. Drawing on Black, we consider metaphor to create similarities: "It would be more illuminating [...] to say that the metaphor creates the similarity than to say that it formulates some similarity antecedently existing." (Black 1962, 37) We follow Black's understanding of metaphor and assume (see page 63):

> that certain qualities of the subsidiary subject come forth from experiencing the principal subject, in which quite particular qualities of the first are "projected upon" the second (Black 1962, 41), or that the first "filters", "transforms", or also "selects" certain characteristics in the second (Black 1962, 42). What is decisive here is that in such an understanding of metaphor as a dynamic interaction, a visual-perceptual principle of figurative thinking is outlined that is not based on given relations of similarity, but produces these (cf. also Schmitt, Greifenstein, and Kappelhoff 2014).

On the macro level, we describe how this visual-perceptive principle of figurative thinking evolves from the affective temporal parcours that film viewers and participants in a communicative encounter engage in. We thus describe the trajectory of expressive movement units that orchestrate a metaphorical theme or the temporal parcours of a cinematic metaphor. Macroanalysis focuses on the unfolding of affectivity and metaphorical themes along the full audiovisual form/multimodal setting (movie, tv-show, dance class, conversation etc.). The goal is twofold: a) describe the temporal orchestration of a metaphorical theme, b) describe potential intertwining of metaphorical themes.

**REPORT MAINZ**

Returning to the televised political report the extension of the analytic perspective to the macro level reveals a second metaphorical scenario that interacts with the first one. On the one hand, losers in the financial crisis are staged as being down and in an excluded exterior and on the other hand, winners are staged as being up and inside in a closed interior.

Figure A.12 shows how the two scenarios intertwine and how they are sometimes even staged on the level of an expressive movement unit (boxes combining dark and light colors). Note that the diagram is slightly varied as compared to the one showing only one metaphorical scenario (Figure A.9). Boxes below the timeline show the staging of 'closed interiors' versus 'excluded exteriors', boxes above the timeline show the orchestrating of upwardness versus downwardness. Succession and alignment of the boxes shows the relative temporal position of the respective scenes. The people/characters to whom those affective qualities of being excluded and included are ascribed in the process of film-viewing are notated above the boxes (fired bankers, consultants, small investors, bank clerks, consultants, and former fired bankers). The four shades of grey align with the four different aspects that characterize the metaphorical scenarios. The big boxes with the round edges on the top and the bottom of the diagram entail descriptive paraphrases of the cinematic metaphors.

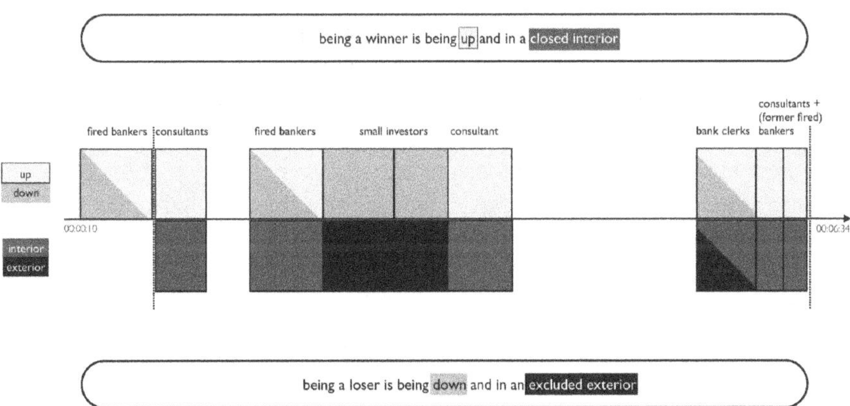


**Figure A.12:** Temporal unfolding and intertwining of metaphorical themes (REPORT MAINZ) (→ Figure 12.7)

Here is how we described the temporal unfolding and intertwining of the two metaphorical themes:

> Summing up, the metaphorical opposition between an upward orientation of the winners and a downward perspective of the losers is embedded in another opposition, namely an "enclosed interior" and an "excluding exterior". Being a winner is not only staged as being up, but also as being in a closed interior. Being a loser, on the other hand, is not only staged as being down, but also being outside and in an excluded exterior. These embedded metaphors unfold in time, i.e., viewers experience a temporal parcours in which the embedded cinematic metaphors intertwine. Figure [A.12] shows that the two metaphorical oppositions forming two scenarios are temporally co-present and intertwined. (see page 204)

## Dance Class

Also, for the analysis of a complete multimodal communicative encounter such as one dance lesson, returning to the macro level of temporal structuring may reveal further dynamic complexities of metaphor trajectories.

Figure A.13 documents two such trajectories that evolve and intertwine along the lesson for one speaker, here the teacher. Both metaphorical realms orchestrate the 'topic' of balance in tango dancing (this was the subject of the class), however they target different aspects of balance: maintaining balance in walking (dark grey boxes) and feeling balance in standing (light grey boxes). The size of the boxes approximates the time length of the metaphorical moments. This documents a temporal profile of interactive intensity, by depicting those moments in which the respective realms of experience are made interactively prominent. This holds, even though the diagram depicts only one speaker, because his activities are analyzed as an interactive engagement with the class. As the analysis of the interactive 'history' of extending the 'dragging anchor chain' scenario has shown, it responds to an interactive affordance of two students expressing non-understanding.

The two metaphorical scenarios are paraphrased at the top of the diagram: balance as axis in a coordinate system, balance as a ship stabilized by a dragging anchor chain.

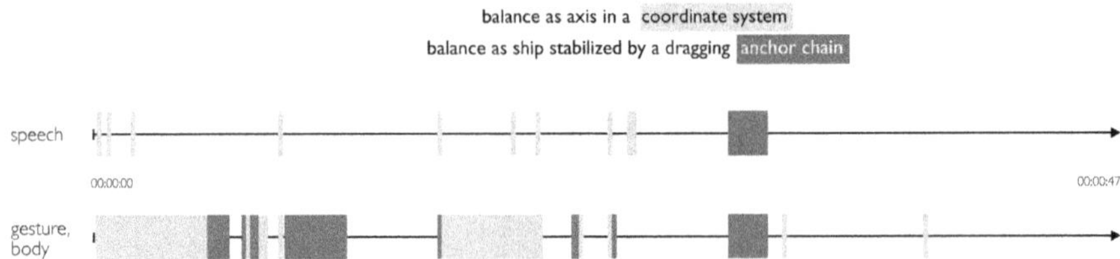


**Figure A.13:** Two evolving and intertwining metaphorical trajectories in a tango class (→ Figure 11.4)

The figure thus documents how, over the time of the unfolding lesson, the coordinate system and the anchoring metaphors develop into experiential metaphorical realms. It visualizes the temporal macro-structure of experienced source domains of metaphors for balance in tango dancing.

This is how we summarized this temporal pattern of unfolding metaphorical themes:

> In this process, the metaphorical scenario that previously established the dancer's vertical (and sagittal) axes in a stable center of a spatial coordinate system connects with a different metaphorical scenario: the anchoring principle as a model for the smooth shifting of the dancer's axis in walking. (see page 190)

## A.4 Concluding remarks

In our collaborative transdisciplinary research, we have developed a range of different methods of analysis and documentation to account for processes of metaphorical meaning-making with audiovisual media as well as within multimodal face-to-face communication. These methods make it possible to uncover temporal structures of metaphorical meaning-making as affective parcours on micro, meso, and macro levels. Our methodological procedure is thus always systematic, but never schematic, meaning that there is not one incremental set of steps to follow and there is not one only way of documenting the analysis. Rather the visualization and the order in which the procedure is carried out are creative responses to the affordances of the material and, obviously, the particular research questions.

Our methods make it possible to document how movement figurations on a micro level form macro level compositional patterns and how metaphorical meaning emerges from and within the affectivity of these movement figurations. The methods also open up new paths to further explore the integration of language, gestures, and body movements as expressive modalities, and relate those explorations to the cinematic movement-image as a specific modality in itself.

# Bibliography

Anderson, Joseph D., and Barbara Fisher Anderson, eds. 2007. *Narration and Spectatorship in Moving Images*. Newcastle: Cambridge Scholars Publishing.

Bakels, Jan-Hendrik. 2014. "Embodying Audio-Visual Media. Concepts and Transdisciplinary Perspectives." In *Body – Language – Communication. An International Handbook on Multimodality in Human Interaction*, edited by Cornelia Müller, Alan Cienki, Ellen Fricke, Silva H. Ladewig, David McNeill, and Jana Bressem, 2048–2061. Berlin/Boston, MA: De Gruyter Mouton.

Bakels, Jan-Hendrik. 2017. *Audiovisuelle Rhythmen. Filmmusik, Bewegungskomposition und die dynamische Affizierung des Zuschauers*. Berlin/Boston, MA: Walter de Gruyter. (English translation in prep.)

Balázs, Béla. 2010. *Early Film Theory. Visible Man and The Spirit of Film*. Oxford: Berghahn Books. Original edition 1924, 1930.

Barcelona, Antonio. 2000. "The Cognitive Theory of Metaphor and Metonymy." In *Metaphor and Metonymy at the Crossroads. A Cognitive Perspective*, edited by Antonio Barcelona, 1–28. Berlin/New York, NY: Mouton de Gruyter.

Barcelona, Antonio. 2009. "Motivation of Construction Meaning and Form. The Roles of Metonymy and Inference." In *Metonymy and Metaphor in Grammar*, edited by Klaus-Uwe Panther, Linda Thornburg, and Antonio Barcelona, 363–401. Amsterdam: John Benjamins.

Barsalou, L. W. 1999. "Perceptual Symbol Systems." *Behavioral and Brain Sciences* 22 (4): 577–660.

Bartenieff, Irmgard, and Dori Lewis. 1980. *Body Movement. Coping with the Environment*. New York, NY: Gordon and Breach.

Bartsch, Anne. 2007. *Audiovisuelle Emotionen. Emotionsdarstellung und Emotionsvermittlung durch audiovisuelle Medienangebote*. Köln: Halem.

Bateman, John, Janina Wildfeuer, and Tuomo Hiippala. 2017. *Multimodality. Foundations, Research and Analysis. A Problem-Oriented Introduction*. Berlin: De Gruyter Mouton.

Baudry, Jean-Louis, and Alan Williams. 1975. "Ideological Effects of the Basic Cinematographic Apparatus." *Film Quarterly* 28 (2): 39–47.

Bellour, Raymond. 2002. "Le Dépli des Émotions." *Trafic* 43: 93–128.

Black, Max. 1962. *Models and Metaphors. Studies in Language and Philosophy*. Ithaca, NY: Cornell University Press.

Black, Max. 1993. "More about Metaphor." In *Metaphor and Thought*, edited by Andrew Ortony, 19–41. Cambridge: Cambridge University Press. Original edition 1977.

Blumenberg, Hans. 1981. "Anthropologische Annäherung an die Aktualität der Rhetorik." In *Wirklichkeiten in denen wir leben. Aufsätze und eine Rede*, 104–136. Stuttgart: Reclam.

Blumenberg, Hans. 1986. *Lebenszeit und Weltzeit*. Frankfurt/M.: Suhrkamp.

Blumenberg, Hans. 1987. "An Anthropological Approach to the Contemporary Significance of Rhetoric." In *After Philosophy. End or Transformation?*, edited by Kenneth Baynes, James Bohman, and Thomas McCarthy, 429–458. Cambridge, MA: MIT Press. Original edition 1981.

Blumenberg, Hans. 2010. *Theorie der Lebenswelt*. Berlin: Suhrkamp.

Bordwell, David. 1985. *Narration in the Fiction Film*. London: Methuen.

Bordwell, David. 1989. *Making Meaning. Inference and Rhetoric in the Interpretation of Cinema*. Cambridge, MA: Harvard University Press.

Bordwell, David. 2008. *Poetics of Cinema*. New York, NY: Routledge.

https://doi.org/10.1515/9783110580785-016

Bordwell, David. 2011. "This is your Brain on Movies, Maybe." In *Minding Movies. Observations on the Art, Craft, and Business of Filmmaking* edited by David Bordwell and Kristin Thompson, 96–102. Chicago, IL: Chicago University Press.

Bordwell, David. 2013. "The Viewer's Share. Models of Mind in Explaining Film." In *Psychocinematics. Exploring Cognition at the Movies*, edited by Arthur P. Shimamura, 29–52. New York, NY: Oxford University Press.

Branigan, Edward. 1992. *Narrative Comprehension and Film*. London: Routledge.

Brewer, William F. 1996. "The Nature of Narrative Suspense and the Problem of Rereading." In *Suspense. Conceptualizations, Theoretical Analyses, and Empirical Explorations*, edited by Peter Vorderer, Hans Jürgen Wulff, and Mike Friedrichsen, 107–127. Mahwah, NJ: Lawrence Erlbaum.

Bruun Vaage, Margrethe. 2009. "Seeing is Feeling. Empathy and the Film Spectator." Ph. D. Dissertation, University of Oslo.

Buch, Robert, and Daniel Weidner, eds. 2014. *Blumenberg lesen. Ein Glossar*. Berlin: Suhrkamp.

Bühler, Karl. 1933. *Ausdruckstheorie: Das System an der Geschichte aufgezeigt*. Jena: Fischer.

Bühler, Karl. 1968. *Ausdruckstheorie. Das System an der Geschichte aufgezeigt*. 2 ed. Stuttgart: Fischer. Original edition 1933.

Bühler, Karl. 1990. *Theory of Language. The Representational Function of Language*. Amsterdam: John Benjamins. Original edition 1934.

Caldwell, John T. 2008. *Production Culture. Industrial Reflexivity and Critical Practice in Film and Television*. Durham, NC: Duke University Press.

Cameron, Lynne. 2003. *Metaphor in Educational Discourse, Advances in Applied Linguistics*. London: Continuum.

Cameron, Lynne. 2006. "Metaphor Analysis Project. Procedure for Metaphor Analysis. Building Metaphor Groupings." The Open University, accessed 25.4.2018 (via the internet archive). https://web.archive.org/web/20111001231254/http://creet.open.ac.uk/projects/metaphor-analysis/building.cfm.

Cameron, Lynne. 2007. "Patterns of Metaphor Use in Reconciliation Talk." *Discourse & Society* 18 (2): 197–222.

Cameron, Lynne. 2008a. "Metaphor and Talk." In *The Cambridge Handbook of Metaphor and Thought*, edited by Raymond W. Jr. Gibbs, 197–211. Cambridge: Cambridge University Press.

Cameron, Lynne. 2008b. "Metaphor Shifting in Discourse." In *Confronting Metaphor in Use. An Applied Linguistic Approach*, edited by Maria Sophia Zanotto, Lynne Cameron, and Maria Cavalcanti, 197–211. Amsterdam: John Benjamins.

Cameron, Lynne. 2008c. "Metaphor Shifting in the Dynamics of Talk." *Pragmatics and Beyond New Series* 173.

Cameron, Lynne. 2010. "The Discourse Dynamics Framework for Metaphor." In *Metaphor Analysis. Research Practice in Applied Linguistics, Social Sciences and the Humanities*, edited by Lynne Cameron and Robert Maslen, 77–96. London: Equinox.

Cameron, Lynne. 2011. *Metaphor and Reconciliation. The Discourse Dynamics of Empathy in Post-Conflict Conversations, Routledge Studies in Linguistics*. New York, NY: Routledge.

Cameron, Lynne. 2018. "From Metaphor to Metaphorising: How Cinematic Metaphor Opens up Metaphor Studies." In *Cinematic Metaphor in Perspective. Reflections on a Transdisciplinary Framework*, edited by Sarah Greifenstein, Dorothea Horst, Thomas Scherer, Christina Schmitt, Hermann Kappelhoff, and Cornelia Müller, 17–35. Berlin/Boston, MA: Walter de Gruyter.

Cameron, Lynne, and Robert Maslen, eds. 2010. *Metaphor Analysis: Research Practice in Applied Linguistics, Social Sciences and the Humanities*. London: Equinox.
Cameron, Lynne, Robert Maslen, Zazie Todd, John Maule, Peter Stratton, and Neil Stanley. 2009. "The Discourse Dynamics Approach to Metaphor and Metaphor-led Discourse Analysis." *Metaphor and Symbol* 24 (2): 63–89.
Carroll, Noël. 1996. *Theorizing the Moving Image*. Cambridge: Cambridge University Press.
Carroll, Noël. 2008. *The Philosophy of Motion Pictures*. Malden, MA: Blackwell Publishing.
Catalano, Theresa, and Linda Waugh. 2013. "The Language of Money. How Verbal and Visual Metonymy Shapes Public Opinion about Financial Events." *International Journal of Language Studies* 7(2): 31–60.
Cavell, Stanley. 1979. *The World Viewed. Reflections on the Ontology of Film*. Cambridge, Mass.: Harvard University Press.
Certeau, Michel de. 1984. *The Practice of Everyday Life*. Translated by Steven Rendall. Berkely, CA: University of California Press. Original edition 1980.
Cienki, Alan. 2018. "Insights for Linguistics and Gesture Studies from Film Studies. A View from Researching Cinematic Metaphor." In *Cinematic Metaphor in Perspective. Reflections on a Transdisciplinary Framework*, edited by Sarah Greifenstein, Dorothea Horst, Thomas Scherer, Christina Schmitt, Hermann Kappelhoff, and Cornelia Müller, 53–68. Berlin/ Boston, MA: Walter de Gruyter.
Cienki, Alan, and Cornelia Müller, eds. 2008a. *Metaphor and Gesture*. Amsterdam: John Benjamins.
Cienki, Alan, and Cornelia Müller. 2008b. "Metaphor, Gesture, and Thought." In *The Cambridge Handbook of Metaphor and Thought*, edited by Raymond W. Jr. Gibbs, 483–501. Cambridge: Cambridge University Press.
Coëgnarts, Maarten, and Peter Kravanja. 2012a. "Embodied Visual Meaning. Image Schemas in Film." *Projections. The Journal for Movies and Mind* 6 (2): 84–101.
Coëgnarts, Maarten, and Peter Kravanja. 2012b. "From Thought to Modality. A Theoretical Framework for Analysing Structural-Conceptual Metaphors and Image Metaphors in Film." *Image [&] Narrative* 13 (1): 96–113.
Coëgnarts, Maarten, and Peter Kravanja. 2012c. "Towards an Embodied Poetics of Cinema. The Metaphoric Construction of Abstract Meaning in Film." *Alphaville* (Issue 4, Winter 2012): 1–18.
Coëgnarts, Maarten, and Peter Kravanja, eds. 2015. *Embodied Cognition and Cinema*. Leuven: Leuven University Press.
Coëgnarts, Maarten, and Peter Kravanja. 2014. "A Study in Cinematic Subjectivity. Metaphors of Perception in Film." *Metaphor and the Social World* 4 (2): 149–173.
Croft, William. 1993. "The Role of Domains in the Interpretation of Metaphor and Metonymy." *Cognitive Linguistics* 4(4): 335–370.
Curtis, Robin. 2008. "Immersion und Einfühlung. Zwischen Repräsentationalität und Materialität bewegter Bilder." *montage AV* 17 (2): 89–107.
Cutting, James E., Catalina Iricinschi, and Kaitlin L. Brunick. 2013. "Mapping Narrative Space in Hollywood Film." *Projections* 7 (2): 64–91.
Damasio, Antonio R. 1999. *The Feeling of What Happens. Body and Emotion in the Making of Consciousness*. New York, NY: Harcourt Brace.
Damasio, Antonio R. 2000. *Ich fühle, also bin ich. Die Entschlüsselung des Bewusstseins*. 2 ed. Munich: List.
Deleuze, Gilles. 2008. *Cinema 1. The Movement Image*. London: Continuum. Original edition 1983.
Deleuze, Gilles. 2008. *Cinema 2. The Time Image*. London: Continuum. Original edition 1985.

Detenber, Benjamin H., and Annie Lang. 2011. “The Influence of Form and Presentation Attributes of Media on Emotion.” In *The Routledge Handbook of Emotions and the Mass Media*, edited by Katrin Döveling, Christian von Scheve, and Elly A. Konijn, 275–293. London: Routlegde.

Dewey, John. 1980. *Art as Experience*. New York, NY: Putnam.

Dohle, Marco. 2011. *Unterhaltung durch traurige Filme. Die Bedeutung von Metaemotionen für die Medienrezeption*. Köln: Halem.

Eco, Umberto. 1976. “Articulations of the Cinematic Code.” In *Movies and Methods. An Anthology*, edited by Bill Nichols, 590–607. Berkeley, CA: University of California Press.

Eder, Jens. 2008. *Die Figur im Film. Grundlagen der Figurenanalyse*. Marburg: Schüren.

Eggertsson, Gunnar T., and Charles Forceville. 2009. “Multimodal Expressions of the HUMAN VICTIM IS ANIMAL Metaphor in Horror Films.” In *Multimodal Metaphor*, 429–449. Berlin/New York, NY: Mouton de Gruyter.

Eisenstein, Sergej M. 2010. “Bela Forgets the Scissors.” In *Writings, 1922–1934. Sergei Eisenstein Selected Works*, edited by Richard Taylor, 77–81. London: I.B.Tauris. Original edition 1926.

Ejchenbaum, Boris. 1974. “Problems of Film Stylistics.” *Screen* 15 (3): 7–34.

Ekman, Paul. 1972. *Emotions in the Human Face*. New York, NY: Pergamon.

Ekman, Paul. 2006. *Darwin and Facial Expression: A Century of Research in Review*. Cambridge, MA: Malor Books.

Ekman, Paul, and Erika L. Rosenberg. 1997. *What the Face Reveals: Basic and Applied Studies of Spontaneous Expression Using the Facial Action Coding System (FACS)*. Oxford: Oxford University Press.

Embree, Lester. 1980. “Merleau-Ponty’s Examination of Gestalt Psychology.” *Research in Phenomenology* 10: 89–121.

Eusterschulte, Anne. 2018. “*Actio per distans*: Blumenberg's Metaphorology and Hitchcock's rear window”. In *Cinematic Metaphor in Perspective. Reflections on a Transdisciplinary Framework*, edited by Sarah Greifenstein, Dorothea Horst, Thomas Scherer, Christina Schmitt, Hermann Kappelhoff and Cornelia Müller, 93–118. Berlin/Boston, MA: Walter de Gruyter.

Fahlenbrach, Kathrin. 2005. “The Aesthetics of Media Perception as ›Aisthesis‹? Considerations on Audiovisual Metaphors.” *CLCWeb. Comparative Literature and Culture* 7 (4): 1–9.

Fahlenbrach, Kathrin. 2008. “Emotions in Sound. Audiovisual Metaphors in the Sound Design of Narrative Films.” *Projections: The Journal for Movies and Mind*.

Fahlenbrach, Kathrin. 2010. *Audiovisuelle Metaphern. Zur Körper- und Affektästhetik in Film und Fernsehen*. Marburg: Schüren.

Fahlenbrach, Kathrin. 2016. *Embodied Metaphors in Film, Television and Video Games. Cognitive Approaches*. New York, NY: Routledge, Taylor & Francis Group.

Fahlenbrach, Kathrin. 2018. “Moving Metaphors. Affects, Movements, and Embodied Metaphors in Cinema.” In *Cinematic Metaphor in Perspective. Reflections on a Transdisciplinary Framework*, edited by Sarah Greifenstein, Dorothea Horst, Thomas Scherer, Christina Schmitt, Hermann Kappelhoff, and Cornelia Müller, 69–92. Berlin/Boston, MA: Walter de Gruyter.

Ferrari, Lilian, and Eve Sweetser. 2012. “Subjectivity and Upwards Projection in Mental Space Structure.” In *Viewpoint in Language. A Multimodal Perspective*, edited by Barbara Dancygier and Eve Sweetser, 47–68. Cambridge: Cambridge University Press.

Fiedler, Konrad. 1991. “Moderner Naturalismus und künstlerische Wahrheit.” In *Schriften zur Kunst I*, edited by Gottfried Boehm, 82–110. Munich: Wilhelm Fink. Original edition 1881.

Fiedler, Konrad. 1991. “Über den Ursprung der künstlerischen Tätigkeit.” In *Schriften zur Kunst I*, edited by Gottfried Boehm, 112–220. Munich: Wilhelm Fink. Original edition 1887.

Fillmore, Charles. 1982. "Frame Semantics." In *Linguistics in the Morning Calm*, edited by Linguistic Society of Korea, 111–137. Seoul: Hanshin.

Forceville, Charles. 2006. "Non-Verbal and Multimodal Metaphor in a Cognitivist Framework: Agendas for Research." *Applications of Cognitive Linguistics* 1: 379–402.

Forceville, Charles. 2008. "Metaphor in Pictures and Multimodal Representations." In *The Cambridge Handbook of Metaphor and Thought*, edited by Raymond W. Jr. Gibbs, 462–482. Cambridge: Cambridge University Press.

Forceville, Charles. 2009a. "Non-Verbal and Multimodal Metaphor in a Cognitivist Framework. Agendas for Research." In *Multimodal Metaphor*, edited by Charles Forceville and Eduardo Urios-Aparisi. Berlin/Boston, MA: Walter de Gruyter.

Forceville, Charles. 2009b. "The Role of Non-Verbal Sound and Music in Multimodal Metaphor." In *Multimodal Metaphor*, edited by Charles Forceville and Eduardo Urios-Aparisi, 383–400. Berlin/New York, NY: Mouton de Gruyter.

Forceville, Charles. 2016. "Visual and Multimodal Metaphor in Film. Charting the Field." In *Embodied Metaphors in Film, Television, and Video Games. Cognitive Approaches*, edited by Kathrin Fahlenbrach, 17–32. New York, NY: Routledge.

Forceville, Charles. 2017. "From Image Schema to Metaphor in Discourse. The FORCE Schemas in Animation Films." In *Metaphor. Embodied Cognition and Discourse*, edited by Beate Hampe, 239–256. Cambridge: Cambridge University Press.

Forceville, Charles, and Eduardo Urios-Aparisi, eds. 2009. *Multimodal Metaphor*. Berlin: Mouton de Gruyter.

Frampton, Daniel. 2006. *Filmosophy*. London: Wallflower Press.

Frome, Jonathan. 2014. "Melodrama and the Psychology of Tears." *Projections: The Journal for Movies and Mind* 8 (1): 23–40.

Fuchs, Thomas, and Hanne De Jaegher. 2009. "Enactive Intersubjectivity. Participatory Sense-Making and Mutual Incorporation." *Phenomenology and the Cognitive Sciences* 8 (4): 465–486.

Gadamer, Hans-Georg. 1960. *Wahrheit und Methode. Grundzüge einer philosophischen Hermeneutik*. Tübingen: Mohr.

Gallagher, Shaun. 2008. "Understanding Others. Embodied Social Cognition." In *Handbook of Cognitive Science. An Embodied Approach*, edited by Paco Calvo and Antoni Gomila, 439–452. Amsterdam: Elsevier.

Gallagher, Shaun, and Dan Zahavi. 2007. *The Phenomenological Mind. An Introduction to Philosophy of Mind and Cognitive Science*. London: Routledge.

Geary, James. 2011. *I is an Other. The Secret Life of Metaphor and How It Shapes the Way We See the World*. New York, NY: Harper Collins.

Gehring, Petra. 2009a. "Das Bild vom Sprachbild. Die Metapher und das Visuelle." In *Begriffe, Metaphern und Imaginationen in Philosophie und Wissenschaftsgeschichte*, edited by Lutz Dannenberg, Carlos Spoerhase, and Dirk Werle, 80–101. Wiesbaden: Harassowitz.

Gehring, Petra. 2009b. "Erkenntnis durch Metaphern? Methodologische Bemerkungen zur Metaphernforschung." In *Metaphern in Wissenskulturen*, edited by Matthias Junge, 203–220. Wiesbaden: VS.

Gehring, Petra. 2014. "Metapher." In *Blumenberg lesen. Ein Glossar*, edited by Robert Buch and Daniel Weidner, 201–213. Berlin: Suhrkamp.

Gendler, Jason. 2012. "Where Does the Beginning End? Cognition, Form, and Classical Narrative Beginnings." *Projections: The Journal for Movies and Mind* 6 (2): 64–83.

Gibbs, Raymond W. Jr. 1998. "The Fight over Metaphor in Thought and Language." In *Figurative Language and Thought*, edited by Albert N. Katz, Cristina Cacciari, Raymond W. Gibbs, and Mark Turner, 88–118. New York, NY: Oxford University Press.

Gibbs, Raymond W. Jr. 1999. "Speaking and Thinking with Metonymy." In *Metonymy in Language and Thought*, edited by Klaus-Uwe Panther and Günter Radden, 61–76. Amsterdam: John Benjamins.

Gibbs, Raymond W. Jr. 2005. *Embodiment and Cognitive Science*. Cambridge: Cambridge University Press.

Gibbs, Raymond W. Jr. 2006. "Metaphor Interpretation as Embodied Simulation." *Mind & Language* 21 (3): 434–458.

Gibbs, Raymond W. Jr., ed. 2008. *The Cambridge Handbook of Metaphor and Thought*. Cambridge: Cambridge University Press.

Gibbs, Raymond W. Jr., ed. 2016a. *Mixing Metaphor, Metaphor in Language, Cognition & Communication*. Amsterdam: John Benjamins.

Gibbs, Raymond W. Jr. 2016b. "Oral Contribution at Cinepoetics Metaphor Workshop Series at Freie Universität Berlin."

Gibbs, Raymond W. Jr. 2016c. "Our Experiences of Film. Paper at Cinepoetics Roundtable 'Cinematic Metaphor. Experience and Temporality'." RaAM 11 Conference, Freie Universität Berlin, 3 July 2016.

Gibbs, Raymond W. Jr. 2018a. "Comments on Cinematic Metaphor." (Private Conversation with the Authors).

Gibbs, Raymond W. Jr. 2018b. "Our Metaphorical Experiences of Film." In *Cinematic Metaphor in Perspective. Reflections on a Transdisciplinary Framework*, edited by Sarah Greifenstein, Dorothea Horst, Thomas Scherer, Christina Schmitt, Hermann Kappelhoff, and Cornelia Müller, 120–140. Berlin/Boston, MA: Walter de Gruyter.

Gigerenzer, Gerd, and Daniel G. Goldstein. 1996. "Mind as Computer: Birth of a Metaphor." *Creativity Research Journal* 9 (2–3): 131–144.

Goodwin, Charles. 2000. "Action and Embodiment Within Situated Human Interaction." *Journal of Pragmatics* 32 (10): 1489–1522.

Goossens, Louis. 1990. "Metaphtonymy. The Interaction of Metaphor and Metonymy in Expressions for Linguistic Action." *Cognitive Linguistics* 1 (3): 323–340.

Goschler, Juliana. 2008. *Metaphern für das Gehirn: Eine kognitiv-linguistische Untersuchung*. Berlin: Frank & Timme.

Grau, Oliver. 2003. *Virtual Art. From Illusion to Immersion, Leonardo*. Cambridge, MA: MIT Press.

Grauwe, Sofie de. 2000. "The Cognitivist Approach to Film in the Light of Systemic-Functional Theory. A Changing of the Guards?" *Image and Narrative* 1.

Greifenstein, Sarah. forthcoming/2019. *Tempi der Bewegung – Modi des Gefühls. Expressivität, heitere Affekte und die Screwball Comedy* Berlin/Boston, MA: Walter de Gruyter.

Greifenstein, Sarah, and Hermann Kappelhoff. 2014. "The Discovery of the Acting Body." In *Body – Language – Communication. An International Handbook on Multimodality in Human Interaction*, edited by Cornelia Müller, Alan Cienki, Ellen Fricke, Silva H. Ladewig, David McNeill, and Jana Bressem, 2070–2080. Berlin/Boston, MA: De Gruyter Mouton.

Griffiths, Alison. 2008. *Shivers down your Spine. Cinema, Museums, and the Immersive View*. New York, NY: Columbia University Press.

Grodal, Torben K. 1997. *Moving Pictures. A New Theory of Film Genres, Feelings and Cognition*. Oxford: Clarendon Press.

Grodal, Torben K. 2009. *Embodied Visions. Evolution, Emotion, Culture, and Film*. New York, NY: Oxford University Press.

Guattari, Félix. 2009. "The Poor Man's Couch." In *Chaosophy. Texts and Interviews 1972–1977*, edited by Sylvère Lotringer, 257–267. Cambridge, MA: MIT University Press. Original edition 1975.

Hackney, Peggy. 2002. *Making Connections. Total Body Integration through Bartenieff Fundamentals*. New York, NY: Routledge.

Hall, Sheldon, and Steve Neale. 2010. *Epics, Spectacles, and Blockbusters: A Hollywood History*. Detroit, MI: Wayne State University Press.

Hampe, Beate, ed. 2017. *Metaphor. Embodied Cognition and Discourse*. Cambridge: Cambridge University Press.

Harcup, Tony. 2009. *Journalism. Principles and Practice*. 2. ed. Los Angeles, CA: SAGE.

Hasson, Uri, Ohad Landesman, Barbara Knappmeyer, Ignacio Vallines, Nava Rubin, and David J. Heeger. 2008. "Neurocinematics: The Neuroscience of Film." *Projections: The Journal for Movies and Mind* 2 (1): 1–26.

Haverkamp, Anselm, ed. 1983. *Theorie der Metapher*. Darmstadt: Wissenschaftliche Buchgesellschaft.

Haverkamp, Anselm, ed. 1998. *Die paradoxe Metapher*. Frankfurt/M.: Suhrkamp.

Haverkamp, Anselm. 2007a. "Die wiederholte Metapher." In *Figur und Figuration. Studien zu Wahrnehmung und Wissen*, edited by Gottfried Boehm, Gabriele Brandstetter, and Achatz von Müller, 183–202. Munich: Wilhelm Fink.

Haverkamp, Anselm. 2007b. *Metapher. Die Ästhetik in der Rhetorik*. Munich: Fink.

Haynes, Todd. 2018. The Film Programme. BBC Radio 4. Interview conducted by Francine Stock. First aired 5 April 2018.

Heath, Stephen. 1981. *Questions of Cinema. Communications and Culture*. London: Macmillan.

Hogan, Patrick C. 2011. *What Literature Teaches Us about Emotion, Studies in Emotion and Social Interaction*. Cambridge: Cambridge University Press.

Hogan, Patrick C. 2013. *Narrative Discourse. Authors and Narrators in Literature, Film, and Art*. Columbus, OH: Ohio State University Press.

Holly, Werner. 2010. "Besprochene Bilder – bebildertes Sprechen. Audiovisuelle Transkriptivität in Nachrichtenfilmen und Polit-Talkshows." In *Sprache intermedial. Stimme und Schrift, Bild und Ton*, edited by Arnulf Deppermann and Angelika Linke, 359–382. Berlin: Walter de Gruyter.

Horst, Dorothea. forthcoming/2018. *Meaning-Making and Political Campaign Advertising. A Cognitive-Linguistic and Film-Analytical Perspective on Audiovisual Figurativity*. Berlin/Boston, MA: Walter de Gruyter.

Horst, Dorothea, Franziska Boll, Christina Schmitt, and Cornelia Müller. 2014. "Gesture as Interactive Expressive Movement. Inter-Affectivity in Face-to-Face Communication." In *Body – Language – Communication. An International Handbook on Multimodality in Human Interaction*, edited by Cornelia Müller, Alan Cienki, Ellen Fricke, Silva H. Ladewig, David McNeill, and Jana Bressem, 2112–2125. Berlin/Boston, MA: De Gruyter Mouton.

Jakobson, Roman. 1987. "Quest for the Essence of Language." In *Language in Literature*, edited by Krystyna Pomorska and Stephen Rudy, 413–427. Cambridge, MA: Belknap Press of Harvard University Press. Original edition 1965.

Jakobson, Roman. 1990. "Two Aspects of Language and Two Types of Aphasic Disturbances." In *On Language*, edited by Linda R. Waugh and Monique Monville-Burston, 115–133. Cambridge, MA: Belknap Press of Harvard University Press. Original edition 1956.

Jensen, Thomas Wiben. 2017a. “Doing Metaphor: An Ecological Perspective on Metaphoricity in Discourse.” In *Metaphor: Embodied Cognition and Discourse*, edited by Beate Hampe, 257–276. Cambridge: Cambridge University Press.

Jensen, Thomas Wiben. 2017b. “The World Between Us: The Social Affordances of Metaphor in Face-to-Face Interaction.” *Rask Internationalt Tidsskrift for Sprog Og Kommunikation*.

Johnson, Mark. 1987. *The Body in the Mind. The Bodily Basis of Meaning, Imagination, and Reason*. Chicago, IL: University of Chicago Press.

Johnson, Mark. 2007. *The Meaning of the Body. Aesthetics of Human Understanding*. Chicago, IL: Chicago University Press

Joost, Gesche. 2008. *Bild-Sprache. Die audio-visuelle Rhetorik des Films*. Bielefeld: transcript.

Kanzog, Klaus. 2007. *Grundkurs Filmsemiotik*. Munich: Diskurs-Film-Verlag Schaudig & Ledig.

Kappelhoff, Hermann. 1998. “Empfindungsbilder. Subjektivierte Zeit im melodramatischen Kino.” In *Zeitlichkeiten – Zur Realität der Künste. Theater, Film, Photographie, Malerei, Literatur*, edited by Theresia Birkenhauer and Annette Storr, 93–119. Berlin: Vorwerk 8.

Kappelhoff, Hermann. 2000. “And the Heart will go on and on. Untergangsphantasie und Wiederholungsstruktur in dem Film Titanic von James Cameron.” In *Über Bilder sprechen. Positionen und Perspektiven der Medienwissenschaft*, edited by Heinz-Bernd Heller, 223–243. Marburg: Schüren.

Kappelhoff, Hermann. 2004a. *Matrix der Gefühle. Das Kino, das Melodrama und das Theater der Empfindsamkeit*. Berlin: Vorwerk 8.

Kappelhoff, Hermann. 2004b. “Unerreichbar, unberührbar, zu spät. Das Gesicht als kinematografische Form der Erfahrung.” *montage/av* 13 (2): 29–53.

Kappelhoff, Hermann. 2006. “Dauer der Empfindung. Von einer spezifischen Bewegungsdimension im Kino.” In *e_motion*, edited by Margit Bischof, Claudia Feest, and Claudia Rosiny, 205–219. Münster: LIT.

Kappelhoff, Hermann. 2008. “Zuschauergefühl. Die Inszenierung der Empfindung im dunklen Raum des Kinos.” In *Tränen*, edited by Geraldine Spiekermann and Beate Söntgen, 195–206. Munich: Fink.

Kappelhoff, Hermann. 2010–2014. Database. Mobilization of Emotions in War Films. Berlin: CeDiS – Freie Universität Berlin, accessed 25 May 2018. www.empirische-medienaesthetik.fu-berlin.de/en/emaex-system/affektdatenmatrix/index.html.

Kappelhoff, Hermann. 2013. “Ausdrucksbewegung und Zuschauerempfinden. Eisensteins Konzept des Bewegungsbildes.” In *Synchronisierung der Künste*, edited by Robin Curtis, Gertrud Koch, and Marc Siegel, 73–84. Munich: Fink.

Kappelhoff, Hermann. 2014. “Artificial Emotions. Melodramatic Practices of Shared Interioirity.” In *Rethinking Emotion. Interiority and Exteriority in Pre-Modern and Contemporary Thought*, edited by Rüdiger Campe and Julia Weber, 264–288. Berlin/Boston, MA: Walter de Gruyter.

Kappelhoff, Hermann. 2018a. *Frontlines of Community. Hollywood Between War and Democracy*. Translated by Daniel Hendricks. Berlin/Boston, MA: Walter de Gruyter.

Kappelhoff, Hermann. 2018b. *Kognition und Reflexion. Zur Theorie filmischen Denkens*. Berlin/Boston, MA: Walter de Gruyter.

Kappelhoff, Hermann, and Jan-Hendrik Bakels. 2011. “Das Zuschauergefühl. Möglichkeiten qualitativer Medienanalyse.” *Zeitschrift für Medienwissenschaft* 5 (2): 78–95.

Kappelhoff, Hermann, Jan-Hendrik Bakels, and Sarah Greifenstein. forthcoming/2019. *Die Poiesis des Filme-Sehens. Methoden der Analyse audiovisueller Bilder*. Berlin/Boston, MA: Walter de Gruyter.

Kappelhoff, Hermann, and Sarah Greifenstein. 2016. "Audiovisual Metaphors. Embodied Meaning and Process of Fictionalization." In *Embodied Metaphors in Film, Television, and Video Games*, edited by Kathrin Fahlenbrach, 183–201. New York, NY: Routledge.

Kappelhoff, Hermann, Matthias Grotkopp, and David Gaertner. 2016. "The Poetics of Mobilization. Gung Ho!" *mediaesthetics* 1.

Kappelhoff, Hermann, and Cornelia Müller. 2011. "Embodied Meaning Construction. Multimodal Metaphor and Expressive Movement in Speech, Gesture, and Feature Film." *Metaphor and the Social World* 1 (2): 121–153.

Kendon, Adam. 2004. *Gesture. Visible Action as Utterance*. Cambridge: Cambridge University Press.

Koch, Gertrud, and Christiane Voss. 2006. *...Kraft der Illusion*. Paderborn: Fink.

Koch, Gertrud, and Christiane Voss, eds. 2009. *"Es ist, als ob". Fiktionalität in Philosophie, Film- und Medienwissenschaft*. Paderborn: Fink.

Kolter, Astrid, Silva H. Ladewig, Michela Summa, Cornelia Müller, Sabine C. Koch, and Thomas Fuchs. 2012. "Body Memory and the Emergence of Metaphor in Movement and Speech. An Interdisciplinary Case Study." In *Body, Memory, Metaphor, and Movement*, edited by Sabine C. Koch, Thomas Fuchs, and Cornelia Müller, 201–226. Amsterdam: John Benjamins.

Kopperschmidt, Josef. 2000. "Was weiß die Rhetorik vom Menschen? Thematisch einleitende Bemerkungen." In *Rhetorische Anthropologie: Studien zum Homo rhetoricus*, edited by Josef Kopperschmidt, 7–37. Munich: Fink.

Krämer, Sybille. 2004. "Was haben 'Performativität' und 'Medialität' miteinander zu tun? Plädoyer für eine in der 'Aisthetisierung' gründende Konzeption des Performativen." In *Performativität und Medialität*, edited by Sybille Krämer, 13–32. Munich: Fink.

Kroß, Matthias, and Rüdiger Zill, eds. 2011. *Metapherngeschichten. Perspektiven einer Theorie der Unbegrifflichkeit*. Berlin: Parerga.

Kuhn, Markus, Irina Scheidgen, and Nicola V. Weber, eds. 2013. *Filmwissenschaftliche Genreanalyse. Eine Einführung*. Berlin/Boston, MA: Walter de Gruyter.

Laban, Rudolf. 1966. *Choreutics*. London: MacDonald and Evans.

Ladewig, Silva H. forthcoming. *Integrating Gestures – Cognitive Grammar Multimodal*: De Gruyter Mouton.

Lakoff, George. 2008. "The Neural Theory of Metaphor." In *The Cambridge Handbook of Metaphor and Thought*, edited by Raymond W. Jr. Gibbs, 17–38. Cambridge: Cambridge University Press.

Lakoff, George, and Mark Johnson. 1980a. "Conceptual Metaphor in Everyday Language." *Journal of Philosophy* 77 (8): 453–486.

Lakoff, George, and Mark Johnson. 1980b. *Metaphors We Live By*. Chicago, IL: University of Chicago Press.

Lakoff, George, and Mark Johnson. 1999. *Philosophy in the Flesh*. 2. [print.] ed. New York, NY: Basic Books.

Larsen-Freeman, Diane, and Lynne Cameron. 2008a. *Complex Systems and Applied Linguistics*. Oxford: Oxford University Press.

Larsen-Freeman, Diane, and Lynne Cameron. 2008b. "Research Methodology on Language Development from a Complex Systems Perspective." *The Modern Language Journal* 92 (2): 200–213.

Littlemore, Jeannette. 2015. *Metonymy. Hidden Shortcuts in Language, Thought and Communication*. Cambridge: Cambridge University Press.

Löffler, Petra. 2004. *Affektbilder. Eine Mediengeschichte der Mimik*. Bielefeld: Transcript.

Marks, Laura U. 2002. *Touch. Sensuous Theory and Multisensory Media*. Minneapolis, MN: University of Minnesota Press.

McDonald, Paul, Emily Carman, Eric Hoyt, and Philip Drake, eds. 2015. *Hollywood and the Law*. London: Palgrave Macmillan.

McLuhan, Marshall. 1964. *Understanding Media. The Extensions of Man*. New York, NY: New American Library.

McLuhan, Marshall. 1966. "An Interview with Marshall McLuhan." *The Structurist. Special Issue on Art and Technology* 6: 61–68.

Merleau-Ponty, Maurice. 1963. *The Structure of Behavior*. Boston, MA: Beacon Press. Original edition 1942.

Merleau-Ponty, Maurice. 1968. *The Visible and the Invisible*. Evanston, IL: Northwestern University Press. Original edition 1964.

Merleau-Ponty, Maurice. 2005. *Phenomenology of Perception*. Translated by Colin Smith. London: Routledge. Original edition 1945.

Metz, Christian. 1991. *Film Language. A Semiotics of the Cinema*. Translated by Michael Taylor. 2 ed. Chicago, IL: The University of Chicago University Press. Original edition 1968.

Metz, Christian. 2000. *The Imaginary Signifier. Psychoanalysis and The Cinema*. Translated by Celia Britton. Bloomington: Indiana University Press. Original edition 1975.

Milburn, Michael A., and Anne B. McGrail. 1992. "The Dramatic Presentation of News and its Effects on Cognitive Complexity." *Political Psychology* 13 (4): 613–632.

Mitchell, William J. T. 2008. *Das Leben der Bilder. Eine Theorie der visuellen Kultur*. Munich: C.H. Beck.

Mitchell, William J. T. 2009. "Vier Grundbegriffe der Bildwissenschaft." In *Bildtheorien. Anthropologische und kulturelle Grundlagen des Visualistic Turn*, edited by Klaus Sachs-Hombach, 319–327. Frankfurt/M.: Suhrkamp.

Mittelberg, Irene. 2006. "Metaphor and Metonymy in Language and Gesture. Discourse Evidence for Multimodal Models of Grammar." Ph.D., Cornell University.

Mittelberg, Irene. 2008. "Peircean Semiotics Meets Conceptual Metaphor. Iconic Modes in Gestural Representations of Grammar." In *Metaphor and Gesture*, edited by Alan Cienki and Cornelia Müller, 115–154. Amsterdam: John Benjamins.

Mittelberg, Irene. 2010. "Interne und externe Metonymie. Jakobsonsche Kontiguitätsbeziehungen in redebegleitenden Gesten." *Sprache und Literatur* 41 (1): 112–143.

Mittelberg, Irene. 2013. "The Exbodied Mind. Cognitive-Semiotic Principles as Motivating Forces in Gesture." In *Body – Language – Communication. An International Handbook on Multimodality in Human Interaction*, edited by Cornelia Müller, Alan Cienki, Ellen Fricke, Silva H. Ladewig, David McNeill, and Sedinha Tessendorf, 750–779. Berlin/Boston, MA: De Gruyter Mouton.

Mittelberg, Irene, and Linda R. Waugh. 2009. "Metonymy First, Metaphor Second. A Cognitive-Semiotic Approach to Multimodal Figures of Thought in Co-Speech Gesture." In *Multimodal Metaphor*, edited by Charles Forceville and Eduardo Urios-Aparisi, 329–356. Berlin/New York, NY: Mouton de Gruyter.

Mittelberg, Irene, and Linda R. Waugh. 2014. "Gestures and Metonymy." In *Body – Language – Communication. An International Handbook on Multimodality in Human Interaction*, edited by Cornelia Müller, Alan Cienki, Ellen Fricke, Silva Ladewig, David McNeill, and Jana Bressem, 1747–1766. Berlin/Boston, MA: De Gruyter Mouton.

Mondada, Lorenza. 2011. "Understanding as an Embodied, Situated and Sequential Achievement in Interaction." *Journal of Pragmatics* 43 (2): 542–552.

Mondada, Lorenza. 2013. "Multimodal Interaction." In *Body – Language – Communication. An International Handbook on Multimodality in Human Interaction*, edited by Cornelia Müller, Alan Cienki, Ellen Fricke, Silva H. Ladewig, David McNeil and Jana Bressem, 577–588. Berlin/Boston, MA: De Gruyter Mouton.

Müller, Cornelia. 1998a. "Iconicity and Gesture." In *Oralité et Gestualité: Communication Multimodale, Interaction*, edited by Serge Santi, 321–328. Montréal: L'Harmattan.

Müller, Cornelia. 1998b. *Redebegleitende Gesten. Kulturgeschichte, Theorie, Sprachvergleich*. Berlin: Berlin Verlag Arno Spitz.

Müller, Cornelia. 2003. "Gesten als Lebenszeichen 'toter Metaphern'." *Zeitschrift für Semiotik* 25 (1–2): 61–72.

Müller, Cornelia. 2008a. *Metaphors Dead and Alive, Sleeping and Waking. A Dynamic View*. Chicago, IL: University of Chicago Press.

Müller, Cornelia. 2008b. "What Gestures Reveal About the Nature of Metaphor." In *Metaphor and Gesture*, edited by Alan Cienki and Cornelia Müller, 219–245. Amsterdam: John Benjamins.

Müller, Cornelia. 2010. "Wie Gesten bedeuten. Eine kognitiv-linguistische und sequenzanalytische Perspektive." *Sprache und Gestik. Sonderheft der Zeitschrift Sprache und Literatur* 41 (1): 37–68.

Müller, Cornelia. 2013. "Gestures as a Medium of Expression. The Linguistic Potential of Gestures." In *Body – Language – Communication. An International Handbook on Multimodality in Human Interaction*, edited by Cornelia Müller, Alan Cienki, Ellen Fricke, Silva H. Ladewig, David McNeill and Sedinha Tessendorf, 202–217. Berlin: De Gruyter Mouton.

Müller, Cornelia. 2016a. "From Mimesis to Meaning: A Systematics of Gestural Mimesis for Concrete and Abstract Referential Gestures." In *Meaning, Mind and Communication. Explorations in Cognitive Semiotics*, edited by Jordan Zlatev, Göran Sonesson and Piotr Konderak, 211–226. Frankfurt/M.: Peter Lang.

Müller, Cornelia. 2016b. "Why Mixed Metaphors Make Sense." In *Mixing Metaphor*, edited by Raymond W. Jr. Gibbs 31–56. Amsterdam: John Benjamins.

Müller, Cornelia. 2017. "Waking Metaphors. Embodied Cognition in Discourse." In *Metaphor. Embodied Cognition in Discourse*, edited by Beate Hampe, 297–316. Cambridge: Cambridge University Press.

Müller, Cornelia, Jana Bressem, and Silva H. Ladewig. in prep. *Gesture and Language*. New York, NY: Routledge.

Müller, Cornelia, Alan Cienki, Ellen Fricke, Silva H. Ladewig, David McNeill, and Jana Bressem, eds. 2013. *Body – Language – Communication. An International Handbook on Multimodality in Human Interaction*. Vol. 1, *Handbooks of Linguistics and Communication Science 38.1*. Berlin/Boston, MA: De Gruyter Mouton.

Müller, Cornelia, Alan Cienki, Ellen Fricke, Silva H. Ladewig, David McNeill, and Jana Bressem, eds. 2014. *Body – Language – Communication. An International Handbook on Multimodality in Human Interaction*. Vol. 2, *Handbooks of Linguistics and Communication Science*. Berlin/Boston, MA: De Gruyter Mouton.

Müller, Cornelia, and Silva H. Ladewig. 2013. "Metaphors for Sensorimotor Experiences. Gestures as Embodied and Dynamic Conceptualizations of Balance in Dance Lessons." In *Language and the Creative Mind*, edited by Michael Borkent, Barbara Dancygier and Jennifer Hinnell. Stanford, CA: Stanford University Press.

Müller, Cornelia, and Christina Schmitt. 2015. "Audio-Visual Metaphors of the Financial Crisis. Meaning Making and the Flow of Experience." *Revista Brasileira de Linguística Aplicada* 15 (2): 311–342.

Müller, Cornelia, and Susanne Tag. 2010. "The Dynamics of Metaphor. Foregrounding and Activation of Metaphoricity in Conversational Interaction." *Cognitive Semiotics* 10 (6): 85–120.

Mulvey, Laura. 1975. "Visual Pleasure and Narrative Cinema." *Screen* 16 (3): 6–18

Münsterberg, Hugo. 2002. "The Photoplay – A Psychological Study." In *Hugo Münsterberg on Film. The Photoplay – A Psychological Study and Other Writings*, edited by Allan Langdale, 45–162. New York, NY: Routledge. Original edition 1916.

Nannicelli, Ted, and Paul Taberham. 2014. *Cognitive Media Theory*. New York, NY: Routledge, Taylor & Francis Group.

Neale, Stephen. 2000. *Genre and Hollywood, Sightlines*. London: Routledge.

Nietzsche, Friedrich. 1989. "On Truth and Lying in an Extra-Moral Sense." In *Friedrich Nietzsche on Rhetoric and Language*, edited by Sander L. Gilman, Carole Blair, and David J. Parent. Oxford: Oxford University Press. Original edition 1873.

Oakley, Todd, and Vera Tobin. 2012. "Attention, Blending, and Suspense in Classic and Experimental Film." In *Blending and the Study of Narrative. Approaches and Applications*, edited by Ralf Schneider and Marcus Hartner, 57–84. Berlin: De Gruyter.

Oben, Bert, and Geert Brône. 2015. "What You See Is What You Do. On the Relationship Between Gaze and Gesture in Multimodal Alignment." *Language and Cognition* 7 (4): 546–562.

Oben, Bert, and Geert Brône. 2016. "Explaining Interactive Alignment. A Multimodal and Multifactorial Account." *Journal of Pragmatics* 104: 32–51.

Oliver, M. B. 1993. "Exploring the Paradox of the Enjoyment of Sad Films." *Human Communication Research* 19 (3): 315–342.

Ortiz, María J. 2014. "Visual Manifestations of Primary Metaphors through Mise-en-Scène Techniques." *Image [&] Narrative* 15 (1): 5–16.

Ortiz, María J. 2015. "Films and Embodied Metaphors of Emotions." In *Embodied Cognition and Cinema*, edited by Peter Kravanja and Maarten Coëgnarts, 203–220. Leuven: Leuven University Press.

Ortony, Andrew, ed. 1993. *Metaphor and Thought*. Cambridge: Cambridge University Press.

Pasolini, Pier Paolo. 1971. "Die Sprache des Films." In *Semiotik des Films. Mit Analysen kommerzieller Pornos und revolutionärer Agitationsfilme*, edited by Friedrich Knilli, 38–55. Munich: Hanser.

Peirce, Charles S. 1960. *Collected Papers of Charles Sanders Peirce (1931–1958). Vol. I. Principles of Philosophy, Vol. II. Elements of Logic*. Edited by C. Hartsthorne and P. Weiss. Cambridge, MA: The Belknap Press of Harvard University Press.

Persson, Per. 2003. *Understanding Cinema. A Psychological Theory of Moving Imagery*. New York, NY: Cambridge University Press.

Plantinga, Carl R. 2009. *Moving Viewers. American Film and the Spectator's Experience*. Berkeley, CA: University of California Press.

Plantinga, Carl R. 2013. "The Affective Power of Movies." In *Psychocinematics. Exploring Cognition at the Movies*, edited by Arthur P. Shimamura, 94–111. Oxford: Oxford University Press.

Plessner, Helmuth. 1970. *Laughing and Crying: A Study of the Limits of Human Behavior*. Evanston, IL: Northwestern University Press. Original edition 1941.

Plessner, Helmuth. 1981. *Die Stufen des Organischen und der Mensch. Einleitung in die philosophische Anthropologie*. Edited by Günter Dux, Odo Marquard, and Elisabeth Ströker. Helmuth Plessner. *Gesammelte Schriften*, Vol. 4. Frankfurt/M.: Suhrkamp. Original edition 1928.

Plessner, Helmuth. 1982. *Ausdruck und menschliche Natur*. Edited by Günther Dux, Odo Marquard and Elisabeth Ströker. *Helmuth Plessner. Gesammelte Schriften,* Vol. 7. Frankfurt/M.: Suhrkamp. Original edition 1957.

Plessner, Helmuth. 1982. "Die Deutung des mimischen Ausdrucks. Ein Beitrag zur Lehre vom Bewußtsein des anderen Ichs [in cooperation with Buytendijk, Frederik J. J.]." In *Helmuth Plessner. Gesammelte Schriften,* Vol. 7. Edited by Günther Dux, Odo Marquard, and Elisabeth Ströker, 67–129. Frankfurt/M.: Suhrkamp. Original edition 1925.

Plessner, Helmuth. 1982. "Lachen und Weinen. Eine Untersuchung der Grenzen menschlichen Verhaltens." In *Helmuth Plessner. Gesammelte Schriften,* Vol. 7. Edited by Günther Dux, Odo Marquard, and Elisabeth Ströker, 201–387. Frankfurt/M.: Suhrkamp. Original edition 1941.

Prince, Gerald. 2003. *A Dictionary of Narratology*. Lincoln: University of Nebraska Press.

Radden, Günter. 2000. "How Metonymic Are Metaphors?" In *Metaphor and Metonymy at the Crossroads. A Cognitive Perspective*, edited by Antonio Barcelona, 93–108. Berlin/New York, NY: Mouton de Gruyter.

Radden, Günter, and Zoltán Kövecses. 1999. "Towards a Theory of Metonymy." In *Metonymy in Language and Thought*, edited by Klaus-Uwe Panther and Günter Radden, 17–59. Amsterdam: John Benjamins.

Ratcliffe, Matthew. 2008. *Feelings of Being. Phenomenology, Psychiatry and the Sense of Reality, International Perspectives in Philosophy and Psychiatry*. Oxford: Oxford University Press.

Robnik, Drehli. 2007. "Kino, Krieg, Gedächtnis. Nachträglichkeit, Affekt und Geschichtspolitik im deutschen und amerikanischen Gegenwartskino zum Zweiten Weltkrieg." PhD, University of Amsterdam.

Rodowick, David N. 1997. *Gilles Deleuze's Time Machine, Post-Contemporary Interventions*. Durham: Duke University Press.

Rorty, Richard. 1989. *Contingency, Irony, and Solidarity*. Cambridge: Cambridge University Press.

Ryan, Marie-Laure. 2001. *Narrative as Virtual Reality. Immersion and Interactivity in Literature and Electronic Media, Parallax*. Baltimore, MD: Johns Hopkins University Press.

Scherer, Klaus R. 1993. "Studying the Emotion-Antecedent Appraisal Process. An Expert System Approach." *Cognition and Emotion* 7: 1–41.

Scherer, Klaus R. 2009a. "Emotion Theories and Concepts (Psychological Perspectives)." In *Oxford Companion to Emotion and the Affective Sciences* edited by Sander David and Klaus R. Scherer, 145–149. Oxford: Oxford University Press.

Scherer, Klaus R. 2009b. "Emotions are Emergent Processes. They Require a Dynamic Computational Architecture." *Philosophical Transactions of The Royal Society B Biological Sciences* 364 (1535): 3459–3474.

Scherer, Thomas, Sarah Greifenstein, and Hermann Kappelhoff. 2014. "Expressive Movements in Audiovisual Media. Modulating Affective Experience." In *Body – Language – Communication. An International Handbook on Multimodality in Human Interaction*, edited by Cornelia Müller, Alan Cienki, Ellen Fricke, Silva H. Ladewig, David McNeill, and Jana Bressem, 2081–2092. Berlin/Boston, MA: De Gruyter Mouton.

Schick, Thomas, and Tobias Ebbrecht. 2008. *Emotion – Empathie – Figur. Spielformen der Filmwahrnehmung, Beiträge zur Film- und Fernsehwissenschaft*. Berlin: VISTAS.

Schmidt, Richard C., and Michael J. Richardson. 2008. "Dynamics of Interpersonal Coordination." In *Coordination. Neural, Behavioral and Social Dynamics*, 281–308. Berlin: Springer.

Schmitt, Christina. forthcoming/2019. *Wahrnehmen, fühlen, verstehen. Metaphorisieren und audiovisuelle Bilder*. Berlin/Boston, MA: Walter de Gruyter.

Schmitt, Christina, and Sarah Greifenstein. 2014. "Cinematic Communication and Embodiment." In *Body – Language – Communication. An International Handbook on Multimodality in Human Interaction*, edited by Cornelia Müller, Alan Cienki, Ellen Fricke, Silva H. Ladewig, David McNeill, and Jana Bressem, 2061–2070. Berlin/Boston, MA: De Gruyter Mouton.
Schmitt, Christina, Sarah Greifenstein, and Hermann Kappelhoff. 2014. "Expressive Movement and Metaphoric Meaning Making in Audio-Visual Media." In *Body – Language – Communication. An International Handbook on Multimodality in Human Interaction*, edited by Cornelia Müller, Alan Cienki, Ellen Fricke, Silva H. Ladewig, David McNeill, and Jana Bressem, 2092–2112. Berlin/Boston, MA: De Gruyter Mouton.
Shaviro, Steven. 1993. *The Cinematic Body*. Minneapolis, MN: University of Minnesota Press.
Sheets-Johnstone, Maxine. 2008. "Getting to the Heart of Emotions and Consciousness." In *Handbook of Cognitive Science. An Embodied Approach*, edited by Paco Calvo and Antoni Gomila, 453–465. Amsterdam: Elsevier.
Sheets-Johnstone, Maxine. 2011. *The Primacy of Movement*. 2 ed. Amsterdam: John Benjamins. Original edition 1999.
Shimamura, Arthur P. 2013. *Psychocinematics. Exploring Cognition at the Movies*. Oxford: Oxford University Press.
Shockley, Kevin, Daniel C. Richardson, and Rick Dale. 2009. "Conversation and Coordinative Structures." *Cognitive Science* 1: 305–319.
Simmel, Georg. 1959. "The Aesthetic Significance of the Face." In *Georg Simmel, 1858–1901. A Collection of Essays, with Translations and a Bibliography*, edited by Kurt H. Wolff, 276–281. Columbus, OH: Ohio State University Press. Original edition 1901.
Simmel, Georg. 1993. "Aesthetik des Porträts." In *Aufsätze und Abhandlungen, 1901–1908*, edited by Rüdiger Kramme and Alessandro Cavalli, 321–332. Frankfurt/M.: Suhrkamp. Original edition 1905.
Sinnerbrink, Robert. 2011. *New Philosophies of Film. Thinking Images*. London: Continuum.
Smith, Greg M. 2003. *Film Structure and the Emotion System*. Cambridge: Cambridge University Press.
Smith, Murray. 1995. *Engaging Characters. Fiction, Emotion and the Cinema*. Oxford: Clarendon Press.
Smith, Murray, and Thomas E. Wartenberg. 2006. *Thinking through Cinema. Film as Philosophy*. Malden, MA: Blackwell Publishing.
Sobchack, Vivian. 1992. *The Address of the Eye. A Phenomenology of Film Experience*. Princeton, NJ: Princeton University.
Sobchack, Vivian. 2004. *Carnal Thoughts. Embodiment and Moving Image Culture*. Berkeley, CA: University of California Press.
Stern, Daniel N. 1985. *The Interpersonal World of the Infant. A View from Psychoanalysis and Developmental Psychology*. London: Karnac Books.
Stern, Daniel N. 2010. *Forms of Vitality. Exploring Dynamic Experience in Psychology, the Arts, Psychotherapy and Development*. Oxford: Oxford University Press.
Streeck, Jürgen, Charles Goodwin, and Curtis LeBaron, eds. 2011. *Embodied Interaction. Language and Body in the Material World*. Cambridge: Cambridge University Press.
Suckfüll, Monika. 2004. *Rezeptionsmodalitäten. Ein integratives Konstrukt für die Medienwirkungsforschung*. Munich: R. Fischer.
Sweetser, Eve. 2012. "Introduction. Viewpoint from the Ground Down." In *Viewpoint in Language. A Multimodal Perspective*, edited by Barbara Dancygier and Eve Sweetser, 1–22. Cambridge: Cambridge University Press.

Tan, Ed S. 1996. *Emotion and the Structure of Narrative Film as an Emotion Machine, LEA'S Communication Series*. Mahwah, NJ: Erlbaum.

Tan, Ed S. 2013. "The Empathic Animal Meets the Inquisitive Animal in the Cinema. Notes on a Psychocinematics of Mind Reading." In *Psychocinematics. Exploring Cognition at the Movies*, edited by Arthur P. Shimamura, 337–367. Oxford: Oxford University Press.

Ulrich, Anne. 2012. *Umkämpfte Glaubwürdigkeit. Visuelle Strategien des Fernsehjournalismus im Irakkrieg 2003*. Berlin: Weidler.

Unz, Dagmar. 2011. "Effects of Presentation and Editing on Emotional Responses of Viewers. The Example of TV News." In *The Routledge Handbook of Emotions and the Mass Media*, edited by Katrin Döveling, Christian von Scheve, and Elly A. Konijn, 294–309. London: Routlegde.

Unz, Dagmar, Frank Schwab, and Peter Winterhoff-Spurk. 2008. "TV News – The Daily Horror?" *Journal of Media Psychology. Theories, Methods, and Applications* 20 (4): 141–155.

Uribe, Rodrigo, and Barrie Gunter. 2007. "Are 'Sensational' News Stories More Likely to Trigger Viewers' Emotions than Non-Sensational News Stories? A Content Analysis of British TV News " *European Journal of Communication* 22: 207–228.

Urios-Aparisi, Eduardo. 2014. "Figures of Film. Metaphor, Metonymy, and Repetition." *Image [&] Narrative* 15 (1): 102–113.

Vertov, Dziga. 1998. "KINOKI – Umsturz." In *Bilder des Wirklichen. Texte zur Theorie des Dokumentarfilms*, edited by Eva Hohenberger, 74–86. Berlin: Vorwerk 8. Original edition 1923.

Visch, Valentijn T. 2007. "Looking for Genres. The Effect of Film Figure Movement on Genre Recognition." Doctors Thesis, Vrije Universiteit Amsterdam.

Visch, Valentijn T., and Ed S. Tan. 2009. "Categorizing Moving Objects into Film Genres. The Effect of Animacy Attribution, Emotional Response and the Deviation from Non-Fiction." *Cognition* 110 (2): 265–272.

Visch, Valentijn T., Ed S. Tan, and Dylan Molenaar. 2010. "The Emotional and Cognitive Effect of Immersion in Film Viewing." *Cognition and Emotion* 24 (8): 1439–1445.

Vorderer, Peter, Hans J. Wulff, and Mike Friedrichsen. 1996. *Suspense. Conceptualizations, Theoretical Analyses and Empirical Explorations*. Mahwah, NJ: Erlbaum.

Voss, Christiane. 2009. "Fiktionale Immersion." In "*Es ist, als ob*". *Fiktionalität in Philosophie, Film- und Medienwissenschaft*, edited by Gertrud Koch and Christiane Voss, 127–138. Paderborn: Fink.

Voss, Christiane. 2011. "Film Experience and the Formation of Illusion. The Spectator as 'Surrogate Body' or the Cinema." *Cinema Journal* 50 (4): 136–150.

Voss, Christiane. 2013. *Der Leihkörper. Erkenntnis und Ästhetik der Illusion, Film Denken*. Munich: Wilhelm Fink.

Weinrich, Harald. 1983. "Semantik der kühnen Metapher." In *Theorie der Metapher – Wege der Forschung*, edited by Anselm Haverkamp, 316–339. Darmstadt: Wissenschaftliche Buchgesellschaft. Original edition 1963.

Wertheimer, Max. 1997. "Gestalt Theory" In *Source Book of Gestalt Psychology*, edited by Willis D. Ellis, 1–11. Goldsboro: The Gestalt Journal Press. Original edition 1925.

Whittock, Trevor. 1990. *Metaphor and Film*. Cambridge: Cambridge University Press.

Wildfeuer, Janina. 2013. "Formal Approaches to Discourse Analysis." *Zeitschrift für Semiotik* 35 (3–4): 393–417.

Wildfeuer, Janina. 2017. "Diskurssemiotik = Diskurssemantik + multimodaler Text." *Diskurssemiotisch: Aspekte multiformaler Diskurskodierung* 14.

Wildfeuer, Janina, and John Bateman. 2017. *Film Text Analysis. New Perspectives on the Analysis of Filmic Meaning*. New York, NY: Routledge, Taylor & Francis Group.

Wilson, George M. 2011. *Seeing Fictions in Film. The Epistemology of Movies*. Oxford: Oxford University Press.

Wilson, Margaret. 2002. "Six Views of Embodied Cognition." *Psychonomic Bulletin & Review* 9 (4): 625–636.

Winkler, Hartmut. 1989. "Metapher, Kontext, Diskurs, System." *Kodikas Code-Ars Semeiotica* 12 (1–2): 21–40.

Winterhoff-Spurk, Peter. 1998. "TV News and the Cultivation of Emotions." *Communications* 23 (4): 545–556.

Wulff, Hans J. 2003. "Empathie als Dimension des Filmverstehens. Ein Thesenpapier." *montage/av* 12 (1): 136–161.

Wundt, Wilhelm. 1900–1920. *Völkerpsychologie. Eine Untersuchung der Entwicklungsgesetze von Sprache, Mythus und Sitte*. 10. Leipzig: Wilhelm Engelmann.

Wuss, Peter. 2009. *Cinematic Narration and its Psychological Impact. Functions of Cognition, Emotion and Play*. Newcastle: Cambridge Scholars.

Yu, Ning. 2009. "Nonverbal and Multimodal Manifestations of Metaphors and Metonymies. A Case Study." In *Multimodal Metaphor*, edited by Charles Forceville and Eduardo Urios-Aparisi, 119–146. Berlin/New York, NY: Mouton de Gruyter.

Zillmann, Dolf. 1996. "The Psychology of Suspense in Dramatic Exposition." In *Suspense. Conceptualizations, Theoretical Analyses, and Empirical Explorations*, edited by Mike Friedrichsen, Peter Vorderer and Hans Jürgen Wulff, 199–231. Mahwah, NJ: Lawrence Erlbaum.

# Audiovisual Sources

ANGELA MERKEL, Agentur Kolle Rebbe, GER 2009
BATAAN, Dir. Tay Garnett, Metro-Goldwyn-Mayer, USA 1943
DEATH AND THE MOTHER, Dir. Ruth Lingford, Channel Four Films, UK 1997
DER KRIEGER UND DIE KAISERIN, Dir. Tom Tykwer, X-Filme, 2000
HER MORNING ELEGANCE, Dir. Oren Lavie, Yuval & Merav Nathan, A Quarter Past Wonderful, ISR 2009
JEZEBEL, Dir. William Wyler, Warner Bros, USA 1938
LOLA RENNT, Dir. Tom Tykwer, X-Filme, GER 1998
MAGNIFICENT OBSESSION, Dir. Douglas Sirk, Universal International, USA 1953
REAR WINDOW, Dir. Alfred Hitchcock, Paramount, USA 1954
REPORT MAINZ, ARD, GER 20 October 2008
SAT1 NACHRICHTEN, Sat1, GER 9 October 2008 20:00h
SPELLBOUND, Alfred Hitchcock, Selznick International Pictures, USA 1945
SUSPICION, Alfred Hitchcock, RKO Radio Pictures, USA 1941
TAGESSCHAU, ARD, GER 21 January 2008 20:00h
TAGESSCHAU ARD; GER, 20 October 2008 20:00h

https://doi.org/10.1515/9783110580785-017

# List of Figures

All figures were created by the authors.
Drawings within figures: Mathias Roloff.
All screenshots were captured by the authors.



https://doi.org/10.1515/9783110580785-018

# Name Index



https://doi.org/10.1515/9783110580785-019

# Subject Index



https://doi.org/10.1515/9783110580785-020

# About the Authors

**Cornelia Müller** is Professor of Language Use and Multimodal Communication at European University Viadrina, Frankfurt/Oder (Germany). She has published on multimodal forms of language use, focusing on gesture as an expressive medium (motivation and conventionalization), on embodied processes of multimodal communication, and on the experiential dynamics of metaphoric meaning in speech, gesture, and audiovisual media. Cornelia Müller directed several interdisciplinary projects researching interfaces between gesture and the dynamics of language. She is Associate Researcher at *Cinepoetics*, Center for Advanced Film Studies at Freie Universität Berlin. As a Cinepoetics Senior Fellow, she co-directed the center's work on the annual focus 'Film Images, Cinematic Thinking, and Cognition' (2015/16, together with Hermann Kappelhoff and Michael Wedel). From 2007 to 2012 she was a principal investigator at the interdisciplinary research center *Languages of Emotion* (Freie Universität Berlin, 2007–2014). Cornelia Müller launched and edited the journal *Gesture* and the book series *Gesture Studies* (until 2010, with Adam Kendon). She is editor-in-chief of *Body – Language – Communication: An international Handbook on Multimodality in Human Interaction* (Mouton De Gruyter 2013, 2014) and co-editor of *Cinematic Metaphor in Perspective. Reflections on a Transdisciplinary Framework* (de Gruyter 2018). Her book *Redebegleitende Gesten* (Spitz) was published in 1998 and in 2008 *Metaphors, Dead and Alive, Sleeping and Waking: A Dynamic View* (University of Chicago Press) came out. Together with Alan Cienki, she edited *Metaphor and Gesture* (Benjamins 2008) and has written several articles on metaphor and gesture. Other publications include further edited volumes, articles, and book chapters on multimodal metaphor and co-speech gestures. She currently prepares a textbook on gesture and language (with Jana Bressem and Silva H. Ladewig, Routledge, to appear).

**Hermann Kappelhoff** is Professor of Film Studies at Freie Universität Berlin (Germany), where he also co-directs the Center for Advanced Film Studies *Cinepoetics* (together with Michael Wedel). Following his research in the history, theory, and analysis of film and audiovisual media, he initiated numerous interdisciplinary projects involving cultural studies, philosophy, aesthetics, literature, fine arts, linguistics, and psychology, and developed various research projects and key activities at Freie Universität Berlin. He was director of the interdisciplinary research center *Languages of Emotion* (2010–2014), where he was also principle investigator (2007–2014). In the Council of the German Research Foundation (DFG – Deutsche Forschungsgemeinschaft) he represented Media Studies (2007–2015). He was a Max-Kade Visiting Professor at Vanderbilt University in Nashville, USA (2009/10) and is Associate Researcher at the Center for Advanced Studies *BildEvidenz. History and Aesthetics*. For the edition project "Hannah Arendt. Complete Works. Critical Edition. Digital and print" he is one of the academic heads (together with Barbara Hahn). He is co-editor of *Cinematic Metaphor in Perspective. Reflections on a Transdisciplinary Framework* (de Gruyter 2018). Besides further editorial projects and the publication of numerous articles and book chapters, Hermann Kappelhoff is the author of several books: *Der möblierte Mensch. G.W. Pabst und die Utopie der Sachlichkeit. Ein poetologischer Versuch zum Weimarer Autorenkino* (Vorwerk 8 1995), *Matrix der Gefühle. Das Kino, das Melodrama und das Theater der Empfindsamkeit* (Vorwerk 8 2004), *The Politics and Poetics of Cinematic Realism* (Columbia University Press

https://doi.org/10.1515/9783110580785-021

2015, German version in 2008), *Front Lines of Community: Hollywood Between War and Democracy* (de Gruyter 2018, German version in 2016), and *Kognition und Reflexion. Zur Theorie filmischen Denkens* (de Gruyter 2018).

For further information: www.hermann-kappelhoff.de

## About the Collaborating Authors

**Sarah Greifenstein** is Assistant Professor for Media, Culture and Communication at European University Viadrina in Frankfurt/Oder (Germany). From 2009 to 2013 she was junior researcher in the project "Multimodal Metaphor and Expressive Movement" headed by Hermann Kappelhoff and Cornelia Müller at the interdisciplinary research center *Languages of Emotion* (Freie Universität Berlin). She is author of the book *Tempi der Bewegung – Modi des Gefühls. Expressivität, heitere Affekte und die Screwball Comedy* (de Gruyter forthcoming/2019). Beyond other publications, she is co-author of chapters for *Body – Language – Communication* (Mouton De Gruyter 2014), including "The discovery of the acting body" and "Expressive movement and metaphoric meaning making in audio-visual media". Together with Hermann Kappelhoff, she published various German and English articles on metaphor and embodiment. She is co-editor of *Cinematic Metaphor in Perspective. Reflections on a Transdisciplinary Framework* (de Gruyter 2018). Her research foci are the relation of audiovisual media and language, embodiment and audiovisual communication, the cultural-historical formation of poetics of affect, and metaphorical meaning constitution in audiovisual media.

**Dorothea Horst** is a postdoctoral researcher at the chair for Language Use and Multimodal Communication at European University Viadrina, Frankfurt/Oder (Germany). She works on intersubjectivity and the experiential dynamics of (figurative) meaning-making in multimodal interaction and audiovisual media. From 2009 to 2013 she was junior researcher in the project "Multimodal Metaphor and Expressive Movement" headed by Hermann Kappelhoff and Cornelia Müller at the interdisciplinary research center *Languages of Emotion* (Freie Universität Berlin). In her PhD research *Meaning-Making and Political Campaign Advertising. A Cognitive-Linguistic and Film-Analytical Perspective on Audiovisual Figurativity* (de Gruyter forthcoming/2018), she has explored the meaning-making role of metaphor and metonymy in German and Polish campaign commercials. Dorothea Horst is co-editor of *Cinematic Metaphor in Perspective. Reflections on a Transdisciplinary Framework* (de Gruyter 2018) and co-author of the book chapter "Gesture as interactive expressive movement: Inter-affectivity in face-to-face communication" (*Body – Language – Communication*, Mouton De Gruyter 2014).

**Thomas Scherer** is *Cinepoetics* doctoral student (working title: *Audiovisual Persuasion. Aggressive Metaphors and Feel-Bad-Movies*) and junior researcher in the digital-humanities project *Audiovisual Rhetorics of Affect* funded by the German Federal Ministry of Education and Research (BMBF) situated at the Freie Universität Berlin and the Hasso Plattner Institute Potsdam (Germany). From 2009 to 2013 he was student assistant in the project "Multimodal Metaphor and Expressive Movement" headed by Hermann Kappelhoff and Cornelia Müller at the interdisciplinary research center *Languages of Emotion* (Freie Universität Berlin). He is co-editor of *Cinematic Metaphor in Perspective. Reflections on a Transdisciplinary Framework* (de Gruyter 2018) and co-author of the book chapter "Expressive Movements in Audiovisual Media. Modulating Affective Experience" (*Body – Language – Communication*, Mouton De Gruyter 2014). His research foci are the aesthetics of utility films and TV news, digital research methods in film studies, as well as audiovisual rhetorics and metaphors.

**Christina Schmitt** is postdoctoral researcher at *Cinepoetics*, Center for Advanced Film Studies at the Freie Universität Berlin (Germany). From 2009 to 2013 she was junior researcher in the project "Multimodal Metaphor and Expressive Movement" headed by Hermann Kappelhoff and Cornelia Müller at the interdisciplinary research center *Languages of Emotion* (Freie Universität Berlin). She is author of the book *Wahrnehmen, fühlen, verstehen. Metaphorisieren und audiovisuelle Bilder* (de Gruyter forthcoming/2019), which is the outcome of her PhD research. In *Building Bridges for Multimodal Research* (Peter Lang 2015) she published the chapter "Embodied Meaning making in audio-visuals. First steps toward a notion of mode". She is co-author of chapters for *Body – Language – Communication* (Mouton De Gruyter 2014), including "Cinematic communication and embodiment" and "Gesture as interactive expressive movement: Inter-affectivity in face-to-face communication". She is co-editor of *Metaphor in the Arts, in Media and Communication* (*mediaesthetics* No. 2 (2017), with Matthias Grotkopp), *Emotionen. Ein interdisziplinäres Handbuch* (Metzler forthcoming/2019, with Hermann Kappelhoff, Jan-Hendrik Bakels, Hauke Lehmann) and *Cinematic Metaphor in Perspective. Reflections on a Transdisciplinary Framework* (de Gruyter 2018). Her research on film and audiovisual media focuses on cinematic expressivity, embodiment, performativity, temporality and metaphorical meaning constitution.

www.ingramcontent.com/pod-product-compliance
Lightning Source LLC
LaVergne TN
LVHW010854110826
845149LV00005B/1406

*9783110709070*